The Sesquicentennial History of Illinois

Published for the
ILLINOIS SESQUICENTENNIAL COMMISSION
and the
ILLINOIS STATE HISTORICAL SOCIETY
by the
UNIVERSITY OF ILLINOIS PRESS
Urbana and Chicago

The Sesquicentennial History of Illinois, Volume Four

Building for the Centuries: Illinois, 1865 to 1898

JOHN H. KEISER

© 1977 by the Board of Trustees of the University of Illinois
Manufactured in the United States of America
C   5   4   3   2

LIBRARY OF CONGRESS CATALOGING IN PUBLICATION DATA

Keiser, John H., 1936-
  Building for the centuries.

  Bibliography: p.
  Includes index.
    1. Illinois—Urbanization. 2. Illinois—
Politics and government. 3. Illinois—Economic
conditions. 4. Illinois—History—1965-
I. Title.
HN79.I3K44   977.3'04   77-1764
ISBN 0-252-00617-8

FOR NANCY, J. J., SAM, AND JOE

With Love

Preface

       What is ordinarily done in prefaces, I have attempted to do in the introduction and conclusion. Yet there are important acknowledgments which must be made, the major one being that the list is selective and incomplete. The research for this volume was partly funded from grants received from the Illinois Sesquicentennial Commission and from the Eastern Illinois University Council on Faculty Research. President Robert C. Spencer, of Sangamon State University, has encouraged me to retain my identity as an historian while assuming the administrative duties of an academic vice president. Over the years I have benefited from the work of countless scholars, and my indebtedness is only partially reflected in my notes. Many of the sections were strengthened by the response of colleagues at EIU and SSU, including Professors Donald Tingley, John Buenker, David Maurer, Judy Everson, David Everson, John Bowman, Dennis Camp, and Arthur Margon. Additional invaluable assistance came from fellow historians Robert Howard, Victor Hicken, Robert Sutton, Roger Bridges, and William Alderfer. My greatest intellectual debt is to my teachers, Professors Robert Wiebe and Ray A. Billington, who taught me to view history with respect and imagination. Their faith in me is a source of undying pride.

       The completion of this volume was due in great measure to the assistance of Ms. Rebecca Veach, my student and colleague at SSU, whose writing, organizational, and critical abilities added quality to many chapters. She is a superb historian. Mrs. Shirley Kinley typed the manuscript "over and over" and tolerated the indecisiveness which made that necessary. Responsibility for interpretations and statements or misstatements of fact is, of course, my own.

       Most important are the debts I owe to my family which can only be paid by love and appreciation. My parents and grandparents instilled in me an unquenchable admiration for scholarship and the state of Illinois, and my only regret is that my mother and my grandfather did not live to read this result. My in-laws, Harry and Iris Peterka, provided constant encouragement. My wife, Nancy, offered stimulating comment, understanding, love, and our own group of Illinoisans—J. J., Sam, and Joe.

Contents

Introduction

The dogmas of the quiet past are inadequate to the
stormy present.
                                                    A. Lincoln.[1]

"The craftiest and most dishonest politician that ever
disgraced an office in America,"[2] sneered a Springfield neighbor.
Sangamon County agreed and gave majorities to his opponents in
both presidential elections. The *Chicago Daily Times* fumed and
sputtered against his supposed despotism, but it was only reflecting
what disgruntled Democrats and many Republicans were mutter-
ing all over the state. The abolitionists hated him for moving too
slowly; the Democrats, for moving at all. In April, 1865, the President of the United States was seen by many Illinoisans as a conniver,
blackguard, scoundrel, black-hearted buffoon, unconscionable
opportunist, and high-handed so-and-so, to whom profane adjec-
tives seemed especially suitable—and then the tocsin tolled.

Abraham Lincoln's funeral cortege limped painfully back to a
state just catching its breath from four years of supporting a devastating Civil War. Illinois volunteers and draftees had fought and
bled in great numbers for the Union cause, and were only now
returning to reclaim their places in the factories and on the farms.
Too many, however, did not return, and their empty chairs stood
sentinel to the memory of the trauma that took them forever away.
The state had been spared the physical wounds of battle. No Sherman marched locustlike across the Shelbyville Moraine, but the
psychological scars were there, and they would not quickly or easily
go away. Those scars were especially raw in the southern counties
for whom the war years had been a long and painful choice between
family and country, between loyalty to deeply felt social beliefs
and loyalty to the ideal of federal union.

xi

Who were they then, those people of Illinois who wept at the bier of the slain president? Even in the midst of war, the state's population had boomed, until in 1865 it ranked fourth among the states, with over 2,100,000 persons. Fewer than half of those were born in the state, and over one-fifth had come to the state within the past five years. They lived primarily in rural districts, with the exception of Chicago—the only metropolitan city in the state. One-fourth of the population was foreign-born, primarily from Ireland, Germany, and other countries of northwestern Europe.

The state's female population lived at the suffrage of their husbands and fathers. They could not vote, hold office, or gain admission to such professions as law or medicine. Their social activities were primarily limited to church work, although the needs of war had propelled them into relief and aid societies, and their men would be dismayed to discover a new self-reliance in their women developed of necessity during the lonely war years. Abolitionism had drained off the energy from the women's rights movement, at least temporarily. Education for girls trained them to sew a fine seam and be adornments for their husbands—not to run a railroad.

State government sat in the sleepy rural town of Springfield where slightly more than 9,000 people lived, largely unaffected by the wheeling and dealing at the Leland House and the St. Nicholas Hotel. The activities of the legislators were restricted by a constitution framed in 1848 to meet the needs of a less complex day. Severe curbs on state debt and short sessions tied the hands of the legislators, but at the same time provisions for unlimited "special bills" left them free to meet individual rather than societal needs. Whatever constitutional safeguards existed could be avoided by adroit finagling. Twenty-five senators and eighty-five representatives, elected from single-member districts, sat in Springfield with war governor Richard Yates. They could override his veto by a simple majority and expected his role to be strictly a housekeeping one —seeing to it that their laws were executed. Executive leadership in the modern sense was neither sought nor contemplated. There was a secretary of state, but no attorney general.

The superintendent of public instruction had general supervision over the $3,000,000 spent on the common schools and the one state institution of higher education, the Illinois Normal School at Bloomington, Illinois. Normal trained students to be teachers, while church-supported colleges and seminaries offered a viable alternative to state-supported higher education.

Other state institutions lacked any central administrative authority, although three of the five charitable agencies were centrally clustered in Jacksonville. The state prison at Joliet was leased as a profit-making venture, and was thus not under direct state control or a matter of administrative function. The first tentative steps toward bureaucratization of state government had come as a response to the exigencies of war, but state agencies had not yet begun to proliferate and the state payroll was well under 5,000 employees. Total state expenditures for the 1864-66 biennium came to just over $5,000,000.

The most outward and visible sign of the state's prosperity in 1865 was a line of track 700 miles long connecting Chicago and Cairo. The Illinois Central was only one of the railroads furiously expanding across the state, bringing the promise of wealth and worldliness on their singing wheels. Local boosters looked to the railroad to put their towns on the map, to carry their goods to market, and to create a financial bonanza. The railroad was seen by most Illinoisans as an economic service to be eagerly courted and supported. For other transportation, the state relied on the Illinois-Michigan Canal and river traffic, for the state's roads were in deplorable and impassable shape.

The Civil War focused attention upon industrial growth in the state as both a military necessity and an unparalleled economic opportunity for individuals. Industry quickly responded to the increased demand, the price rise, and the growth of home markets assisted by high tariffs and population growth. Correspondence to and from the office of the McCormick Harvester Company revealed the emphasis: "Fredericksburg signified that the premium on gold might rise, and Lee's march to Gettysburg that fewer reaper sales might be expected in Maryland and Pennsylvania. Judging from the silence of the correspondence, there was no Emancipation Proclamation, the siege of Vicksburg and Petersburgh are myths, Lee did not surrender and Lincoln was never assassinated. Business did not go on as usual, but it was all absorbing."[3]

The end of the war left the state tooled up and ready for phenomenal growth. The year 1865 saw the production of the state's first Bessemer steel rail, the incorporation of the Union Stockyards, and the creation of the Chicago Clearinghouse. Mines produced 1,078,000 tons of coal. The Elgin Watch Company and Pullman Palace Car Company were in the planning stage. Basically, however, industry was unorganized, consisting of local operators functioning independently of other firms in the same industry.

Seventy-six national banks helped provide the financing, but the state banking system was generally in a state of flux. Illinois was ready to build—but had the skills and vision for building only for today.

With 15 percent of the available work force away at war, the climate for the laborers who remained was salubrious indeed. When 72,000 soldiers re-entered the work force, they found that the boom of the war years was over and there were no jobs to be had. Although the depression of 1857 had seriously weakened organized labor, it was still viable in spots. The Chicago typographers were still active, as were the American Miners Association and the railroad brotherhoods, but unionism was not the prevalent mode, and even the union leaders themselves were unsure of the goals and methods to pursue. The rural, individualistic majority of the state viewed unions as alien and unnecessary, and most had experienced little if any actual contact with strikes and boycotts.

In sheer bulk and profit, the state's largest industry was agriculture. Large portions of the state's fertile mid-section lay still undrained and unfenced, but farm production composed the state's greatest wealth. The plainly adorned farmstead symbolized the simple sturdy credo of the prairie farmer—serviceable and non-frivolous, dedicated to hard work and perseverance. The farm was neither mechanized nor fertilized, and most farmers owned and worked their own land.

The fertile prairie soil was matched by an equally fertile political seedbed. The prewar years had seen wild political swings as Democrats, Free Soilers, and Whigs attempted to rationalize their moral and economic reactions to the slavery issue within the confines of a political party. As abolitionists found a home in the new Republican party, the Democrats found themselves increasingly parochial, and as the war began, an increasingly defensive minority. Views that were once merely controversial were now dangerous, if not treasonable. The sympathies of southern Illinois were by inheritance and family loyalty pro-slave, and the trauma of fighting both honest conviction and blood kin scarred the southern counties. A vocal enclave of Chicago's alleged "Copperheads" kept the Democrats alive in the North, but the party's star was definitely on the wane. Not only had Illinois Republicans helped place their man in the White House with all the power and patronage that office implies, but they also were in the enviable position of claiming their party as the sole arbiter of patriotism and the savior of the union.

Culturally, Illinois in 1865 was firmly entrenched in the

"McGuffey's Reader" period of its maturity. Writing was sentimental, attempts at architecture derivative, and the theater arts largely confined to traveling circuses and minstrel shows. Children learned patriotism, protestantism, and puritanism, along with the most basic rudiments of the "three R's" at the nearest one-room school.

By 1865 Chicago was already set apart from downstate. One out of ten people in the state lived there in an ethnic mix not matched elsewhere. Chicago's acres of wooden buildings housed a burgeoning array of industries and the potential of great fortunes. A foreign-language press, and social clubs which kept alive the cultural heritage of the many immigrant groups, gave Chicago an eclectic culture with a richer flavor than the dour protestant gruel of downstate. Crime was on the rise in the city by the lake, with a thriving levee gaining fame and notoriety throughout the country. But although Chicago was bigger and more powerful than any other city in the state, it was still an aberration to be smugly dismissed as unimportant by the dominant downstate farmers who believed their way of life was what was and is and is to be.

That complacency was shattered for all time on Good Friday, 1865. Word of Lincoln's death coursed like streaks of blood-poisoning back to Illinois. To the 158,724 who had only months before marked a ballot against him came a schizophrenic relief-guilt-laugh-bitter grief. The Great Emancipator was dead, crucified on Good Friday, and the parallels to another Savior were too obvious for orators to miss. In Washington the bickering over his body began; in Illinois the dead of the war seemed killed again, and in that catharsis the martyr became for the first time president of all the people in his home state.

The bunting went up—a phantasmagoria of crepe and black roses to welcome the slain hero home. His life had embodied all the deepest beliefs of the Prairie State: rural and self-sufficient, self-taught, and possessed of a native wit superior to the decadent easterners. Needing only his own ability and hard work to rise from poverty to the nation's highest honor, Lincoln confirmed the deeply felt frontier myths and personified what seemed lasting and good in American life. Now he was dead.

And so they laid him away, and loosed millions of words in eulogy over his body, little knowing it was the ideal itself that was being interred. For times were already changing, and in the new urban-industrial age the Lincoln values could not compete and would become anachronistic touchstones done lip service by men whose lives denied them. The thousands weeping over the bier could have also been weeping over the passing of their age, for in the confusing years ahead those values that were then the center would not hold. Or as a later poet would mourn, "a formula, a phrase remains. But the best is lost."[4]

[1] Abraham Lincoln, "Annual Message to Congress," Dec. 1, 1862, *The Collected Works of Abraham Lincoln*, Roy P. Basler, ed. (New Brunswick, N.J., 1953), 537.

[2] David Donald, *Lincoln Reconsidered: Essays on the Civil War Era*, 2nd ed. (New York, 1961), 3-4.

[3] William T. Hutchinson, *Cyrus Hall McCormick: Harvest, 1856-1884* (New York, 1935), 99.

[4] Edna St. Vincent Millay, "Dirge without Music," *Collected Poems* (New York, 1956), 240.

Building for the Centuries

1
Of People and Places

First come the pioneers, lean fierce, dirty
. . . .
Then the fat years arrive when the fat drips
Then come the rich men, baffled by their riches
Bewildered by the silence of their tall possessions

Carl Sandburg[1]

Who were they, the people of Illinois? What did they look like? How did they live? What were their cities like, and the spaces between them? There was buying and selling. Of what goods? If they danced and sang, to what tune? When they died, of what pain? Many came as aliens. What did they find? And what change? They were male and female. In what scale did they measure their value as sexes? As people? What were their lives like, the people of Illinois?

They were, at first, people close to the soil. In 1870 over 76 percent of them lived in what the census defined as rural districts. Their trading centers dotted the prairie every six to ten miles. Horsepower provided the farmer's only transit, and his trading centers had to be within a one-day journey by wagon from his home. The isolated farm trading center was just beginning to realize a new dimension with the coming of the railroads. Illinois Central officials plotted towns every ten miles along their route, and simplified planning by standardizing each town. North-south streets were numbered; east-west streets were named for trees. Oak Street, Maple Street—every new city had one, and "the boxlike station, the grain elevator, the water tank, and the inevitable main street were part of virtually all."[2] In 1874 the Chicago *Inter-Ocean* ran a series of sketches of these prairie towns which illustrated the importance of the railroad: "Four years ago this prairie was a corn field," came the report from Varna. After the Chicago, Alton and

1

St. Louis railroad "wormed its way along toward this Eden-like spot," the corn was replaced by a city of 400 with "six dry goods, grocery and hardware stores, two drug stores, one dressmaker, one milliner, and one confectioner shop, two elevators, one coal and one lumber yard, one livery stable, several merchandise shops, a school house—two room, four churches, and two hotels."[3]

In every town the livery stable was a festival of boyish delight. It could house "courting buggies and hearses for hire, and probably a back room poker game complete with jug of home brew."[4] There was no better spot for loafing and swapping tall tales. Although their mothers protested the presence of "gentleman horses" (kept for stud service), many a young Illinois boy got his first glimpse of a man's world while hanging around the livery stable.

After leaving his team to be fed and watered, the farmer and his family walked to the general store to pick up mail and buy supplies. Out front were brooms and rakes and seasonal supplies, while in the window crowded a sample of the items for sale within. Before the shopper's eyes adjusted to the dim light he knew the whole of the store by its smell. "Molasses, vinegar, damp cellar floors, freshly ground coffee, rope, rubber boots, dress goods in bolts, fish, cheese, leather goods or kerosene," according to Louis Atherton, "permeated the whole of the store." Canned goods were still new in 1865, although J. L. Mohler advertised 1,000 cans of peaches that year at $4.50 a dozen. Most foodstuffs came out of common containers: the vinegar, pickle, and molasses barrels, bins of dried peas and beans, long plugs of tobacco in "fruity-smelling strips which could be cut at conveniently marked lengths by a hinged blade."[5]

The general store was a favorite meeting place, but as an unspecialized monopoly it was under little pressure to control either the price or the quality of merchandise. A housewife who complained of bugs in the meal or dust on the crackers usually had to buy or go without—or travel to the next village where conditions were much the same. Store-bought cloth was apt to fade or shrink—and there was no alternative brand to choose.

Ownership of the stores remained local. Chains of two or more stores did not appear nationally until the early 1880s, and in 1872 there was only one such chain offering twenty-six lines of merchandise. By 1900 the United States boasted 120 chain store groups of various kinds, indicating a future trend, but local ownership remained the common experience.[6]

In the century's final decades, pressures from national advertising had forced most local stores to upgrade their merchandise. Led by Singer Sewing Machine, firms began extensive advertising of brand names after the Civil War. Money spent on advertising increased by more than 1,000 percent between 1867 and 1900, indicating the national "brand name" drive. As Pillsbury Flour, Ivory Soap, Wrigley's Gum, and Bayer Aspirin became known through advertising, country store owners were forced to stock more than one brand. Shoppers could compare both quality and price as the cracker barrel gave way to sealed packages of clean, fresh crackers. National brands competed successfully with local producers, and local flour mills found that they could not fight the advertising budgets of the giants. The nonspecialized disorder of the postwar country general stores was on the endangered list by the turn of the century as customer demand for standardized quality, mail-order houses, and national corporate brand-name competition imposed the impersonal order of standardization.

Shoppers at the close of the Civil War may have bought bolts of cloth at a store, but their clothing was primarily made at home. By the turn of the century, however, a thriving ready-to-wear clothing industry challenged the homemade wardrobe. For females, the new look included some downright uncomfortable items: corsets, for example, or some styles of shoes. The *Chicago Evening Journal* found both contemptible, scolding: "The absurd and ungainly practice of mounting the hinder part of the feet on stilts while the toes press the ground and bear the weight, as in the use of high heels, is one against which it is not easy to write with temper. The practice of strangling the waist with tight-laced corsets was contemptible for its ignorance, that to which we now allude is outrageous in its defiance of the laws of gravity."[7] To which Dr. Ira DeVer Warner could sadly reply seventeen years later, "women will wear corsets; they always have and they always will."[8]

Ladies fashions also furnished a clue to character, according to one presumably serious newspaper account. "Ridiculous toilets, bunches of feathers and rosettes" supposedly equaled an "amiable nature," but men were warned to "beware of women who always and for no apparent reason wear yellow dresses bound with red." Such garments indicated "artful women who are fond of dress" and possessed of "numberless ambitions,"[9] especially if they were not pretty.

The pocket made its appearance as a fashionable item in 1878. Religious newspapers were offering ladies' pistols as premiums to subscribers as a defense against "crime in the streets," and the pocket was advocated as a necessary repository for the weapon. The

Chicago Evening Journal facetiously suggested that women "carry their pistols on a chain in hand. It would be notice to good people that they mean business."[10]

By 1897 the well-dressed, middle-class family could achieve the height of sartorial splendor ordered direct from a "wish book." Here stands father in his derby ribbed balbriggan undershirt and long drawers. His undershirt is a thirty-eight cent special, but it includes "silk taped front, pearl buttons, French Collorette neck . . . same as all high priced garments." Over it goes a very proper shirt front, for "shiftless he who shirtless goes." A celluloid collar and cuffs complete the shirt. A cotton-lined "cassimere" suit, full-length mackintosh coat, calf dress boots, peccary hogskin gloves, and nutria fur crusher hat complete his ensemble.[11]

Mother is protected from the elements in a warm union suit ("in Union there is strength"), topped by a fifteen-ounce corset "stripped with sateen, bone bust, two side steels, six hook clasp, embroidered at top and bottom." Next comes a shoulder brace and skirt supporter, lisle hose, and a suit "in Bolero cape style," appliqued and embroidered, with braid and ribbon trim. The skirt is lined with "rustling taffeta and bound with velvet all around." This creation costs $9.00, and is set off by high button shoes, kid gloves, and an elegant black hat, "wire frame covered with lace, straw crown edge trimmed with ruffle around crown, loops of ribbon in front and two sides, two pretty bunches of roses, steel ornaments, a band underneath with chiffon ribbon, finished with buds."[12] At their sides are their dutiful children, dressed like miniature adults. Little Betsy wears a cotton vest covered by a modest waist. In public view is a readymade dress with "large butterfly collar, newest style large puff sleeves . . . trimmed with fancy novelty braids."[13] Brother Tom is the epitome of style in his ruffled front sateen blouse.

The trend away from personalized retailing capitalized on by the mail-order houses became an increasingly evident part of big city shopping when such department stores as Carson, Pirie, and Scott and Marshall Field's consolidated all the shopper's needs under one roof. These great stores catered primarily to women and were located in central urban shopping districts. They compensated for their relatively lower prices by great volume. Technological innovations warmed the big stores with central heating, whisked customers to upper floors in elevators, and lured them into the store with advertising in the daily mass-circulation newspapers. Horse cars, cable cars, and electric street railways brought all city dwellers within walking distance of the new stores.

Chicago's central shopping district saw a 700 percent increase in land value between 1877 and 1896, with a corresponding decline in outlying business districts. Small and middle-sized retail merchants were at a competitive disadvantage, a disadvantage aggravated by swings in the business cycle. During the depression of 1893-97, business failures in this class spread alarmingly. In 1896, 817 Illinois trading and commercial firms died in bankruptcy while the large department stores continued to prosper.

The small retailers formed the Cook County Businessmen's Association in 1897 in an attempt to fight the big stores. The Chicago Federation of Labor allied itself with the group in an effort to break the anti-union stand of the big stores, which also earned labor's wrath for their use of child labor. The association failed to attract support from civic reform groups which admired the efficiency of the big stores as well as their lower prices, but it was actively endorsed by Cook County Republican boss William Lorimer. On March 24, 1897, the Illinois senate passed an anti-department store bill over the anguished protests of the department store owners. Momentum slowed, however, as attention in the House was diverted to other issues, and downstate suspicion of Chicago cooled enthusiasm for the bill. The problem was still a local one, and downstate legislators began to wonder if helping Chicago's small merchants might not hurt the general stores in rural districts which could fall into the department store category. On April 8, 1897, the bill failed in the House.[14]

Just as the stores, so did the towns themselves change. As they moved into the 1870s, many small towns began providing services to the people—especially gas lights. The larger towns of Champaign, Urbana, LaSalle, Jerseyville, Mattoon, and Rock Island all installed gas lighting in 1870, amid much jubilation. The 1890s saw gas streetlights replaced by electric lights in places like Marion and Knoxville. Banks, barber shops, and hotels now lined the square, and more than one church summoned the faithful on Sundays. Larger cities gained in importance, with only 45.7 percent of the population living in towns of less than 2,500 by 1900. The greatest rural decline, 14.1 percent, occurred during the 1880s, followed by the 1890s with 9.6 percent and the 1870s with 7.2 percent.

Towns of moderate size were proud of the special features that made them unique. Jacksonville was the home of two private colleges and three of the state's charitable institutions. Galesburg was proud of Knox College, and the Chicago *Inter-Ocean's* roving reporter was equally impressed. "The groves of academe were blueberry swamps compared to the groves of Galesburg," he declared. "Our republic would stand another hundred years if it could rest upon the intelligence of Galesburg."[15]

New towns with nothing much to be proud of were also appearing. Mine owners built company towns to provide the manpower needed to get out the coal. Central to this type of community, of course, was the company store, surrounded by the grey-board houses of the miners. A plain church and tavern ministered to the soul of the place, and the road to the mine shaft reminded one and all of their dependence on the company. Glen Carbon and Zeigler rose and fell on the mine's prosperity, as did "those other bitter, unkempt mistresses of a single industry."[16]

For a mining community to really prosper, it needed other industries as well. Madison County's Collinsville, for example, was completely undergirded by coal shafts by the 1890s. The width of the city could be transversed without ever seeking daylight. Much of the population depended on the mines for work, but the city was also the home of a large zinc smelter, a machine shop, a race track, a canning factory, brick yards, breweries, a small packing plant, and two large bell foundries. Although the mines dominated the economy, the city's other natural resources, combined with a diversified population of Germans, Bohemians, Slavs, Croats, Austrians, Italians, English, Welsh, and Lithuanians, kept the financial base diversified enough to avoid the sad plight of the one-industry town.

As in other Illinois cities, the industries which developed were closely tied both to the soil and to the immigrant background of the population. Basic to all of these growing cities were the agricultural foundations of their infancy. From these developed diversified industries to convert the area's natural resources into finished goods. The more industries a city could generate—either separate or as a spin-off of others, the better able it was to continue to grow. Collinsville's clay topsoil became bricks, its corn became liquor, its coal fueled the smelter. Tomatoes from surrounding fields fed the canning factory and wafted a hunger-making smell over the town at canning time. Across the state similar combinations of natural resources and knowledgeable men turned Elgin into a watch center and Peoria's abundant pure water into whiskey.

Labor from the immigrant stream was another necessity. It was the presence of the immigrants that gave much of the flavor to

Illinois towns. Every railroad town might have its Maple Street, but not all had a *Saengerbund* or a *Schuetzenfest*. Identical in the conglomerate, houses designed by builders instead of architects, city hall, tavern, slum, the cities of Illinois individually had personality shaped by the people who lived there. Much of that personality was the same from town to town: Calvinist morals, Republican politics, optimism. But interspersed in the sameness were the Amish of Arcola, the English settlement of Albion, the German intelligentsia of Belleville, the Swedes of Galesburg.

Immigrants buttressed the work force that sped industrialization, the consumers who supported the economy, and the cultural diversity that lifted the state out of tedium. Without them there could have been no Second City—no Chicago the Giant. Between 1870 and 1900, over 450,000 immigrants entered the state, bringing the total foreign-born population to 966,747. The foreign born in Illinois constituted 8 percent of all foreign born in the United States in 1870, a figure that increased to 9 percent in 1900. The importance of Illinois as a destination of immigrants, and the importance of that group to the state, is more clearly shown, however, by the fact that although immigrants accounted for 20 percent of the state's population throughout the period, they counted only 15 percent of the national population in 1870 and only 13 percent in 1900.[17]

By 1890 Illinois ranked fourth in the nation as a residence for the natives of Great Britain; second, for the natives of Germanic nations; fourth, for the natives of Ireland; second, for the natives of the Scandinavian nations; third, for the natives of the Slavic nations; seventh, for the natives of Canada and Newfoundland; and sixth in the nation in the number of natives of Latin America.

The foreign-born population of the state in 1890 was 842,347 of the 9,249,547 foreign born in the nation. The figure included 39,525 Canadians; 622 South Americans; 70,510 English; 20,465 Scots; 4,138 Welsh; 124,498 Irish; 366,226 Germanics; 128,897 Scandinavians; 8,407 Russians; 3,126 Hungarians; 26,627 Bohemians; 28,878 Poles; 8,540 French; 8,035 Italians; 661 other Latins; 778 Chinese; 297 Asiatics; and 2,117 "others." See Table A in Appendix for additional statistics.

In spite of their numbers, only two nationality groups constituted over 5 percent of the state's population—and all major groups declined in comparison to the native born during the period. The Germans, numbering 40.16 percent of the foreign born in 1890, reached a peak of 8.89 percent of the total state population that year. Immigrants from the British Isles declined from 7.59 percent of the total state population in 1870 to 4.21 percent in 1900. English dominance among the foreign born declined proportionately from 37.45 percent to 20.57 percent. Chicago's concentration of ethnic groups exerted considerable political influence. The city's German contingent gained approval of an ordinance closing all city offices in honor of the Kaiser's birthday in 1893, to which the *Denni Hlasatel* sardonically suggested that the Bohemians should now demand the same honor for Jan Amos Comenious Day.[18] Chicago became the ultimate destination of a majority of the foreign born, although not the only one. All over downstate, communities of ethnic groups gathered in the midst of old-line settlers, and the Springfield *Illinois State Journal* noted a "Swede theater" in Galesburg and two German language newspapers in 1871. In 1898 Joliet was the center of the Austrian population of the country and the headquarters of the Carnolian Slavonic Catholic Union.

The transplanted citizens frequently maintained ties to their homelands, and the upheavals in Europe in 1870 saw sharp divisions of loyalty. Bloomington Germans raised $500 for the "first German soldiers . . . that take the first French flag."[19] Mass meetings were held for both the French and Germans across the state, and the Chicago Scandinavians met to decide which warring nation should have their sympathies. (They chose the Germans.) In 1898 the Holland Society was still refighting the war between Spain and William of Orange at an annual banquet.

Native sons had ambivalent feelings about the newcomers. "Progress" and "growth," two bywords of the age, demanded new people to work the land and man the factories. The universal frenzy of real estate speculation demanded an unending supply of buyers, and boosters and railroad agents encouraged immigrants to settle. In 1880, the *Chicago Times* reported "one thousand tickets have been sent from Streator, this year, to bring immigrants from the old country."[20] And in 1893 the *Joliet Daily News* reported at great length a speech given before the Populist Club entitled "Why We Should Not Prohibit Immigration."[21]

Those who encouraged the immigrant (and hoped to exploit him), however, met a solid wall of defensive parochials who saw the increased work force as a threat to their financial security and the strange dress and customs of the foreigners as a threat to the sanctity of their cultural institutions. Rural Illinois was an inbred place, hostile to outsiders. "All outsiders were alien and a foreigner was doubly so. His knowledge of a foreign tongue was a count against him. Why didn't he speak English, as all decent people did?"[22] In 1870, when the Chinese population of Illinois was .003 percent of the state's population, 300 Belleville isolationists petitioned Congress "to take some action against the importation of Chinese Coolies."[23] See Table B in Appendix for additional statistics.

Labor strife in 1873 was blamed by the press on demoralized foreigners. Continued labor agitation served to alienate the immigrant both from the working man who saw his job threatened by foreign scabs and from the employers who feared the pro-union European background of many of the newcomers. Immigrants became scapegoats for both unemployment and riots as hysteria reached a peak following the Haymarket incident in 1886. The *Chicago Evening Journal* pinned blame for the affair squarely on "the Polish rioters," and agreed with Russian suppression of the Poles as "unfit to enjoy liberty regulated by law and reason."[24] Anti-Polish feeling persisted, and by 1893 the Populists were also listening to tirades against "Polacks" in Joliet. The Steamboatmen's Protective Union was urging action against aliens.[25]

If the foreign-born often found Illinois inhospitable, they were not alone in feeling so. Throughout the period a steady flow of native farmers left the state, hoping always for a better life elsewhere, and contributing to the feeling that the state was a crossroads, a halfway point. Lebanon and Charleston reported "large numbers of emigrant wagons bound for the far west . . . daily."[26] Groups of neighbors, families, and ethnic groups often traveled west together, piling aboard trains to Kansas or Arkansas, or taking the rougher wagon route to the Pacific Northwest. The Veterans' Colonization Society and a colony of 250 Germans organized in Chicago in 1870; the Germans left by rail for Colfax, Colorado, under the auspices of the National Land Company. While farm land in central Illinois was among the best in the nation, the climate fluctuated between bitter cold winters and scorching, humid summers. Still the water was sweet and plentiful, and by the 1870s farmers were becoming used to the treeless prairie, while westward lurked hostile Indians, drought, unfamiliar land, and all of the hardships of beginning life anew. Nevertheless, devils or dreams drove trainloads of pioneers out of the cultivated gardens of Illinois into the wilderness.

Rising land prices in Illinois motivated some to move on. By the 1890s, a 200-acre farm near Bloomington could be sold and the money exchanged for 400 to 500 acres in the unfilled lands over the rainbow. Dream-spinning was big business, and emigrant associations and land agents promised to turn the emigrant's itchy feet and boundless hope into pots of gold. Some agencies were unscrupulous, especially those whose clients were foreign born. A mass meeting of Scandinavians in 1871 protested one such agency which had been sending Swedes South into "most odius oppression and shocking misery."[27] In spite of abuses, however, the emigrant business continued to find customers. A trainload of 100 Champaign County persons left Chicago for Kansas in 1893, pilgrims for whom Illinois had not made the American dream come true.

The success of that dream had been predetermined for many long years before man came to the prairie. For before man, there was the glacier, moving relentlessly southward, bringing rich and fertile soil as far south as the thirty-ninth parallel, as far south as Vandalia, Robinson, Alton, before it stopped. The land it left north of the Shelbyville Moraine was an inviting one with soil deep and full of life. South of prosperity lie the thirty-nine counties of what Baker Brownell calls "the other Illinois"—Little Egypt. The glacier did not enter there, and the soil is thin, poor clay. The region gets more rain than the rest of the state, but it runs off and the clay washes with it.

Southern Illinois is river country. The Mississippi, Ohio, and Wabash meet on its borders, and "from the Southern Illinois country to the north, south, east, west there are 15,000 miles of navigable rivers."[28] The rivers should have meant wealth, but brought with them instead devastating floods. Shawneetown went under every year until 1884, when a series of levees were built. But these were not high enough, for in 1893 the waters rose over the walls. Eighteen ninety-three, in fact, was a bad year for floods all over the state. The *Knox County Republican, East St. Louis Daily Journal,* and *Mattoon Commercial* all contained stories similar to the warning in the *Galesburg Spectator* that "it is but a question of time when it (levee) will go and the town of Brooklyn will be swept away."[29] East St. Louis was sure that "insecurity against floods is the prime, chief, and almost only cause why our city has not long since achieved much greater proportions than its present ones."[30]

Nevertheless, huddled behind their walls, the river towns in the 1860s were full of hope, decking themselves out like brides for the Prince of Prosperity who was sure to come after the war. Cairo, lowest spot in the state, was bustling with importance, serving as a staging area and shipping point for Grant's drive South. Commanding the confluence of the rivers, its future looked boundless.

Fruit from 700,000 trees was shipped out of Little Egypt during the war, and the barges and steamboats that plied the rivers promised much. Life was full of zest in a river town then. Populations swelled with southerners fleeing the war, and with Negroes newly freed. They joined a population already deeply tinged with accents of the South: Mississippi gamblers awaiting the next steamer, taciturn Appalachians loading cargo, and roistering spiritual sons of the legendary Mike Fink. Bales of cotton and kegs of molasses sat upon the docks, and the industry of the river towns turned around their shipment. Boardinghouses and hotels served sturdy fare to the river men, and more intriguing amusements were also available. The pirates of Cave in Rock left a legacy time could not soften, and crimes of violence were as much a part of these towns as the violent floods perpetrated by the Mississippi and Ohio. It was in a river town that Robert Ingersoll, making an uncouth remark or gesture to a farmer's daughter, narrowly missed death when the righteously indignant father piously shot the man he thought was Ingersoll, and was acquitted of murder by reason of insanity.

The *Illinois State Journal* described the typical river port of Grafton in 1871: "The resident population of this place approximates 2,000; as a river town Grafton claims no rival in point of shipping and general commerce. The facilities for transportation of freight, produce, livestock, etc., are such that shippers and buyers at this point can cope with many towns that boast of their lines of railroad. Almost every packet and propellar that cruises the waters of the Upper Mississippi, and those of the Illinois River land here; which makes Grafton a port of considerable magnitude. Aside from the commercial traffic there is an immense local trade."[31] Cairo was the most important commercial river city in Illinois, but its dreams of becoming the Chicago of the south rapidly vanished as the value of its commerce declined by nearly two-thirds between 1869 and 1886, and its receipts, mostly from the North, now consisted of bulky goods for local consumption. River towns in the southwest suffered a similar fate, but it was less crushing in terms of their expectations. The towns which were involved in any way in river commerce on the Wabash, the state's southeast boundary, included Mound City, the most important at the end of the period, Shawneetown, Metropolis, Brookport, Rosiclare, Elizabethtown, Cave in Rock, Golconda, and Hamletsburg.

As the years went by, river freight shifted from cotton and molasses to coal, and while river shipping continued, the focus of the country turned West instead of South, with the railroads carrying the east-west freight. The river towns of Egypt were geared to a north-south economy, and the South no longer had anything to offer. Stuck with the seemingly terminal plague of war-sickness, it nursed its wounds, and left Cairo a port without a purpose. Life went on in the river towns as the 1870s, 1880s, and 1890s crept by. Traffic still flowed on the river, but it took wealth away and left little behind. The boardinghouses boarded up, the dockmen sat on the wharves chewing tobacco and wondering. When is it coming? Where did it go?

The land between the rivers was settled long before the northern two-thirds of the state. Up the Wilderness Trail through Tennessee and Kentucky came the progeny of freed indentured servants, old-line Americans whose lineage went back to the country's infancy. These hill and woodland people found Egypt much like home. They were farmers in 1865, scratching in the anemic soil for the richness promised by the heart-stopping beauty of redbud and magnolia, peach, and plum. The air was sweet in Little Egypt; the streams that washed off the farmer's topsoil were also swollen with delicious fish and the woods were full of game. Ducks and geese flew South overhead. A woodsman could be happy if not prosperous there.

They were a stiff-necked people, those farmers of Mt. Vernon and Herrin, rugged and proud and above all, independent. They lived in what Paul Angle calls "a dispersed city," on isolated farmsteads. Fundamentalists of Methodist or Baptist faith, these folk held a deep distrust of education and outsiders. Their lives were bound by the black and white of simplistic codes, and in that strong soil the more delicate plant of liberal learning had not yet taken root. Nearby villages served as trading posts, but it was the family that provided the real focus of social life and social control. The southern Illinoisan did not look to city or state to provide for his needs—or to hand out justice. He settled his own feuds, and it did not take much to get one of those feuds started.

Williamson County is the bleeding heartland of Egypt, and between 1839 and 1876 a total of 285 victims fell murdered there while another 495 were assaulted. The courts punished six of the murderers; the rest took their chances with the vengeance of their victim's families. On the 4th of July, 1868, "Field" Henderson sat down in a tavern near Carbondale for a hand of cards with several of his neighbors, all Bulliners. The game went badly for Henderson, who incautiously questioned both the veracity and the parentage of the Bulliners who beat him to show their displeasure and left. The feud was on!

The two Bulliner brothers had moved into Williamson County from Tennessee, while the three Henderson brothers had settled their families nearby after leaving Kentucky. All were growing prosperous and influential in the area. A dispute with the Bulliners over a crop of oats led the Sisney family to join the feud on the side of the Hendersons when similar charges of dishonesty and a gun battle left George Sisney with four bullet wounds. The courts fined the gunmen $100, but did not settle the poisoned feelings, and the feud was now a blood vendetta. For the next eight years the county was the scene of murder and ambush while the state looked the other way. No one was ever convicted for any of the killings, although at one point the state contemplated allocating $10,000 to catch the "Williamson County outlaws."[32]

While the Bulliners and Hendersons were seeking their vengeance, a fundamental change disrupted the county's economy and contributed to its violent reputation. In 1869 Laban Carter opened the area's first coal mine. By 1890 Williamson County was producing 200,000 tons of coal per year, and the bleakness of the soot-covered company town stood in sharp contrast to the green and peach of the woodlands. The men who came out of the hills to work the mines changed their occupations but retained the fierce independence and love of the outdoors that the first farmers and hunters brought with them into the county. Life in the coal pits did not fundamentally change the men of Bloody Williamson, and when confronted with another enemy, they would again take the law into their own hands.

In 1890, Samuel Brush of Carbondale, backed by St. Louis and Cincinnati money, opened the St. Louis Big Muddy coal shaft near Carterville. By 1897, the mine had weathered the depression of 1893 and was the largest producer in the state. Brush considered himself a benevolent employer, but was unalterably opposed to unions. Mine wages were low, with yearly income averaging $235-$273 per year in 1895. The United Mine Workers struck for thirty-six cents a ton in 1897, and Brush was dismayed to find his men had organized. He offered thirty cents a ton, and 80 percent of the men walked out.

Brush filled their jobs with Negro strikebreakers imported from Tennessee. In spite of community fears, no major trouble occurred until 1899, when the union, this time including some of the original

Negro strikebreakers, again walked out. Brush decided to import more Negroes from strike-torn Pana, and this time violence exploded. On June 30 the train carrying the strikebreakers was attacked and the wife of one of the men was killed. Twenty Negroes were wounded. The National Guard moved in to keep order, but rioting broke out again six days after they left. This time five blacks died and others were wounded. Local authorities acted quickly, and nine men (seven of them black) were indicted for the first murder, and twelve men (all white) for the others. The trials were couched in drama, as large crowds gathered to hear the oratory. As in the vendetta trials, all were acquitted. Williamson County protected its own.[33]

Egypt promised great prosperity. Long-settled, breathtaking in its beauty, accessible to ancient river routes of trade, and possessed of incredible mineral wealth, the region should have blossomed. Instead, the hopes of the war years washed off in floods, were shipped north and east and west by trains which carried off wealth to mine owners and food processors far away. And by the turn of the century, the land was noticeably scarred with slag, bitter with disillusionment, and notorious for its violence.

The black strikebreakers brought to Williamson County were some of only 57,028 Negroes in the state. Blacks constituted 0.45 percent of the state's population in 1860; 1.13 percent in 1870. By 1890 there were 1,513 Negroes to every 100,000 whites, and that figure rose to 1,797 to 100,000 in 1900. In all of those years, Ohio and Indiana had higher percentages of Negro population, and in 1860 Michigan's percentage was also greater. The Illinois percentage of Negro population differed from the national, both in proportion and in trend, for while the national percentage declined from 14.13 percent in 1860 to 11.6 percent in 1900, the much smaller figures in Illinois steadily rose.

The total black population of the state in 1870 showed a decrease in proportion to the white population of seventeen per 100,000 from ten years earlier. Negro migration to Chicago by 1890 was insignificant in terms of population density, and the entire state, with the exception of the southern river counties, showed less than one Negro inhabitant per square mile. The proportion of the black-white population in Chicago in that census year was 1 to 7 percent black to 99 to 93 percent white. Census records for both 1870 and 1880 are considered largely inaccurate as guides to actual Negro population, but what they show is an increase of 13,332 between 1860 to 1870; an increase of 10,660 between 1880 to 1890, and an increase of 32,050 in 1900 to a total of 85,078.[34]

For the Negroes who did come, there were few important changes in status, although in 1871, John Jones of Chicago was elected county commissioner. In 1874, the General Assembly forbade segregation in the public schools, and in 1876 John Thomas of Chicago became the first black state representative. The first Illinois Negro newspaper, the *Conservator*, was printed in Chicago in 1878.

In 1885 the General Assembly passed a Civil Rights Act forbidding discrimination in restaurants, hotels, theaters, railroads, streetcars, or public accommodations, but legal guarantees did not mean actual enforcement of equality of treatment. In spite of the imposed status of blacks, in 1891, Dr. Daniel Hale Williams performed the world's first successful heart operation on a fellow black at Provident Hospital in Chicago, the first facility in the country to offer nurses' training to Negro women.[35]

While Illinois was a man's state, nearly one-half of those viewing it were women, but prior to 1860 they functioned almost totally in terms of their relationship to men. Their ideal role was seen as the nurturers of children and the preservers of Christian morals, while their gentle spirits provided a haven for their husbands, a place of retreat from the harshness of the outside world. They existed to serve as submissive partner in the bedroom, cook and servant in the kitchen, and hostess in the parlor.

Marriage was the normal state for most women, and when the census takers first recorded conjugal statistics in 1890, they discovered that 81.9 percent of all women in the census district which included Illinois were or had been married. Divorce was rare, with only 0.46 percent of both sexes admitting to that state. In 1900, the number of women fifteen years old and older in Illinois who were or had been married was 68.8 percent. For the north central district, the group studied in 1890, the percentage was still 81.9.[36]

The coming of the war had had a profound effect on many of the state's women, as they were thrust, willing or not, into the sphere of business and public life. Farm wives whose husbands and sons were marching with Grant had no choice but to cultivate their fields themselves and learn to deal with shipping rates, grain prices, and mortgage and banking politics. The bureaucracy spawned by the war forced state and federal government to open clerical jobs to women for the first time. Before the war only 10 percent of the nation's teachers were women, but by 1865 fully half of all teachers were female, and even the medical profession was pried open by the needs of war, as more and more male physicians were pressed into duty as army doctors. In Chicago, Mary H. Thompson filled the void left by departing male doctors and was named head of the Chicago Hospital for Women and Children.

Women were not content to let their men make all of the sacrifices of war, and many followed the troops into battle as nurses. They inspected army hospitals and supplies, and reported their findings to military authorities with demands that unsatisfactory conditions be improved. Such nurses as Illinois' "Mother" Mary Bickerdyke infuriated military commanders with their insistence on reforms in the hospitals, continuing to heal in spite of male sputtering. Other women became involved in the great sanitary fairs that were held to raise money for bandages and supplies, and a Chicago woman, Jane Hogue, is credited with organizing the Great Sanitary Fair of 1863 which netted $70,000 for such supplies.

Mary Livermore rationalized the need for a temporary change in the role of women in a speech in 1864: "Some would say that women ought to keep quiet and not put themselves before the public so prominently, and be around begging for money all the time. Well, when the jubilant bells shall ring in the return of peace ... then we are going to quit begging and be quiet and sew and embroider nice little ornaments and let the men be the lords of creation, and we will be ladies of creation."[37]

Livermore found returning to her embroidery unfulfilling after the challenge of her Sanitary Commission work, and on February 11, 1869, she organized and chaired the first Illinois Women Suffrage Convention in Liberty Hall, Chicago. On March 13 of that year she published *The Agitator*, a women's rights weekly, and she was later active in the formation of the American Woman Suffrage Association. The Illinois Equal Suffrage Association formed at the Chicago convention named her president, although the founding group included several men, among whom were Judge Charles B. Waite and Judge J. B. Bradwell, whose wife Myra was refused admission to the Illinois bar in 1869. A major victory for the group that year was passage of a bill securing women's wages to their own use.

One of the less traumatic ways for a woman to try out her newly found self-confidence was to join with other women in social clubs, and the history of those organizations parallels in many ways the trend toward order and consolidation among other elements during the era. Jacksonville claimed the only two women's organizations founded before the Civil War: the Ladies Education Society, founded in 1833, and the coed Plato Club, founded in 1860. The close of the war saw the first literary club, the Friends in Council, begun when "twelve ladies agreed to meet weekly for reading and conversation."[38] The Jacksonville Sororsis and Art Association met in 1868, but the rest of the women in the state were not yet ready to branch out from membership in church societies. Aware of the gaps in their own education, and content that they had found a respectable outlet for their newly found determination to seek fresh goals, Illinois women set about organizing literary societies. The Chautauqua Plan for Home Study entered the state in 1874 and by the turn of the century had 675 circles: 200 in towns of 500 to 3,500, sixty in hamlets, and the rest in cities. The Ladies Reading Club of Mattoon, the Monday Club of Rockford, the Tuesday Club of Pana, and the Cleonian of Pontiac, organized in 1877, were followed by the Every Wednesday of Elgin in 1879. Chicago reflected the activities of downstate with the formation of the Fortnightly in 1873, the Friends in Council in 1875, and the Women's Literary Club of Willard Avenue in 1878.

Cultivation of art was also a respectable pastime, and Lincoln led the growing art appreciation movement with the formation of an Art Club in 1876. Champaign's Art Society began the same year, followed by the Springfield Art Society in 1877. Decatur opened two women's art classes in 1879, Bloomington's Palladan and a Historical and Art Society began the same year, and in 1880 the Central Illinois Art Union, with representatives of those local clubs, organized in Lincoln. It met once a year, and later included art clubs in Peoria, Carlinville, and Pana. Cairo had a successful women's club and library association "with the double purpose of raising funds for a library and of improving of its members through discussion of domestic, moral, social, and political questions." The women purchased 1,257 books, which became the start of the Cairo Public Library.

Moral crusades were also popular in the 1870s, and the Illinois Women's Christian Temperance Union elected Frances Willard its first secretary in Bloomington in 1874. Four years later she became national president, and by 1904 the movement had grown to 475 circles in ninety-one counties. An enthusiast wrote, "In the forty departments of the great body, women find not only occasion for benevolent service but the opportunity of self-development as well."[39]

The WCTU served a second cause. In 1876, Willard became convinced that the solution to the temperance problem lay in securing votes for women. Equal suffrage was too radical and revolutionary a concept to gain easy acceptance from most women of the day, but the educational program of the temperance crusade won over its adherents to the suffrage cause. Local Home Protection elections were a chief goal of the WCTU, and it was women who signed petitions demanding these referenda on the temperance question. They also demanded that they be allowed to vote on this one crucial issue, securing 180,000 names on such petitions in a nine-week period in 1879.

Those petitions served two purposes. "Everyone who signed the petition became a convert to their cause," wrote a women's rights author, "and every woman who presented a petition became unconsciously a convert (to suffrage)." Willard's plan was "to urge the women to go before the legislature and plead, in order that they might thus realize how futile the method is."[40] Once women became convinced that the only hope for the temperance cause lay in securing the vote in local elections, and once they personally experienced the contempt with which most male legislators viewed their demands and efforts, the step to a commitment to full political equality was a short one.

Monmouth claimed the honor in 1888 of being the home of "probably the first women's political club in the country."[41] The Democratic Women's Club campaigned unsuccessfully for Grover Cleveland, but remained active after the election, and one of its members was elected county superintendent of schools. The fact was remarkable not only because the winner was a woman, but also because she was a successful Democrat in heavily Republican Warren County. The group earned further acclaim in 1896 as the only women's group to successfully schedule William Jennings Bryan as a speaker.

In the 1890s women's groups began looking beyond improving their own mind to the possibility of improving society. The earliest example had been the Cairo club, but it was the Chicago Women's Club, founded in 1876, which established a format that combined culture with an action program aimed at specific answers to obvious social problems facing women and children. The club was organized into six departments: reform, home, education, philanthropy, art, and literature. The Chicago club had 900 members by the turn of the century and claimed credit for hiring women physicians for women patients in insane hospitals in Cook and Kankakee

County hospitals; for seats for girls in retail stores; for a kindergar-
ten for poor children; for a school for boys in jail; for $10,000
donated to vocational schools; and for the creation of the Public
School Art Association, the School Children's Aid, the Municipal
Order League, the Political Equality League, and the Protective
Agency for Women and Children.

National movements for women's rights had some adherents, but
the main thrust of women's groups was toward order and organization as they took on the corporate structure so familiar to their
husbands. The General Federation of Women's Club was organized in 1889 with seventy-seven chapters. The number increased
rapidly to 225 by 1904, at which time the federation had nineteen
standing committees and 11,000 books in 225 traveling libraries.
The Association for the Advancement of Women was founded in
New York in 1873, with Mary Livermore as its first president. The
group's second and eleventh annual conventions met in Chicago. It
was joined on the national scene by the National and International
Councils of Women in 1888. The National Council of Mothers
organized in 1897.

The projects of the groups varied. The Ravenswood Women's
Club lobbied for domestic science classes in the public schools. In
Champaign, Elgin, and Danville the city hospitals were supported
by women's groups, as was the Chicago Children's Hospital. During
the depression of 1893, Chicago women's clubs provided work-
rooms where the poor could do sewing in exchange for hot meals,
groceries, and clothing. The Klio Club's famous "noon Day Rest"
provided a cultural midday meal and lecture for working women.
The Austin, Park Ridge, and Rogers Park women gave outings to
poor children, and the Settlement Women's Club installed a public
bath and gym in the stockyards' area.

Leaders of the suffrage movement regretted that by the 1890s
women's clubs were involved in so many projects that energy was
diverted from seeking the vote. Some women, however, attempted
to combine those two: Elizabeth Bayton Harbert served as president of the Illinois Equal Suffrage Association from 1877 to 1884;
edited "The Women's Kingdom" in the Chicago *Inter-Ocean*;
founded the Evanston Women's Club; served as president of the
Social Science Association of Illinois; and was on the board of
managers of the Girls Industrial School of South Evanston. She was
also active in the Woman's Congress.[42]

Paralleling social and educational developments, the legal status
of women slowly changed. When the state's first equal suffrage

association met in Earlville in 1855, Illinois women were barred not only from voting but also from property ownership and equal guardianship of their own children. A bill to eliminate those two restrictions was defeated in the Illinois legislature in 1861. In 1870, the chief justice of the State Supreme Court held "that a woman could not be admitted to the bar or hold any office in Illinois,"[43] and months later Governor John Palmer refused a notary public's license to a Chicago woman on the grounds that "the custom not to grant such commissions is accepted as the law in the case."[44] Susan B. Anthony, speaking in Chicago, declared "a woman married is a slave," and called for such revolutionary changes as "equal pay with men for the same work" and for the ballot.[45] Someone was listening, and in 1871 the Domestic Relations Committee of the Senate recommended passage of a bill allowing married women "to carry on business as if single," and permitting women access to the professions of medicine and law. Although women were made eligible for appointive office in 1872, the "radical" recommendation of the Domestic Relations Committee that they "become lawyers, physicians, clerks, etc." was defeated 63 to 53.

Judges Bradwell and Waite had successfully lobbied against a clause in the 1870 constitution which would have barred women from public office, and although Mrs. Bradwell was still unable to practice law, her cause was joined in 1870 by Ada H. Kepley, who claimed to be the world's first law school female graduate.[46] The Supreme Court refused to hear Myra Bradwell's appeal, but she and Alta M. Hulett circumvented the court by lobbying for passage of a state law admitting women to all professions in 1872. In the same year Catharine Waite filed a petition requesting to vote—but was predictably refused. The legislature did approve, however, a bill making fathers and mothers equal in inheritance from a child. In 1873 women were made eligible for elective school posts, and by 1874 ten were elected county superintendent of schools. Another victory in 1874 was a law declaring that both spouses' interest in real estate constituted dower rights. Mrs. Bradwell was instrumental in 1875 in getting the word "person" substituted for "man" in the law relating to public notaries. Dr. Sarah Hackett Stevenson became the first woman admitted to the American Medical Association in 1876, and in 1879 Helen Schuhardt was upheld by the Supreme Court as a master in chancery.

Many prominent Illinois women were writers, and in 1885 the Illinois Women's Press Association was organized in Chicago by Frances A. Conant. Mrs. Bradwell, who published *Legal Notes*, Mary

Bannister, Frances Willard, Dr. Mary Weeks Burnett, and Caroline Alden Huling were all charter members of the group which admitted only women who wrote professionally and received a salary for their work. Another member was Dr. Julia Holmes Smith, a homeopathic physician and Dean of the National Medical College. She later became the first woman appointed to the University of Illinois Board of Trustees. Dr. Smith was joined on the University of Illinois Board of Trustees in 1894 by Lucy L. Flower, the first woman elected to the post. As the century closed, Governor John Tanner appointed Mary M. Bartelme Public Guardian of Cook County.

The age of consent in Illinois, as in much of the country, was ten years when the Equal Suffrage Association began its work. Changing this antiquated concept was a chief goal of women's groups which realized that "consent" often meant the privilege of going to work at the age of ten, as well as rape and forced marriage. In 1887 the age of consent in Illinois was raised to fourteen years.

The woman activist was still viewed with hostility, however, and the *Chicago Evening Journal* was quick to castigate the "Polish and Bohemian women" it held partly responsible for the Haymarket riots. "Civilized, elevated and cultured womanhood is the better part of humanity," it declared; "savage womanhood, influenced by its native instincts . . . is the worst part of humanity."[47] By the 1890s, Illinois men were feeling defensive about women's rights groups, and the *Evening Journal* waxed ironic about the prevalence at the World's Fair "not of the serpent, but its historic associate, the petticoat." The *Journal* deplored women's tendency to "go swishing into the realm of business" and stated that in spite of "the woman's rights doctrinaires" who "are harping on from morning till night . . . this talk of bringing womanly qualities into business is preposterous twaddle."[48]

For women who did work, career opportunities remained limited, both in kind and in location. Excluding housekeeping, 16.3 percent of all women in the state were employed in 1900. They numbered 20 percent of the actors, 37 percent of the literary and professionals, 40 percent of the artists and teachers of art, 55 percent of the musicians and teachers of music, and 74 percent of the teachers.

In downstate communities, utilitarian professions such as medicine, law, journalism, dentistry, and ministry were strictly a man's province. Chicago offered the only real opportunities for women, and among the state's "professional" women, 44 percent made their homes in Chicago. In less utilitarian fields, such as art and music, women were expected to fill the need for services downstate. A man who would not dream of letting a female pull his tooth gladly sent his daughters to lady piano teachers. A man in these nonbusiness fields was suspect, and most male artists, architects, sculptors, writers, and musicians congregated in the more cosmopolitan atmosphere of the lake city.

The effect of the women's rights struggle of the 1870s is evident in the census figures of 1880 as more and more occupations and professions were pried open for women. In that year, 106,101 Illinois women were working for wages. Of those, 2,575 were employed in agriculture, 72,383 in professional and personal services, 3,044 in trade and transportation, 28,099 in manufactures and mechanical and mining industries. Of that number, 7,096 were between the ages of ten to fifteen, a testament to the need to raise the age of consent. In professions not usually open to women, Illinois had 12 of the nation's 165 female clergymen, 9 of the nation's 75 female lawyers, 349 of the nation's 7,316 female officials and employees of (civil) government, 155 of the nation's 2,432 female physicians, and 22 of the nation's 426 female manufacturers and officials of manufacturing companies. In more typically female professions, the state employed 51,106 of the nation's 938,910 domestic servants and 10,768 of the nation's 154,375 female teachers. Only Texas and Ohio had more female clergy, and no state in the union had more female lawyers than did Illinois in 1880.[49] The state ranked fifth in the number of female physicians; third in the number of female teachers. In comparison, Illinois' male lawyers and physicians ranked fourth.

Women's groups began slowly in the 1870s, as middle-class women found new time and a modicum of freedom to improve and expand their own minds. Once experienced in the art of group action, they turned their vision outward, first to other women's groups with whom they could ally themselves, then still further outward to the plight of poverty-stricken children and of women forced to work in sweatshop conditions. By 1900 they had yet to win the vote, and the temperance crusade had not yet spawned the Volstead Act. In terms of what women had managed to achieve inwardly, in terms of their increased self-awareness and consciousness of worth, in terms of their practice in the skills of power through united action, and in terms of their real, if limited, betterment of civic and social problems, however, Illinois women by 1900 had come a long way.

Neither sex had much free time for entertainment, but they enjoyed what they had all the same. Some of the new rich were "hotfoot after Cultyre," according to poet Bert Leston Taylor. For them there were symphony concerts and the ballet. Others enjoyed more simple entertainment. Whether traveling circus or Chicago Symphony, those entertainments provided a needed escape from the loneliness of the farm or the impersonality of the city. They could be a reminder of a life left behind in the German university and European metropolis, or a status symbol of newly achieved wealth and leisure.

Reminiscing in 1871, the *Kewanee Independent* recalled "the earlier residents of Illinois seemed to have a great fondness of music, and concerts were among their favorite recreations. . . . Every town and village had its singing society and chorus."[50] A fondness for music and concerts continued after the Civil War, and such amateur productions as Freeport's "Married Life," presented in 1873 with intermission music by the Modoc Band of Serenaders, gave an outlet for suppressed talents as well as entertainment for the audience.

Minstrel shows remained popular, as did traveling circuses which crisscrossed the state. Tent repertory theaters, of which the Toby Players was one of many organized in the 1880s, presented plays around the state. Curiosity about exotic places assured the popularity of such groups as the Japanese Troupe, which featured "the slack rope trick by Otoksen, the Belle of Japan."[51] P. T. Barnum, "the celebrated showist," toured with his circus and freak show —and picked up spare change as a temperance lecturer. The *Chicago Evening Journal* noted with approval, "in the course of an eventful life, the lecturer has come in contact with as many of the vices and bad effects caused by intoxicating liquors as any other person in the country. . . ."[52] No doubt.

The Belleville area was already established as a cultural center downstate, and its Germans formed a symphony there in 1860. Buffalo Bill began his stage career in Illinois, appearing in "Scouts of the Prairie" in 1873. McVickers Theater, rebuilt after the fire of 1871, offered Chicago a variety of cultural events. A presentation of "Shenandoah" in 1898 featured a detachment of artillery, 200 people, 50 horses, and 28 "rough riders."

When not performing themselves or enjoying the antics of performers on stage, music lovers could buy copies of popular music, and the "Hit Parade" of 1878 indicated the kind of music that found favor:

1. "Put Me in My Little Bed"	250,000 copies
2. "Tramp, Tramp, Tramp"	180,000 copies
3. "Nora O'Neil"	100,000 copies
4. "Silver Threads among the Gold"	75,000 copies
5. "Come Home, Father"	50,000 copies
6. "Mollie Darling"	40,000 copies
7. "Evangeline"	25,000 copies
8. "Sweet Genevieve"	20,000 copies

The author of the popular "Put Me in My Little Bed," lamented "it surely can't be possible. . . . the public wants such miserable stuff as this?"[53] But he managed to write the piece and collect his royalties despite his astonishment.

Civic groups across the state raised money and enlightened their communities with lecture series which brought Ralph Waldo Emerson, Louis Agassiz, Horace Greeley, James Russell Lowell, Oliver Wendell Holmes, and a host of lesser (much lesser) lights to Dixon and Mattoon and Belvidere. Emerson was a star attraction, drawing a munificent fifty dollar lecture fee, although he received uniformly bad reviews and cold audiences. The people came to look, even if they did not want to listen. A frontier inferiority complex was hidden behind reports of Shakespearean lectures and self-congratulatory press notices that "it is a high compliment to the Western people that an Oxford Professor should consent to address them on a purely scientific topic."[54]

Lectures by the clergy had a respectability Japanese belles might lack, and groups such as the Mattoon Lecture Association leaned heavily toward ministers of various sorts for their lists of "noted speakers and readers."[55] Excitement seekers were not disappointed in the "religious" lectures available from such speakers as Miss Edith O'Gorman, "The Escaped Nun" with her "startling and thrilling lecture on CONVENT LIFE and the ROMANISH SCHOOL SYSTEM and . . . How She Escaped."[56] With a semistraight face, the Chicago Inter-Ocean reported in 1875 a lecture by Elder William P. Thurinou "to prove that the Second Coming of the Messiah will take place on the 19th." "William," sympathized the Inter-Ocean, "won't get back to Boston in time to see the trouble."[57]

For social life, citizens of Illinois' small towns turned to churches and lodges. "The second story is to be occupied by the Odd Fellows Hall"[58] was a frequent note in descriptions of towns in the 1870s. Frontier folk shunned the decadent titles of Europe, substituting instead the elaborate ritual and regalia of Masonic pomp and Odd Fellows circumstance. "Your Highness" was scorned, but "Most Worshipful Grand Sultan" was a title to be eagerly sought by farmers and merchants throughout the state. The Woodmen, with their insurance programs, and the Grange were also popular into the 1890s, but they never elbowed out the older orders.

In Springfield, for example, 1892 found seven lodges of Masons; three lodges, Colored Masons; three lodges, one Encampment, one Canton, one International Order of Odd Fellows; three lodges, Knights of Pythias; five lodges, Ancient Order of United Woodmen; seven lodges, Benevolent and Protective Order of Elks; three Posts, Grand Army of the Republic; six Camps, Modern Woodmen of America; three Tents, Knights of the Maccabees; four Courts, Catholic Order of Foresters; several Rulings, Fraternal Mystic Circle; two Tribes, Improved Order of Red Men; and many more.[59] The GAR and its auxiliary appealed to the martial spirit, and the DAR touched the chord of ancestor worship. Animal clubs (Elks, Moose, and so on) all had their own appeal to the aspiring middle class.

Outdoor activities emphasized the closeness of the Illinois farmer to the life and death realities of nature. Wolf hunts were common throughout the 1880s, with bounties offered for scalps. The *Chicago Evening Journal* sounded an early call for ecological awareness in 1886 in a story on importation of quail in central Illinois: "The quail was formerly very plentiful . . . but the merciless trap and shotgun of indiscriminate hunters have eradicated them. If the game laws were more stringently enforced, there would be some chance of a revival career for both the quail and the prairie chicken in this state."[60]

Although hunting remained a widespread "sport" in the state in spite of the *Journal*'s warning, other far less lethal games swept in faddish waves from village to village. The Bardolph trustees leaped to the defense of morality and "passed an ordinance prohibiting the game of croquet inside the corporation."[61] Cock fighting had its enthusiasts, but it was baseball, challenged by college football, which really caught fire.

Recess and noontime saw schoolchildren outside playing improvised games, the type depending largely on the weather. Teachers left the children to themselves, for "the play of children was not a matter of adult concern, whether at school or at home."[62] Baseball was the most popular sport, with variations like "Town Ball" or "One Old Cat" or "Rotation": "Batters stayed in until they hit the ball, and base runners were put out by throwing the ball across the runner's path in front, or better still, hitting him with it."[63]

On the college level, baseball was also the most popular sport in the 1870s, described as "fascinating, and . . . much more American than the boat races which the eastern colleges so much indulge in."[64] The game held as much fascination for adults as it did for students, and newspaper columns detailed the glories and woes of the Chicago team. A popular sport also paid its players well, as the *Chicago Tribune* pointed out in 1876: "Three years ago a young man graduated at Evanston with high honors. . . . He is now filling a $350 pastorate in Kansas, while the dullest young man of the class, the butt of his classmates and the despair of his teachers, gets $3,700 a year as a pitcher for a professional baseball nine."[65]

Baseball as a college sport had stiff competition from football. The first intermural teams clashed at the University of Illinois in 1878, leaving "boys with limping gaits, bandaged shins, and skinned noses." Athletic activities were still informal, unsupervised fun, however, until 1888 when "the athletic association erected seats on the campus, stretched ropes around the diamond and charged an admission fee of 10¢."[66] Football joined the intercollegiate schedule in 1890 when the Illini lost their first game against Purdue 62-0. The loss was attributed to "a coacher from Indianapolis" who had apparently taught the Purdue eleven some successful "trick plays."[67] For adults, handball and shooting clubs, the YMCA and YWCA, as well as the German Turner Clubs, all promoted physical fitness.

For the not-so-physically-fit, patent medicine hawkers offered to cure every ailment from cancer to impotence—often with the same elixir. As part of a generation generally considered prudish, Illinois' Victorians took an amazing interest in the distresses of their generative organs. Amid the aids for Reliable Worm Cakes and Obesity Powder, the 1897 Sears Catalogue lists intriguing compounds such as Dr. Beaumont's Pennyroyal Pills, "with useful information and instructions to ladies concerning their troubles." A half-page ad (with a picture of the plungerlike apparatus) extolled the virtues of the "Princess Bust Developer and Bust Cream or food." Cures for drinking, smoking, and the opium habit treated specific weaknesses, but such all purpose drugs as Dr. Baker's Blood Builder cured "scrofula, cancer, rheumatism . . . exzema and other skin diseases arising from impurity of the blood, nasal catarrh, acne or pimples, chronic ulcers, carbuncles, boils . . . syphilis in its primary, secondary, or tertiary form."[68]

For somewhat less specific disorders, readers were urged to "Beware of Quack Doctors" and take Dr. Chaises' Nerve and Brain Pills to be cured of:

> a thousand and one indescribable bad feelings . . . low spirits, nervousness, weariness, lifelessness, weakness, dizziness, feeling of full-

ness or emptiness of stomach in morning, flesh soft and lacking firmness, headache, poor memory, chilliness alternating with hot flashes, blurring of eyesight, specks floating before the eyes, nervous irritability, gurgling or rumbling sensation in the bowels, with heat and nipping pain occasionally, palpitation of heart, short breath on exertion, slow circulation of blood, cold feet, pain and oppression in chest and back, pain around the loins, aching and weariness of the lower limbs, drowsiness after meals, but nervous wakefulness at night and a constant feeling as if something awful was going to happen . . . impotence, spermatorrhoea, night sweats, emissions, caricocele (or swollen veins), weakness of both brain and body, arising from excesses and abuses of any kind.[69]

A hypochondriac's delight! There was good reason for hypochondria. Mortality rates were high—especially for children under three—and modern medical techniques were unknown. Children under four years old continued to be the group with the highest mortality rate nationally throughout the period. By 1900 the national death rate per 100,000 was 179.1 for male infants under one year of age and 145.4 for females in the same age group. In the five to fourteen year age group the figure had dropped to 3.8 for males and 3.9 for females. Although medicine had made some advances, the infectious diseases which killed in 1869 were still virulent nationally by 1900. The national death rate per 100,000 population for 1869 is shown in Table 1.

TABLE 1. NATIONAL DEATH RATE PER 100,000 POPULATION, 1869

Tuberculosis	Major Cardio-vascular, Renal Diseases	Pneumonia Influenza	Gastritis Guc-denitis Enteritis, Colitis	
194.4	345.2	202.2	142.7	
Accidents	Malignancies	Diphtheria	Typhoid	
72.3	64	40.3	31.3	
Measles	Whooping Cough	Cirrhosis Liver	Diabetes	Suicide
13.3	12.2	12.5	11	10.2[a]

[a]U.S. Bureau of Census, *Historical Statistics*, 26.

The urban slums of Chicago had a national impact on one field of medicine. In 1893 Dr. John Harvey Kellogg of Battle Creek, Michigan, father of prepared breakfast cereals and devout Seventh Day Adventist, visited the city on the lake and opened a branch sanitarium with funds donated by wealthy Chicagoans Francis and Henry Wessels. Dr. Kellogg advocated direct church aid to feed and clothe slum dwellers as a missionary service, and in June, 1893, he opened the Chicago Medical Mission. This approach to social medicine involved more than healing specific complaints, and the mission offered baths, laundry facilities, a penny lunch, and a medical dispensary. In the first three years, 38,000 baths, 26,000 other treatments, 9,000 nurses' visits, 75,000 penny lunches, 17,000 religious conversions, and the distribution of 13,500 tracts were recorded.[70] Kellogg's work expanded in 1896 with the opening of a Workingmen's Home and a Missionary College Settlement Building. Indigent men were offered shelter at the 400-bed Workingmen's Home, and a chance for rehabilitation into the economy by reweaving carpets and making brooms.

Medical students training in Battle Creek began taking their clinical training at the American Medical Missionary College in 1895. The Chicago facility offered the chance for medical students to receive clinical training and at the same time to serve the desperate medical needs of the city's slum dwellers. The scope of the total medical operation in Chicago, however, made it a continual drain on the finances of the Adventists, and Dr. Kellogg was forced to sever his relationship with the religious body.

Dr. E. Andrews introduced the state's physicians to the new idea of antiseptic surgery in an article in the *Chicago Medical Examiner* in 1869. He carefully explained the method for preparing carbolic acid, noting its beneficial effect on open wounds: "the effusion of pus from any raw tissue may be wholly prevented by simply applying carbolic acid and killing all the animalcules . . . the patient is saved from hectic [*sic*], grows fat and vigorous, and his life is commonly saved."[71] Despite its advantages, however, Andrews warned doctors not merely to "make a hobby of it,"[72] and sterile surgery was not introduced into hospitals until 1879.

In October, 1869, Chicago listed 597 deaths. Seven were from "teething," one from "excessive gymnastics." The leading cause of death was convulsions (45), closely followed by still birth (44), consumption (44), scarlet fever (42), typhoid fever (36), cholera infantum (33), diphtheria (27), tapes mesenterica (24), diarrhea (20), pneumonia (16), and old age (12). One hundred sixty-five of the victims were under one year of age, and one hundred thirty-one were between one to three.

A yellow fever epidemic hit the southern portion of the state in 1878—one of the first emergencies faced by the new state board of health. The state board ran most of the quack doctors from the state, but in 1878 downstate still had many physicians without medical degrees. The State Medical Register for that year lists thirteen of the first eighty as uncertified, compared with one of eighty in Chicago. Rush Medical School supplied most of the state's physicians, and the growth of consolidation and professionalism so evident in industry was evident in the medical profession as specialties, notably obstetrics "and diseases of women," formed their own "colleges." In addition to their specialty groups, doctors organized—the American Medical Association and county medical associations—to promote professional medical practice.

Some health hazards were more optional than others. An editorial campaign in the 1880s cited "pale-faced lads . . . puffing their little lives away" on cigarettes. Women were urged in 1885 to "ignore the attention of every smoker as a smoker could not be a perfect gentleman." By 1893 the *Egyptian Press* sadly noted that "young girls are being secretly led into the same course by boys who indulge." Delegates from the cigar-makers' union also urged organized labor "to renew the fight against the deadly cigarette"—presumably in favor of the benign cigar. The *Chicago Tribune* in 1898 printed a lurid account of a fourteen-year-old Indiana youth who lay dying of "excessive cigarette smoking," but reported a minor victory a week later when "gumbacco" was taken off the market.[73]

The health-damaging effects of alcohol were also a cause of the many temperance groups in the state. The Sons of Temperance and the Independent Order of Good Templars joined with Catholics in a drive to "rout forever that accursed Hireling of Satan—King Alcohol."[74] In 1874 women across the state began a physical attack on the enemy, starting with an invasion of the saloons of Chicago, followed by an appeal for the closing of saloons on Sundays. In 1883 the WCTU successfully pushed through the legislature the Harper Bill, which assessed license fees for liquor sellers. Unable to completely close the bars, the WCTU extended its efforts to women's suffrage and aids to drunkards and prostitutes through such organizations as the Washington Home Association and the Florence Crittendon Anchorage.

The WCTU was not able to dry out all the state's alcoholics, but an obscure Dwight physician believed he could. In 1866 Dr. Leslie Keeley began trying to find a chemical cure for the disease of alcoholism. In 1880 he opened a small sanitarium in Dwight to treat alcoholics with a rigid regimen of treatments based on injections of double chloride of gold. The treatments proved effective in eliminating the physical craving for alcohol, and by 1890 Dr. Keeley had franchised sanitariums operating around the state and in other states as well. Joseph Medill publicized the Keeley cure in 1891, the same year a group of former patients formed the Bi-Chloride of

Gold Club, an organization which became the Keeley League. The league "had a membership exceeding 30,000 in 1897, and had auxiliaries in which wives, daughters, mothers and sisters were enrolled." In 1895 there were

> local leagues in forty-two states, plus Indian and Oklahoma territories. Tennessee led with forty-seven leagues; Illinois had forty-five; Pennsylvania, twenty-six; Colorado, twenty-four; Missouri, twenty-one; New York, nineteen; Iowa, fifteen; and Maine and Michigan fourteen each. There were leagues in the soldiers' homes at Leavenworth, Kansas; Togus, Maine; Bath, New York; Los Angeles, California; Hampton, Virginia; and Milwaukee, Wisconsin, as well as the posts at Fort Leavenworth and Fort Riley, Kansas.[75]

As more "cured" alcoholics joined the league and returned sober to their communities, the reputation of the treatments grew. The Chicago World's Fair celebrated "Keeley Day" in 1893, and six states passed "Keeley Laws" providing public aid for indigent inebriates in institutions. The cure dried out drunks but it provided no reassurance against recurrence of the problem. The leagues served as prototypes of the Alcoholics Anonymous organizations of the future.

Whether drunk or sober, the population of the state more than doubled between 1865 and 1900. The increase from 2,141,510 to 4,821,550 moved the state from fourth in population in the nation (behind New York, Pennsylvania, and Ohio) to third. The decades of greatest growth both in absolute numbers and in the percentage of growth were the 1860s, with an increase of 48.4 percent, and the 1890s, with an increase of 26 percent. While the foreign-born portion of the population remained constant at 20 percent, the number of Illinois-born among the aggregate American-born portion of the total increased from 47 to 60 percent.[76]

Much of the increase in population must be explained by the expansion of Chicago. The city grew from 109,260 in 1860 to over 1,698,575 in 1900 when 35 percent of the state's population lived there. In 1860 the city's population counted only 10 percent of the state's, and rural districts were in the majority, with only three cities having populations of 10,000. By the turn of the century urban dwellers outnumbered rural, and twenty-five cities in the state numbered over 10,000. Peoria was the state's second city, with a population of 56,100 in that year.

More and more of the population were becoming city dwellers. They were dour New England merchants and fiercely independent Appalachian clansmen, soot-grimed Welsh miners and sun-burned prairie farmers. They were robust German brewers and anemic Polish tailors; Irish stockyards workers and descendants of the Mayflower. They were Swedes, Canadians, Chinese, and Frenchmen, Italians and fifth-generation Americans. They came to Illinois in the years following the Civil War, or they were born there, swelling the population and giving vitality to both economy and culture. They were not all one thing, the people of Illinois. Their towns varied as much as the people. Sleepy farm trading centers, river ports, grey company towns were home to some. For others it was the smoky bustle of growing industrial centers or the bewildering, dynamic chaos of Chicago.

The people shopped in various ways: from wandering peddlers, at the general store, in specialty shops, from "wish books," and in the new urban phenomenon—the department stores. They dressed in the fashions of the day, sang maudlin ballads, and listened to earnest lecturers. They skirmished in the coming battles of race and sex. They coughed the fatal rattle of tuberculosis and dosed themselves with patent medicine; they smoked and drank and tried to stop doing both.

Although they were not easily classified, their predominant characteristic as a group was optimism. They lived in a state undergoing an economic revolution, a population explosion, a reorganization of government and industry, and they lived in an age which believed business organization and technology, combined with earnest endeavor, made all things possible. They lived in a state that was building for the centuries.

1. Carl Sandburg, "Good Morning, America," *Harvest Poems 1910-1960* (New York, 1960), 74.
2. Lewis Atherton, *Main Street on the Middle Border* (Chicago, 1966), 6. James B. Hedges, "The Colonization Work of the Northern Pacific Railroad," *Mississippi Valley Historical Review* XIII (Dec., 1926), 311-342.
3. Chicago *Inter-Ocean*, July 21, 1874.
4. Atherton, *Main Street on the Middle Border*, 6. Paul W. Gates, *The Illinois Central Railroad and Its Colonization Work* (Cambridge, Mass., 1934), chap. 7.
5. *Ibid.*, 44, 46.
6. United States Bureau of Census, *Historical Statistics of the United States: Colonial Times to 1957* (Washington, D.C., 1960), 523.
7. *Chicago Evening Journal*, July 27, 1878.
8. Marion Harland, ed., *Plain Talks upon Practical Subjects* (New York and Chicago, 1895), 119.
9. *Illinois State Register*, Sept. 8, 1880.
10. *Chicago Evening Journal*, May 2, 1879.
11. Fred L. Isreal, ed., *1897 Sears Roebuck Catalogue* (New York, 1968), 237, 211.
12. *Ibid.*, 240, 306, 280, 302.

13. *Ibid.*, 304.
14. Joel Tarr, "The Chicago Anti-Department Store Crusade of 1897," *Journal of the Illinois State Historical Society* LXIV (Summer, 1971).
15. Chicago *Inter-Ocean*, July 14, 1875.
16. Baker Brownell, *The Other Illinois* (New York, 1958), 101.
17. See Table 1.
18. *Denni Hlasatel*, March 21, 1893.
19. *Chicago Times*, July 18, 1870.
20. *Ibid.*, Oct. 14, 1870.
21. *Joliet Daily News*, Feb. 8, 1893.
22. Albert Britt, *An America that Was: What Life Was Like on an Illinois Farm Seventy Years Ago* (Barre, Mass., 1964), 141.
23. *Chicago Republican*, July 14, 1873.
24. *Chicago Evening Journal*, May 4, 1886.
25. *Joliet Daily News*, March 13, 1893.
26. *Chicago Times*, Oct. 15, 1870.
27. *Ibid.*, April 8, 1871.
28. Brownell, *The Other Illinois*, 25.
29. *Galesburg Spectator*, May 2, 1893.
30. *East St. Louis Gazette*, Feb. 12, 1870.
31. *Illinois State Journal*, March 15, 1871.
32. Paul Angle, *Bloody Williamson: A Chapter in American Lawlessness* (New York, 1969), chap. 5.
33. *Ibid.*, chap. 6.
34. United States Bureau of Census, *Report on the Population of the United States at the Eleventh Census: 1890*, pt. 1 (Washington, D.C., 1895), xciii-cii.
35. Helen Horney and William E. Keller, "The Negro's Two Hundred Forty Years in Illinois—A Chronology," *Journal of the Illinois State Historical Society* LVI (Autumn, 1963).
36. United States Bureau of Census, *Report on the Population of the United States at the Eleventh Census: 1890*, pt. 1, clxix-clxxivii; *Twelfth Census of the United States, 1900*, pt. 11, lxxiii-xcvii.
37. Louise R. Noun, *Strong-Minded Women: The Emergence of the Woman-Suffrage Movement in Iowa* (Ames, Iowa, 1969), 106.
38. Belle Short Lambert, "The Woman's Club Movement in Illinois," *Transactions of the Illinois State Historical Society* (1904), 317.
39. *Ibid.*
40. Belle Squire, *The Woman Movement in America* (Chicago, 1911), 225.
41. Sarah Bond Hanley, "Political Pioneering in '88," *The Democratic Digest* (Feb., 1941), 23.
42. Noun, *Strong-Minded Women*, 270.
43. *Chicago Republican*, Sept. 18, 1870.
44. *Chicago Evening Post*, Dec. 1, 1870.
45. *Chicago Times*, May 29, 1870.
46. Catharine Waugh McCulloch, *Chronology of the Women's Rights Movement in Illinois* (Chicago, circa 1903).
47. *Chicago Evening Journal*, May 7, 1886.
48. *Ibid.*, May 25, 1893.
49. United States Bureau of Census, *Compendium of the Tenth Census, 1880* (Washington, 1883).
50. *Kewanee Independent*, June 30, 1871.
51. *Peoria Transcript*, Jan. 16, 1871.
52. *Chicago Evening Journal*, Oct. 4, 1872.
53. *Ibid.*, July 27, 1878.
54. *Chicago Tribune*, Nov. 9, 1874.
55. *Chicago Evening Journal*, Oct. 11, 1872.

56. *Peoria Transcript*, May 15, 1873.

57. Chicago *Inter-Ocean*, April 15, 1875.

58. *Illinois State Journal*, Aug. 16, 1871.

59. Rebecca Monroe Veach, *Growing Up with Springfield: A History of the Capital of Illinois* (Springfield, 1974), 37. *Illinois State Journal Souvenir Supplement*, 1892.

60. *Chicago Evening Journal*, May 9, 1886.

61. *Chicago Evening Post*, Sept. 28, 1870.

62. Britt, *An America that Was*, 72.

63. *Ibid.*, 172.

64. Roger Ebert, ed., *An Illini Century: One Hundred Years of Campus Life* (Urbana, Chicago, London, 1967), 30.

65. *Chicago Tribune*, April 9, 1876.

66. Ebert, *An Illini Century*, 41.

67. *Ibid.*, 42.

68. Isreal, ed., *Sears Catalogue*, 27, 8 page insert between pages 32-33.

69. *Ibid.*

70. Richard W. Schwartz, "Dr. John Harvey Kellogg as a Social Gospel Practitioner," *Journal of the Illinois State Historical Society* LVII (Spring, 1964); United States Bureau of Census, *Historical Statistics*, 26.

71. E. Andrews, "The Sum and Substance of Antiseptic Surgery," *The Chicago Medical Examiner*, N. S. Davis, ed., X (Chicago, 1869), 734.

72. *Ibid.*, 737.

73. *Chicago Evening Journal*, Jan. 10, 1881; *Chicago Evening Journal*, Dec. 14, 1885; *Egyptian Press*, April 13, 1893; *Chicago Tribune*, March 14, 1898.

74. Bessie Louise Pierce, *A History of Chicago: The Rise of a Modern City*, III (New York, 1957), 456.

75. George A. Barclay, "The Keeley League," *Journal of the Illinois State Historical Society* LVIII (Winter, 1964), 341.

76. See Table 2.

2
Structure of Governmental Power

Let us bear in mind in all we do that we are legislating
for one of the greatest states on earth, a State that is yet
in its infancy, and has already won the admiration of
mankind: a State which if guided by those principles of
liberty and true republican government ordained by the
fathers, must have a career of unparalled grandeur and
glory. Therefore let us build for the centuries.

John Peter Altgeld[1]

To many people of Illinois from the close of the Civil
War to the turn of the century, Springfield was synonymous with
state government, and to many of them the only reason to go there
was for governmental purposes. The capital had been the functioning center of government in Illinois since December, 1839. Because
of inadequate transportation facilities, the city remained in relative
isolation until the 1850s, and this remoteness contributed greatly to
its importance in state affairs. Legislators and their wives had little
choice but to spend the entire session of the General Assembly in
residence, giving a flair to the social life and inadvertently a continuity to the government.

In 1847 Julie Trumbull commented on the holiday festivities in
the community, including a party to be held at the Lincoln's for
which "the tickets issued were pretty gether [sic] up, and I think it
probable that it is all of style that will be in the affair."[2] Mrs.
Trumbull's complaints at the lack of style in Springfield's social life
were to be alleviated somewhat by the hectic pace of the war years,
but by 1865 Springfield still held to its small-town ways and was a
far cry from the sophistication of eastern capitals.

From the arrival of the railroads until Appomattox the growing
fissures threatening the union of the North and South, the divided
sympathies of the people of Illinois on the issues of slavery and

35

states' rights, and the intimate connections of the capital city with such prominent statesmen as Abraham Lincoln and Stephen A. Douglas, kept it at a high pitch of excitement. Demands upon the state government made by the Civil War focused great attention upon the little city. During all these years the relationship between Springfield and the state government was intimate, and the majority of the business conducted in the city was affected by the official business transpiring in the capitol building. The stage for these activities was a graceful buff-colored stone structure that had housed the state government since 1853.[3] It stood in a three-acre square in the center of the city about one-fourth mile east of the present capitol.

The visitor to Springfield in the spring of 1865 could find many new homes and businesses. The *Illinois State Register* was settling into its new building and a new city waterworks was being built to pump water from the Sangamon River for the capital city. Four primary schools, one high school, and a commercial college served the educational needs of the community.

Needs of a more frivolous nature were met by Varney's Theater (now known as Capitol Hall), the Opera House, and Madame Levant, the clairvoyant. Madame Lucinda Taylor ran a less mystical establishment known as "Fort Taylor" because of its popularity with soldiers from Fort Butler. Sixty-three saloons, including the new Reisch Saloon, quenched the prairie thirsts of the city—and one such business was reputed to dispense 4,000 glasses of beer per day.

There were 15,000 residents in Springfield in 1865. Forty of them owned Singer sewing machines. When they went out to eat they could patronize Halfen and Company on East Adams Street, or Doul's Restaurant, "the Delmonico's of Springfield."[4] Visitors to the city were encouraged by hotel facilities: "The St. Nicholas Hotel has just been enlarged by a 60-by-157-foot addition, and the Chenery House had added a wing 120-by-157 feet. Work had started on a new hotel which was to cost $200,000 and would be called the Leland. . . . It would have in its basement a billiard room, saloon, barbershop, bathroom and reading room."[5]

Between 1865 and 1898, however, Springfield developed characteristics which made having the state government within its limits seem less important to the city than ever before or since. The change in the atmosphere inspired a *New York Daily Tribune* reporter covering Lincoln's funeral to write, "The importance of the city has consisted mainly in its being the state capital, yet it has a large trade with the surrounding country, and railroads intersect here, which gives communication north, south, east and west."[6] Improved transportation took legislators out of the city more frequently, thus making the central location of the state capitol less important. The burning issues of maintaining the union and abolishing slavery were no longer present to draw the constant attention of the citizens toward the city, and had not been replaced by others commanding equal interest.

In addition, the state government was not ready as yet to benefit Springfield as the city's largest employer. The citizens of Illinois, for the most part, seemed to have been left to themselves by the state and national governments, or at best to the will of the county or municipal governments in solving everyday problems. The population of Springfield grew from 9,320 in 1860 to 34,159 in 1900, but commercial and industrial activities grew faster than those associated with government. Typical of the period, even the capital city seemed anxious to develop identity outside of government. Business was relatively more important to the city than it had been in the turbulent, though in many ways simpler, period before the Civil War or than it was to be after the expansion of government in the twentieth century. In 1890 there were, for example, 3,269 factory workers in the city when it had a population of 24,963, and only 5,111 in 1940 when Springfield's population numbered 75,503. Even the state fair, after the first was held in the capital in 1853, did not return on a permanent basis until 1894.

Since geographical location was no longer a major concern, Springfield fell into the category of other cities of its size, sharing with them many of the problems of a developing urban area which could not offer the diversions of a metropolis like Chicago. In contrast to earlier years, politicians sought entertainment instead of providing it, and legislators became less colorful as committees and commissions replaced the compelling oratory of the prewar period. Hotels and amusements were available, and sanitation problems were not much greater than elsewhere. Only a few roads and sidewalks had been planked before the war. The hazards of perambulation caused the *Journal* to observe in January, 1865, that "owing, probably, to the execrable condition of the streets and crossings not a single drunken person was seen upon the streets yesterday. A drunken man falling in gutter must have smothered in the mud."[7] Gas lights appeared on the streets in 1855, a date comparable to other cities. Local transportation consisted of street railway-cars pulled by horses until 1890 when electricity became the motive power. As a result of Springfield's loss of special appeal, politicians made several attempts to remove the capital. Chicago, Peoria, East St. Louis, and other cities made bids between 1865 and 1871. The members of the legislature toured Peoria in March, 1871, and were impressed with the city's political, financial, and aesthetic possibilities as a capital site. But the *Chicago Tribune* observed that agitation to move the capital to Peoria was "a shrewd Chicago trick," for if it were ever decided to move the seat of government "all [the] reasons which have been urged in favor of Peoria will apply with equal force to Chicago, and, if the issue is reduced to a financial test, the latter city can and will outbid the former at the rate of ten to one, if necessary."[8] Although it was a clear violation of the law, the legislature planned to meet in Chicago in 1871. Only the Great Fire prevented the experiment.

Perhaps the most pressing and justifiable complaint was that the capitol at Springfield was too small for the governmental offices, many of which occupied rented quarters throughout the city. The demand for increased facilities led the Twenty-Fifth General Assembly to pass an act on February 25, 1867, which provided for the construction of a new statehouse. This construction took dispute-filled years amid frequent charges of corruption. On March 11, 1868, ground was broken on an eight-and-one-half acre plot. The legislature first occupied the unfinished building in 1876, although construction continued until 1888. The total cost, the subject of most of the controversy, was over $4,000,000.

The building, in the form of a Latin cross, was of a composite architectural style. Constructed of Niagara limestone from the quarries of Joliet and Lemont, the capitol consisted of a basement, three upper stories, a gallery floor, and a dome. Large murals and statuary of varying aesthetic quality took their place over time. In 1898 the first floor contained the offices of the various state boards; the second floor contained the executive offices and chambers of the Supreme Court; and the third floor was the province of the General Assembly, with the north wing containing the senate chamber and the south quartering the house of representatives. The two remaining wings housed the multiplying state agencies. Other facilities and buildings in the present capitol complex did not materialize until well into the twentieth century, but with the construction of the capitol itself the state government was permanently settled in Springfield.

As the physical surroundings changed, so did the structure of state government itself demand modification. It was obvious before 1865 that the growth and modernization of the state required a corresponding centralization and awareness of the government to meet new problems and to eliminate abuses. The constitution became increasingly unpopular when enterprising legislators found ways to avoid its restrictions. Imaginative increases in appropriations for legislative and executive maintenance helped to solve the personal financial problems of the politicians, and they increased this item of the budget from $256,878 in 1858 to $840,380 in 1868. Although the public agreed that the lawmakers were underpaid, their methods of helping themselves provoked criticism. The *Journal* contended that the Constitution of 1848 "was made for totally different times, that the state was now reaping the evils of what, at the time of its adoption, was considered one of its chief excellences—the check upon profligate legislatures. But does that," it questioned, "justify the Legislature of today in seeking to evade or set it aside?"[9] Others pointed out that it was simply impossible "to run the state government for three months without violating"[10] the constitution.

The constitutional safeguards against unlimited chartering of corporations became paper tigers when a general agreement among the legislators made every case exceptional. Operating in this manner, the Twenty-Sixth General Assembly passed some 1,700 private laws incorporating a tremendous variety of schemes which filled three volumes. In contrast, without definite mandates to meet the new problems of the industrial era, the public laws of the same General Assembly fit nicely into one modest volume. Governor Palmer observed in 1870 that under the old constitution "the Executive Department was destitute of influence, the Judicial Department was unequal to its greatly increased duties, while the Legislature, regardless of the limitations upon its authority, was practically the supreme power in the State. Before the adoption of the constitution of 1870, the history of the American States presented no example of a government more defective or vicious than that of the State of Illinois."[11] Vast numbers of new people, the expanding economy, and the growth of urban centers, especially Chicago, required a change in the basic law.

Efforts to prepare a more elastic and positive constitution failed in 1862 because of the partisanship of the convention. In a more successful attempt in 1869, the voters instructed the General Assembly to order an election of delegates to a constitutional convention. The eighty-five members elected met at Springfield, December 13, 1869, to begin their task. Generally an able group, it included forty-four Republicans, most of whom came from the

counties north of the National Road (U.S. 40), and forty-one
Democrats, from the southern and western counties. There were
fifty-three lawyers, twelve farmers, ten merchants, bankers, and
traders, six doctors, two blacksmiths, one minister, and one
editor.[12]

In general, the delegates agreed upon the need to centralize
power and to turn the state into a more adequately rational and
cohesive unit. To make the government more responsible to all the
people, the convention, after defeating a blanket motion against all
special legislation, agreed to prohibit such favoritism in all cases
"where a general law can be made applicable."[13] Twenty-three
specific prohibitions were included in the constitution which covered the most common infractions of the past. After long and
bitter debate over the suffrage question, it was decided that Negroes should have the vote but that women and unnaturalized
foreigners should not. And to help unify the state and to break the
political sectionalism which had developed in the years immediately
before and after the Civil War, the principles of cumulative voting
and minority representation were included. To secure representation of the minority party in heavily one-party districts, and to make
the division in the General Assembly more nearly equal to that
between the total number of voters in the state, each voter was
permitted to cast as many votes for one candidate as there were
representatives to be elected, or he could distribute his votes "or
equal parts thereof, among the candidates as he shall see fit."[14]
According to Joseph Medill, who chaired the committee that produced it, this plan would allow the majority to rule, but at the same
time, it would give "the disenfranchised minority, who may amount
to almost one-half of the community, some voice, some representation in government, some chance to be heard."[15]

To provide continuity to government, the new constitution
abolished the prohibition against a governor succeeding himself.
The salaries of most officials of the state were established by law,
thereby preventing the irregular efforts to increase incomes of the
past. The process of legislating was made more rational by requiring that all bills, without exception, as possible under the old constitution, be read on three different days, that all bills and amendments be printed before their final passage, and that only one
subject be embraced in each bill. The judiciary was enlarged by
adding four justices to the Supreme Court and by providing for
appellate courts and county courts of record. Downstate delegates
were suspicious of any "favoritism" for Cook County, but finally

agreed to additional court facilities to enable that cauldron of business and crime to keep up with its legal problems.

Responding to the problems of industrialization, the convention made important decisions regarding transportation and warehousing. Under the persuasive and informed eloquence of Reuben M. Benjamin of Bloomington and others, the delegates underwent a drastic change in their original attitude toward railroads. At the outset, the majority favored increased competition as the only workable regulative force. But loud voices called for state regulation, one delegate insisting that "we must have a new deal and new decisions on this subject."[16] In the closing days of the convention, a four-day debate changed their hands-off approach and they declared railroads to be "public highways" subject to the control of government. The General Assembly now had the mandate to "pass laws establishing reasonable maximum rates of charges for the transportation of passengers and freight on the different railroads in this State."[17] And, should the courts prevent the operation of that section, a famous mandatory provision provided a second line of defense, enforceable by no other means than the oath of the assemblymen to obey the constitution. "The General Assembly shall pass laws to correct abuses and to prevent unjust discrimination and extortion in the rates of freight and passenger tariffs on the different railroads in this state, and enforce such laws by adequate penalties to the extent, if necessary for that purpose, of forfeiture of their property and franchises."[18] In the grain trade, where, in the words of Medill, "competition has been blotted out and combination has seized the business,"[19] grain elevators which were operated for profit became by law "public warehouses." Their owners made weekly statements of their business activities, and the General Assembly passed laws providing "for the inspection of grain, for the protection of producers, shippers and receivers of grain and produce."[20]

An extended debate concerning the future of the Illinois and Michigan Canal brought sectional feelings to a high point as delegates from the northern part of the state wished it to maintain ownership, management, and maintenance of the canal while those from the south felt that it should be sold or leased. Common sense broke the deadlock and led to the adoption of a compromise providing that it should never be sold or leased until the voters agreed at a general election.[21]

In other areas the delegates agreed with Daniel Cameron and colleagues that "the special wants and dangers to which the miners, as a class are exposed, entitle them to special protection,"[22] and the convention wrote requirements into the new constitution demanding laws to increase the health and safety of working conditions for miners. The new constitution encouraged liberal homestead and exemption laws, as well as drainage districts. The General Assembly should "provide a thorough and efficient system of free schools,"[23] but public money could not be contributed to the support of sectarian or church-affiliated educational institutions. Amendment of the new document required the two-thirds vote of both houses of the General Assembly in addition to a majority of the votes cast at the general election or two-thirds of the votes cast on the issue. The General Assembly was restricted to proposing amendments to no more than three articles of the constitution in a single session and to the same article only once in four years.[24]

The convention adjourned on May 13, 1870, after ninety-five days of debate. The majority of public comment seemed favorable to the work of the convention, and the debate over its merits never became really heated. Richard Oglesby informed Lyman Trumbull in June, 1870, that "it looks up to this time as though the new constitution will be accepted. There is, however, no organization for or against it."[25] The delegates placed eight separate articles containing the most drastic changes on a separate ballot. These were the articles relating to counties, warehouses, railroads, the Illinois Central railroad tax, removal of county seats, minority representation, municipal subscription to railroads or private corporations, and the Illinois-Michigan Canal. The entire package was endorsed by the voters on July 2, 1870, and the constitution replaced the old document on August 8, 1870.

The basic structure of state government did not change as a result of the document, although each branch made several important internal adjustments. The bicameral General Assembly continued to be the most powerful section of the state government exercising "every power not delegated to some other department, or expressly denied to it by the Constitution."[26] New apportionment provisions nearly doubled the numbers of legislators in the General Assembly. In 1868 there were only twenty-five senators and eighty-five representatives. Under the new document the state was apportioned into fifty-one senatorial districts, each of which elected a senator for a four-year term. Three representatives were elected to two-year terms from each of the senatorial districts, for a total of 153. Regular sessions began early in January following the election, with additional sessions for stated special purposes at the call of the governor. State and national politics continued their close relationship as members of both houses faced election on the same day as did the President, the members of Congress, and the governor.

The presiding officer of the senate was the lieutenant governor, but a president *pro tem* presided in the former's absence. The speaker of the house was in many ways the most powerful political leader in the state. He personally appointed all committees, paying off political debts and rewarding friends in the process. The chairmanships of such important committees as corporations, railroads, appropriations, insurance, judiciary, and printing were objects of great competition. Their formal power lay in the fact that only a resolution of the house, an infrequent occurrence, could overcome the will of the chairman in calling bills out of committee where important ones could be buried in subcommittees or at times simply "lost" or "misplaced."

The speaker had the power to recognize or ignore members of the house during regular debate and to declare the results of votes except when the yeas and nays were recorded. Elijah M. Haines (Independent, Lake County), Speaker in the Twenty-Ninth General Assembly, illustrates the power of this official to frustrate opposition. Having established a record of obstreperousness at the constitutional convention, he lived up to his independent label by his refusal to recognize members, be they Democrat, Republican, or Independent, who desired to oppose any measure he favored. On April 11, 1875, widespread dissatisfaction with Haines's arbitrary use of parliamentary law and the house rules led to a free-for-all in the chamber. To quote the *Chicago Times*, "Hell broke loose." The *Tribune* explained that "the tumults [were] precipitated by efforts to exclude a Republican protest. A splenetic and rash Republican (Representative Alfred M. Jones, Jo Daviess) hurls a book at [Lewis F.] Platen [Democrat, Hardin]. Whereat that incomparable idiot flounders like an acephalous rooster. Drawn up in a plug-ugly affray, cowardice and not shame prevents a Tipperary head-smashing."[27]

Three men served two terms as speaker. Shelby M. Cullom (Republican, Sangamon, 1860-62, 1872-74) used the knowledge of the state and political machines, as well as the contacts he made, to elevate himself to the governorship and later to the United States Senate. Franklin Corwin presided over the house in the Twenty-Fifth and Twenty-Sixth General Assemblies, opening the gate to a flood of private legislation. Horace H. Thomas (Republican, Cook) was the first resident of Chicago to hold the position (Thirty-Second General Assembly, 1880-82), and Clayton E. Crafts (Democrat, Cook) was the only Democrat to hold the position during the period (Thirty-Seventh and Thirty-Eighth General Assemblies, 1890-94).

The members of the General Assembly were personally similar during the period, regardless of party affiliation. It was made up of upper-middle-class men who were relatively wealthy and accomplished. Neither the very rich nor the very poor won seats with any frequency. Only one member could be classified as a laborer in the Twenty-Fourth General Assembly (1864-66), seven in the Thirty-Third (1882-84), and two in the Forty-First (1898-1900). Farmers, most of them owning over 300 acres of land, numbered thirty-nine in 1864, fifty in 1882 (the General Assembly had nearly doubled in size), and the same in 1898. Thirty-nine members were lawyers in 1864, and sixty-one in both 1882 and 1898, the only noticeable shift being from lawyers of general practice in the early period to those representing special business interests and corporations in the latter. Those who might be classified as nonlegal professional people numbered seventeen in 1864, increased to nearly forty in 1883, but dropped to seventeen in 1898. The most marked difference, reflecting the change in Illinois society, involved the numbers of businessmen, the category increasing from sixteen in 1864, to forty-eight in 1882, and then to sixty-one by 1898. The increase in members of foreign birth reflected both the increase in immigration during the period and the material and political success of the various groups. In the legislature of 1868 there were ten members of foreign birth; in that of 1874 there were twenty-three; thirty-three in 1888; and thirty-nine in 1898. Those of German and Irish descent predominated. In 1876 John W. E. Thomas from Chicago's third district was the first Negro to become a state representative in Illinois, and he served in the Thirtieth, Thirty-Third, and Thirty-Fourth General Assemblies. The three other blacks who served in the period were Edward Morris, 1890, 1902; William Martin, 1898; and John Jones, 1900.

The operating expenses of the General Assembly amounted to over $475,000 in 1870 to 1872, dropped to around $250,000 for most of the remaining biennia, and rebounded to $422,000 in the biennium, 1898 to 1900. Legislators found that special interest lobbies were available to increase their personal incomes. The exact influence of the "third house" is impossible to measure, and, of course, lobbyists were not then required to register. William P.

Peirce told the Constitutional Convention of 1870 that "the 'Chicago horse railroad' bill, of the session of 1865, the new 'State house' bill, of the session of 1867, and the 'lake front' bill of the last session—went through the Legislature of this State by the purchase of votes with money." More specifically, when the Twenty-Fifth General Assembly of which Peirce was a member, was considering the statehouse bill, any member of the lower house, in his words, "could have gone to the Leland House any day for two weeks before the passage of that bill and received $2,000 by promising to give his vote and support to that measure."[28] In the last days of consideration of the bill, the price of a vote apparently rose to $5,000. Although Chicago traction magnates and bankers would attempt to buy favors in Springfield in the 1890s, the methods which legislators used in tapping this source differed somewhat after the Constitution of 1870 curtailed special or private legislation. After 1870 it was easier to collect by threatening to introduce or to support regulative legislation, or, unless properly rewarded by the groups involved, to advocate strict enforcement of available laws.

The executive power in Illinois did not divide neatly into departments under the supervision and responsibility of the governor. Instead, a complex assortment of local and state officials made decisions in major problem areas, dividing and confusing the responsibility. The Constitution of the United States concentrated executive authority in a single office providing that "the executive power shall be vested in a president of the United States of America." But the Constitution of 1870, while it stated that "the supreme executive power shall be vested in the governor," qualified that statement by declaring that the "executive department shall consist of a governor, lieutenant governor, secretary of state, auditor of public accounts, treasurer, superintendent of public instruction, and the attorney general."[29] Each officer ran for election independently of the governor and had no real obligation to support his program.

Most observers felt that the key function of the governor in this period was his constitutional duty "to take care that the laws be faithfully executed."[30] The general attitude toward the governor as an innovator and policymaker led a delegate to the Constitutional Convention of 1870 to insist that "the power to inaugurate and mature the policy of the State belongs exclusively to the General Assembly, and that the duty of the Governor is to execute that policy, not to say what the policy shall be."[31] In his inaugural address Governor Oglesby spoke of the government's duty "to guard with special care the local interests of the State, and to contribute our best energies in developing its resources. I am thankful that this duty falls chiefly upon the legislative branch of government."[32] Beginning his second term, Governor Cullom exclaimed, "I have no policy to announce other than that contained in those principles of economy, faithfulness to duty, and impartial administration of the laws."[33]

It is not surprising, then, that the legislature continued to grant administrative authority which should have remained with the governor to other state officers or to newly created administrative commissions and agencies. These limitations caused John M. Palmer to exclaim when being urged to accept the nomination in 1868, "the Governor of Illinois is a mere figure-head. To be a governor for four years is to waste four years, take it out of my life at a time that I am profitably and most pleasantly employed."[34] For much the same reasons John Peter Altgeld remarked that during the decade of the 1880s, none of the nation's governors had "done anything of an enduring character for their country or for the progress of civilization . . . anything that can be regarded as raising the standard of public morals, creating a healthy public sentiment, or solving in a proper manner any of the great questions, both economic and social, that are calling for solution."[35]

Within these limitations, however, the governor's constitutional duties were still broad enough for a strong man to exert considerable leadership. If he had a program or recommendations, he could give them wide publicity through his duty to address the General Assembly on the condition of the state at the beginning of each session and at the conclusion of his term of office. He was obliged to accompany this statement with an account of finances received and expended by him, as well as his estimate of tax money necessary to realize his goals.

Unfortunately, no governor during the period delivered a real budget message. This fact reflected the lack of assistance in preparing financial estimates (Governor Beveridge called this a "legislative wrong"),[36] but more important, program-oriented reform or any long-term policy at all was obviously impossible without a carefully prepared budget presented early in an administration. No governor made use of his power to prorogue the General Assembly as Governor Yates had done in 1863, but numerous special sessions dealt with emergencies. The governor possessed the veto power over legislation; he was granted the item veto by amendment to the constitution in 1884, but a majority vote of the

General Assembly could override it before 1870 and a two-thirds vote after the adoption of the new constitution.

Patronage appointments proved both a blessing and a curse as governors daily faced long queues of favor seekers eager for jobs. Wise dispersal of patronage may have helped governors who had ambitions for the Senate (Yates, Oglesby, Cullom, and Palmer became United States Senators), but it was time consuming and drained energies needed in other areas. The press of appointments contributed to governor-elect Altgeld's complete physical breakdown before his inauguration.[37]

An increasingly important function of the governor during this period was his position as commander-in-chief of the military forces of Illinois. The wide use of the militia in industrial disputes had great effect upon labor-management relations and upon the lives of those laborers directly involved with the conflicts. The tribulations involved with his power to grant pardons, reprieves, and commutations of sentences of prisoners led Governor Palmer to say "any person unfamiliar with the exercise of the pardoning power, and with the various methods employed to deceive or impress the executive, will often be induced to grant pardons under improper circumstances."[38] Widespread publicity was given this power when Governor Altgeld pardoned the Haymarket rioters. As a result of the complexities of this duty and as a partial backlash against Altgeld's pardoning of the Haymarket "murderers," the board of pardons was created in 1897 to assist the governor in making decisions. In contacts with the national government, strong governors found that assertion of state authority at the expense of federal was unpopular, even though most citizens opposed positive actions from Washington in most spheres. When Governor Palmer in his inaugural message tried to delimit areas for exclusive state action, the press was hostile, and a political opponent exalted that "John D. Calhoun must have had a hand in it. From his almost unknown grave in South Carolina came a deadly vapor. Palmer inhaled it and he is no more."[39] When Palmer vigorously protested the use of a federal army officer, General Phil Sheridan, to command the state militia, and when he objected to the employment of federal troops to maintain order in Chicago following the Great Fire without his request, he faced a similar reaction from the public. The same outcry greeted Governor Altgeld's firm objections to President Grover Cleveland's use of federal troops in the Pullman Strike of 1894 without a request from the state executive. Altgeld "has put Illinois to shame"[40] was the *Chicago Tribune*'s verdict. Thus, although the governor bore responsibility for his administration's record, the structure and operation of government often made it difficult for him to exercise actual control.

Among the remaining offices, that of lieutenant governor assumed the greatest importance in the periods when Governors Oglesby and Cullom resigned to take seats in the United States Senate and John L. Beveridge and John M. Hamilton, the respective lieutenant governors, succeeded to the governorship. The office of attorney general was held in abeyance until created by statute in 1867. It became a constitutional office in 1870. He was to "perform such duties as prescribed by law," but he actually had limited influence as a legal adviser to the state. Special attorneys for the various commissions, boards, departments, and local states attorneys divided the real legal authority. The state's legal business was never concentrated in the hands of one officer. The secretary of state's office kept the records of the state and performed a variety of other duties such as issuing charters to corporations under the general state laws and then exercising some supervisions over them. Fees collected by the secretary of state for his duties rose from $12,659 in the biennium 1874 to 1876 to $195,135 in the biennium 1896 to 1898.

The state treasurer and the auditor of public accounts worked together in dispersing and accounting for public monies. The treasurer, elected for a two-year term and unable to succeed himself, received and disbursed public funds, posting bond to insure against loss. Operating on an independent treasury system, the treasurer kept the money in his office until legally drawn out. An order or warrant from the state auditor was necessary before any funds were received or withdrawn officially. The auditor had no voice over the purpose of expenditures. Loose administrative practices made it customary during the period for both officers to appropriate funds for their own use from tax money collected for the registration and the disbursement of income from municipal bonds. In addition, many officials used for private purposes fees collected for services rendered. And in January, 1893, Governor Altgeld noted that "while it may be true that the law does not contemplate that funds shall be deposited at interest in banks, it is a notorious fact that all custodians of public funds actually draw interest on the balance of such funds."[41] Centralized supervision of state monies did not exist. For example, the treasurer received tax money from the county collectors who were required to register reports with the auditor, but neither state officer had supervisory powers over the county collectors.

A similar diffusion of power grew up as the educational system expanded. The superintendent of public instruction had general supervision over the common schools and state colleges. He had advisory and quasi-judicial powers over local authorities, some administrative and financial powers to examine teachers, to control the distribution of state school funds, and to serve as an ex-officio member on various institutional boards. Capable superintendents such as Newton Bateman and others provided leadership, and expenditures for the common schools rose from over $3,000,000 in 1865 to over $12,000,000 in 1890. In 1880 Illinois ranked second in school expenditure, although it ranked fourth in population. The 704,041 Illinois students used $10.70 per capita in state expenditures for education. Only New York spent more on its school system. Administratively, however, by 1898 there were nearly a dozen officials or agencies in Illinois whose functions were primarily educational. Each normal school had a separate board of trustees appointed by the governor with the consent of the senate, while the board of trustees of the University of Illinois consisted of nine members elected by popular vote with three ex-officio members. These institutions were coordinated neither with the public schools nor with one another in terms of appropriations, educational standards, fees, or admission standards. The several libraries and scientific bureaus established by the state operated with little reference to the others or to the school system.

The Civil War crisis presented Illinois with new kinds of problems for which the apparatus of state government was not adequate. Governor Yates responded to one of them on August 20, 1862, by establishing a state sanitary bureau to provide "hospitals with appliances for the sick and wounded."[42] A board of army auditors was appointed January 3, 1865, and Governor Yates noted in his last message to the General Assembly, "The nation is passing into a new era of its existence. Old forms must be abandoned and enlarged views of the principle of government accepted. The garments of the youth are too contracted for the man."[43]

Enlarged views, however, were out of keeping with the prevalent view that "the general political proposition that government is to be regarded as best which interferes with the people the least will remain forever true."[44] A systematic enlargement of government to deal with the demands stemming from increasing population, urbanization, and industrialization did not materialize. Instead, an ever increasing proliferation of boards and commissions, each dealing with an isolated problem, emerged.

In the relatively simple days at the close of the war, Governor

Oglesby effusively complimented the work done during the conflict by the United States Christian Commission, but warned that "it
is greatly to be feared that any attempt to give it the appearance of
an institution supported by law, will divest [it] of its real character,
and in a short time, discourage those voluntary and unselfish efforts of the public."[45] Four years later, in 1869, the same governor
urged the creation of a state board of public charities. At that time
the state's charitable institutions included the Hospital for the Insane, Institute for the Deaf and Dumb, and the Institute for the
Education of the Blind, all in Jacksonville, an Eye and Ear Infir-
mary in Chicago, and an experimental school for "idiots and
feeble-minded children."[46] Pointing to these institutions with pride,
Oglesby stated, "It may be truly said of Illinois that she does not lag
behind her sister states of the West in zeal, liberality, and intelligent
effort to look after and provide for her children of sorrow."[47]

The legislature approved Oglesby's request for a state board of
charity in 1869. This board of five members, appointed by the
governor, served without pay, except for expenses. Each of the
separate state institutions retained its separate board of trustees,
and the state board failed to set up a central purchasing department
for all the hospitals.

In 1875 the legislature enacted a law to regulate state charitable
institutions, and for the first time required that the superintendents of the asylums and institutes for the feebleminded be "educated and competent physicians."[48] The state's chief concern, however, was fiscal, and eleven of the state institutions expected to be
able to turn back part of their yearly appropriations. Governor
Cullom summed up the situation: "How to care for all the unfortunates in Society without imposing upon the taxpayers of the state
too great burdens, is a serious and perplexing question the consideration of which constitutes one of your most important and labori-
ous duties. . . . It is the duty of those responsible for the administration of affairs to see that it is done at as little cost to the body of the
people as possible."[49]

In 1879 he found "a gratifying evidence" of fiscal responsibility.
In that year the state board of charities advised a decrease in the
next biennium to $1,200,000, down from $1,333,275 and far short
of the $1,400,000 requested. The governor was "substantially in
accord with the recommendation,"[50] despite the fact that all the
state institutions were overcrowded. This overriding concern with
keeping down costs gave Illinois the distinction in 1878 of having
the lowest per capita cost per pupil in deaf and dumb institutions in

the country. The Illinois low of $194.92 compared with $525 for California, $343 for Iowa, and $245 for Pennsylvania. By 1893 the per capita figure for all Illinois charities was reduced to $163. At that time the most expensive public charity was the Soldier's Widow's Home at $254.56 per capita. The least expensive was the Soldiers and Sailors' Home at $108.26 per capita.

By 1885 the state was operating nine homes (including two reformatories) to care for the 14,121 insane, idiots, blind, and deaf and dumb in the state—that census figure not counting those in private charitable institutions. This number was also the total of those afflicted and not the total number actually cared for by the state. By 1897 the total number of persons in state homes was only 8,948. Governor Hamilton reiterated the emphasis on cost in 1885: "It has been demonstrated beyond question that the cheapest and best way of taking care of these unfortunates is in State Institutions, aggregating and accommodating large numbers under one system of care and management."[51]

Although Governor Hamilton voiced the problem of centralizing control, nothing was done to actually put all of the state institutions under one management. By 1900, fifteen charitable institutions were in operation, with forty-nine trustees, five board of charities' members, plus fifteen local treasurers. Each institution purchased its own supplies. The trustees were unpaid, except for per diem expenses, and their performance "tended to become merely perfunctory."[52] The problems of such inefficiency were brought to light in 1899 when the General Assembly spent $50,000 to construct an insane asylum in Peoria. The asylum was built "over an abandoned coal mine, which was found upon examination to be so badly planned and constructed that it was declared unsafe for occupation"[53] and was torn down.

The prison system was considered part of the charitable function of the state, and prison problems plagued all of the administrations during the period. The first state prison was built in Alton in 1827. The state sold the Alton prison in 1857 when it built a new prison in Joliet. In 1865 Governor Yates recommended that "the head of our State benevolent institution [prison] should have a fixed salary and not a percentage of the profit."[54] The state's involvement in the Joliet enterprise at that time was as an absentee landlord—the policy being to lease the prison (and prisoners) to private individuals as a profit-making venture.

A real crisis occurred in 1867 when the lessees announced their intention to give up their contract on June 30. Governor Oglesby called a special session of the legislature to ask for an appropriation to feed and clothe the more than 1,000 prisoners who were about to become dependent on a state that legally could not spend any money for their support. Rather than look for a new lessee, the governor suggested that the state undertake to run the prision itself "and dispense with the service of all intermediates . . . whose object will never be punishment or reformation of the criminal, but the realization of profit from his labor."[55]

TABLE 2. STATE CHARITABLE INSTITUTIONS

Institution	Location	Date Authorized
Central Hospital for the Insane	Jacksonville	1847
Southern Hospital for the Insane	Anna	1869
Northern Hospital for the Insane	Elgin	1869
Eastern Hospital for the Insane	Kankakee	1877
Western Hospital for the Insane	Watertown	1895
Hospital for Incurable Insane	Bartonville	1895
Asylum for Insane Criminals	Chester	1889
Asylum for Feeble-Minded Children	Jacksonville	1865
Institution for the Deaf, Dumb, and Blind	Jacksonville	1839
Institution for the Blind	Jacksonville	1848
Industrial Home for the Blind	Chicago	1887
Charitable Eye and Ear Infirmary	Chicago	1858
Training School for Girls	Geneva	1893
Soldiers' Orphans Home	Normal	1865
Soldiers and Sailors Home	Quincy	1885
Soldiers' Widows Home	Wilmington	1895
State Prisons		
State Penitentiary	Joliet	1857
State Reformatory	Pontiac	1867
Southern Penitentiary	Chester	1877

The state did take over the prison, and after attempting unsuccessfully to contract out the labor of the convicts, worked them for four years on the state account. For the ten-and-one-half years the prison was leased, the total cost to the state was $145,188.37. From July, 1867, to the fall of 1871, the state worked the prisoners at a cost of $874,000. "An experience of four years of loss to the State . . . induced a change from the state account to the contract plan."[56] Unwilling to incur such a loss, the state once more attempted to sell the labor of the convicts on a contract basis—this time with great success. The prison became self-supporting.

The state itself became one of the chief contractors, hiring 300 convicts to help build the new statehouse. This had the double advantage that "it will hereafter give steady employment for nearly

¼ of the number of convicts now in the Penitentiary, [and] that it will require but a small outlay of capital."[57] Not only could the state save on building costs; it also could be sure that one of its biggest prison contracts was promptly paid.

Agitation from free labor, which was unable to compete success-fully with the low cost of convict labor, led to a constitutional amendment in 1886 abolishing the convict contract system. After dismissing the possibility of an educational apprenticeship pro-gram as too expensive, and a piece-price system as essentially the same as the outlawed contract system, the prison system went back to the 1867 to 1871 model and began working prisoners on the state account. A large captive work force, even working directly for the state, still seemed an unfair competition with free labor, and Gov-ernor Tanner in 1897 attempted to lessen the impact on the market by limiting the number in any one trade to 100.

Until 1897, all applications for pardon went directly to the gov-ernor, a practice that was both time consuming and fraught with possibilities for political abuse. With the new board of pardons, three persons (no more than two belonging to the same party) at salaries of $2,000 a year investigated and recommended action on pardons and commutations. The salary went up to $3,500 per year in 1894 when the board assumed parole powers. The board actually served to reduce rather than increase the number of pardons. In 1895 the state board of pardons "considered 123 applications for pardon and recommended to the Governor a full and free pardon in one case and a commutation of sentence in nineteen cases."[58] As Governor Tanner commented in 1901, "in a very large number of cases where the trial judge and states' attorney have recommended a pardon, it has been denied."[59]

The governor appointed the first state board of health in 1877. The board consisted of seven members, each serving a seven-year term, with one member rotating off the board every year. Members did not have to be physicians, and they served without pay. A $10 per diem was paid for expenses, plus the salary of a full-time secretary. Not always popular, "there were doubts in the minds of many good people as to its necessity, and for a time a prejudice against its work."[60] The board began with a modest $1,669 yearly expenditure, an amount which rose gradually. It spent a total of $25,248 in 1889 to 1890, dropping back to $18,861 in 1891 to 1892.

The board's initial success was in the field of certifying physicians and medical schools in compliance with the Medical Practices Act. In its first two years "more than 5,000 persons practicing medicine have complied with the law and received certificates, and it is estimated that 1400 persons who had been practicing medicine and were unable to comply with the law, have left the State."[61] It also broke up fraudulent medical colleges, and Governor Cullom rejoiced that "much has been accomplished at little expense to the State."[62] The work of the board changed somewhat in 1881 to 1882 when it was credited with saving the state $3,500,000 during a smallpox epidemic "through preventative and protective measures."[63]

Much of the success of the board of health goes to its president, Dr. John H. Rauch. Rauch served in 1876 as president of the American Public Health Association, and attempted to coordinate the work of the Illinois board with national and regional health activities.

Rauch believed smallpox outbreaks were caused by the influx of unvaccinated immigrants, and he worked tirelessly to pressure the national board of health to require effective vaccinations of all who entered the country. The board soon found that immigrants were not alone in avoiding vaccination. Some Illinois doctors feared the procedure and blamed it for everything from syphilis to tuberculosis.[64] Parents often distrusted it as well, and when vaccinations for smallpox became mandatory for all school children, the board of health found itself innoculating 600,000 children in a six-month period.

Dr. Rauch supplemented the effect of his vaccination program with publications describing "rules and instructions for quarantine, disinfection and sanitation"[65] for such diseases as diphtheria, scarlet fever, and smallpox. Rauch's office also set up prohibitions and regulations for transporting the dead.

An early effort of the board of health in supervising medical education was a resolution on November 15, 1877, not to recognize medical schools with less than two-year programs. More specific requirements set in 1883 included the stipulation that medical schools: 1. exclude candidates with questionable morals; 2. require candidates to show diplomas from liberal arts colleges or a high school—or pass an equivalency test; 3. require courses in anatomy, physiology, chemistry, materia medica, and therapeutics, theory and practice of medicine, pathology, surgery, obstetrics and gynecology, hygiene and medical jurisprudence.[66] These standards made Illinois a leader in the drive for professional medical training, and were copied by other states.

The legislature was so pleased with the work of the board of health that in 1881 it established two similar boards. The board of pharmacy had the responsibility for examining pharmacists and licensing drugs and patent medicines. It had five members, all with at least ten-years' experience as pharmacists, and all appointed by the governor. They received $8 per diem and an annual salary was provided for a secretary. The board of dental examiners also had five members, but they needed only five-years' experience, and received $10 per diem.

In addition to its original duties, the board of health also superintended vital and mortuary statistics and "all details which pertain to sewerage, drainage, inspection of private residences and the general policy as to violations of health laws and accumulations of filth."[67] Governor Tanner requested in 1901 that the examination of medical schools and doctors be placed under a separate board of medical examiners and that the board of health be allowed to concentrate on "sanitary duties."

By 1900 the commission structure included a claims commission, a board of canal commissioners, a food commission, a board of equalization, a practice commission and a revenue commission, state board of examiners of architects, and state board of examiners of horseshoers, as well as numerous agricultural agencies.

The history of government by commission in Illinois was basically a history of improvisation, of action taken to deal with a crushing imperative without integrating the new program into a well-defined comprehensive operation. In attempting to limit government spending, the legislature unwittingly created a monster of budgetary inefficiency. By 1893 it was apparent to Governor Altgeld that "there has been a tendency to create unnecessary boards . . . many of these should be abolished and their duties, so far as they perform any necessary service, be assigned to some of the regular county or state officers."[68]

Not to be lost sight of, however, in the jumble of secretaries' salaries and per diem expense accounts, were the very real accomplishments performed by those boards. Very early in its existence Illinois had accepted its obligation to "promote the general welfare" through positive action, and by 1900 that positive action was touching the lives of every Illinoisan who visited a dentist, or purchased Chicago-butchered beef, filled a prescription, fertilized a farm, or became insane.

The increase in the number of semi-independent agencies gave the appearance of state action in problem areas, but at the same time their creation tended to divide authority and increase the governor's patronage burden. Governor Altgeld regretted the ex-

pense of "unnecessary boards," and he pointed out that "experience has shown that division of responsibility in public bodies is
productive of corruption and unjust measures; that when the public can put its finger upon the individual and hold him responsible,
he will be more careful and circumspect in his actions and will make
more effort to keep up, at least a semblance of fairness, than he will
if there are a large number of others to share responsibility with
him."[69] Most of the agencies, often having overlapping jurisdiction,
had only investigatory power, and their actions were in nearly all
cases subject to judicial review. Most important, these multiple
agencies, fractionalizing major areas of governmental concern,
were indicative of the transitional nature of administrative government between a simpler period when a small number of constitutional and elected officers were sufficient and the twentieth
century when large departments operated in those earlier-defined
areas of constant involvement.

State supervision of corporations was more rational and effective
than many other areas of administration. The secretary of state
under the corporation law of 1872 had general charge of certification of corporations. In a unique provision of that law, in operation
in only one other state, persons desiring to form a corporation first
had to obtain permission from the secretary of state before solicit-
ing subscriptions to the capital stock. This provision safeguarded
the investor by supervising the work of corporations during the
period of promotion. Foreign corporations were put under the
control of the secretary of state in 1897. He did not require annual
reports, however, until 1901. The attorney general as well as the
secretary of state enforced the state's antitrust law of 1891. Separate
acts to incorporate and govern fire, marine, and inland navigation
insurance companies and to organize and regulate the life insurance business went into effect in 1869. The attorney general and
the secretary of state divided supervisory duties. In 1893 the insurance department was created and put under the control of the
insurance superintendent, to whom the execution of all laws relating to insurance and insurance companies doing business in
the state was entrusted. The general banking law of 1887 put the
supervision of banks in the state under the control of the auditor.

Of greatest importance was the creation of the railroad and
warehouse commission in 1871 with important powers of supervision and regulation of railroads and warehouses. In this area Illinois had claim to genuine administrative innovation. The body
had power to investigate the condition, management, and policy of

railroads and warehouses and to inquire into charges of unfair discrimination, to sue for the enforcement of penalties, and to require annual reports from both. After 1873 the commission was authorized to establish a schedule of reasonable maximum rates for passenger and freight on railroads within the state. The pioneer efforts of this group resulted in a maze of litigation which attracted national attention, established precedents, and improved transportation and warehousing within Illinois.

A fairly extensive list of labor laws had been passed by 1898, but one of the most significant features of its administration was the division of power between the various state inspectors and agencies and other state and local authorities involved. A bureau of labor statistics was formed in 1879, a state mining board providing for mine inspectors in 1883, a factory inspectors office in 1893, and a state board of arbitration in 1895. As in the other areas, administration suffered from lack of centralization, real authority, and appropriations.

The history of the bureau of labor statistics was typical of the entire system of government by commission. An attempt to create a bureau of labor statistics failed in 1877, bills to the effect being introduced into the house by Henry F. Sheridan (Democrat, Cook) and David H. Zepp (Republican, Montgomery). Sheridan's bill received an unfavorable recommendation by the committee of manufactures, while Zepp's bill passed the house but died when the senate judiciary committee recommended that it lay on the table. Reformist elements within the council of trade and labor unions of Chicago had hoped for some time to initiate increased concern on the part of the government with the conditions of the labor force in Illinois. In response to their request, Christian Meyer (Socialist, Cook) introduced a resolution into the house on February 17, 1879, asking "that the speaker of this house shall appoint a special committee of five, who shall visit the City of Chicago and Braidwood to obtain such information as may be required for the members of this House, to enact such laws as will ameliorate the conditions of the working people of this state."[70] The speaker appointed a seven-man special committee on labor consisting of three Republicans, two national Republicans, one Democrat, and one Socialist to conduct the requested investigation.

The committee briefly toured several working-class neighborhoods in Chicago and heard the grievances of the Council of Trade and Labor Unions, and Socialist Labor party, and the various Chicago trade unions. It learned of the appalling conditions of the coal miners during a brief visit to Braidwood. The establishment of a bureau of labor statistics, among other suggestions, was requested by each group heard, in the belief that accurate information must precede legislation, and the committee's report contained the recommendation. Six bills introduced in the house in 1879 sought the creation of a bureau of labor statistics. Three of them received "Do Not Pass" recommendations from the committee on labor and manufactures; the committee on the judicial department reported a fourth, with the recommendation that it be printed for the use of the house, but it, too, was lost; the fifth passed the house but received a "Do Not Pass" recommendation from the senate committee on labor and manufactures.

The bill, which finally became law, had been introduced into the senate on January 9, 1879, before the special committee had conducted its investigation by Sylvester Artly (Socialist, Cook). After deleting the sections empowering the prospective bureau to subpoena witnesses and to compel employers to submit statistical data, senators passed the bill on May 6, 1879, the house on May 28, and Governor Cullom signed it into law two days later. Credit for the law goes to its sponsors in the Socialist party and to the support it received from sympathizers in the major parties, more from the Republicans than from the Democrats. It was the only proposal which became law from the long list contained in the report of the special committee on labor.

According to the law, the governor appointed a board of five commissioners. They were to elect one of their number president and to appoint a secretary, in practice frequently a nonmember, into whose hands leadership and direction was to fall. The bureau of labor statistics was "to collect, assort, systematize, and present in biennial report to the General Assembly, statistical details relating to all departments of labor in the State, especially in its relations to commercial, industrial, social, educational, and sanitary conditions of the laboring classes, and to the permanent prosperity of the mechanical, manufacturing, and productive industry of the State."[71] Neither labor nor industry could be compelled to submit information. John S. Lord, the bureau's secretary, lamented the limitations thus imposed in 1883. "At present," he said, "the bureau cannot call upon county, municipal, or other public officials for either assistance or special information; it has no access to official research, save by courtesy; it has no power to summon witnesses, or administer oaths. Consequently, we are wholly dependent upon such voluntary information as may be obtained through personal effort, and the use of printed forms containing interrogatories, sent through the mails."[72] George Schilling, appointed secretary of the bureau during Governor Altgeld's administration, regretted the lack of funds; the secretary received $1,200 a year, and out of the additional $6,000 appropriated annually came $150 salary for each of the five members (exclusive of expenses), the salaries of secretaries and canvassers, incidental expenses, and, after 1883, those related to the issuance of the annual coal report. (The appropriation was increased to $8,000 in 1895 and $10,000 in 1899.)

In spite of the restrictions of power, finances, and the relatively unsophisticated collection and use of statistics, the bureau's biennial *Reports* proved to be valuable sources of information for contemporaries. They are often the exclusive source for scholars investigating topics related to commerce, manufacturing, and labor during the period. Little objection came from the bureau as to the quality or the quantity of responses of those from whom it solicited information. This fact demonstrated the need and the use the collected statistics met for labor, industry, and government. The *Reports* were as objective as possible, and Governor Fifer spoke of their "integrity and impartiality."[73] As such, they revealed a host of inequities and lent support to ameliorative legislation. Governor Hamilton in 1885 recommended the bureau's *Report* to the General Assembly: "The statistical information therein contained of the manufacturing and mining industries of the State, and especially of the wages, cost of living, and general condition of the laboring classes; the relations between capital and labor, as showing the legitimate profits of each, is suggestive and instructive."[74] As a result of its investigations over the years, the bureau recommended the abolition of convict labor and the reorganization of the prison system, measures to protect the health and safety of miners, the abolition of child labor, and the establishment of compulsory education for children, the creation of a state board of arbitration, the abolition of the sweating system, and the enactment of major tax reforms. In each case, buttressed by additional agitation, the General Assembly responded with investigations or some type of legislation.

Between 1865 and 1898 the judiciary in Illinois expanded, centralized, and made special provisions for Cook County. Several major differences between the state's courts and their federal counterparts are important to note from the outset. The people elect state judges, whereas the President appoints federal justices. Although federal judges hold office for life or good behavior, state judges have definite terms of six or nine years. These limitations make the state courts somewhat more dependent upon the people and deprive the governor of an important appointive power and control possessed by the President.

According to the Constitution of 1870 the Supreme Court was empowered to exercise original jurisdiction in cases relating to the revenue, *mandamus*, and *habeas corpus*, but in general it functioned as a court of appeals from the appellate, circuit, or county courts. The circuit courts possessed general, original jurisdiction in cases of law and equity. City courts in existence prior to the new constitution continued unless abolished by the voters. These courts held concurrent jurisdiction with circuit courts in all civil and criminal cases, excluding murder, treason, and appeals from city justices of the peace. In 1898 Alton, Aurora, Canton, East St. Louis, Elgin, Litchfield, and Mattoon all had such courts.

In 1873 the General Assembly divided the state, exclusive of Cook County, into twenty-six judicial circuits. In the election of that year one judge served a six-year term in each district. In 1877 the state was divided into thirteen districts, exclusive of Cook County, and an additional judge was elected for each district to serve a two-year term resulting in three judges per district and thirty-nine for the state. In the same year the Supreme Court assigned twelve of the circuit judges to appellate duty, the remainder holding circuit court in their districts. The legislature neglected, however, to appropriate funds for the appellate court, which was forced to exist on credit until the legislature met again in 1879. A new court of claims sat for the first time that year. In 1879 three judges gained election in each of the thirteen judicial circuits, and a second assignment of appellate justices was made. Continuing to respond to the demand for increased judicial facilities, the state divided into seventeen circuits, exclusive of Cook County, in 1897.

The Constitution of 1870 recognized the special judicial problems of Cook County and made it a unit in the judicial system. The Supreme Court held one or more sessions each year in Chicago, and Cook County became a separate judicial circuit not subject to redistricting. The constitution provided for the increase of justices of the Circuit Court in Cook County with the increase in population, and the continuation of the Superior Court of Cook County. It also made provision for an increase of justices. The Recorder's Court of Chicago became the Criminal Court of Cook County, and like the remaining counties in the state, there was a county court to decide matters of probate, taxes and assessments, and other matters. Although the state had only 4,025 lawyers (.004 of the population) in 1880, court expenses rose steadily from $395,869 in 1871 to 1872 to $606,308 in 1891 to 1892.

The rhetoric of government officials when it came to the problem of the judicial system had a strikingly ageless ring. Governor Cullom characterized one viewpoint in 1883 when he said, "the criminal class should be dealt with promptly and punishment made certain."[75] Governor Oglesby had earlier voiced the same sentiments: "A too tender regard for human life must not allow the criminal code to be so written or executed as to encourage or indulge daring violations . . . or to afford the means under the indulgence or mere technical construction of it for the escape of prisoners. We must limit and restrain the opportunity for escape."[76]

Decrying the state's reliance on outmoded English common law, both governors repeatedly urged sweeping changes in the legal system. Both asked that provisions for a change of venue be eliminated in criminal cases, Governor Oglesby noting that while he "adored in principle" the idea of innocence until proven guilty and trial by jury, "I would in practice decline to carry the indulgence of this constitutional right to such extremes" as to baffle the other principle of human and divine justice, "that the guilty shall suffer."[77]

A second proposed change would eliminate the accused's right to twenty peremptory challenges to prospective jurors. In this manner "the defendant increases his opportunity for getting his friends and incompetent persons on the jury."[78] According to Governor Cullom, "our jury law sets a premium on ignorance."[79] Governor Cullom also asked that the court be given the power to instruct the jury in points of law. "I do not believe that the framers of our Constitution intended to place the decisions of law questions in the hands of persons who never read a law book."[80] He also asked (without success) that a revision committee be appointed to make penalties more uniform and asked for legislation restricting the granting of continuances when the defendant's witnesses were not able to appear in court, because "the defendant has no constitutional right to be confronted by his own witnesses."[81] Governor Palmer added the abolition of the grand jury system, and abolition or restriction on pardoning power to the suggested "reforms."

Although Cullom, Oglesby, and Palmer were concerned with protecting society from the "criminal class" by swift and sure punishment, other governors were concerned with the injustice of delays for those falsely accused or too poor to hold out in civil suits against wealthy corporations or individuals. "The dockets are so crowded as to amount almost to a denial of justice,"[82] was a phrase that recurred throughout the period. This was especially true in Cook County, despite an increase in the number of judges. "It takes years to get a case finally settled by the court [in Chicago] . . . the poor cannot stand it and the business man cannot afford it."[83] Governor Palmer also noticed the unequal application of the laws in 1873: "The wealthy and influential do disregard or violate them with a measure of impunity not permitted to the poor and friendless."[84] The poor also suffered for lack of legal council, and Governor Palmer stated, "it is time that the practice of delivering the living bodies of poor prisoners to legal students for professional instructions was abandoned."[85]

The magistrate court system was especially vulnerable to abuse. In order to secure a jury trial in magistrates' court, the defendant had to pay the jury fee. "While a judge of a higher court, could not imprison a man for an hour without a jury trial, a simple magistrate actually does imprison scores every day," noted Altgeld.[86] In 1891 the Chicago police arrested 70,550 men, women, and children. Of these, 32,500 were released after they had been "arrested, sometimes clubbed through the streets . . . and sometimes kept in prison several days."[87] Something over 8,000 were actually sent to prison, most for inability to pay fines. All but ninety were convicted of trivial offenses. One reason for abuse was "the subject of permitting any officer connected with the administration of justice to keep fees. This is the very foundation upon which the whole structure of fraud, extortion, and expression rests."[88] It was common in Chicago for police to arrest 50 to 100 women and a few men every night on no particular charge. "Then the justice gets a dollar from each for taking a bond . . . the machinery of the law is used to gather a harvest off of vice."[89]

Another problem related to the inequities of the court system was the practice of corporations and wealthy individuals "to introduce their private counsel into the management of public prosecutions," so that the courts "are practically superseded by counsel who represent private purposes if not personal resentments and passions."[90]

As early as 1873, Governor Palmer urged the legislature to abolish the death penalty as "a worn-out vestige of barbarism, that hardens and depraves."[91] In 1895, a year in which seven men were hung, Governor Altgeld revived the plea. In 1899, Illinois created the world's first juvenile court "regulating treatment and control of dependent, neglected, and delinquent children."

Stretching across the legislative, executive, and judicial branches, the amount and variety of state expenditures were indicative of the real extent of state power. Following the accepted pattern of the era, and still chafing under the large debts acquired in the 1830s, the government contracted its spending in times of economic difficulties and increased it somewhat in prosperous years. Pay-as-you-go was the general rule. On occasion, however, the state rose to real need, as when it provided assistance to Chicago after the disastrous fire of 1871.

A special session of the legislature advanced the ravaged city $2,955,340 as a refund on the Illinois and Michigan Canal. The state also issued $1,500,000 in bonds to rebuild the courthouse and jail, purchased the books of the three abstract firms which survived the fire, transferred Chicago reform-school inmates to the state reformatory in Pontiac, and passed a reassessment bill for collection of state and local taxes. Total warrants drawn on the state treasury amounted to $5,273,768 in the biennium 1864 to 1866, but increased to $13,207,030 under the additional demands of the new constitution and the payment of $4,000,000 on the state debt in the period 1871 to 1872. Expenditures never exceeded that total until the biennium 1898 to 1900, and then only moderately. In the two-year periods between 1875 to 1886 they were less than $9,000,000. Per-capita expenditure by the state was approximately $.94 in 1870, $1.39 in 1880, $1.28 in 1890, and $1.46 in 1900. These figures do not include funds expended by county and municipal governments, which were significantly larger. Funds went primarily into administration, and the amount actually spent on dispensing services remained quite low.

The maintenance of a balanced budget was a firm rule in the period, militating against large deficit spending on any occasion. Except for a nearly $2,500,000 imbalance between receipts and expenditures in the period from 1871 to 1872, and a similar amount in 1892 to 1894 (lesser infractions occurred in 1879 to 1880, 1885 to 1886, and 1895 to 1896), rigorous measures of retrenchment and economy kept the treasurer's books balanced. Regular increases occurred in administrative and judicial salaries because of expressed need and the provisions of the constitution, but legislative expenses were amazingly even. New areas of administration classified as industrial supervision entailed an increased but modest outlay of $275,024 in the period 1897 to 1898, but this was some $140,000 less than that expended on the militia in the same period. A gradual increase in spending to 1898 occurred in education due to expansion of facilities, in various charitable institutions because of the state's assumption of previously local functions, and in the militia because of industrial strife. But budget items such as internal improvements decreased from nearly $2,500,000 in 1873 to 1874 to less than $20,000 in eight of the remaining thirteen biennia.

Another index of the extent of governmental influence involves the number of the state's citizens employed in public service. This number increased from 4,771 in 1870, or .64 percent of the total work force, to 18,912 in 1900, or 1.05 percent of the total work force. These figures include federal, county, and local employees, as well as those who worked for the state. Since some 676 men were employed as firemen and policemen in Chicago alone in 1870 and must, therefore, be subtracted from the total figure, it is obvious that the state was not the large employer it was to become in the twentieth century.

Illinois' tax system proved adequate to finance its programs only because they were of the administrative and limited nature described. The Constitution of 1870 made a few changes in the revenue article by eliminating the capitation tax, increasing the list of businesses subject to special taxation, lengthening the exemption list, and regularizing provisions for tax sales and redemptions. It also put limits on tax rates for counties and on local indebtedness while authorizing special assessments for local improvements. In 1872 the tax law was in the form it maintained throughout the period. The property tax remained the main source of income.

Money from property tax found its way to the state treasury in a fashion which allowed local influence to reduce its total, which discriminated against owners of real estate as opposed to personal property, and which in practice favored large owners against small. The *Illinois State Journal* complained in 1865 that "horses are valued at from two to three times as much in some counties as the same kind of stock in others, though there is probably no considerable difference in their real value. Almost all classes of property are assessed at a rate far below their real value, while much escapes assessment altogether."[92] Assessment of the value of all real estate and personal property was to be made by local officials before June 1 every fourth year. Governor Oglesby regretted the "custom which left each assessor to fix values substantially after his own notion of things."[93]

Boards of review and equalization to correct inequities existed at the state level after 1867, in the towns until 1898, and in each county. The state board of equalization was a cumbersome body of twenty-six members, elected by congressional districts, with limited powers and a casual attitude toward those they had. "It was soon discovered, that where individuals made return of their effects at honest valuation, and generally others in the same locality did not, an increase of the county assessment by the State Board of Equalization resulted most injuriously to the honest tax-payer."[94] Under-evaluation and inequities of assessment between the various counties, the cities, and the farms, and between large and small holdings, were subject to only minute adjustment. Illustrative of the greatest violation under this system of almost personal assessment was the fact that while all indexes show industrial activity outstripping agriculture during the period, assessed personal property, including the paper evidence of industrial wealth, accounted for 25 percent of the total in 1861 and declined to merely 16 percent in 1898. The burgeoning wealth represented on paper by bonds, stocks, and credits proved nearly impossible to tax equitably, forcing tangible productive property of the type found on farms to bear an unfair share of the burden. The tax rate was set by combining a variety of bases after assessment, and the county clerk determined individual bills. Collection by town or county officials depended upon local organization.

A revenue commission appointed in 1885 reported a year later in favor of significant changes in the tax laws and their administration, but it had no important result. In 1894 the bureau of labor statistics published an extended report on taxation, pointing out inequities and urging changes. An act of 1898 made some modifications in the local administrative machinery, providing among other things that the taxable value of property should be one-fifth of its full value, in this way hoping to increase fairness and revenue. But significant and workable improvements remained unmade. "The poor, who cannot afford, and the wealthier classes who are not inclined to resist payment, bear the burdens of government,"[95] according to Governor Beveridge. Governor Oglesby said of the property tax: "The theory is sound; the practice is wretched."[96] And Governor Altgeld characterized the revenue system as "a giant of injustice" and "a gigantic fraud."[97]

Attempts to increase revenue included minor revisions of the property tax and the addition of other taxes. The law of 1872 contained a provision to tax the "corporate excess," the value of securities of corporations with valuable franchises which assured their increase in value as the general economy expanded. But there were many exceptions, and assessment was haphazard. Local officials assessed the tangible property of railroads, and the state board of equalization, their rolling stock, track, and corporate excess. Reported capital excess dwindled rapidly from $64,611,071 in 1873, and after 1877 assessment of the corporate excess of railroads simply disappeared. Additional revenue was supplied by the Illinois Central, which instead of taxes paid the state 7 percent of its gross receipts. An inheritance tax became law in 1895. It brought in $3.5 million in the biennium ending September, 1898. Other taxes and fees brought in increasing but relatively modest amounts. From all sources, the total general revenue fund grew from $3,445,387 to $13,010,229 in the biennial period ending in 1898. The property tax accounted for over 90 percent of the total in the first biennium and over 70 percent in the last.

The structure of government during the period 1865 to 1898 changed in a formal and quantitative sense, but there was a qualitative continuity. The primary concern of government was administration rather than regulation, direction, or welfare, even though agencies and expenditures expanded. The new constitution made provisions for dealing with some of the problems created by industrialization in that it made the railroad and warehouse commission possible. Government by commission, at least to the extent it was employed, was an innovation, but the actual power of the various commissions created during the period remained limited. There was little coordination between the various agencies, and the governor found it difficult to establish a uniform long-term policy. A programmed approach to government had to await the progressives, the twentieth-century apostles of efficiency.

The attitudes of people toward the function of government changed more slowly than the needs of society. Frontier tradition and the isolation imposed by long distances had necessitated a reliance upon local self-government before the war. The railroad had only recently broken that isolation, while itself posing a problem which could be handled only by increased governmental influence, but the tradition remained. Many people had reacted against unprecedented governmental controls during the war, and in the succeeding generation, traditional attitudes had been strengthened by the influence of Social Darwinist Herbert Spencer, supported by business interests who found his ideas convenient. *Laissez-faire* became an article of faith. As early as 1871 the *Chicago Evening Mail* observed that "with three railroad commissioners, and three grain commissioners, and three State prison commissioners, and we

know not how many more, our State ought to be able to run itself."
It seemed that an unfortunate trend toward unwieldy and expensive government had begun, and the paper asked, "Why not have three dry goods commissioners, and three grocery commissioners, and three live stock commissioners, and three beef and pork commissioners, and while we are about it, three newspaper commissioners, so that every interest will have its commissioners, all having a gentle salary of $2,000 or $3,000 a year each?"[98] Governor Oglesby summed it up when he told the General Assembly in January, 1873, that he did "not believe the laws of trade are to be materially affected by the laws of legislatures."[99]

An article in the Illinois Bureau of Labor Statistics *Report* for 1881, entitled "Communism in Illinois," seems to reflect the imprecise knowledge as well as the attitude of many workers and citizens of the state toward enlarged, centralized government. Most revealing was the close link made between communism and the general topic of increased governmental controls. Communism, in this view, was an organization around a "commonality of property" where needs rather than deeds received reward. And socialism meant "that all agents of production and distribution, and all the products themselves, shall be controlled by a coercive political" state. These approaches to government were lumped as "state control," and to prove the evil of that possibility the author turned to Herbert Spencer's *Essays, Moral, Political, and Aesthetic*. From this catechism of the period, the question was put that since "greed, rapacity, and dishonesty characterize the people individually," how could a collective agency, government, composed of men, eliminate these evils? Illinoisans could well believe the allegation that "most of the duties now assumed by the Government are but poorly performed," and that charges of "fraud, jobbery, and corruption" were partially true.

The substitute for government was "nature's law and nature's teachings," or the tested virtues of self-reliance, self-restraint, self-control, and sobriety. Government could not be substituted for these things, and "any agency used as a prop for mass weakness but prevents the acquisition of strength." What was needed in modern society was unfettered opportunity to accumulate "a large capital." The tinge of racism inherent to this argument appeared when the author moralized that "the Anglo-Saxon seeks room for individualism and is justly jealous of an over-towering, all-absorbing, inquisitorial state."[100] Although this approach was being gradually overcome by reformers and the actions of government, it reflected a climate of opinion that had to be changed before the function of government could be basically altered.

The period was one of transition in state government from one based on serving the limited needs of a rural and agricultural society to one which faced the problems of an urban and industrial state. That economic developments outstripped governmental is not surprising. Governmentally, the period is one of halfway measures. The judicial article of the constitution recognized the special interests and judicial needs of Chicago, for example, but other unique problems faced by that metropolis got only lip service. The sectionalism of the 1850s and 1860s crumbled under the principle of minority representation, but that noble experiment also helped prevent positive action by the General Assembly by contributing to an opposition strong enough to block action. And even in times of need and depression, the state felt little compulsion to increase expenditures and services. Budget increases remained quite normal.

What was accomplished, however, was not without significance. Adequate or not, the agencies and commissions established to deal with the problem areas of an industrial society formed the elements of modern state government, and having been organized in a more or less efficient pattern during the nineteenth century, could be pulled together more rationally and strengthened when necessary. It was evident also that from 1865 to 1898 Illinois was a relatively prosperous state and that although discontent existed, most citizens were fairly well satisfied with their government. The predominant sentiment was that an increase in the power and action of government was likely to create more problems than it solved. Most citizens, for example, preferred to see inefficient tax collection than have an equitable system which would increase their own levies.

At one time or another most Illinoisans found it necessary to concern themselves with what was happening in Springfield, and in this sense the government was constant in that it represented a center of power, if not policy. United States Senators depended upon the General Assembly for their election, farmers and shippers depended upon the executive for regulation of the railroads, and the corporations were determined that regulation would not get out of hand. Miners were concerned that the mandates of the constitution for their protection be carried out, while factory workers, late in the period, depended upon government for the publication and improvement of their plight. Both labor and management were increasingly forced to turn to the governor and the militia to see that disputes did not get out of hand. The powers of the General Assembly forced all elements to petition it—from the people who wished to prevent political corruption through a voter registration law to cities who wished to have permission for special action. And the state political machines were constant factors in their interests in state government. Reformers knew that only government could solve their problems. Everyone was concerned with the taxing power. And strong, ambitious men learned that state government was useful when they sought "power, to get hold of the handle that controls things."[101]

1. Gov. John Peter Altgeld, Illinois House of Representatives, *Journal of the House of Representatives*, Jan. 10, 1898, 49.

2. Julia Jayne Trumbull to Julia Trumbull, Oct. 3, 1847. Lyman Trumbull *MSS*, Illinois State Historical Library.

3. Efforts to preserve the old structure began in 1898 when the Sangamon County Board of Supervisors agreed to raise the structure eleven feet to add an additional floor rather than to tear the building down. The Abraham Lincoln Association, formed in the 1920s, interested the state in the possibilities of restoring the building as an historical site in 1931, but the legislature did not approve the project until April 6, 1961. The building, then in very poor condition, was dismantled stone by stone, and each stone was numbered and stored at the state fairgrounds while a two-story underground parking facility and the State Historical Library were constructed as the new foundation of the old building. The "new" old state capitol then rose in its former location on the courthouse square. On December 3, 1968, Governor Samuel Shapiro dedicated the building and opened it to tourists. Furnishings, including half-smoked pipes, were carefully reconstructed to give the building the feeling that Lincoln and the other legislators had only moments before stepped out for lunch.

4. James T. Hickey, "Springfield, May 1865," *Journal of the Illinois State Historical Society* LVIII (Spring, 1965), 23.

5. *Ibid.*

6. *New York Daily Tribune*, May 8, 1865.

7. *Illinois State Journal*, January 14, 1865.

8. *Chicago Tribune*, May 12, 1871.

9. *Illinois State Journal*, May 13, 1865.

10. *Debates and Proceedings of the Illinois Constitutional Convention of 1869*, II (Springfield, 1870), 1317.

11. *Journal of the House*, Jan. 5, 1871, 32.

12. The document they produced served the state until a new constitution was approved by the voters in 1870.

13. *Debates and Proceedings*, I, 576-612; 11, 960. *Illinois Constitution*, 1870, Art. III, Sec. 22.

14. *Debates and Proceedings*, I, 523-540; *Constitution*, Art. IV, Sec. 13.

15. *Debates and Proceedings*, II, 1727.

16. *Ibid.*

17. *Constitution*, Art. XI, Sec. 12.

18. *Ibid.*

19. *Debates and Proceedings*, II, 1629.

20. *Ibid.*, 1622-37; *Constitution*, Art. XIII, Sec. 52.

21. The state ceded the canal to the federal government in 1882, at which time it became part of the lakes-to-gulf waterway.

22. *Debates and Proceedings*, I, 266.

23. *Ibid.*, II, 1732-61; *Constitution*, Art. VIII.

24. Before 1898 voters accepted five amendments and rejected three.

25. Richard Oglesby to Lyman Trumbull, June 13, 1870. Oglesby *MSS*, Illinois State Historical Library.

26. *Ibid.*

27. *Chicago Times*, April 11, 1875; *Chicago Tribune*, April 11, 1895.

28. *Illinois State Journal*, Feb. 16, 1870.

29. *Constitution*, Art. V, Sec. 6, i.

30. *Ibid.*

31. *Debates and Proceedings*, 1, 759.

32. *Journal of the House*, Jan. 15, 1865.

33. *Journal of the Senate*, Jan. 10, 1881, 33.

34. Governor John Palmer to John Mayo Palmer, in George Thomas Palmer, *A Conscientious Turncoat: The Story of John M. Palmer, 1817-1900* (New Haven, Conn., 1941), 206.

35. *Chicago Evening Post*, July 30, 1891.

36. *Journal of the House*, Jan. 5, 1877, 27.

37. *Chicago Evening Mail*, March 28, 1871. Wm. O. Thompson Memorandum in Harry Barnard, *"Eagle Forgotten": The Life of John Peter Altgeld* (Indianapolis, 1938), 166. *Journal of the House*, Jan. 11, 1897, 27.

38. *Journal of the House*, Jan. 6, 1871, 44.

39. Robert G. Ingersoll to Richard Oglesby, Jan. 14, 1869. Oglesby *MSS*, Illinois State Historical Library.

40. *Chicago Tribune*, July 7, 1894.

41. *Journal of the House*, Jan. 10, 1893, 50.

42. *Ibid.*, Jan. 3, 1860, 54.

43. *Ibid.*, 27.

44. John Palmer, *Journal of the House*, Oct. 13, 1871, 41.

45. *Journal of the House*, Jan. 16, 1865, 221.

46. Governor Richard Oglesby, *Journal of the House*, Jan. 4, 1869, 23.

47. *Ibid.*, 22.

48. *Appleton's Annual Cyclopaedia and Register of Important Events* (New York, 1899), 369.

49. *Journal of the Senate*, Jan. 7, 1881, 140.

50. *Journal of the House*, Jan. 10, 1879, 29.

51. *Ibid.*, Jan. 30, 1885, 71.

52. *Appleton's Annual*, 369.

53. *Journal of the House*, Jan. 4, 1899, 19.

54. *Ibid.*, Jan. 3, 1865, 33.

55. *Ibid.*, July 14, 1867, 34.

56. *Journal of the House*, Jan. 6, 1887, 34.

57. *Ibid.*, May 24, 1871, 12.

58. *Appleton's Annual*, 329.

59. *Journal of the House*, Jan. 9, 1901, 61.

60. *Ibid.*, Jan. 7, 1881, 22.

61. Governor Cullom, *ibid.*, Jan. 10, 1879, 25.

62. *Ibid.*, Jan. 7, 1881, 22.

63. Governor Oglesby, *ibid.*, Jan. 10, 1889, 22.

64. F. Garvin Davenport, "John Henry Rauch and Public Health in Illinois, 1877-1891," *Journal of the Illinois State Historical Society* L (Autumn, 1957), 277.

65. *Ibid.*, 292-293.

66. *Ibid.*

67. *Journal of the House*, Jan. 6, 1886, 41.

68. *Ibid.*, Jan. 10, 1893, 51.
69. *Ibid.*, Jan. 12, 1897, 50.
70. *Blue Book of the State of Illinois* (Springfield, 1903), 33.
71. Illinois, *Laws*, 1879, Sec. 2, 61.
72. National Convention of Chiefs and Commissioners of State Bureaus of Statistics of Labor, *Proceedings of First Annual Convention* (Columbus, Ohio, 1883), 30-31.
73. *Journal of the House*, Jan. 5, 1893, 27.
74. *Ibid.*, Jan. 30, 1885, 76.
75. *Ibid.*, Jan. 5, 1883, 33.
76. Governor Oglesby, *ibid.*, Jan. 13, 1873, 57.
77. *Ibid.*
78. *Ibid.*, Jan. 13, 1873, 97.
79. Governor Cullom, *ibid.*, Jan. 5, 1883, 33.
80. *Ibid.*, 13.
81. *Ibid.*, 14.
82. Governor Beveridge, *ibid.*, Jan. 5, 1877, 39.
83. Governor Tanner, *ibid.*, Jan. 12, 1907, 48.
84. *Journal of the Senate*, Jan. 8, 1873, 14.
85. *Ibid.*, 15.
86. *Journal of the House*, Jan. 10, 1893, 50.
87. *Ibid.*
88. Governor Tanner, *ibid.*, Jan. 12, 1897, 48.
89. *Ibid.*, 49.
90. *Journal of the Senate*, Jan. 8, 1873, 12.
91. *Ibid.*
92. *Illinois State Journal*, March 7, 1865.
93. *Journal of the House*, Jan. 4, 1869.
94. *Ibid.*, Jan. 6, 1887, 29.
95. *Ibid.*, Jan. 5, 1877, 38.
96. *Ibid.*, Jan. 6, 1887, 28.
97. *Ibid.*, Jan. 12, 1897, 49.
98. *Chicago Evening Mail*, Feb. 21, 1871.
99. *Journal of the Senate*, Jan. 13, 1873, 55.
100. Illinois Bureau of Labor Statistics, *Report, 1881,* 163-169.
101. Barnard, *"Eagle Forgotten."*

3
Politics: Of Men and Machines

I realize . . . that both men and parties are judged by what
they do, rather than by what they profess or promise . . .
the recent action of our people at the polls is a warning
that their patience has a limit and cannot be long fed on
empty and delusive promises.

John Peter Altgeld[1]

Political trends from 1865 to 1895 are deceptively easy to
follow. Seemingly, success crowned the Republican party, and the
Democrats appeared hopelessly unable to shake the disloyal image
painted of them by their antebellum proslavery stand and by opposition to the Civil War. Disaffection with the dominant party was
diffused into third, fourth, and fifth party movements, never able
to attract broad-based support. In a very real way, Republican
historian C. A. Church was correct when he asserted that "the
history of the Republican party has for sixty years . . . been the
political history of the nation. Illinois has from the first," wrote
Church in 1912, "been a stronghold of Republicanism. Only once
since 1856 has the enemy successfully stormed the citadel."[2] The
citadel was safe from enemy attack with that one exception
throughout the last half of the century, but warring factions clustering about a relatively small group of leaders kept the political pot of
Illinois' politics boiling.

As a group, the governors of Illinois from 1864 to 1896 were a
homogeneous lot. They saw their roles as administrators, limited to
managerial functions. Altgeld stands out as a social reformer with a
new view of the possibilities of government. Oglesby is remembered for his oratory, Cullom for his agrarian beliefs, Palmer as a
"conscientious turncoat," but their similarities far outweighed
minor flashes of individualism. None were born in Illinois. All were
from farm families. All became lawyers. Their most important

72

common characteristic was the trauma of civil war. All but Cullom served in battle, and this experience profoundly influenced their reactions to the turbulent era in which they found themselves. They looked for simple answers.

The Civil War was an emotional catharsis for a nation burdened too long by struggles over slavery. It was a "simple" answer that gave a terminal point to conflict, and if the awesome problem of slavery could be eliminated in one swoop, there must be another simple answer to the uncertainties of the postwar years. Higher tariff? Lower tariff? Gold standard? Greenbacks? Prohibition? The people pinned their hopes on simple answers and expected the state government to remain inert once it had taken that "simple" step. The mystique of "Honest Abe" hung over state politics, and the successful politician folded himself in the cloak of Lincoln and posed as carrying on in the Lincoln tradition. The challenges of industrialization and urbanization were too new, too powerful, and too complex to be met squarely by the politics of the era.

Reformers had looked to the ballot box to solve the ills of society, especially in Chicago where local unsavory politicians were frequently singled out for purging by zealots of reform coalitions. It was not yet time for change, and the reformers met defeat for they were asking the impossible. Vachel Lindsay could have appreciated their dilemma, for they were asking, "come let us vote against our human nature,"[3]—never an auspicious plea.

It was John Peter Altgeld, a one-term reform governor, who seems most to embody the conflicts which this new age presented to the state's politicians. In this one man the old icons of Jeffersonianism, agrarianism, individualistic protestant materialism—all of the rural, native, simplicity of the Lincoln mystique—warred with the realities of an age of big cities, big business, immigration, and stratifying economic classes. Altgeld's feet were planted in both the country soil of the old days and the city soot of the new—and he met that challenge with both great success and great failure. Altgeld was a Democrat in a state dedicated to Republicanism, and his statewide political prominence came at the close of the period.

The extent of Republican success is reflected by the party's hold on the Illinois General Assembly. Of the seventeen General Assemblies that met between 1865 to 1898, ten were indisputably Republican, four of them meeting before the adoption of cumulative voting and six after. Only one was controlled by the Democrats (1892 to 1894), and the remaining seven had Republican majorities in one house and Democratic in the other (1890 to 1892), or third parties held the balance of power (1874 to 1876, 1876 to 1878). The Republican majorities were razor thin in the senate from 1878 to 1880 and in the house from 1882 to 1884 and from 1884 to 1886. Actually, the Republican party controlled the General Assembly comfortably only a little more than half the time, and the speakership went twice to an independent and to a Democrat.

This fairly equal division in party strength in the General Assembly, due mostly to the principle of minority representation after 1870, as well as to the frequent breakdown of party discipline, was of great importance in the actual operation of the governmental structure. Only in a relatively few matters where party lines nearly always held, as in the elections of United States Senators, did the Republicans make maximum use of their numbers. Of the thirteen senators elected by the General Assembly during the period, eleven were Republicans; one, David Davis, classified himself as an Independent, and another, John M. Palmer, was a Republican turned Democrat. Davis had also been a Republican early in his career, and was closely associated with the Lincoln mystique.

Northern Illinois was the stronghold of the Republican party, with Winnebago, Boone, McHenry, DeKalb, Kendall, and DuPage counties giving majorities for that party in nearly three-fourths of all elections. Lesser Republican majorities prevailed across the rest of northern Illinois. Below a line drawn roughly diagonally across the state from Hancock County on the west down to Clark County on the east, Democrats were in control in approximately 50 to 60 percent of the elections. Northern Democratic counties of Peoria, Woodford, and Tazewell jutted into Republican territory, but their advance was offset by a solid stronghold of Republicanism across the tip of otherwise Democratic Egypt. The normally Democratic Ohio River counties of Pope, Massac, and Pulaski registered Republican wins 60 to 70 percent of the time. Madison, St. Clair, Jackson, and Clay counties, also in the southern region, swung from one party to the other, with neither winning more than 50 percent of the elections.

A comparison of maps (see Appendix) of the presidential vote at the beginning (1864), middle (1880), and end (1900) of the era shows slight changes in the strength of the majorities and minor swings of individual counties, but no change in the basic geographic distribution of the vote. County returns both in presidential and gubernatorial balloting tended to merely confirm the vote of the largest city in the county, for a polarization into rural versus urban voting blocks had not yet crystallized. As the state's most thoroughly urbanized city, Chicago had the greatest possibility of voting contrary to rural Cook County. Chicago's voting patterns were consistent with those of the county throughout the era. Grover Cleveland's presidential victory in 1892 was the only instance in which Chicago and the county were strikingly at odds. In 1888, pluralities differed between county and city when Chicago went Democrat, 51 percent to 48 percent, and the county went Republican, 49.40 percent to 48.93 percent, but there was actually only 2 percentage points difference between the two.

TABLE 3. CHICAGO AND COOK COUNTY VOTING PATTERNS, 1864-1900

	CHICAGO Percent of Vote		COOK Percent of Vote	
Year	Democrats	Republicans	Democrats	Republicans
1864	47	53	18.90	81.10
1868	43	57	44.97	59.03
1872	40	60	37.68	62.32
1876	50	50	51.37	48.23
1880	47	53	44.18	54.66
1884	49	51	46.02	52.82
1888	51	48	48.93	49.40
1892	57	43	42.57	55.33
1896	41	58	40.14	58.61
1900	48	50	46.53	49.77

By 1900, in isolated elections, the city vote was slightly different from that of the county, illustrating that Chicago had not yet assumed political identity markedly different from the surrounding countryside. City and county dwellers alike voted with an awareness of party rather than an awareness of the special needs and problems of their type of environment, and the goal of political parties was to win and exercise power rather than to impose ideologically consistent, unified programs.

One common political denominator, whether in urban or rural areas, was a concern over currency. Depressions in 1837, 1857, 1873, and 1893 hit nearly everyone, and tended to make money itself, whether gold or paper, a subject of morbid interest. The West, including Illinois, was substantially a debtor territory, and any effort to appreciate the dollar met with political resistance in the state. Responding to the depression of 1873 and the passage of the Resumption Act of 1875, which would resume specie payment, pro-inflationists, mainly farmers and laborers, "reckless brokendown speculators and equally brokendown politicians,"[4] launched the Greenback party.

The affection for specialty parties never seriously threatened the two-party system in Illinois, but it did voice the discontent of certain areas of the state with the fiscal policies of the Democratic and Republican parties. More important, the new parties continued a trend of the prewar years in which the most outspoken, liberal, and/or radical members of the old parties left to form parties of their own. The Republican party had benefitted from this trend in its formative years as the most dynamic, ambitious, and "liberal" leaders of the Whigs, Democrats, Free-Soilers, Know Nothings, and Anti-Nebraskaites forsook their old allegiances to form the antisouthern, antislavery, anti-Democratic, Republican party. The smaller of the old parties died out without their leadership, and the Democrats were left with a conservative leadership and constituency with which to enter the war years.

Those same forces remained at work in the second half of the nineteenth century. The dissidents who had flocked to the Republican banner to protest the slave question or to demonstrate loyalty during the war remained discontented with the harsh realities of political life. If the Republican party refused to live up to its ideals, these restless and fire-eyed leaders marched into a new party that would. And so the radicals, the liberals, the idealists left the Republican party to become Liberal Republicans, Greenbackers, Gold Democrats—or regular Democrats again. What remained was a Republican party growing increasingly into the mold of the conservative Whigs, allied with big business and remote from the idealism that characterized it during its early years.

If the party mourned its loss of youth and idealism, it was not apparent in the campaign oratory that fogged the night air at Republican rallies. An Illinoisan had captured the White House in 1860, and except for the Andrew Johnson years, Illinois politicians would hold the White House until 1876. They were good years to be a Republican politician in Illinois. Exciting years. Hope-filled years. Political campaigns rivaled circuses as entertainment for both featured brass bands, torchlight parades, and chanting voices filled with excitement.

Carl Sandburg was a boy in Illinois then, and he remembered one of those parades, complete with brass band, twenty flambeaus, and "a tall man in yellow pants with a red coat and a red velvet hat nearly as tall as I was." It was a Republican rally that Sandburg remembered, but:

> I heard a man on the sidewalk yell out "Hurrah for Cleveland." Right away came howls from the procession "And a rope to hang him" . . .

[My father] gave me the idea that Republicans are good men and Democrats are either bad men or good men gone wrong or sort of dumb. I wondered if someday I would march with a torch. Maybe I might even have a flambeau someday and blow into a pipe and watch a line of fire go up and up and wriggle into a big fine flower. And I had the feeling that Cleveland was an ugly man, ugly as you could think of, and if the Republicans got a rope and hanged him I wouldn't be sorry.[5]

That kind of enthusiasm was pervasive and no campaign was complete without violent denunciations, veiled charges, or outright slanders. After four years of a traumatic and tragic war, emotional responses were easy to evoke, and the specter of that war lifted its head in every election. Republicans "waved the bloody shirt," and Democrats responded by pointing to the exploits of their own loyal war heroes and shaking a finger at the disgrace of radical reconstruction. For the Old-Whigs-now-Republicans there was a delightful irony in hurling charges of "treason" at the same Democrats who had smeared them with that brush after the Mexican War. Across the door to elective office in Illinois hung an almost tangible sign: ONLY WAR HEROES NEED APPLY!

State and national politics remained intertwined as they had become in the 1850s and during the war itself. After the uneasy Johnson presidency, the people turned to its new pantheon of generals for a leader to set things right again, the most illustrious of whom was the shopkeeper from Galena, Ulysses S. Grant. Grant was a West Pointer whose first Civil War position was a desk job for Illinois Governor Richard Yates. He came to prominence late in the war, amid rumors of heavy drinking and violent criticism for his bloody campaigns in the wilderness, at Cold Harbor, and at Spotsylvania Courthouse. While his battle tactics produced gory results, an affront to those who saw war as an exercise in chivalry, they turned the tide of the war, and for the man who accepted Lee's surrender no honor was too great.

For his achievements, Grant was awarded the presidency of the United States. He did not participate in the campaign, or declare himself in favor of any policy, and some who knew him as a military man were uneasy at the thought of Grant in the White House. If the public expected dynamic leadership from Grant to offset the increasing power of Congress, they misread him. Grant saw his role as administrative and he was content to let Congress have its head in most areas. Somewhat naturally, in choosing assistants to help him in that administrative role, Grant looked to Illinois. He named John

Rawlins secretary of war, and his friend Elihu Washburne secretary of state. A critic described Washburne as "half-illiterate, ill-mannered, and incredibly undiplomatic,"[6] but his role at state was strictly for show. After a few days in office, he resigned to become minister to France, where, according to Grant's grandson, "Washburne distinguished himself greatly"[7] and was the only foreign minister to remain in Paris throughout the days of the Commune.

Other Illinois Republicans chosen by Grant for national posts included Giles Smith, second assistant postmaster general; Buford Wilson, solicitor of the treasury, and General Green B. Raum, commissioner of internal revenue. Raum had served as a Republican in the Fortieth Congress, and in the revenue post "he distinguished himself by suppressing illegal distilling and eliminating the violence against revenue agents."[8] After leaving the revenue post, Raum headed a law firm specializing in pension claims. His pension experience caused him some later difficulty when after initial success as President Harrison's commissioner of pensions he was accused of using the office for personal gain.

The Grant appointees followed other Illinoisans into the federal bureaucracy. David Davis already sat as Illinois' first United States Supreme Court Justice. He had been joined in Washington during the Lincoln years by Secretary of Interior Orville Browning, Secretary of War John Schofield, Secretary of War John Rawlins, Director of the Mint Horatio Burchard, and Public Printer S. P. Round.

Whatever Grant and his Illinois friends may have accomplished during his administration was long overshadowed by the fumes of corruption rising from his staff. He would later be coupled with President Warren Harding as the only two "failures" in the American presidency. "Theirs were the only administrations," according to a poll of historians in the 1950s, "riddled by corruption. As president they were beyond their depth. Grant allowed himself to become the dupe of crafty swindlers, speculators and plain grafters."[9] However, in the quarter-century following that poll, with the publication of Grant's long-neglected presidential papers, and in comparison to other presidents on the matters of civil rights, Grant's reputation as a politician and a statesman has begun a revision upward.

Perhaps their familiarity with Lincoln and Grant took the mystery from the presidency; or perhaps it was only the supreme confidence of western men fresh from military and political triumphs. Whatever the reason, Illinois abounded in active rivals for the nation's highest office, and Grant's seeming ineffectiveness encouraged them. Former Governor John Palmer, Judge David Davis, and Senator Lyman Trumbull all fought for the nomination of the Liberal Republican party in 1872. The three Illinoisans split western strength, and the party turned fatally to Horace Greeley.

The Liberal Republican movement was an offshoot of a political revolt in Missouri led by Carl Shurz. It consisted primarily of Republicans repulsed by the despotic conditions in the Reconstructed South and the unsavory reputation of the Grant administration. It was also symptomatic of an era in which answers to pressing political problems were sought in a proliferation of new parties. John Palmer, for example, belonged to five different parties during the course of his career—three of which he helped found. He was first a Democrat, then a Free-Soiler, then a Republican, a Liberal Republican, a Democrat again, and finally a Gold Democrat presidential candidate. Trumbull left the Democratic party to become a Republican, a Liberal Republican, a Democrat, and a Populist. The Liberal party was especially strong in Illinois, and all the members of Governor Yates's cabinet joined, as did Superintendent of Education Newton Bateman and several other former state officeholders. "The schism was great and alarming even to the most stout-hearted Republicans."[10] The party joined forces with the Democrats in the campaign of 1872, and after its disastrous defeat, many of the Liberals returned to the Democratic party.

In 1875 Secretary of the Treasury Benjamin H. Bristow exposed a scheme which was defrauding the government of two-thirds of the taxes due on whiskey. The investigation led to Grant's personal secretary, Orville E. Babcock, who had served as Grant's aide-de-camp beginning in 1864, and had won acclaim for his gallantry, courage, and efficiency. Grant refused to believe that the man who proved so trustworthy on the battlefield would be dishonest, and his deposition to that effect was instrumental in gaining Babcock's acquittal on charges of defrauding the revenue office.

As more unsavory schemes came to light, Grant's own reputation suffered. His friends were indignant, and blamed the stories on "a concerted effort on the part of personal and political enemies to bring his name into utter disgrace."[11] Grant himself was never implicated in the schemes, and he apparently took a philosophical view of the problem, writing to a friend two years before his death that, "I have never felt the slightest concern for myself through all the abuse that has been heaped upon me. I was, of course, much annoyed that such things would happen as did while I was the executive of the nation. I was probably too unsuspecting."[12]

Despite the scandals, Grant remained popular and efforts were made to renominate him for a third term. The efforts failed, leaving him bitter with former allies, especially Washburne, who had exposed him to a humiliating defeat in the Republican national convention. The bugles had ceased to blow for the general, and he spent his remaining years in dusty near-poverty in New York and Galena. His death in 1885 stirred memories of his victories in battle, and around the state memorial processions honored the man whose leadership on the battlefield had seemingly failed him at the executive desk.

Presidential hopefuls were not the only Illinois politicians to capture the spotlight in Washington. The Illinois Congressional delegation was also active, and received wide public attention during the congressional fight over Reconstruction. The Republicans had come to power in 1860 as a sectional party, and Negro suffrage in the South was crucial to the establishment of truly national Republican power. An unreconstructed South would not only escape its "just" punishment for the lamented war, but would also quickly unite its Democratic strength with the Democratic minorities in the North and West and drive the Republicans from office.

An ultimately more crucial issue was the constitutional question of separation of powers inherent in the conflict between Lincoln-Johnson and the Congress. The radical Republicans in the legislature were determined to appropriate to themselves powers to conduct the reconstruction of the South which both presidents believed to be solely vested in the executive branch. The Senate and House defiantly set up the joint committee of reconstruction, including Illinois' Representative Washburne of Galena, in the belief that the Confederacy had reverted to territorial status and was therefore within the province of congressional action. The executive held to the belief that the rebellious states forever remained states, and were therefore under jurisdiction of the executive branch.

Binding both issues together was the most complex subject: the rights of the newly freed Negro. The assassination of President Lincoln complicated an already tense situation. Lincoln was by no means in a strong enough position to carry out his conciliatory program without some real problems from a Congress already smarting over his high-handed use of "war powers" during the conflict. Before his death the legislature passed the Wade-Davis Bill, a harsh reconstruction measure which Lincoln pocket vetoed. Lincoln's legislative liabilities were mild, however, compared with those of the new president, Andrew Johnson. Johnson was southern, agrarian, and Democrat—all anathema to the Republican majorities in the House and Senate. Convinced he would try to rebuild both the South and the Democratic party at the expense of the industrial North and the Republicans, Capitol Hill looked askance at the new president.

The Illinois delegation to Washington included Republican senator Lyman Trumbull and former Governor Richard Yates. Trumbull, a former Democrat, had joined the new party as a result of the Nebraska Controversy in 1854. Yates, an ardent Whig in the 1840s, became a Republican when his party died out. Four of the eleven Republican representatives were former Democrats. There were only three avowed Democrats in the delegation: Samuel Marshall of McLeansboro, Lewis Ross of Lewiston, and Anthony Thornton of Shelbyville.

Although not identified with the most virulent radicals, the Illinois delegates reflected the will of their constituents when they voiced definite hostility to the idea of mild reconstruction. Representative Shelby Cullom of Springfield stated indignantly in 1866: "We are told by the gentlemen that after all this . . . national debt, taxes . . . sacrifice on the battlefield . . . and the civilized world startled by the death of the Chief Executive . . . that these people, fresh from all these scenes of carnage, are to defiantly take their place in the national council."[13]

Jehu Baker was also incensed at the idea of the old slavocracy regaining power, stating, "the rebel states, under the old ruling class, will each for itself, burden the labor of its poor, both white and black, with the payment of the rebel debt it has contracted."[14] Senator Trumbull also did not mince words addressing the Thirty-Ninth Congress: "We may treat them [rebels] as traitors, and we may treat them as enemies, and we have the right to be both belligerent and sovereign as far as they are concerned."[15]

The Democratic delegation was vastly outnumbered, but nonetheless vocal in its opposition to the harsh reconstruction planned by the radicals. Anthony Thornton reflected his southern Illinois background when he pleaded: "If those states are ever to be bound together in an equal and enduring union by us, we must . . . bury forever the feelings of distrust. . . . Can they accept your conditions . . . tendered in such Spirit? Never!"[16] Such polarity on so emotionally charged an issue virtually guaranteed that party lines would harden into insurmountable barriers to compromise and cloud most issues.

Senator Trumbull introduced the first reconstruction bill in January, 1866, asking for an extension of the powers of the Freedman's Bureau. The bureau combined both humanitarianism and crass opportunism as the newly freed slaves were turned into party-line Republicans in anticipation of the Fifteenth Amendment. The bill passed the Senate 37 to 10, and the House 137 to 37. The Illinois delegates voted along straight party lines, and President Johnson vetoed the bill.

Trumbull then introduced the first Civil Rights Act, giving citizenship to all persons except Indians born in the United States. The Illinois delegates again voted on straight party lines, and the bill passed. Johnson again vetoed, but the veto was overturned 33 to 15 in the Senate and 137 to 47 in the House. Republican Anthony Kuykendall of Vienna was absent, providing the only change in the Illinois vote.

The Fourteenth Amendment granting due process to the newly freed slaves passed both houses in June, 1866, with the *Chicago Tribune* pompously warning Mississippi that the North would turn her into a "frog pond"[17] if she tried to reinstitute slavery. A second Freedman's Bureau Bill passed over Johnson's veto in July. The vote on that bill marked the first break in the solid Republican ranks in the Illinois delegation. Kuykendall sided with the Democrats in voting not to override, and continued to vote with the Democrats against the Command of the Army Bill and against overriding President Johnson's veto of that bill. The veto was overturned, predictably, 38 to 10 in the Senate, 138 to 51 in the House. (The absence was Washburne of Illinois.) The Second Reconstruction Bill divided the South into five military districts under army commanders. It passed handily despite Kuykendall's continued maverick Democratic vote.

Kuykendall's defection should have come as no surprise. He had not been a Republican very long, and as early as March 3, 1866, he delivered a lengthy speech in Congress supporting President Johnson's stand on the territoriality of the Confederate states and questioning the motives of the radicals. "I believe their object to be, first," he declared, "to reduce those states to a territorial condition, and then to legislate for them by Congress, and . . . declare universal suffrage, or in other words, give the negroes the right to vote in those eleven seceded states. To this I am opposed."[18]

Kuykendall remained, however, in partial agreement with the radicals. He was opposed to abandoning the loyalty oath, and raised the specter of Jefferson Davis and Alexander Stephens sitting unquestioned in the sacred halls of Congress. The Democratic viewpoint, as explained by Representative Marshall of McLeansboro, was that each officeholder should be judged on his merits, not by an unconstitutional oath. He lamented the Republican practice of applying the term "copperhead to the members of this side of the House, around whom are clustering all the hopes of people of this country who desire an immediate restoration of the union."[19]

Kuykendall then voiced his concern that "the question of the African Race" would have to be settled before Congress could return to its normal business. His solution was typical of the views of southern Illinois:

> I come, sir, from the great Northwest, where our people are a producing people, and more interested in the price of beef, pork, corn, wheat, oats . . . than they are in the negroes being made their equals at the ballot box. . . . I would make a treaty with the Republic of Mexico and arrange with them to colonize the American citizens of African descent in the warm climate and rich valleys of Mexico. . . . I would enforce the Monroe Doctrine and drive Maximillian out of the country . . . secure to the negroes lands, give them a fair start in the world, give them all the assistance incumbent on a Christian people to do, and then let them . . . mark out their own destiny.[20]

Kuykendall's suggestion, similar to earlier schemes of Lincoln and others to colonize the former slaves out of the country, was not adopted.

On November 25, 1867, the House judiciary committee recommended impeachment of the President, Democrat Samuel Morrison of Illinois voting nay. The resolution was defeated in the House 57 to 108 as Republicans Jehu Baker of Belleville, Burton Cook of Ottawa, Ebon Ingersoll of Peoria, and Elihu Washburne of Galena joined the three Illinois Democrats in voting against the impeachment bill. When Johnson exercised what he considered a vested executive right, however, and removed Secretary of War Stanton, the House took another impeachment vote and this time the Republicans voted overwhelmingly for the measure, 128 to 42. When voting on the articles of impeachment, Ebon Ingersoll read a telegram from Illinois Governor Richard Oglesby: "The people of Illinois demand the impeachment of President Johnson," wired the governor, "and will heartily sustain action by our congress." Ingersoll commented that "good government depends on the prompt impeachment of the president,"[21] and John Logan of Illinois was selected one of the seven managers to conduct the trial before the Senate.

Much to the shock of his colleagues and constituents, Senator Lyman Trumbull, champion of radical reconstruction, voted "No," and removal failed by one vote. Trumbull had voted for every reconstruction act, and had sponsored two of them himself, but impeachment of the President went too far. Explaining his vote, he said with great insight: "Once set the example of impeaching a president for what, when the excitement of the hour shall have subsided, will be regarded as insufficient cause, and no future president will be safe who happens to differ with a majority of the House and two-thirds of the Senate on any measure deemed by them important."[22]

In January, 1869, the Tenure of Office Act was defeated in the Senate, Senator Trumbull being one of those voting "No." He was joined in the House by Baker, Brownell, Farnsworth, and Hardin, all Republicans. Radical reconstruction was winding down, and its final effort was the passage of the Fifteenth Amendment granting voting rights to all male citizens. All Illinois Republicans voted "Yes," all Democrats, "No." Later, Shelby Cullom recalled the mood of those years: "The nature of the opposition to the Johnson plan of Reconstruction was a firm conviction that its success would wreck the Republican party, and by restoring the Democracy to power, bring back Southern supremacy and Northern vassalage."[23]

Trumbull's Republican colleagues viewed his vote to acquit the President as something less than a profile in courage. Wrath poured down from such spokesmen as Horace Greeley of the *New York Tribune*. "Senator Trumbull never gave his Republican colleagues a hint of his hostility to impeachment," raged Greeley. "We are assured that his Democratic son had quietly made bets through third parties by which he expects to win $5,000 by his father's resistance to impeachment." Hinting of a conspiracy with the Democrats, Greeley asserted, "The leading Copperheads of Chicago were fully apprised that Senator Trumbull would vote to acquit long before his Republican brethren. . . . Was that done like Cassius?"[24] Mere political skulduggery could not account for such an unbelievable act of treachery, according to the Republican press. "Considerable sums were obtained expressly to buy the votes of Senators," broadly hinted the *New York Tribune*.[25]

The controversy remained alive throughout Trumbull's remaining political career. During the exposure of the Grant scandals,

Trumbull issued a broadside defending himself from "Slanders." "My public record is before the world," Trumbull said. "By it I am willing to be judged."[26] By this time criticism of Trumbull's vote had crystallized around a reputed conflict of interest involving legal work done by Trumbull in the prosecution of one of the reconstruction cases. The *Chicago Tribune* pompously proclaimed: "In April 1868, while Senator of the United States, he [Trumbull] received out of the federal treasury $10,000 as a remuneration for an opinion, written at the request of President Johnson in the McCardle case. Four weeks later, he . . . voted for the acquittal of President Johnson. . . . Anyone not so blinded as to be unable to see daylight between the steps of a ladder will at once perceive the connection between the $10,000 and the singular acquittal."[27]

Despite Trumbull's explanation that the legal work had been originally commissioned by Secretary Stanton and was fully legitimate, his fee being unconnected with his work as a Senator, critics continued to allege wrongdoing. In 1880 a campaign pamphlet revived the charges, concluding that Trumbull's fee was "estimated at the rate of one million dollars a year."[28]

Senator Trumbull's career had already been marked by much controversy. One of his earliest public acts was authorship of a scheme repudiating the state debt, an act according to Stephen A. Douglas, "which if successful would have brought infamy and disgrace upon the fair escutcheon of our glorious state."[29] He then made unsuccessful bids for Congress, the Senate, the governorship, Congress again, and a judgeship. He was successful at last in a bid for Democratic Congressman from the Belleville district. Breaking with the Democrats over Nebraska, Trumbull served next as a Republican Senator, and was especially influential during the war years as an adviser to President Lincoln.

In 1872 Trumbull unsuccessfully sought the presidency as a liberal Republican, and party regulars retaliated in 1873 by denying him re-election to the Senate. Trumbull explained his decision to leave the regular Republican party in a letter in 1876:

I became satisfied in 1872 that the Republican Party had become as a body corrupt, and that the people were being plundered in almost all branches of the public service. . . . That General Grant is personally corrupt I would not intimate, but he has been singularly unfortunate in some of the men and influences that have surrounded him. . . .

I do not believe the Republican organization or General Grant which is really in most cases but its instrument, will allow the Secretary

[Bristow] to prove even this whiskey business, to say nothing of the corruption in other branches of government. . . .

You see I have no hope of reform and purification through the Republican organization. Its power must be broken. Public sentiment in the west . . . is unsettled. The public are dissatisfied [sic] but know not what to do.[30]

In 1880 Trumbull once again ran for office, this time as a Democrat, his fourth party affiliation, and it left him open to charges of opportunism which his opponents were quick to voice. Campaign pamphlets accused him of making denigrating remarks about his current party throughout the years, especially at the Liberal party convention in Cincinnati in 1872. "They are a body of men, mostly traitors, who cannot be made useful for any purpose,"[31] he is quoted as commenting on the Democrats.

Trumbull's shift to the liberal viewpoint was also ridiculed: "In expectation that the liberal party of that day . . . might be successful over the Republicans [he] very promptly discovered that the Republican party was corrupt and that its mission had ended."[32] Trumbull's bid for the governorship as a Democrat was unsuccessful, and he was flirting with the Populist movement at the time of his death in 1896. The virulence of Trumbull's detractors had no lasting effect on the reputation of the man remembered for placing conscience above party.

On the state scene, the Republican party had first gained the governorship under William Bissell in 1856, ousting the Democrats for the first time since the formal organization of parties in the state. Richard Yates guided the state through the war years, and the party had high hopes of maintaining that dominance in 1864. The onus of alleged treason and conspiracy clung to the disorganized Democrats, and the sanguine expectations of the Republicans were fully realized in the election of 1864. According to an obviously partisan historian, "The gallant Oglesby and patriotic Moulton [congressmen-at-large] boldly met their adversary and routed him horse, foot and dragon."[33] The state would stay in Republican hands throughout twenty-six of the next thirty years.

Richard Oglesby was a man of many talents, and a wanderlust that had taken him, after an adolescence spent wandering with an itinerant uncle, to the California gold fields and the Mexican War. He early abandoned the family farm in Decatur, and was admitted to the bar in 1845. Law sustained him between adventures, but in 1856 he left his practice again to make the Grand Tour of Europe. The tour launched his political career, for upon his return he was an instant celebrity and much in demand as a speaker. His style was described as "electric, full of penetrating enthusiasms which communicated itself to his listeners."[34]

Oglesby began his political career as a Whig, but first ran for Congress as a Republican in 1858. He is credited with giving Lincoln the "railsplitter" title, and worked hard for his election in 1860. He resigned from Congress in 1861 to enlist in the Union army, from which he retired as a major general after sustaining a near-fatal wound. Throughout his career he was known as a champion of the soldiers' interests, and it was his secretary who worked out a ritual for a fraternal order of Union soldiers to be known as the Grand Army of the Republic. The GAR's first charter was issued to Oglesby's hometown of Decatur. The organization proved an ideal political arm for former generals with eyes on elective office. Its first state commander was Major General John Palmer, who was the logical choice for Oglesby's successor.[35]

Because the Constitution of 1848 denied governors two successive terms, the Republicans had to turn to another war hero to be their standard bearer in 1868. They settled on a reluctant John M. Palmer, who, like Lincoln, Oglesby, and Civil War Governor Yates, was born in Kentucky. He peddled clocks, taught school, and finally became a lawyer. He entered politics as a Democrat, but split with his friend Stephen A. Douglas over the Kansas-Nebraska bill. Defeated for county clerk in 1839, he was elected probate judge, county judge, and state senator.

When the war broke out, Palmer enlisted and, as a major general, commanded the military district of Kentucky where he was under indictment for helping slaves escape when the Thirteenth Amendment was passed and the charges were dropped. He retained his interest in military affairs after the war, however, and his state GAR post proved an auspicious one from which to launch a political career as a Republican.

Writing to his son in 1868, Palmer expressed his doubts about running in the upcoming election:

I am pressed on all sides to be a candidate for governor, but my repugnance to the thing is definite. The emergencies of the party may make my nomination a necessity and the same necessity may compel me to accept it, but I don't want to do it. . . . My income for January was $1,186 and for February $1,602 which is for two months $788 more than a whole year's salary as governor. Now stop income and our situation is mere gilded poverty. With six children at home and two sisters-in-law can I wisely pay that enormous price for a very empty honor?[36]

TABLE 4. MAJOR VOTING PATTERN IN ILLINOIS, 1864-97

Year	Governor		U.S. Senator	U.S. Senator	Presidential Vote in Illinois	
1864	Richard Oglesby	190,376	Lyman Trumbull	Wm. A. Richardson	Abraham Lincoln-Johnson	189,519
	James Robinson	158,701			John McClelland	158,724
1865				Richard Yates		
1868	John Palmer	249,912			U. S. Grant	250,293
	John R. Eden	199,813			Horatio Seymour	199,143
1871				John Logan		
1872	Richard Oglesby	237,774			U. S. Grant	241,237
	Gustave Koerner	197,084			Horace Greeley	184,772
	B. G. Wright	2,185			Charles O'Connor	3,138
1873	John Beveridge		Richard Oglesby			
1876	Shelby Cullom	279,263		David Davis	Rutherford B. Hayes	278,232
		xx			Samuel Tilden	258,601
	Lewis Steward	272,465			Peter Cooper	17,207
1877						
1879			John A. Logan			

Year					
1880	Shelby Cullom	314,565		James Garfield-Arthur	318,037
	Lyman Trumbull	277,532		Winfield Hancock	277,321
	A. G. Streeten	28,898		James Weaver	26,358
	John Hamilton				
1883			Shelby Cullom		
1884	Richard Oglesby	344,234		James G. Blaine	337,469
	Carter Harrison	319,635		Grover Cleveland	312,351
	James B. Hobbs	10,905		John St. John	12,074
	Jesse Harper	8,605			
1887			Charles Farwell		
1888	Joseph Fifer	367,860		Benjamin Harrison	370,475
	John Palmer	355,313		Grover Cleveland	348,371
	David Harts	18,874		Clinton Fisk	21,703
1891			John Palmer		
1892	John Altgeld	425,555		Grover Cleveland	426,481
	Joseph Fifer	402,676		Benjamin Harrison	399,288
	Robert Link	24,808		James Weaver	22,207
	Nathan Barnett	20,103		John Bidwell	25,871
1896	John Tanner	587,637		Wm. McKinley	607,130
	John Altgeld	474,256		Wm. J. Bryon	464,523
	George W. Gere	14,559		Joshua Levering	9,796
1897			Wm. E. Mason		

Apparently he could, for when the convention appeared dead-locked, Palmer agreed to serve. "This was the first instance in Illinois," he observed, "of the office seeking the man rather than the man seeking the office."[37]

Palmer's nomination short-circuited the budding political career of Colonel Robert Ingersoll, whose friends were "nearly crazy to have [him] run for governor."[38] Among Ingersoll's supporters was Governor Oglesby, who considered him, after Palmer, "most acceptable to our people."[39] Oglesby was not convinced, however, that Palmer was sincere in declining the nomination, for although he "said he was not a candidate . . . he did not say or even intimate he could not accept a nomination."[40] Oglesby's judgment proved sound, and Colonel Ingersoll turned his energies in other directions, thus depriving Illinois of the distinction of having a professing atheist for its governor.

Ingersoll's reputation in 1868 rested, as did Illinois' other Republicans, on military exploits and rhetoric. The *Marshall County Republican* rested his qualifications for governor on the fact that "he hates treason, rebels and Democrats, and says 'that during the entire war a Democrat without a musket was a rebel; a rebel without a musket was a Democrat!'"[41] Ingersoll may have been in 1868 "the best stump speaker in the state,"[42] but his stumping was not yet on behalf of his moral philosophy. Woe to the unmusketed Democrat in the election of 1868, for he was about to pay at the polls for causing the Civil War. Both Generals Grant and Palmer carried the state by large majorities.

The most important act of the Palmer years was the calling of a constitutional convention which rewrote the state charter and eliminated many of the abuses of the Constitution of 1848. Although a nominal Republican, Palmer's views of government were more in keeping with those of the party he left behind him. He was a firm believer in states' rights, distrusted the eastern financial leadership of the Republican party, and was repulsed by congressional reconstruction policies. Within the state, he saw his role as a restricted one, and was happy to keep it that way. In his inaugural address he stated, "The Constitution has wisely given to the governor but little power to influence legislation,"[43] and he held to that course throughout his term.

Not only did Palmer not actively seek to influence legislation himself; he was also quick to veto bills he felt had overstepped the limited constitutional role of government. In all, he vetoed seventy-two bills, and according to a member of the legislature, "if there is a question of constitutionality on a bill we will not discuss the question here; if there is anything constitutional in the bill, Governor Palmer will find it."[44] The governor also found a way to solve his financial dilemma, by keeping his law practice going throughout his term in office, a practice also followed by his predecessor, Governor Oglesby.

One of Palmer's few initiatives was a request for regulation of railroad rates. He then vetoed the first bill passed as too extreme, but eventually signed the first railroad regulation act. General Fuller of Belvidere was named chairman of the senate committee on railroads, and his next-door neighbor, Jess S. Hildrop, was named chairman of the house committee. "These gentlemen," noted D. W. Lusk, "invested with the power of shaping the railroad legislation of Illinois were from the same little town of three thousand people, with only one railroad."[45]

The crisis sparked by the Chicago Fire of 1871 involved the governor in an imbroglio with Mayor Mason and President Grant. Mason had requested and Grant had supplied federal troops to keep order in the city, but Palmer was outraged at this usurpation of state authority and demanded the troops be withdrawn. Even though "the first impulse of many of our Republicans is for Sheridan (the general sent to Chicago) no matter what side he is on,"[46] the public response to Palmer's states' rights stand was remarkably favorable. J. Newton Crittendon of Chicago attempted to take the blame for Grant's call out of troops by writing Palmer to confess he was the one who saw the flames and in a panic wired President Grant to "send help immediately."[47]

The governor's other correspondence indicates the variety of problems brought to the state's chief executive for solution. Reverend Peter Cartwright, eighty-five-year-old Methodist missionary, sought help to get a railroad pass to California; an antislavery society protested Chinese coolie "slaves"; a reprieve in "the Walsh murder case" brought letters of praise and condemnation; the GAR requested a speech; George Morrison wanted an appointment to the Blackburn College board of trustees. And amid all of the mundane demands was the growing possibility that Palmer would bolt the party and head the Illinois delegation to the liberal Republican convention in 1872.

"Don't go near Cincinnati!,"[48] warned A. J. Norton of Alton. "Its nominees will not be elected." Harley E. Haynes of Jerseyville offered the governor some concord grape wine to soothe his "political stomach," noting "your old political friends have experienced alarm for you and hope that you will not delay a proper application of the remedy . . . with sentiments of the highest personal respect and the deepest political disgust."[49] Palmer did not heed Haynes's warning, and after the ill-fated Liberal campaign of 1872 he turned to the Democratic party. He was much in demand as a speaker at Democratic rallies across the country in the election of 1876, but after the campaign devoted himself once more to his legal practice. Many of his clients had invested heavily in Macoupin County bonds, and they were most unhappy with the results. "I have written to you several times without a reply,"[50] complained client after client. Palmer ran for governor again in 1888, this time as a Democrat, and was soundly defeated by Republican Joseph Fifer.

When Palmer refused the Republican nomination in 1872, the party turned to reliable Richard Oglesby. The regular Republicans attended the national convention and cheered their own Shelby Cullom as he nominated Grant for a second term in a brief, one-sentence speech. That speech, according to Cullom's "recollections," was outshadowed by another speaker from Illinois. Wrote Cullom: "I do not recall that I ever saw a man electrify an audience as did Governor Oglesby on that occasion. It was the first convention where there were colored men admitted as delegates. . . . Old Garret Smith the great abolitionist was in the Gallery. . . . Oglesby took for his theme first the colored men represented there on the floor and then Garret Smith. He set the crowd wild. They cheered him to the echo."[51] The Civil War was over, but obviously not forgotten.

Oglesby's campaign was destined for success as the nomination of Greeley killed the hopes of the national Liberal party. The Democrats were unable to forgive his radical past, and the more moderate Republicans also had their doubts. The election was a sweep for Grant and the Liberal coalition broke up in disillusionment. Liberal Democratic gubernatorial candidate Gustavus Koerner, a leader of the states' German intelligentsia, fell to Oglesby by 40,000 votes. The breakup of the liberal Republicans sent most of its adherents into the arms of the Democrats, but some returned to the regular Republican party. "Treason to party is not easily forgiven," writes a Republican historian, "and no wandering prodigals had fatted calfs killed in honor of their return."[52]

Oglesby's inauguration for his second term was a mere formality, for he resigned two days later to become United States' Senator. Lieutenant Governor John Beveridge, who had three weeks earlier resigned his position as congressman at large, succeeded to the office. Beveridge had moved to Illinois at eighteen from Tennessee. He returned to Tennessee, went broke through business mismanagement, and returned to Illinois with twenty-five cents and the clothes on his back. By 1855 he was a prosperous Chicago attorney, and after serving in the war, he was elected Cook County sheriff, and then state senator. Beveridge approached the office as a caretaker, content to carry on the policies of his predecessor. Although his Illinois experience was in Chicago, his administration did not reflect any particular awareness of urban problems. His strong prohibition stand was not appreciated, and he was not renominated.

The midterm election of 1874 was the first Republican defeat since 1862, as currency reform and railroad legislation rallied dissident groups into another fusion party calling itself the Illinois State Independent Reform party. It demanded repeal of the national bank law and the issue of legal tender currency direct from the treasury and interchangeable for government bonds; a declaration favoring railroad legislation; elimination of railroad passes for public officials; and opposition to the protective tariff. The Independents nominated David Gore for state treasurer and Samuel Ettor for superintendent of education.

In the meantime, the Democratic liberal party entered the field, calling for restoration of gold and silver as the basis of currency, the resumption of specie payments, no protective tariff, individual liberty, and opposition to sumptuary laws. They also nominated Ettor, and he defeated Republican nominee William B. Powell. All over the state Republicans lost votes and elected only seven congressmen instead of their usual eleven.

The Republican state platform of 1876 condemned leniency toward the South and endorsed paper currency. Shelby Cullom, farmer-turned-lawyer, headed the Republican ticket. Both the Greenback and Democratic parties nominated Lewis Steward, "the Democratic apology for a governor."[53] As the campaign progressed, rumors began to circulate that Cullom was involved in the Pekin whiskey frauds, which he denied vigorously: "I desire to brand all such charges and insinuations as false and caluminous and to assure my personal and political friends that they need have no apprehension that any credible evidence can or will be produced showing culpable connection on my part with their transactions."[54] If credible evidence existed, it was not uncovered.

Shelby Cullom took office as governor in 1876 with the smallest majority of any Republican governor. His concept of the role was expressed in his inaugural address: "The state may be regarded as a great business enterprise."[55] Cullom followed the Republican pattern of seeing himself as an administrator, not an innovator, and he proudly recalled years later, "I no more thought of influencing the legislature than I have thought of attempting to influence the judiciary."[56]

Cullom's agrarian background had a profound influence on his perception of government, and he firmly believed "agriculture is now and always will be the chief industrial and productive interest of Illinois, the foundation of our material prosperity."[57] Farmers were convinced that banking and railroad laws victimized them, and Cullom agreed by strengthening the railroad and warehouse commission and eliminating the state debt. He vetoed a bill requiring payment to labor only in United States currency. The bill was an attempt to eliminate scrip payments, worth sixty cents on the dollar, and good only at a company store, but Cullom remembered the common practice of paying for farm work with produce, and he declared the bill an abridgment of individual rights.

Cullom was the first governor to win two successive terms under provisions of the Constitution of 1870. His opponents in 1880 were Lyman Trumbull, now a Democrat, and A. J. Streeter of the Greenback Reform party. Trumbull was unable to overcome the skepticism caused by his frequent changes of party, and he gave Cullom little trouble. Cullom's chief opposition came in the form of charges that he was antiforeign. The *Illinois State Register* accused him of being a know-nothing, of voting against a congressional resolution supporting Ireland. Cullom was, it claimed, "at heart opposed to and prejudiced against foreign-born citizens."[58] Like the whiskey-ring charges of 1876, the antiforeign charges against Cullom in 1880 were ineffective.

David Davis's term in the Senate ended in 1882, and Governor Cullom was elected to fill the next term. He left office satisfied that "my administration as Governor of Illinois was a very quiet, uneventful one."[59] He continued his agrarian thrust during his thirty years in the Senate. In 1887 he saw passage of the Cullom Act establishing the interstate commerce commission which extended railroad regulation to the national level, and he chaired that commission until 1901, when he became chairman of the foreign relations committee.

From Washington, Cullom spent the next thirty years keeping his political machine in line, for his election rested on keeping both a Republican and a friendly majority in the Illinois General Assembly. Opposition was ferreted out, and as a friend suggested, "it would not cost you a great deal to have these districts discreetly canvassed."[60] Discreet canvassing was coupled with encouragement of the Republican Editors Association and a continuing correspondence regarding possible rivals. One was dismissed as a threat in 1886 because "his stronghold is philosophy and I never saw that used much in securing votes from an Illinois Legislature."[61] Cullom's most faithful adviser and errand runner was John Tanner, who warned the Senator in 1887 that his chance for the presidency looked slim and therefore, "isn't it political wisdom to hold fast to the political machinery of our state?"[62]

Illinois politics and an Illinois candidate figured prominently in the presidential election of 1884. Ulysses S. Grant, soldier-turned-politician, received the presidency as a gift. General John "Black Jack" Logan, politician-turned-soldier, sought the prize eagerly but was turned away. Grant was simply the most spectacular hero when battle ribbons were the only qualifications needed for the job, but by the time Logan's name came up times had changed. Logan was a particularly southern Illinoisan who entered politics as a fire-eating Democrat and was elected to the legislature in 1852. When he ran for Congress in 1858, the *Mound City Emporium* noted with approval, "in him abolitionism finds a foe who will be satisfied only with 'war to the knife and the knife to the hilt.'"[63]

The firing on Fort Sumpter and secession of the southern states brought moments of cheer in southern Illinois, and there was talk, egged on by the *Chicago Tribune*, of the southern counties seceding and joining the Confederacy. Logan was on record as stating, "he hoped his right arm might wither and his tongue cleave to the roof of his mouth if he ever gave any aid, comfort or countenance to any attempt at conquering the rebellion by force of arms."[64] His in-laws and relatives were active in the building secession movement, and he was well known, as the author of Illinois' most recent Black Laws, to be violently opposed to abolition. More damning to his later career, as the weeks slipped by and the war intensified Logan refused to commit himself to one side or the other. His wife would later claim that he always intended to fight for the Union, but at the time many of his constituents were not that sure. In June, 1861, however, Logan put his southern sympathies aside and plunged into the northern cause, recruiting volunteers for the army. So strong was his pro-southern image at home that there was a general feeling that he was recruiting for the South.

John Logan was not a halfway man. Once committed to the

Union cause, he fought with bravery and distinction, and as commander of the army of Tennessee in the battle of Atlanta he earned national fame. He returned from the war a radical Republican and was immediately elected congressman at large from Illinois. When Richard Yates's Senate seat came up for election in 1870, Logan went after it with determination, courting the legislators in a statewide canvass and holding open house, hosted by Mrs. Logan, at Springfield's Leland House.

His opponents for the seat were Gustavus Koerner and Richard Oglesby. Oglesby was critical of Logan, writing to a political adviser in December, 1870:

> The growing opinion upon all hands justified it, that it would be unwise, unjust and most unpolitic to lift Logan above us all and place him in the high position of trust and responsibility at the expense of every other hard-working meritorious and devoted Republican. And that his place is good enough for him. He sought it, let him keep it. It is becoming more apparent that his anxious aspiration to the place [the Senate] is little less than inexcusable selfishness, having in view his own rather than the glory of the public.[65]

Logan's bid in 1870 proved successful and he succeeded Yates in Washington, where he continued making flamboyant speeches—sometimes to the embarrassment of his new Republican colleagues. One speech was termed "the oddest performance I ever saw. Such ghastly rubbish," noted the critic, "would disgrace a freshman in a Western College."[66] Independents controlled the balance of power when the seat came up for re-election in 1876, and the nod went to David Davis by a margin of one vote on the fortieth ballot. The next two years Logan spent building a political machine, and when Richard Oglesby's seat came up for election his forces swept his old enemy aside. Oglesby's own popularity was no match for the dashing general and the solid support of the Grand Army of the Republic.

Since 1860, nomination by the Republican party had been tantamount to election to the presidency, and Logan mustered his forces in 1884 for a bid for the top office. By this time, however, military victories were not enough, and the eastern press was scornful of the dashing general. "Nature made him a soldier and a politician," sneered *The Nation*, "but neither nature nor art ever designed him to be a statesman."[67]

Logan's military image and political contacts at the Republican convention could not get him the nomination, but it did win him the second spot on the ticket. Even that honor unexpectedly evaporated when the election results showed a surprising Democratic comeback. Grover Cleveland was President of the United States, and a disappointed John Logan returned to Illinois to battle for his Senate seat. Holding his forces in line through 103 ballots, Logan retained his seat in that body. His death two years later ended one of the state's most exciting political careers, and brought forth reams of memorial oratory. Robert Todd Lincoln declined to serve as pallbearer, but Roscoe Conkling accepted. Logan was, according to his eulogists, the "ideal soldier, bold, brave, generous, but careful, calm and considerate. In personal appearance he was the most remarkable figure of the war."[68]

Cullom's successor to the governorship in 1883, John M. Hamilton, was a scholar and lawyer, elected state senator at age twenty-three. At thirty-six he became the state's youngest governor and immediately was forced to deal with an election scandal. Balloting in the nineteenth-century elections was a very individual thing. Each party printed its own tickets, which were then distributed in the hopes that voters would choose to deposit them at the polling places. The opportunities to stuff ballot boxes, vote gravestones, and bribe voters did not go unnoticed, and the election of 1884 was a case in point.

Ex-Governor Richard Oglesby was once more nominated by the Republicans in that race. Carter Harrison of Chicago led the state Democratic ticket and the prohibitionists and Greenback parties also entered slates, the prohibitionists having the honor of nominating the first woman for state office, Frances Willard, defeated for state superintendent of schools. It was the election of "rum, romanism and rebellion," the first Democratic victory since the war. The Republicans were shocked, and some cried foul. Republican historian Church piously recalled, "the impartial historian must record the fact that enough votes were stolen in New York to defeat Mr. Blaine and give the presidency to Grover Cleveland."[69]

The Republicans elected twenty-six state senators in the disputed election. The state election canvassing board was unable to reach a decision in a disputed Chicago race, and Governor Hamilton made the arbitrary decision to seat Republican Henry Leman. Leman's original plurality of 390 votes was changed following the canvass of the Cook County board of canvassers to a 10 vote plurality for Democrat Rudolph Brand, but the state board was unable to certify either man. In making his decision for Leman, Governor Hamilton declared, "There is no precedent in the commission of such a heinous crime. . . . That I have the right to construe the meaning of the Constitution as to the duties pertaining to my office and am clothed with power to do so, independent of the co-ordinate branches of the State Government, is established by the best authority."[70]

Richard Tuthill, United States District Attorney from the northern district, gathered evidence in the case and presented it to a grand jury. One instance of erasure of returns was cited in the second precinct, eighteenth ward, in which numbers had apparently been transposed from 420 Leman to 274 Brand to 220 Leman to 474 Brand. Michael Ryan, Cook County clerk, was ordered by the court to produce the disputed ballots, and Baker Printing Company, apparently on instruction of Joseph C. Mackin, printed facsimile Republican ballots, substituting the name Brand for Leman. These ballots were printed three weeks after the election and delivered to the grand jury as original ballots on November 25. Mackin, Arthur, Gleason, and Henry Biehl were indicted, and William J. Gallagher was added to the group to be tried after evidence was uncovered that he was the actual forger. The men were all convicted, but the case was appealed to the Supreme Court on a writ of error.

Meanwhile, Mackin was arraigned, tried, and convicted of perjury and began serving a five-year term in Joliet prison. On March 22, 1886, the convictions of Mackin, Gallagher, Gleason, and Biehl were set aside by the United States Supreme Court because Gallagher had not been indicted by a grand jury.

The Democrats in the Senate did not appreciate Governor Hamilton's decision to seat Leman or agree that his right to do so was established by the best authority. A move was made to censure the governor because "the rights of this Senate have been invaded, because a coordinate branch of the state government has dared to cross the threshold of the Senate and usurp its rights."[71] Republicans countered with a resolution quoting the grand jury's findings "that out of 171 precincts . . . there were but seven in which there were not violations of the election laws, and that the evidence indicates that fraud was attempted or committed at every step as the election progressed."[72] After much bitter wrangling, both motions were dropped.

Controversy continued into 1887 as the evenly split assembly attempted to elect a United States Senator. Neither side had a quorum, so failure to vote by either party would block election. The Democrats backed first William Morrison, then Lambert Tree, and the Republicans stuck with John Logan. Voting began on February

10 and continued into May. By this time two members had died and been replaced by men of their own party. The balance held. Democrat Henry Shaw was the third man to die during the term; he came from a safe Democratic district, and a special election was called for May 6. It was to become a famous Illinois election coup:

> A few days before the senatorial election, pursuant to the plan arranged in Springfield, trusted emissaries were sent through the thirty-fourth district, some in the guise of stock-buyers, others as insurance agents, others as sewing machine agents—all with plausible excuses for being in the neighborhood. They visited Republicans whom they could trust with the secret and left with them tickets bearing the name of Captain Wm. H. Weaver, a Republican of Menard County. Instructions were given that the Republicans were to manifest the utmost indifference and were to remain away from the polls until three o'clock or later in the afternoon of the day of the election. Then they were to go quietly to the polls and deposit the Weaver tickets.[73]

Weaver was elected by 336 votes, and on May 10 Logan was re-elected to the Senate on the 120th ballot. His victory was a brief one, for the general died in office on December 26, 1887, and once more the Republicans had to fill the vacant spot. Charles Farwell of Chicago and Governor Hamilton were both contenders for the spot, and the ubiquitous Tanner scurried to Chicago to interview both and report back to Cullom. He was disgusted with both men. "The trouble with Charlie," reported Tanner, "he seems to think that everybody is for sale."[74] After talking with Hamilton, however, Tanner was forced to conclude, "I ventured to say that it seemed to me that the chances were against him."[75] Farwell got the nod.

Oglesby's last term was disrupted by the Haymarket incident, and the third-term governor found himself in 1887 the center of an emotional appeal for pardon or clemency for the condemned men. August Spies pleaded with him to spare the other men even if he himself must die. "If a sacrifice of life there must be," pleaded Spies, "will not my life suffice? I offer it to you so that you may satisfy the fury of a semi-barbaric mob, and save that of my comrades!"[76] Oglesby was not impressed by the eloquent plea. "My opinion at the time," he commented, "was that it was intended for publication at some time by friends of the anarchists. It was of course not expected to have any impression upon my mind in deciding the cases. Its suggestions are too absurd for serious consideration by me upon whom would fall the duty of deciding the cases in the light alone of the exercise of clemency."[77]

Another of the condemned men, Albert R. Parsons, also wrote to the governor with savage irony: since he was convicted of merely being present at the meeting, Parsons suggested delaying the execution until his wife, two small children, and Mrs. Lizzie M. Holmes who had accompanied him could also be "arrested, tried and condemned to die upon the scaffold in company with their equally guilty husband, father, and friend."[78] Oglesby was not amused. The suggestions, he wrote, contained neither "law or decency."[79]

Among the pleas for clemency came a letter from "clar huntz (age eight years)," who offered to name the guilty party, an "offle bad man" who had told her father "his watch has not kept such a time as it did the day he thrown the Dinemont . . . thy mans name Fritz Benz." Countering young Clar's plea was realistic advice from George White, who warned Oglesby that "the people are talking hard of you if you let up on the four anarchists. Of course, do as you please. But it will cost you and the Republicans thousands of votes if you do."[80]

Oglesby managed both to offend and to please both sides. He commuted the sentences of the two most contrite of the men, and allowed the others to hang. Many disapproved of his "opening the door away from the gallows for two enemies of good government, fireside safety, and supremacy of the law."[81] Another "life-long republican" raged that "to you, Sir, in free and civilized America belongs the unenviable distinction of having first used the halter as a mode of punishment for such offenses [political offenders]."[82]

In spite of the criticism, however, Oglesby managed to finesse a tricky political decision by carefully couching his commutation statement in the most soothing terms and giving both sides enough to keep wrath from falling on himself. Governor Altgeld would not be quite so diplomatic.

Former Republican Governor Palmer, now a Democrat, sought re-election in 1888. His Republican opponent was Joseph Fifer, a private wounded at Vicksburg who ran as a common man and friend of the worker. Fifer's greatest asset was his political innocence and lack of enemies—and the strength of the Republican party. "It would be sheer hypocracy," commented the *Chicago Tribune*, "to pretend that the convention placed in nomination the strongest candidate."[83] Three generals, a colonel, a major, and a captain were passed over for Republican nomination, but this did not mean that the war had faded from memory. Fifer ran on his war record, and his campaign slogan gained him a permanent nickname: "Joe-Joe-Private-Joe . . . Fifer-Fifer-Jos-eph-Fifer."[84] Despite the cries of "down with the infidel," Private Joe defeated Palmer by a slim margin.

His first two years went fairly well, and he fulfilled his promise to the working man by asking for mine and factory safety laws and a law prohibiting aliens from working for the state unless they planned to become naturalized. He was also concerned with education, and asked for stringent teacher certification laws and a truant officer to enforce the new compulsory attendance law. By midterm, Fifer's middle-of-the-road approach was drawing fire from all sides. He was able to get only two measures approved— a change in the pardon law and the State Ballot Box Act which provided official ballots with all candidates listed and the Australian ballot system of voting. The previous legislature had also acted to correct election abuses by making the offering of a bribe a criminal offense. Fifer summed up his administration saying, "[my] administration was not a reform administration in any sense, but it did not mark time. It was earnest for enlightened measures . . . as administrations go mine was free from any great trouble."[85]

Fifer's greatest trouble was the enmity of the Hamilton-Tanner-Cullom wing of the party. "I shall continue to oppose Fifer during his miserable lifetime,"[86] wrote Tanner. When Fifer threw his support to Harrison against presidential aspirant Cullom, the Cullom faction declared war on Fifer, the *Chicago Tribine*, and the *Inter-Ocean*. Fifer's opponent in 1892 would be a giant in the state's history, John Peter Altgeld.

That historical giant was actually a small-statured man, known as "the Little Dutchman" to both friends and enemies. Altgeld was both an immigrant and a native son, brought to the United States from Germany at the age of three months by peasant parents. His childhood was spent in "Johnny Appleseed" country near Mansfield, Ohio, in a very typical midwestern American farm community. That rural, yeoman-farmer background, however, was combined with autocratic German methods of childrearing that had young Pete doing a full day's work while still a child. His labor was hired out to neighbors when free time appeared, and he was frequently beaten by his stern, narrow father. The father was suspicious of schooling, and the son got only two summers and one winter of formal education.

Those early years were often painful ones, for in addition to the bleak severity of his home life, the boy felt physically unattractive due to a slight harelip, a squat stature, and uneven features. "I have thought there is something about me that repels others,"[87] he told "Buck" Hinrichson. His devoted friend, socialist organizer George Schilling, recalls Altgeld musing, "Hell, if I had to depend on my looks I'd have been hung long ago."[88]

His inability to speak fluent English deepened his sense of alienation from his comrades. He remembered that in those early years "in school the boys all picked on me. No one of them ever thought of protecting me from abuse. It was the crowd on one side and John Peter Altgeld on the other."[89] Altgeld's sensitivity to his foreign background is clearly evident in an article entitled "The Immigrant's Answer," published in *The Forum* in 1890 in answer to an article condemning immigrants and urging restrictive legislation. The leading Republican papers, including Joseph Medill's *Chicago Tribune*, were in the forefront of the antiforeign crusade, and Altgeld marshaled statistics to remind them that "in every state carried by Lincoln there was a large immigrant foreign population, which was mostly, and in some states, entirely, Republican."[90] Medill replied that Altgeld was a Marxist.

He was still an adolescent when the Civil War broke out, but when he became old enough to enlist, lured by "the enthusiasm of those days, the drums and flags and all the rest of it,"[91] he received the $100 bounty for entering the service. Unlike Oglesby, Palmer, Grant, and Logan—unlike Private Joe Fifer—Altgeld relegated his war experience to insignificance. He "did not bleed and did not die, but was there; always reported for duty, was always on deck, never shirked and never ran away."[92] That perspective is more in keeping with Lincoln's attitude toward his Black Hawk War duty than the obsessive glorification of conflict which Republican would-be Lincolns affected. The most significant memento Altgeld carried home from the war was a malarial-type fever which plagued him throughout the rest of his life.

Altgeld's young manhood was marked by struggle, rejection, and failure. He went to school against his father's wishes, tried teaching, and was rejected by a young lady whose father did not approve of him. In 1869 he joined the American migrant stream, walking westward in search of himself. He ended his journey in Kansas, hospitalized with a near-fatal recurrence of his fever while employed on a railroad section gang. The railroad hospital ate up his savings, and he was refused a job by the company upon his partial recovery. Wandering back east he was befriended in Savannah, Missouri, where he regained his health, studied law, and began his political career.

It was the high-hope time of Grangerism, 1873 to 1874, when lawyer Altgeld, fancy dresser, ladies' man, and Bourbon Democrat, took up politics. After solidifying his position with the Democrats, he attended the Granger convention and received their nomination for prosecuting attorney of Andrew County. Ignoring his opponents' charges of the "cheapest kind of know-nothingism"[93] (an absurd charge considering his immigrant background), Altgeld campaigned on the Jeffersonian, Granger issues and won. A year later he resigned, took $100, and headed for Chicago.

Lawyer Altgeld struggled to establish himself in the big city, sleeping in his law office to save rent, until he once again made friends who would help him. He disliked the law, believing it a profession in which "its strongest men sold themselves to destroy people, to perpetuate and intensify the poverty of the oppressed and enlarge their burdens."[94] With his first bit of extra money he turned to real-estate speculation, buying and selling lots, building office blocks, and working himself into the paper-millionaire ranks. He profited mightily from the laissez-faire economic dogfight of Chicago, as did his friends and backers, Vanderbilt attorney William Goudy and antilabor editor William Story. A third friend from this period—and the most lasting—was professional gambler Joseph Martin.

The Man of Property, however, had another side. In 1884 Altgeld brought out his first book, *Our Penal Machinery and Its Victims*, in which he recognized that crime is bred by social conditions—the same social conditions which were creating his own wealth. "The law," he declared, is directed against "the poor, the unfortunate, the young and neglected."[95] The boy who had tramped penniless into the West deplored the practice of arresting boys whose only crime was to sleep in someone's shed for the night. He deplored the brutality of the police in arresting often innocent men. "Can clubbing a man reform?" asked this oft-beaten man, "will he not wish to be avenged?"[96] It was a point he would return to time and again. "Brutal treatment brutalizes," he noted, "and thus prepares for crime."[97]

Although the book made no appreciable literary mark, Altgeld used it effectively to promote his political career. George Schilling and Clarence Darrow both received copies and turned toward Altgeld. By the senatorial election of 1885 Altgeld could travel to Springfield and be seriously considered as a dark-horse Democratic candidate.

The next year saw the Haymarket incident and the trial of anarchy in Chicago. When the hysteria cleared, 60,000 Chicagoans, including almost all lawyers and sitting judges, signed petitions seeking clemency for the seven men condemned to die. John Peter Altgeld did not sign. The incident led, among other things, to the formation of the United Labor party. Because of his friendship with Schilling, his book, and an article in April, 1886, advocating the compulsory arbitration of strikes, Altgeld was assured of the party's support in a campaign for judge in the superior court of Cook County. With that backing he secured the nomination of the regular Democratic party. Again he used the tactics employed in Andrew County—he ignored the charges of his opponents and spent his own money on the campaign.

Once again Altgeld was successful—winning an office for which he had little good to say. Although he appeared to relish his autocratic role on the bench, he claimed a low opinion of judges and the criminal justice system. In an article on the subject of "the Administration of Justice in Chicago," marked as were all of his writings by clear, logical accumulation of facts and statistics, he examined the plight of a litigant who customarily found that "it is apparently not the justice of his cause which is the main subject of inquiry, but that instead, it is the rules of procedure about which great solicitude is shown."[98] He felt that all the judge could do "is to blow dust off volumes . . . drawing learned distinctions between tweedledum and tweedledee,"[99] and he resigned his judgeship.

His resignation, however, did not come before he demonstrated some of the conflicts that made his career so much a reflection of the conflicts of the period. In 1889 builder Altgeld sued the city of Chicago for damages when the grade leading to some of his property was changed. It was a questionable action in view of his position as Superior Court judge. The more he appeared to be in the wrong, the more fiercely he defended himself. He was fined $100 for contempt of court for one angry outburst, and later filed an angry and intemperate brief and sent a bitter, contemptuous letter to all three appellate judges who had given him a "good character" in their decision. Altgeld's chief adversary was Mayor John Roche. In the mayoral election of 1889 Roche was defeated by a questionable but legal scheme which cost Altgeld $5,000, certainly an unusually vigorous response to a legal adversary.

Judge Altgeld's greatest joy remained building, and the greatest of his buildings was the Unity Block. For financing, Altgeld turned to politico-banker John R. Walsh. The project got off to a bad start due both to Walsh's recalcitrance at issuing the necessary bonds and the fact that it was thrown out of plumb by construction sloppiness and had to be substantially rebuilt. The building was a financial albatross almost from the beginning, and in the end its builder lost it. But still, when asked what achievement had given him the greatest personal satisfaction, he replied "The Unity Building."[100] This from the man deemed one of the state's great reform governors.

Reformers are expected to adhere to a higher system of ethics than most mortals. That did not appear to be the case in 1890 when Altgeld once more sought the senatorship. Working clandestinely he apparently sought to undermine support for General Palmer and win the seat for himself—to no avail.

He appeared just as ordinary in 1892. His candidacy for governor was boosted in Chicago by "King Mike" McDonald, boss of the city's gambling interests, and his big appeal downstate was his wealth. Touted as a "man with a barrel," Altgeld presented a solid, conservative image as a millionaire who would finance his own campaign. To charges that he was a socialist, he replied that "the country people will know it is absurd to talk about a man being a socialist or anarchist who has spent his whole life endorsing the majesty of the law and who has built some of the finest business blocks in Chicago."[101] He ran as a "law and order" candidate, campaigned tirelessly throughout the state blaming Fifer for passage of the Edwards Act requiring compulsory school attendance, and he spent $100,000 of his own money.

Altgeld was supported by former Governor Palmer, leading one Republican to complain that "Palmer has again appeared in his favorite role of the demagogue aspiring to the leadership of the Anarchists and promises to be more of an issue in the state than Altgeld himself."[102] Altgeld's candidacy received another boost from division within the Republican party. The Cullom faction had backed Tanner for the post, and was convinced that if Fifer was renominated "he will be snowed under by the people."[103] The nominees for state office, moaned one Republican, "are below average. . . . Governor Fifer has never been a great success as a statesman and national leader of the party. Perhaps his early education has been so curtailed that he could not rise above it . . . to secure his nomination, of course, he made an alliance with men of the same character as himself."[104] Senator Cullom agreed. "The Governor," he wrote back, "seems not to possess those elements of manhood and gratitude which every honorable and, to any extent, great man possesses. However, we must make the best we can of it and elect it [the state ticket] if we can."[105]

With such lukewarm support from his own party, Fifer was unable to overcome Altgeld's skillful use of the Edwards Act—a measure Altgeld had strongly favored but which most immigrants feared and disliked—and Altgeld's strenuous campaign. Altgeld was elected with a 22,000 vote plurality and became the first Democratic governor since the Civil War, as well as the first foreign-born.

To make the election results even more gratifying to Illinois Democrats, Adlai Ewing Stevenson, an attorney from Bloomington, was elected vice-president of the United States. Stevenson had been elected to Congress in the Democratic sweep of 1874, and after a defeat in 1876 was re-elected in 1878 with support of the Greenback party. He was a personable man, and made friends on both sides of the aisle. He retained his low-tariff, soft-money views, but managed to avoid antagonizing the Republican opposition.

When Grover Cleveland became president in 1884 he chose Stevenson for the politically difficult and critical post of first assistant postmaster general. The Republicans had been in power for twenty-five years, and it became Stevenson's job to as gently and painlessly as possible fire 40,000 patronage postal workers to make way for the long-hungry, deserving Democrats. Despite some scathing denunciations from the unhappy Republican machine, Stevenson's diplomatic tactics pleased his own party, and won him the post of justice of the Supreme Court of the District of Columbia. In 1892 Stevenson led the Democratic delegation to the national convention and worked hard for the renomination of Cleveland. When the factions within the party looked for a man to run with Cleveland, they chose Stevenson for the second spot on the ticket. The Illinois Democrats now had taken power in Washington and control of the governorship after a long dry spell.

Unfortunately for the reform governor, the Democrats had been out of power for thirty-six hungry years, and patronage appointments resulted in some unhappy choices. In 1893 the governor fired Robert Oldroyd, the Republican curator of the Lincoln home. The home contained one of the country's most comprehensive collections of Lincoln memorabilia, but it belonged to Oldroyd and not the state. He promptly packed up his priceless collection and moved with it to Washington, D.C., where he became curator of the house where Lincoln died. Appointments to the University of Illinois board of trustees proved equally embarrassing when a bank chosen by the trustees crashed with a loss to the university of several thousand dollars. "I am nearly heartbroken over the loss to the

University," wrote Altgeld. "I had done more for that institution than all other governors put together."[106]

Altgeld was hardly exaggerating his interest in the state's university system. In 1896 he requested that President A. J. Draper of the University of Illinois set up a series of free lectures on law and medicine with a view toward starting departments in those areas. "I am exceedingly anxious," wrote the governor, "that your institution shall be a complete university in the highest meaning of the term before the expiration of my term of office."[107] He was also instrumental in establishing the new normal schools at DeKalb and Charleston, and increasing state support of the existing teacher-training schools. The governor extended his interest into the architecture of the new schools—insisting that his favorite "English castle" style was best suited to the prairie colleges.[108]

The potentially disastrous effects of so many patronage appointments were tempered by Altgeld's zeal in personally overseeing the operation of the state's institutions. He required them to publish their payrolls and seek competitive bids for supplies. In his first days in office he also obliquely recommended an inheritance tax and municipal ownership of utilities. His future policies as governor were both fair and far-seeing. His appointment of Florence Kelley as state factory inspector was a master stroke, and his veto of Charles T. Yerkes's "eternal monopoly bills" a victory for personal integrity.

Thus far, there is little in Altgeld's career to distinguish him from Shelby Cullom or Richard Oglesby. His writing betrayed an identification with the poor and oppressed more typical of Lincoln than his Republican successors, but his actions were those of a conservative man of wealth. Those who remembered his statement that "the history of the country demonstrates that the common people are swayed by a patriotic impulse or impulse in favor of the right— something which cannot be said of the wealthy or the book men,"[109] or that he also claimed that "labor's only hope for the future lies in united action,"[110] saw nothing in his conduct to cause them concern. That was about to change.

Public support for pardons for the three anarchists still jailed for the Haymarket incident had grown by 1892 to include the most respected and influential leaders of society. It was the unspoken understanding of much of this group that Altgeld would pardon the men on grounds of mercy. He might very well have chosen that course had not trial Judge Joseph Gary seen fit to publish a lengthy article justifying the decision and casting snide aspersions on the convicts, their friends, families, and defenders. Instead of choosing a politically safe course—a suggestion he received very angrily— Altgeld published an 18,000-word pardon statement to support his contentions:

> First—That the jury which tried the case was a packed jury selected to convict.
>
> Second—That according to the law as laid down by the Supreme Court, both prior to and again since the trial of this case, the jurors, according to their own answers, were not competent jurors, and the trial was, therefore, not a legal trial.
>
> Third—That the defendants were not proven to be guilty of the crime charged in the indictment.
>
> Fourth—That as to the defendant Neebe, the State's Attorney had declared at the close of the evidence that there was no case against him, and yet he has been kept in prison all these years.
>
> Fifth—That the trial judge was either so prejudiced against the defendants or else too determined to win the applause of a certain class in the community, that he could not and did not grant a fair trial.[111]

Altgeld's arguments were buttressed by affidavits and by cold, clear, irrefutable logic. Its moral impact was lessened, however, by his obvious personal vendetta against Judge Gary, coincidentally one of the three appellate judges to whom his blistering letter had been addressed in his suit against the city. Even his supporters were dismayed by Altgeld's unnecessary wrath. The press, led by Medill's *Tribune*, heaped abuse on the governor. Not since Abraham Lincoln had such concentrated community hate been focused on a public figure. And that was just the beginning.

The years 1893 to 1897 were not good years to be governor of any state. A severe depression shattered the economy and brought on the Pullman Strike in 1894. Altgeld's position was clear: "The state must not pursue such a policy as to convince the masses of the laboring people that the authority of the state is simply a convenient club for the use of the employers."[112] President Cleveland apparently disagreed, and federal troops were sent to break the strike. As had Governor Palmer in 1871, Governor Altgeld upheld the state's right to handle internal matters without interferences from the federal government. His imbroglio with Cleveland unleashed another fire storm of attack in the press. Both the strike and Altgeld were "beaten" in the actual dispute, but once more the governor got his revenge.

Altgeld's first target was George Pullman himself, the feudal lord of the sleeping-car factories and owner of the town of Pullman. Altgeld started a public outcry, impossible for even the *Tribune* to ignore, over starvation in Pullman's enclave. He then directed a reassessment of the company's taxes and eventually saw court action to divest Pullman of his control of the community.

Altgeld's need to avenge himself had already been at work in his attempts to retaliate against Roche, Gary, and Pullman. Revenge was a theme to which Altgeld continually returned. Much of the Haymarket pardon message, in fact, was given over to proving that whoever threw the bomb must have been motivated not by politics but by the need to seek revenge for clubbings administered by Bonfield and the police. Now his own deep feeling was turned against Grover Cleveland.

In spite of the howling of Medill, Altgeld controlled the state's Democratic political machinery. In 1895 he called a special convention to set the policy of the Illinois delegation to the national convention on the hottest national political issue, free coinage of silver. The convention backed Altgeld's pro-silver stance, and he went to the Chicago convention controlling a key delegation and determined to eradicate Cleveland and "Clevelandism" from the party forever. That successful determination led to one of Altgeld's most lasting political contributions.

The Democratic convention of 1896 began a new era in politics. After forty years of drift toward a pro-business position identical to the Republicans, the Democratic party took a drastic turn back to its philosophical beginnings. And the man who wrote that platform (complete with thinly veiled personal insults to Cleveland) was John Peter Altgeld. "For the first time," writes Altgeld biographer Harry Barnard, "since the rise to dominance of industrialism, of monopolies and of corporations and of corporation finance, one of the major parties took a clear stand on the basic economic issues which were dividing the nation between 'haves' and 'have-nots.'"[113] It was the first national recognition that the nation had entered a new era, that the old articles of faith—still so righteously mouthed by Illinois Republican politicians, must be modified to a completely new set of circumstances. As early as 1888 Altgeld had recognized that "times have changed, so that now there are tens of thousands of men in our large cities and a good sprinkling all over the country who are ready and willing to work, but can get nothing to do."[114] That recognition, coupled with the belief that government must be involved in a new way in order to deal humanely with this new set of problems, sets Altgeld apart from the other governors of the period.

He devoted his energies in the 1896 campaign to the hopes of Democratic presidential candidate William Jennings Bryan. Ignoring the continuing personal attacks of the press, the "anarchist" governor exhorted rallies to support Bryan, free silver, and the new Democratic platform. His own campaign for re-election as governor was a secondary concern.

Not so with faithful John Tanner, at last the candidate. He ran a masterfully programmed campaign. Tanner managed to suppress his dislike of Fifer and Oglesby, and begged for their support. The state and national Republican committees set up a whistle-stop, campaign-train canvass of the state, and all surviving Republican governors were scheduled to appear on the train, preceded by "surviving generals and old heroes of the War."[115] It was the past against the future, and the people chose the past. Amid the usual charges of vote fraud in Chicago, Tanner was elected with the highest majority ever received by a governor of Illinois.

Tanner contrived a final insult to the man who had already weathered so much abuse. With Altgeld seated on the platform, Tanner refused to allow him the customary honor of delivering a farewell address. Perhaps it was just as well, for Altgeld was surely unreasonably optimistic. In his prepared speech, released later to the press, he had rejoiced that "passion is retiring and reason is mounting the throne."[116] He noted that:

> The presence of the defeated and retiring party is not necessary for the peaceful change of administration, yet in order to add the graces to republican form it is customary for the retiring party to be represented and participate in the ceremonies of inauguration, and to-day the great party which I have the honor to represent, not only assists in these ceremonies, but it expresses the hope that the new administration will direct the destinies of this mighty state along the paths of honor and of glory. While politically divided we are all Illinoisans and the greatness and the grandeur of this State rise above all considerations of persons or of party. Her past thrills, her present awes, and her future dazzles the intellect of man.[117]

He left office "conscious of having struggled for a great cause, [smiling] at the frowns of fate and . . . with renewed hope and a firmer purpose."[118]

His successor John Tanner was a "Republican of Republicans" and a man who "despised a party bolter from the bottom of his heart."[119] He enjoyed a good relationship with the Republican-held

General Assembly, and vetoed few bills. Aware of the political dangers of pardoning criminals, Tanner shifted the spotlight from the governor's chair to a newly created board of pardons. He was hardly an idealist, and he considered the police "an instrument for the sole benefit of the political party which happens to be in control after each election."[120] As a good Republican he wanted a state police board created to control the police department in Democratic Chicago. His request was denied.

All of the governors struggled with the problems of unjust tax assessment, and Tanner's solution was quadrennial assessment at one-fifth value. He felt that "the taxpayers would be more willing to make honest schedules if they could be fooled into the idea that they were paying taxes on only one-fifth of their property."[121] The governor never forgot political realities, and when the United Mine Workers struck in the election summer in 1898 he refused to send troops to put down the strike. "The laboring man's only property," he declared, "is the right to labor which is as dear to him as the capitalist's millions."[122] When violence broke out in Pana and Virden, he finally sent troops to restore order, but put blame squarely on the mine owners who had brought in Negro strikebreakers "who bring this blot upon the fair name of our state."[123] At the same time he was courting the labor vote, however, he signed the Allen Bill giving Chicago street railroads a fifty-year franchise and a transportation monopoly. Efficiency and economy were bywords of Tanner's administration. He did his job as his party expected him to and stepped down as the century closed.

Tanner's term closed a half-century of primarily Republican, conservative, big business control of state government. The party of Lincoln dominated the political scene, split into factions to be sure, but remained basically homogeneous. Republican governors held fast to the frontier touchstones of their rural backgrounds and applied those simple answers to an urban-industrial age. The results were an increasingly cozy relationship between success (that is, big business) and government, often at the expense of the urban poor, the immigrant laborer—even the farmer himself. For a key idol on the shrine of the past was the protestant work ethic at its Social Darwinist worst—the belief that material success could always be earned by the man who persevered—and that his success or lack of it was proof of God's pleasure (or lack of it).

The one Democratic governor during the period held to many of those beliefs, as did his party. He was rural, farm-bred, dedicated to material success. He was equally, however, foreign, urban, aware of what industrialization means for the common man. Altgeld identified with the alien, the oppressed. He combined Lincoln's shrewd political skills with the Great Emancipator's eloquence and compassion. He accepted the realities of the new situation and sought to bring to government that awareness. While Tanner and his cohorts were still conjuring away the present by holding up their Civil War glories, Altgeld endeavored to build for the ages with faith and optimism. His final speech, after which he collapsed and died, affirmed that vision: "I am not discouraged. Things will right themselves. The pendulum swings one way and then the other. But the steady pull of gravitation is toward the center of the earth. Any structure must be plumb if it is to endure or the building will fall. So it is with nations. Wrong may seem to triumph. Right may seem to be defeated. But the gravitation of eternal justice is upward toward the throne of God. Any political institution if it is to endure must be plumb with that line of justice."[124]

1. Governor Altgeld, *Journal of the House*, Jan. 10, 1893, 48-49.
2. Charles A. Church, *History of the Republican Party in Illinois 1854-1911: With a Review of the Aggressions of the Slave-Power* (Rockford, Ill., 1911), 2-3.
3. N. Vachel Lindsay, "Why I Voted the Socialist Ticket," *Collected Poems by Vachel Lindsay*, rev. ed. (New York, 1969), 302.
4. *Chicago Tribune*, Jan. 1, 1876.
5. Carl Sandburg, *Always the Young Strangers* (New York, 1953), 32.
6. W. E. Woodward, *Meet General Grant* (New York, 1929), 391.
7. U. S. Grant, III, *Ulysses S. Grant: Warrior and Statesman* (New York, 1964), 298.
8. William Barlow, "U.S. Commissioner of Pensions, Green B. Raum of Illinois," *Journal of the Illinois State Historical Society* LX (Autumn, 1967), 299.
9. Arthur Schlesinger, "Historians Rate U.S. Presidents," *Life* 25:17 (Nov. 1, 1948), 66.
10. Church, *History of the Republican Party*, 115.
11. D. W. Lusk, *Eighty Years of Illinois, 1809-1889* (Springfield, 1889), 289.
12. U. S. Grant to D. W. Lusk, Oct. 10, 1883. Lusk, *Eighty Years*, 313.
13. *Congressional Globe*, 39th Cong., 1st Sess., Feb. 11, 1866, 91.
14. "Speech of Jehu Baker of Illinois on Reconstruction," House of Representatives, Jan. 27, 1866, 4-6. Illinois State Historical Library.
15. *Congressional Globe*, 39th Cong., 1st Sess., 943.
16. *Ibid.*, 1169.
17. *Chicago Tribune*, Dec. 1, 1865.
18. "Speech of Honorable A. J. Kuykendall," House of Representatives, March 3, 1866, 28. Illinois State Historical Library.
19. *Ibid.*
20. *Ibid.*
21. James G. Blaine, *Twenty Years of Congress*, II (Norwich, Conn., 1893), 360.
22. "Opinion of Lyman Trumbull, May 16, 1868," *Congressional Globe*. Kenneth Stampp, *The Era of Reconstruction, 1865-1877* (New York, 1965), 153.
23. Shelby Cullom, *Fifty Years of Public Service–Recollections of Shelby M. Cullom* (Chicago, 1914), 146.
24. *New York Tribune*, May 14, 1868.
25. *Ibid.*, July 4, 1868.

26. "Trumbull's Slanderers," broadside, NI. Trumbull *MSS*, Illinois State Historical Library.
27. *Chicago Tribune*, Sept. 13, 1868.
28. "Forty Years an Office Seeker—Lyman Trumbull—Why He Should Not Be Elected Governor—The Inconsistencies of His Political Career." Trumbull *MSS*, Illinois State Historical Library.
29. *Ibid.*, 3.
30. Lyman Trumbull to James Wilson, Jan. 4, 1876. Wilson *MSS*, Library of Congress. James P. Jones, "Trumbull's Private Opinion of the Grant Scandals," *Journal of the Illinois State Historical Society* LIV (Spring, 1961), 51.
31. "Forty Years an Office Seeker," 7.
32. *Ibid.*
33. Lusk, *Eighty Years of Illinois*, 163.
34. Jane M. Johns, *Personal Recollections of Early Decatur, Abraham Lincoln, Richard J. Oglesby and the Civil War* (Decatur, Ill., 1912), 105. Frank B. Wilkie, *A Sketch of Richard Oglesby* (Chicago, 1884), 5.
35. Robert Howard, "The G.A.R. Goes G.O.P.," *Illinois: A History of the Prairie State* (Grand Rapids, Mich., 1972), 327.
36. Palmer, *A Conscientious Turncoat*, 416.
37. *Ibid.*
38. Robert Ingersoll to Bro, March 3, 1868. Ingersoll *MSS*, Illinois State Historical Library.
39. Richard Oglesby to Robert Ingersoll, March 19, 1868. Ingersoll *MSS*, Illinois State Historical Library.
40. *Ibid.*
41. *Marshall County Republican*, April 6, 1868. Ingersoll *MSS*, Illinois State Historical Library.
42. *Bloomington Pantagraph*, April 6, 1868. Ingersoll *MSS*, Illinois State Historical Library.
43. John Palmer, *Journal of the House*, Jan. 11, 1871, 202.
44. Palmer, *A Conscientious Turncoat*, 218.
45. Church, *History of the Republican Party*, 115.
46. Harley E. Haynes to John Palmer, May 13, 1872. Palmer *MSS*, Illinois Historical Library.
47. J. Newton Crittendon to John Palmer, Nov. 7, 1871. Palmer *MSS*, Illinois State Historical Library.
48. Harley E. Haynes to John Palmer, May 13, 1872. Palmer *MSS*, Illinois State Historical Library.
49. *Ibid.*
50. S. June to John Palmer, Nov. 14, 1878. Palmer *MSS*, Illinois State Historical Library.
51. Cullom, *Fifty Years of Public Service*.
52. Church, *History of the Republican Party*, 127.
53. *Illinois State Journal*, Oct. 20, 1876.
54. Wm. C. Searles, "Governor Cullom and the Pekin Whiskey Ring Scandal," *Journal of the Illinois State Historical Society* LI (Spring, 1958), 36.
55. Shelby Cullom, *Journal of the House*, Jan. 8, 1877, 52.
56. Cullom, *Fifty Years of Public Service*, 168.
57. James Neilson, *Shelby M. Cullom: Prairie State Republican* (Urbana, 1962), 168.
58. *Illinois State Register*, Sept. 22, 1880.
59. Cullom, *Fifty Years of Public Service*, 168.
60. John Moses to Shelby Cullom, April 10, 1886. Cullom *MSS*, Illinois State Historical Library.
61. Otis Humphrey to Shelby Cullom, Dec. 2, 1886. Cullom *MSS*, Illinois State Historical Library.

62. John Tanner to Shelby Cullom, Nov. 17, 1887. Cullom *MSS*, Illinois State Historical Library.
63. *Mound City Emporium*, Oct. 14, 1858.
64. Broadside, NI. Logan *MSS*, Illinois State Historical Library.
65. Richard Oglesby to ?, Dec. 4, 1870. Oglesby *MSS*, Illinois State Historical Library.
66. Isaac N. Phillips to Shelby Cullom, July 14, 1876. Cullom *MSS*, Illinois State Historical Library.
67. *Nation*, April 3, 1884. Ernest Bogart and Charles Thompson, *The Industrial State, 1870-1883. Centennial History of Illinois,* IV (Springfield, 1920), 146.
68. May Strong Hawkins, "The Early Political Career of John A. Logan," M.A. thesis (Chicago, 1934). See also Mrs. John A. Logan, *Reminiscenses of a Soldier's Wife* (New York, 1912). Alexander Davidson and Bernard Stuve, *A Complete History of Illinois from 1673 to 1884* (Springfield, 1884), 661. James P. Jones, "John A. Logan, Freshman in Congress, 1859-1860," *Journal of the Illinois State Historical Society* LVI (Spring, 1963).
69. Church, *History of the Republican Party.*
70. Lusk, *Eighty Years of Illinois*, 479.
71. *Ibid.*, 498-499.
72. *Ibid.*
73. Church, *History of the Republican Party*, 157-158.
74. John Tanner to Shelby Cullom, Jan. 2, 1887. Cullom *MSS*, Illinois State Historical Library.
75. *Ibid.*
76. August Spies to Richard Oglesby, Nov. 6, 1887. Oglesby *MSS*, Illinois State Historical Library.
77. *Ibid.*, Oglesby's comments written on the letter.
78. A. R. Parsons to Richard Oglesby, Nov. 8, 1887. Oglesby *MSS*, Illinois State Historical Library.
79. *Ibid.*, Oglesby's comments written on the letter.
80. Clar Huntz to Richard Oglesby, Nov. 2, 1887. George White to Richard Oglesby, Oct. 27, 1887. Oglesby *MSS*, Illinois State Historical Library.
81. R. J. Bringhurst to Richard Oglesby, Nov. 10, 1887. Oglesby *MSS*, Illinois State Historical Library.
82. E. B. to Richard Oglesby, Nov. 11, 1887. Oglesby *MSS*, Illinois State Historical Library.
83. Bogart and Thompson, *Industrial State*, 176.
84. James O'Donnel Bennet, *"Private Joe" Fifer* (Bloomington, Ill., 1936), 78.
85. *Ibid.*, 79.
86. John Tanner to Shelby Cullom, April 24, 1892. Cullom *MSS*, Illinois State Historical Library.
87. Barnard, *"Eagle Forgotten,"* 18. William H. Hinrichson, "Illinois Giants I Have Known," *Chicago Inter-Ocean*, March 16, 1902. Waldo R. Browne, *Altgeld of Illinois: A Record of His Life and Works* (New York, 1924), 6. See also Howard Fast, *The American: A Middle Western Legend* (New York, 1946).
88. Barnard, *"Eagle Forgotten,"* 18.
89. *Ibid.*, 17.
90. John Peter Altgeld, "The Immigrant's Answer," *The Forum*, Feb., 1890. Henry M. Christman, ed., *The Mind and Spirit of John Peter Altgeld: Selected Writings and Addresses* (Urbana, Ill., 1965), 36.
91. Barnard, *"Eagle Forgotten,"* 19. Browne, *Altgeld of Illinois*, 9.
92. *New York World*, July 17, 1894. Barnard, *"Eagle Forgotten,"* 20.
93. *Andrew County Republican*, Sept. 24, 1874. Barnard, *"Eagle Forgotten,"* 37.
94. Clarence Darrow, *The Story of My Life* (New York, 1932), 107-108.
95. Barnard, *"Eagle Forgotten,"* 86. John Peter Altgeld, *Live Questions* (Chicago, 1890), 68.

96. Barnard, *"Eagle Forgotten,"* 87. Altgeld, *Live Questions*, 179.
97. Barnard, *"Eagle Forgotten,"* 87. Altgeld, *Live Questions*, 179.
98. Altgeld, "The Administration of Justice in Chicago," Feb. 12, 1889, in Christman, *Mind and Spirit*, 17.
99. Barnard, *"Eagle Forgotten,"* 119. John Peter Altgeld, *The Cost of Something for Nothing* (Chicago, 1904), 73-74.
100. Barnard, *"Eagle Forgotten,"* 150.
101. *Chicago Daily News*, Aug. 28, 1892. Barnard, *"Eagle Forgotten,"* 150.
102. Paul Selby to Shelby Cullom, July 13, 1892. Cullom *MSS*, Illinois State Historical Library.
103. John A. Roche to Shelby Cullom, Jan. 15, 1892. Cullom *MSS*, Illinois State Historical Library.
104. George Scheider to Shelby Cullom, July 6, 1892. Cullom *MSS*, Illinois State Historical Library.
105. Shelby Cullom to George Scheider, July 11, 1892. Cullom *MSS*, Illinois State Historical Library.
106. John Peter Altgeld to My Dear Judge Tree, May 11, 1897. Altgeld *MSS*, Illinois State Historical Library.
107. John Peter Altgeld to A. J. Draper, March 6, 1896. Altgeld *MSS*, Illinois State Historical Library.
108. Neil Thornburn, "John P. Altgeld: Promoter of Higher Education in Illinois," *Essays in Illinois History: In Honor of Glenn Huron Seymour* (Carbondale and Edwardsville, Ill., 1968).
109. Altgeld, "The Immigrant's Answer," in Christman, *Mind and Spirit*, 34.
110. Altgeld, "The Immigrant's Answer," in Christman, *Mind and Spirit*, 36.
111. Altgeld, "Reasons for Pardoning Fielden, Neebe and Schwab, the So-Called Anarchists," in Christman, *Mind and Spirit*, 63-104.
112. *Journal of the House*, 1893, 52.
113. Barnard, *"Eagle Forgotten,"* 359.
114. Altgeld, *Live Questions*, 74-79. Barnard, *"Eagle Forgotten,"* 129.
115. John Tanner to Richard Oglesby, Sept. 6, 1896. Oglesby *MSS*, Illinois State Historical Library.
116. Altgeld, "Retiring Address as Governor of Illinois," in Christman, *Mind and Spirit*, 176.
117. *Ibid.*
118. *Ibid.*, 178.
119. *Oration by Honorable Isaac N. Phillips,* Oak Bridge Cemetery, Springfield, Illinois, May 26, 1901 (Bloomington, Ill., circa 1901), 26.
120. *Journal of the Senate*, Dec. 7, 1898.
121. Robert M. Haig, *A History of the General Property Tax in Illinois* (Urbana, Ill., 1914), 147.
122. Victor Hicken, "The Virden and Pana Mine Wars of 1898," *Journal of the Illinois State Historical Society* LII (Summer, 1959), 274.
123. *Ibid.*
124. John P. Altgeld, speech in *Chicago American*, March 12, 1902. Barnard, *"Eagle Forgotten,"* 435. Browne, *Altgeld of Illinois*, 331. Fast, *The American*, 332.

4

Agriculture: More Machines, Fewer Men

The fertility of her soil is unsurpassed by any in the world and furnishes boundless resources for agriculture which industry constitutes the real basis of our great wealth and prosperity.

Governor Joseph Fifer[1]

The basic concern of the state between 1865 and 1898 was agriculture, which built the state, fed the cities, and created the capital and raw materials on which the industrial state developed. Farming was above all an individual enterprise, based on the family. Farm neighbors helped each other raise barns, shared machinery and labor, but saw themselves as individual units when it came to prices, rents, and costs of production. The period saw major but only partially successful attempts to move toward organization.

Whether north or south, the population of Illinois was overwhelmingly agrarian at the close of the Civil War. Only Chicago, Quincy, and Peoria had populations over 10,000 in 1860, and Springfield, Bloomington, Aurora, Rockford, and Galesburg were the only five to join them in 1870. As the surge toward the cities began, the rural dwellers declined proportionately, so that by 1890 less than one-third of the state's workers were engaged in farming and by 1900 the number was down to less than one-fourth. By the turn of the century, over one-half of the state's population lived in towns of more than 2,500, although East St. Louis remained the only large metropolitan area in the southern part of the state.

An absolute decline in farm population, however, still left the state with over 250,000 farms in 1900, with farming by far the most populous industry in the state. The average Illinois farmer at the turn of the century lived in a saltbox house on 124 acres of land. If

116

he were a tenant farmer, he probably lived in the central or northern part of the state, as the less productive acreage in Little Egypt remained in the hands of owner-operators. His farm was worth $7,500 on the average, and if he were especially prosperous and progressive he might own an Illinois-invented wheat shocker, cow milker, or silage cutter to help in the work.

Manure remained the main fertilizer, and the turn-of-the-century farmer might spend $3 per year fertilizing his land. His farm was probably planted 80 percent in corn and 20 percent in wheat to correspond to the 10,000,000 acres of corn and 2,000,000 acres of wheat grown in that year, although other crops were grown as well. His gross income was $1,300, supplemented with produce from his truck garden which made him largely self-sufficient. He probably lived on land inherited from his father, for 55 percent remained on family land. Kerosene lamps lit his home, fireplaces and stoves heated it, and hard work kept it going.

A typical farmhouse throughout the period depended more on the carpenter's skill and imagination than on architectural design. Two rooms downstairs and two up was the rule, with the stairway often being outside. After 1875 full frame construction with filled weatherboarding and shingle roofs predominated for the exterior, with plastered, ten-foot ceilings inside. Halls or closets were rare, but the bare walls were frequently decorated with wallpaper or pictures. Some French homes were heated by huge fireplaces, but wood or coal stoves were more prevalent. Sewing machines were the only mechanical appliances available to the farm housewife. Her other "tools" in 1865 included "a few dishes, knives, spoons, a skillet or spider, a pot or kettle, drinking gourds, a coffee pot, a coffee mill, and where cookstoves were not modernized, a dutch oven."[2] Kitchen sinks were "hardly known" and wooden bathtubs lined with zinc were few and far between. The family's Saturday night bath might come from "a quart of water in the tinned washbasin."[3] The ever present privy sat out back, for few homes had water pipes, and kitchen slops went into the chicken and hog pens. "Wash, bath, and dish water quite often flew out the kitchen door"[4]—an efficient if not aesthetic system of garbage disposal.

The needs of the agricultural calendar determined the school term, as did the amount of money available for the teacher's salary. The transplanted southern farmers of Little Egypt distrusted education at the taxpayer's expense, and salaries there remained lower than in the rest of the state. Thirty dollars per month was average, with the teacher doubling as janitor.

Nationally, the number of people engaged in agriculture increased from 6,287,000 in 1860 to 10,609,000 in 1900, but the farmer's proportion in respect to the rest of the population decreased from 59.7 percent to 36.8 percent. The farm population "increased barely half while the total nonfarm population leaped from 12,000,000 to 48,000,000, or by a multiple of four."[5] According to one source, "more farmers sought refuge in the city than on new lands," and "for every city laborer who took up farming, 20 farmers flocked to the city to compete for the vacated job or place in the breadline."[6] The trend held in Illinois where over half the state's population was engaged in agriculture in 1870, compared with one-fourth in 1900. There was not only a proportional decline, but absolute numbers declined as well. The exodus of workers from the farm was vital to Illinois, as the burgeoning industrial cities demanded more and more unskilled labor.

Why did men leave the land? One impetus was "the steady transference during the period of various industries from the household to the factory,"[7] and the increased efficiency which required fewer "hands" to do farm work. Emigration also took large numbers of the farm population to greener pastures to the west. Illinois lost the greatest number (320,000) of any state between 1870 to 1880, and again between 1880 to 1890. Tenants had no strong ties to hold them and they left in such great numbers for the higher wages offered in cities that by 1890, "there was a farm labor shortage."[8] Over a half-million Kansans that year were from Illinois, as competition from the new western grain states affected both agricultural prices and the number of farmers willing to stay on Illinois' more expensive land.

There may have been fewer farmers, but all other indexes rose, with 1880 generally representing the peak year for the period. The number of farms increased from 202,803 in 1870 to 255,741 in 1880, before declining to 240,681 in 1890. The percentage of land area in farms rose from 72.2 percent in 1870 to 88.3 percent in 1880, down to 85.0 percent in 1890. More important, the percentage of improved acreage rose steadily from 74.7 percent to 84.2 percent. The average acreage remained fairly stable, declining slightly from 127.6 acres per farm in 1870 to 126.7 acres in 1890, and the average value of land and buildings per acre increased —from $26.30 in 1870 to $31.90 in 1880 to $50.50 in 1890.[9] Land and buildings represented the major value, followed by domestic animals, poultry and bees, implements and machinery.

Averages may be deceiving, however, for the pattern of landholding differed markedly in the various divisions of the state.

The southern region, the bottom one-third of the state, remained in the hands of small owner-operators, with tenancy extremely rare and the value of the farms low. In the northern division farm size increased, while in the central division large landholdings were common and tenancy a major factor. Central Illinois farms were valued at $11,000, or $75 per acre[10] in 1890.

The opening of the central division prairie to agriculture was vastly complicated by the need for fencing and the necessary drainage of the heavy soil. Unimproved land was cheap in the 1840s and 1850s, but large holdings were usually sold off in order to acquire the capital necessary to improve the remaining land. Lack of trees made wooden fences impossible, and Jonathan Baldwin Turner's highly touted osage orange hedges were extremely costly to plant and maintain. It took 17,000 plants, costing $1.50 to $2.50 per thousand, two to six years to provide one mile of fence. Total cost was estimated at $165 per mile the first year and $105 the next three. The hedges required annual trimming and exhausted the soil for forty feet on each side. Necessity, however, forced their use in spite of the cost, and by 1871 hedges were used in fifty-six counties and "comprised a significant proportion of the total fencing in 34 counties."[11] Kankakee County's hedges accounted for 75 percent of all enclosures that year.

The cost of improving prairie land led many large landholders to let portions of their land to tenants in return for improving it and paying the taxes. Tenants hoped to make enough from their crops to advance to landholding status, an expensive proposition, as it cost a minimum of $1,000 to break and fence forty acres of prairie between 1850 to 1860—not counting the cost of the land.

Retirements of original owners led to an increase in tenancy after 1880. Often grown children rented their father's land until it became theirs by inheritance, but farmers who retired without heirs willing to stay on the land found leasing to outsiders a good investment. Mortgage foreclosures in the late 1870s also increased the number of absentee holders, as banks and businessmen gained title to the land. Most important, as land values rose, the cost of buying a farm became prohibitive for the tenants.

Another factor leading to increased tenancy was the rise of the landlord-entrepreneur. The *Chicago Tribune* in 1871 described the Sullivant farm, a 50,000-acre enterprise whose value had risen from $2 to $40 per acre. Sullivant had divided his estate into eight farms "of 5,000 acres each which are known by their numbers. . . . Each farm is enclosed and entrusted to a reliable tenant."[12] The 4,500 men employed on the farms lived in "quite a village" near

Sullivant's home, and Sullivant was described in 1872 as "the baronial farmer of Ford County."[13] His corn yield that year was 500,000 bushels. Sullivant's farm of 40,000 acres in Ford and Livingston counties, known as Burr Oaks, harvested its largest corn crop in 1871, but the farm was also mortgaged that year for $478,000 to Hiram Sibley of New York at 10 percent interest plus 5 percent commission. In 1874 Sullivant tried renting out eighty-acre tracts, but the move came too late. The land was assigned in 1877 and foreclosed two years later, when Sibley sold one-half of the acreage and divided the remaining 17,680 acres into 146 tenant farms. He laid 376 miles of drains and shipped in 500 purebred calves. Sibley's tenant contracts required crop rotation in contrast to Sullivant's reliance on corn alone, and under his management the entire farm began showing a profit.

Sullivant was not the only large landholder who lost his land to creditors. John T. Alexander's Broadlands farm, a 26,500-acre plot, was run much like Sullivant's Burr Oaks—with migrant labor as one large-scale operation. And like Burr Oaks, Broadlands went into bankruptcy.

William Scully, an Irish landlord, was more successful. He accumulated an estate of 211,000 acres, "making him the largest landholder in the United States."[14] Scully returned to England in the 1880s, leaving his holdings in the hands of an agent who was free to raise the rents and impose rigid cultivation requirements. Such a feudal domain seemed "un-American" to Illinois legislators, and in 1887 the Illinois legislature attempted to prevent its continuance by the passage of an Anti-Alien Landlord Bill.[15] Scully circumvented the bill by establishing residence in Washington, D.C., and taking out citizenship papers.

The Anti-Alien Landlord Bill was signed in Illinois on June 16, 1887, for the "legislature was in no mood to deal with tenancy in a constructive way but was blindly striking at Scully, possibly to soothe its conscience for its failure to solve the problems of the tenants."[16] That failure may be traced in part to the number of high-ranking state officials, including Governor Oglesby, David Davis, and representative David Littler, who were themselves among the large landholders and landlords.

The men who bought large parcels of land for speculation played key roles in the development of their counties, for "in practically every town, large or small, the local squire, the bank president, the owner of numerous mortgages, the resident of the 'big house,' the man whose wife was the leader of 'society,' got his start—and a substantial start—as a result of the upward surge in land values in the nineteenth century."[17]

Many speculators found their land purchases unprofitable and their mortgages and taxes impossible to meet. However, "if the expected profits did not materialize within a short period, their taxes remained unpaid, tax titles of dubious value were issued, and patronage was thereby created for lawyers and the courts, and further financial aid was given to the newspapers in the form of the much fought-over tax delinquent list."[18]

The number of land owners fell by 17,000 during the period. Tenancy increased statewide from 31.4 percent in 1880 to 34 percent in 1890 and 39 percent in 1900. By 1890 Illinois ranked third in the country in the number of farm tenants: Logan County had over 50 percent tenancy in 1880, and Ford County by 1890 had 53.7 percent. Grundy, Marshall, Livingston, Ford, Macon, Logan, Christian, Madison, and St. Clair counties all had tenancy rates over 45 percent in 1890 as more and more of the most productive land in the state was falling into the hands of absentee landlords.

A high tenancy rate was not peculiar to Illinois. Of the 4,008,907 farms in operation in the country in 1880, 1,024,601 were worked by tenants. As land values rose, so did the rate of tenancy, until the national figures in 1900 show 5,737,372 farms with 2,024,664 tenants. The rise in land values largely explains this demise of the "agricultural ladder," especially in the Midwest.

Not everyone was happy with the trend. In 1897 Governor Altgeld deplored "landlordism" and warned the General Assembly:

> There seems to be a tendency now . . . to allow the land to pass into the hands of men who live in cities and feel no interest except to get money out of it . . . the conditions of the tenant will be constantly lowered, and in time produce a lower class of citizenship that will in no way be equal to the independent farmers that have been the boast of our country. It is far better for the state that the farmer should own his own land even though he be in debt for it, than he should feel no interest in the soil, and see all his earnings go to the landlord.[19]

Governor Altgeld's fears were well founded, as investigators found that "tenancy had long been associated with sloppy farming."[20] In 1866 the *Prairie Farmer* noted that "men prefer to let their land lie idle rather than run the risk of letting to unworthy, lazy, stealing tenants."[21] Short-term leases of one to three years gave the tenant little incentive to improve the land or experiment with crop rotation. Early leases stipulated the cash or share required, although after 1876 more specific requirements concerning actual cultivation were often included.

The tenant farmers were not alone in practicing "sloppy farming." The richness of the prairie soil led almost all farmers in the state to believe manuring and rotation were unnecessary. If Illinois farmers did not wear out the soil as rapidly as "the early Virginia planters, it was only because of great original fertility and the less exhaustive nature of the crops grown."[22] Agricultural colleges slowly impressed farmers with the value of fertilizing and rotating crops, but careless and exploitive practices continued into the twentieth century, employed by prairie farmers who had lands rich enough to get away with it.

As farms in the central division were improved and drained, competition among potential renters for these good farms drove rents up. In the early 1870s renters paid one-third of their crop and furnished labor, seed, work animals, and equipment. By the mid-1880s rents had climbed to one-half the crop and some landowners in Macon County "reportedly asked a three-fifths rental in 1893."[23] Sharecropping was the most common rental arrangement, but cash rents in the central division became more prominent as more and more land fell into the hands of absentee landlords, businessmen, and bankers. In 1880, 2,268 farms in the east central division rented for cash compared with 9,596 rented for shares. By 1900 the figures showed 6,117 for cash and 7,794 for shares.[24] Cash rents for improved farms rose from $3 per acre in the early 1870s to $6 to $8 in the 1890s, although unimproved pasture land still could be rented for $1 per acre.

Life for the tenant farmer became more bleak as rents increased and landlords began demanding more specific types of cultivation. Tenant homes were often little better than shacks, with neither the landlords nor the tenant holding a lasting interest in the buildings. While, in fact, rising land values made the move from tenant to owner virtually impossible by the 1880s, this was not generally understood. It would not be until the twentieth century that a permanent tenant class would appear and long-term lease arrangements would make substantial improvements worthwhile.

By 1900, "prairie landlordism frequently provided expert farm management [but] . . . the old dream of owning one's farm was coming to be practically unattainable to a large proportion of prairie residents."[25] The increasing value of land and the relatively more expensive demands of modern farming in the 1890s encouraged efficient, businesslike management of acreage through carefully drawn tenant contracts, but made the rags-to-riches hopes of the farmer of Lincoln's day idle and unattainable daydreams.

By the 1870s small farms of three to ninety-nine acres had begun to decline in the central and northern divisions and the turn of the century saw definite agricultural trends: "In general the broad lines of distinction between the different sections of the state were now being drawn: mixed farming in the northern division, grain farming in the central division, cattle raising, and the production of horticultural and other special products for which it is particularly adapted in the southern counties."[26]

Statewide, four-fifths of all farm land was improved in 1890 —with very little unimproved land existing in the north and central divisions. Land values had also risen, for by 1900 over 90 percent of the land area of the section with the richest soil (east central Illinois) had been turned into farms. Very desirable tracts were then selling for $90 to $100 per acre compared with the $2 to $3 per acre for unimproved land in the 1860s.

The increase in land value depended upon the quality and quantity of crops produced on improved land. The winter of 1865 to 1866 was devastating for Illinois corn as the price dropped to ten cents per bushel, making it the cheapest fuel for farm stoves, but not otherwise profitable. The number of acres planted in corn increased to a peak for the decade of 8,935,911 in 1877, but large crops (305,913,377 bushels in 1879) meant lower prices. The lowest price during the 1870 to 1890 period was twenty-two cents per bushel in 1878. The highest price for the period followed a drought in 1873 to 1874, and was fifty-six cents per bushel.

Between 1870 to 1874, 16.6 percent of the corn crop in the state was grown in the southern division, but the proportion of the state's corn crop grown south of a line from East St. Louis to Terre Haute, Indiana, fell to 10.5 percent by the years 1890 to 1894, as more and more southern farmers gave up hope of profitable corn yields in that area. The northern and central regions also faced hardships, as between 1870 to 1893 the state board of agriculture estimated that "there were . . . only ten years in which growers of corn received a profit over and above all their costs of production; that is to say, in three years out of five the farmers suffered a loss."[27] Losses even on the state's most valuable crop were more common than not.

New studies confirm the depression in farm prices in the 1870s and the peak in prices in the 1880s, but contend that farm prices actually moved upward during the period, and that the farmer's position in relation to other sectors of the economy actually improved, or at least remained stable. What the farmer saw in those years, however, was his own industry remaining much as it had since the seventeenth century while all other industries changed, grew, and became more profitable, seemingly at his expense. If that impression was a false one, the farmer at the time was unaware of it.[28]

By the turn of the century the Illinois corn belt clearly spanned the state's bulging middle, and Champaign County dominated all others as the central division out-produced the north and south. Corn yields depended greatly on the skills of the individual farmer as much as location, however, with high individual yields in each county often far outstripping the county average. The average yield in DeKalb County in 1879, for example, was forty-two bushels—while the individual high yield was 105.

The state's preoccupation with corn led to improvements in both cultivation and varieties. Shallow cultivation was introduced by George Morrow of the University of Illinois, and new corn varieties included Golden Eagle produced in 1871 by H. B. Perry of Toulon, a standard variety called White Superior originated by C. R. Sperry of Monmouth in 1880, and introduced in 1890 by J. C. Sibley.[29] As a result of its advantages and the efforts of its farmers, Illinois ranked as the leading corn state from 1860 to 1900.

Wheat ranked second in importance to corn. In 1870 the national center of wheat production was eighty-three miles northeast of Springfield, and in 1880 it was sixty-nine miles northwest of the capital city. By 1890, however, the bulk of national wheat production had largely moved into Iowa and Minnesota. Wheat acreage increased to 3,642,589 in 1881, after which a steady decline began and the state board of agriculture reported that "in more than half of the fifteen years ending in 1894 . . . the Illinois farmer lost money on his production of wheat."[30] In fact, "the profit per acre on winter wheat fell from $7.44 in 1877-1879 to 14¢ in 1890-1894." Spring wheat was even worse, with the farmer who planted it in 1890 to 1894 actually losing "16¢ on every acre planted."[31]

Not only could the wheat states of the new northwest better compete because of new railroad access, but also their wheat made a cheaper and whiter flour than that grown in Illinois. Wheat was well adapted to those areas where land was cheap and labor dear. Illinois no longer fit that category as land prices soared and the increase in the state's population lent itself to a more labor-intensive type of agriculture.

Lack of success with wheat led many farmers to turn to oats, and oat production increased from 37,000,000 bushels in 1870 to 1874 to 104,000,000 bushels by 1890 to 1894. Illinois ranked first in oats production in both 1870 and 1880, although like wheat, oats was generally unprofitable. Rye, barley, and buckwheat were only locally important, with most of the barley used by the liquor industry and located near distilleries.

Hay and pasturage were much less important to the state's economy than the cereal grains. Prairie grass was grown in the northern division, clover in the south, and 72.6 percent of all hay was in timothy, mostly in the central division. Pasturage increased until the 1880s, as had hay, then declined. It developed chiefly in the cattle-raising lands of the northern division.

The climate of Little Egypt lent itself to fruit production, and peaches, apples, and cherries were a major crop there. Tobacco was introduced during the war years, and over 9,000,000 pounds were harvested in 1862 from 8,585 acres. In 1863, 30,627 acres were in tobacco with a yield of over 20,000,000 pounds. That was the high point for the crop, which fell off markedly to minor importance by the 1890s.

The importance of agriculture stimulated one of the state's most important industries—the invention and manufacture of farm implements. The Civil War accelerated the search for labor-saving devices, for in 1861 Illinois took out eighty patents, or over one-seventh of the patents for such machines granted by the government; "seventeen for cultivators, fifteen for harvesters machines, eleven for ploughs and ten for corn planters."[32] "The First Actual Success in Steam Plowing in America!"[33] was realized in Grundy County in 1860. Although the steam plow covered 2.63 acres in seventy-two minutes, it proved unwieldy. Enthusiasts continued to push its virtues, however, and in 1872 the *Chicago Evening Journal* concluded that "a revolution is at hand: after watching a public exhibition of Parvine's 'Steam Motor and Farmer's Engine,'" which "moved over the ground in nimble and businesslike way, dragging after it a gang of six plows which were made to harrow up the breast of Mother Earth in a most savage manner." The *Journal* estimated the machine could "go through about fifteen acres per day."[34] Steam power did not catch on for plowing, however, but found a place as belt power for threshers, water pumps, hay baling, and shredding and cutting silage.

The developments of farm machinery focused in factories of Cyrus McCormick and his kind. Between 1877 to 1882 McCormick sold 50,000 binders. While McCormick's reaper dated from the

1830s, and other important implements, including the Marsh Harvester, steel plow, sulky plow, and manure spreader also predated the war, mass production did not come until after 1866. George Spaulding of Rockford built a grain binder in 1869 to 1870, followed by the first successful twine binder in 1878. In 1884 G. W. Hunt patented the three-wheeled riding plow, and a grain drill was introduced by J. P. Fulghum in 1877, the same year J. S. Kemp brought out an improved manure spreader. Further improvements on the spreader were made in 1884 and 1890. Hay loaders, rake, and tedders also were improved at this time. It is possible to assert that "by 1893 most of the important machines had been pretty well developed, but improvements are constantly being made. Those which were of chief importance in the Illinois corn belt were the following: the improvement on the check row planter and the introduction of the edge drop. . . ."[35] Other important improvements were the potato digger, solo-feeding machinery, and the gasoline tractor.

Plows, wagons, harvesters, and implements of all kinds were produced in the factories of Illinois in increasing quantities so that by 1890 it was the third highest capitalized industry in Chicago, where one-seventh of the nation's farm machines originated. Almost one-half of the production of agricultural implements in Illinois originated in three large Chicago works employing 4,000 men. By 1900, the value of products of this industry for the entire state was over $42,000,000, an increase of 70 percent from 1890. The production at the turn of the century was 41 percent of the nation's total, and it came from ninety-four establishments around the state. National investment in farm implements and machines tripled during the period, from $246,000,000 in 1860 to $750,000,000 in 1900, part of the increase being replacement of worn-out older machines.[36]

Some of the most important mechanical innovations were not "tools" or machines at all. In 1875, the *Illinois State Journal* noted the completion of the Shy Levee, which would "reclaim 100,000 acres of very fertile lands now subject to overflow by the Mississippi River."[37] Even lands not threatened by flooding were impossible to till in the central division due to their heavy, wet soil. The Constitution of 1870 provided for drainage districts, but drainage was expensive, so much of the wet land was allowed to remain as pasturage. Those who could afford it drained with ditches and tile, and in 1879, after a constitutional amendment in 1878 overcame Supreme Court objections, the state legislature finally authorized the formation of drainage districts with taxing power. By the 1880s many districts had been formed, and extensive tiling and ditching were underway. "Rails, brush, slabs, sawed boards, brickbats or stones" were all used for tiling, and "all [were] rather dear items in Prairie areas."[38]

A mole ditching machine was introduced in the 1860s, but was of limited value. Large landholders experimented with tile, but it was not until the 1880s that small farmers could benefit. Tax levies from drainage districts and the decreased cost resulting from more local tile factories resulted in massive tiling of wet lands by the end of the 1880s.

Even with lower costs, drainage was expensive. Between 1879 to 1883 B. J. Gifford of Champaign County purchased 7,500 acres of wet lands. By 1884 his expenses for drainage had reached $300,000, and by the time the project was completed in 1887 an estimated 2,500,000 tiles had been laid. The expense was justified, for between 1884 to 1908 Gifford sold those lands, which had originally cost him between $14 and $40 per acre, for $60 to $75 per acre.

Another improvement was the development of barbed wire by W. H. Glidden of DeKalb. The new wire made enclosure cheap and required much less upkeep than did the bulky hedges. DeKalb County became the center of a barbed wire battle that would rage into the 1890s throughout the west. Charles Kennedy bought the barbed wire patent of William D. Hunt in DeKalb County in 1873. The Hunt patent proved impractical, but Glidden and Jacob Haish, also of DeKalb, both secured patents on effective and economical barbed fencing and began production of the wire. Isaac L. Ellwood, a DeKalb hardware merchant, purchased half of the Glidden patent in 1874 for a few hundred dollars, and in 1876 the Massachusetts firm of Washburn and Moen bought out the remainder of the patent. The simplicity of the wire and its quick success led to numerous imitators, and Washburn and Moen brought suit in 1876 against fourteen companies for infringement of patent. Haish was named principal defendant. The trial dragged on until 1880, when a decision in favor of Washburn and Moen was finally handed down. The decision's chief effect was to encourage scores of quacks to spread over the West selling fake licenses for manufacture of the wire. Illegal manufacture of the wire continued, and farmer indignation mounted as Haish and others stirred up resentment over the monopolistic aspects of the decision. The barbed wire battle focused in Iowa during the 1880s, with Haish leading the fight to get the Washburn and Moen patents set aside. The original Glidden patent was finally upheld in the United States Supreme Court in 1892, after it had expired and after the barbed wire industry had already begun the consolidation that would lead to the American Steel and Wire Company.[39]

All of these machines and improvements increased the value of the farmer's land and increased his productivity as well, but the "most obvious result was the reduction of spirit-deadening toil. . . . This helped the man who was fortunate in his selection of soil and wise in management—and if factors outside his control permitted—to acquire prosperity and leisure, and give his family added cultural advantages . . . academies, high schools, colleges, and universities springing up in all predominantly agricultural states, after 1869, were created out of the wealth produced, directly or otherwise by farmers."[40]

Approximately one-fourth of the value of Illinois agriculture came from animal products. Once again the southern division was overwhelmed by the north and central which accounted for almost 85 percent throughout the period. As the livestock industry became more specialized, in fact, the southern division's share decreased —from 16.3 percent in 1870 to 13.8 percent in 1890. The two other divisions were almost equal, with the northern division forging a slight lead as the dairy industry in the Elgin area increased in importance. Also important was the pioneering work in improving the breeding of shorthorn cattle done by John O. Gillette, "cattle king of the world," by 1868.

The late 1860s and 1870s witnessed a revolutionary change in the character of the Illinois cattle industry. Dominated in the prewar days by large holders who bred native cattle and fed them on unimproved pasturage and cheap corn, the industry shifted by 1880 to the mass feeding of Texas cattle for market. Thus "the first stage was that in which cattle were fed on corn as the most profitable method by which to bring the corn to market. The second stage was reached when the ranges were broken up; the object became not so much to raise cattle as a means of marketing corn as to raise corn in order to make beef."[41]

Several factors combined to discourage the local breeders and convince them that stock feeding was more profitable than raising and breeding local cattle. Texas cattle purchased in 1866 for $15 to $20 per head sold in Illinois at $20 to $40 per head. The price differential was as much as 30 to 75 percent less than the cost of similar Illinois cattle—with appropriate differences in profit at marketing time. Both the Mississippi River and the Illinois Central Railroad were important adjuncts to the cattle traffic, carrying as many as 70,000 cattle to a single firm in 1867.

The boom in land prices and subsequent increase in taxes also caused the northern and central divisions to turn more and more to intensified cultivation. Improved and less expensive drainage could convert the wetlands left in pasture into productive tillage—a more rational and profitable use of the land. And as the land values rose, taxes rose with them, further pressuring the livestock breeder to make his land pay by intensive cultivation and convert his livestock interests to feeder enterprises.

Transportation of large herds of cattle, and the new practice of shipping livestock by rail, drew attention to the problem of dehorning. The horns on cattle held a special place in agrarian mythology, being credited as a source of a bull's virility and necessary to the production of a cow's milk. They were also a danger, however, when large groups of heavily horned animals were enclosed in cramped quarters—both to themselves and to the men who handled them. In 1878, Henry Haaff, a wealthy Henry County farmer, was attacked by a bull. He retaliated by removing the animal's horns with a handsaw. The operation proved such a success that Haaff became an evangelist for it. In 1885 Haaff was charged with cruelty to animals by the Illinois Humane Society, and his trial became a nationwide forum for debate on the dehorning issue, ending with such a favorable public response to Haaff's arguments that the society requested that the case be dismissed. Haaff continued to work for dehorning after his trial, and developed and sold tools and instruments for the process. His book, *The Practical Dehorner, or Every Man His Own Dehorner*, and his slogan, "The Horns Must Go," were both widely known. "The testimony at his [Haaff] trial first acquainted the American public with the basic arguments for and against dehorning and the essential techniques used in the operation. Secondly, the notoriety created by the trial gave the dehorning movement such momentum and popularity that in a short time it flowered into one of the nationwide crazes that periodically swept over rural America."[42]

Statistically, the number of nondairy cattle increased 43.5 percent between 1870 and 1880 and another 29.4 percent between 1880 and 1890, with the average number of animals per farm increasing from 5.2 in 1870 to 8.2 in 1890. The northern division held a commanding lead in the number of cattle, with 51.2 percent in 1890 compared to the central division's 36 percent and the south's 12.2 percent. The number of beef cattle sold increased steadily at from 12 to 25 percent per year until 1890 to 1894 when it decreased 22 percent. The peak years were from 1885 to 1889 when an average 545,314 beef cattle were sold. The highest price, however, was between 1870 to 1874 at $55.90. The gain per animal (if fed on corn) those years was high for the period at $11.90. The gain dropped sharply to $4.50 per animal in 1875 to 1879 when the price per animal was $43.25. The price per animal rose to $50.10 in 1880 to 1884, but the farmer's gain continued to decline—to $2.22 per animal. By 1885 to 1890 the price had plummeted to $37.05 per animal, down again to $36.10 in 1890 to 1894. The farmer feeding corn lost fifty-eight cents per animal in 1885 to 1889 and $12.92 in 1890 to 1894 on each steer sold.

The changeover from breeding local cattle to feeding western cattle drew the state into a forty-year struggle to control a disease, and ultimately into an active role in regulating the health of Illinois livestock. With the introduction of Texas cattle came a tick carrying deadly Texas cattle fever. The Texas cattle themselves seemed immune, but their presence brought death to local livestock. The Illinois legislature voted in 1867 to ban Texas or Cherokee cattle from the state, and in 1868 a national convention of cattle commissioners met in Springfield to study the problem—without result. The state agricultural society studied the disease and the Chicago board of health attempted to quarantine infected animals at the stockyards. In 1869, under pressure from large-scale cattle interests, the law was amended to bar importation only between March and October. Challenges to the constitutionality of the law were settled in favor of the state in 1870 and 1871.

In 1877, however, the United States Supreme Court declared a similar law in Missouri an unlawful regulation of interstate commerce, and the Illinois law was thus null. The need for protection remained. In 1875 an epidemic of "epizootic" had struck the state's equine populine. Elgin, Greenville, Peoria, and Joliet all reported the disease in the Chicago *Inter-Ocean*. "The epizootic is afflicting the equine family here," ran a typical report, "and scarcely a farm can muster a team."[43] Mattoon reported "cholera is destroying the hog crop."[44] In 1879 and 1881 Governor Cullom mentioned "the necessity of legislation . . . to prevent the introduction and spread of infections and contagious diseases among animals."[45]

Humane agents were appointed in 1877 to inspect the stockyards at Chicago, East St. Louis, and Peoria, and report any undue cruelty to the animals. A board of livestock commissioners, appointed in

1887, dealt with "contagious or epidemic diseases."[46] The board originally inspected only "foreign" livestock brought in from other states, which was fine with the stockyards' managers who inspected Illinois stock. Calling the setup a "farce," Governor Altgeld and the board met with the livestock merchants and told them all inspections of out-of-state cattle would cease if they refused to cooperate. Altgeld reported in 1895, "it is believed that the traffic in diseased cattle has been substantially broken up."[47]

In 1883 a veterinary surgeon was appointed to inspect herds and slaughter infected animals. His two-year appropriation of $10,000 proved wholly inadequate, for it was to include compensation paid for the slaughtered animals. An epidemic of Texas fever in 1884 brought quarantine requests to Governor Hamilton, but after "learning that it could not be communicated to Illinois native cattle,"[48] the governor declined to quarantine. He asked only that "provisions should be made to constantly inspect shipments from the Southwest to Chicago markets so as to guard against diseased animals being sold in the stockyards."[49]

Cattle were not the only animals affected by contagious diseases. In his first year the state veterinarian also slaughtered forty-eight mules and horses, and in 1885 a glanders epidemic was raging. Governor Hamilton noted that "the most revolting feature of this disease is that the contagion may be communicated from equine species to persons . . . with certainly fatal results."[50] In 1884, pleuro-pneumonia also hit cattle, although it was "confined to a few Jersey herds."[51]

In 1885 and 1887 laws providing for a state board of livestock commissioners were passed. They reported in 1888 livestock in the state valued at $47,901,581. The breakdown showed:

998.031 horses	valued at $24,826,145
100.613 mules	valued at $ 2,517,970
2,423.484 cattle	valued at $17,229,377
555.910 sheep	valued at $ 534,764
966.700 hogs	valued at $ 2,793,326[52]

The value in livestock represented "one-third of the assessed valuation of the entire personal property of the State."[53]

Governor Hamilton's happy assertion that Texas fever could not infect local cattle had been proved false, and Governor Fifer in 1883 regretted that "little is known save that native cattle exposed to the fresh trail of southern cattle are condemned to almost certain death."[54] The livestock commissioners that year slaughtered 2,548 animals afflicted with actinomycosis (lumpy jaw), and the work of the state board of agriculture was so effective that its "chief benefit" was thought to be "increased trade in native stock cattle during the summer months."[55]

The state was now involved in a massive regulatory effort, policing the health of livestock throughout the state and slaughtering animals carrying an increasing number of diseases. In 1899 tests made with the United States Department of Agriculture near Rockford uncovered the real source of Texas fever. The southern cattle tick (*Boophilis bovis*) was declared "the only carrier of Texas . . . fever."[56] Dipping the cattle in "extra dynamo oil and sulphur" killed the tick and eliminated the danger, and forty years of state-sponsored research was responsible for the solution. It is not surprising that it took forty years to find the cause of the disease. Veterinary medicine remained in the hands of a few poorly trained graduates of eastern schools, local "cow leeches," and outright quacks until the 1890s. Cures were produced by bleeding, firing with irons, blistering with caustics, and purging with "dragon's blood, black antimony, sulphur, spices and condiments of all kinds mixed together in various unsavory concoctions, often including the animal's excretion . . . strong mineral poisons, acids and preparations of arsenic, antimony and mercury. . . ."[57] One reputable Illinois veterinarian, Dr. N. H. Paaren, remarked in 1880 that "in the curing of animal diseases men still had not progressed very far along the road toward civilization."[58] Animals which failed to respond to the attentions of the local "hoss doctor" were proclaimed too far gone in advance to respond to care. It is a wonder that any survived at all.

Discovering the cause of Texas fever neither ended the state's involvement in regulation of livestock industry nor the controversy that accompanied it. Although it was cattlemen who originally asked state aid in fighting the Texas fever problem, cattle interests by 1901 were complaining about the low assessments which compensated them for slaughtered stock. Payment was made according to the value of the stricken animal—based on how far the disease had progressed—not what it could be worth if well. Between July 1, 1889, and November 1, 1900, 522 dairy animals were slaughtered. They were appraised at $49.73 per animal, or $21,262.50, but actual payment amounted to only $17.60 per head.

A connection was shown in 1899 between tuberculosis in dairy cattle and infection to humans. Governor Tanner was shocked: "It startles the mind," he wrote, "to contemplate the knowledge that thousands of infants are taking into their stomachs through their nursing bottles the enemy that will destroy their lives." He was especially disturbed that "the value of a cow whose milk had recently begun to produce death, [was worth] five times greater than that of a cow whose milk had been planting the deadly germ for three years. I cannot," he said, "conceive a difference in the intrinsic value of rattlesnakes." Tanner was an arch-Republican, opposed to state expenditure, but in this area he was firm. "Let the cost be what it will."[59]

Opposition to state regulation of livestock came, as expected, from those whose animals were slaughtered. But by the turn of the century the necessity of state inspection was accepted. New knowledge increased the scope of the state board as new diseases came under its jurisdiction. The health of each herd had become the joint concern of the state as police protection of the public health outweighed the priorities of individual enterprise.

Regulation of diseased animals was only one area of state involvement in agriculture. Agriculture was big business in business-minded Illinois, and the growing number of boards and institutes financed by the state to promote it testified to its importance. The Illinois Agricultural Society received $1,000 from the state in 1853 to run a state fair. It was joined by the State Horticultural Society in 1856, the office of the state entomologist in 1867, the Department of Agriculture (which took over the state fair, held county fairs, inspected and licensed fertilizers, and received the reports of the Canadian thistle inspectors, among other tasks) in 1872, the Illinois Dairyman's Association in 1874, the state veterinarian in 1885, the fish commission in 1879, the board of veterinary examiners and the Milk Producers Institute in 1889, the Beekeepers Association in 1891, the Illinois Farmers Institute in 1895, the State Poultry Association in 1896, the board of inspectors of commission merchants (later declared unconstitutional) in 1899, and the Stallion Registry Board in 1909. Despite the number of agencies, the state did not usually interfere with individual farming operations.

The fish commission illustrates the practical nature of those boards. In 1888 it introduced carp into the Illinois River in which coarse fish were practically extinct. By 1896 the river yielded 7,000,000 pounds of carp which sold for $207,000. In 1897 the commission rescued 24,950 yearling bass, 28,150 crappie, and 360,000 riny perch which would otherwise have perished when flooding rivers receded.

The office of state entomologist was one which brought national acclaim to the state, for it was filled in its first years by men whose experiments into the nature of insects advanced world knowledge. The first man to hold the post was Benjamin Walsh, founder and editor of the *Practical Entomologist*, the first journal of its type. He wrote numerous articles on natural selection in the insect world, based chiefly on his research into the sexual habits of ladybugs.

William LeBaron took over the office at the death of Walsh in 1870. His experiments led to the use of Paris green against codling moths. State funds were not available for widespread distribution of this valuable information, but newspapers and the *Prairie Farmer* carried the news to farmers looking for a weapon in their battle against the insect.

The third state entomologist, Cyrus Thomas, was appointed to the United States entomology commission in 1867 to 1877. His research led to an important essay on the chinch bug, but he is better remembered for his annual reports which included a compilation of information on insect pests. Thomas later joined the Bureau of American Ethnology.

After 1882 the multitalented Stephen Forbes served not only as state entomologist but also as director of the Illinois State Laboratory of Natural History and professor of zoology and dean of the College of Science at the University of Illinois. Forbes was an expert on the food of fish and birds, and won later acclaim as one of the founders of the ecology movement for his research into the importance of the food chain.

A state entomologist performed many services for the farmers of the state. "When aroused growers announced that the fruit bark beetle was destroying all the orchards in the state, it was the entomologist who calmed their fears and promised that something would be worked out. The entomologist served the farmer, the schoolteacher, and the scientist. He was a combined soothsayer, medicine man, educator, researcher, and politician."[60]

Forbes's work was complicated by lack of funds and public support. When state orchards were threatened by the San Jose scale in 1895, it took two years for funds to be authorized by the legislature to combat the insect, and another two years for the law makers to authorize the necessary quarantine measures to contain it. Armed with money and state assistance, Forbes discovered another enemy in the farmers he was trying to help. They were suspicious of sprays and hesitant to invest in their application. When another disastrous failure wiped out the apple crop in 1898, 60 percent of the loss was blamed on negligence.[61]

While the total value of animal products was declining steadily from $68,484,171 in 1880 to 1884 to $56,001,579 in 1895 to 1899, the percentage of that value represented by dairy products rose from 13.4 percent in 1870 to 1874 to 30.1 percent in 1895 to 1899. As with other kinds of animals, the northern division predominated as the industry grew up to supply the growing needs of Chicago and Peoria. The metropolitan St. Louis area also created a demand met by dairies in St. Clair, Washington, and Randolph counties, although St. Louis breweries offered stiff competition in the form of cheaper milk obtained from swill-fed cows fattened on brewery slops.

The value of all dairy products rose steadily from approximately $7,000,000 in 1877 to 1879 to over $18,000,000 in 1884 to 1889, but declined by 7 percent in 1895 to 1899 to $16,851,326. The northern division controlled between 84 to 89 percent of this value throughout the period, while the share of the central division fell from a high of 11.4 percent to 5.2 percent, with the southern division taking the remainder—never more than 6.3 percent.

Commercial dairying led to a search for a breed that would consistently produce high yields of milk. Shorthorns were the most common purebred, but jerseys, holstein-friesians, Ayrshires, and brown Swiss herds were all increasing. By 1890, while only 1.4 percent of all cattle were pureblooded, these being divided into 368 dairy herds, 35 percent were "high grades," with some pureblood breeding. One study shows that "the jerseys led with 234 (herds), the holsteins coming next with 115 herds, while the guernseys had only 19."[62]

The major product of the dairy industry was milk, comprising a steadily rising percentage of the total. In forty years that percentage rose from 36 percent to 76 percent. Of this, Chicago consumed the major amount, slugging down 20,112 gallons daily as early as 1872. As refrigerator cars made longer shipment feasible, the farmers supplying the Chicago market expanded until nine-tenths of all milk produced in Illinois was destined for the lake city. The total amount of milk sold increased both in quantity and price. In the two-year period 1877 to 1879, the price for 26,450,588 gallons of Illinois milk was 9.6¢ per gallon. The figure rose to 13.1¢ for the 97,652,247 gallons sold in 1894 to 1899. Freight charges, however, cut into the profit of the farmer, as did the fact that he sold his milk at wholesale prices to a distributor. Lack of a large metropolitan center and shortage of rail transport actually aided the dairy farmer in the central division, for he was forced to haul his milk to the nearest town in his own wagon and sell it himself—thus reaping the entire retail cost. Such personalized activity was only feasible on a relatively small scale, and the central division's proportion of all milk sold declined from 3.8 percent in the years 1877 to 1879 to 1.7 percent in 1890 to 1894.

Dr. Joseph Tefft established the Elgin Butter Factory in 1870, the first creamery in the new west. Elgin was already a center of commercial dairy products when Tefft opened his historic creamery since in 1865 Gail Borden had begun production of condensed milk in Elgin and opened a cheese factory there as well. Butter production decreased as the price for whole milk rose until an industry which comprised 53.5 percent of all dairy products in 1870 to 1874 could claim only 17 percent in 1895 to 1899. The volume of butter rose slightly by 2,000,000 pounds (or 9 percent) between 1877 to 1879 and 1880 to 1884, but declined by 2,000,000 in the next half-decade and another 3,000,000 (14.2 percent) in 1890 to 1894, when the total was 17,747,601 pounds.

In addition to butter, Chicago packers improved upon the patent of Frenchman Hippolyte Megé-Mouries for a butter substitute or margarine. The new product was a natural one for the packers to promote as it utilized hitherto useless by-products of slaughtered animals. Although the product was not introduced in the United States until 1873, by 1884 "no less than 180 patents were applied for."[63] A new product called butterine was introduced by the Chicago packers in 1883, consisting of 25 percent creamery butter, 20 percent oleo oil, and 15 percent ordinary milk. By 1886 the Chicago firms were producing 30,000,000 pounds of butter substitutes, or 3 percent of the total butter production. Although butter interests claimed that margarine frequently contained deadly germs and animal filth, the same charges were leveled against the often rancid product sold by farmwives as butter. Butter interests in several states achieved protective legislation against imitation products in the 1880s, but the Chicago packers successfully lobbied against such bills in the Illinois legislature. A federal statute in 1886 placed a special tax on margarine products, but after an initial production decrease, the new industry revived in the 1890s.

The greatest decrease in the dairy industry resulted not from technological changes or natural forces, but the greed and shoddy practices of the commercial producers. J. H. Wanzer began the state's first cheese factory near Elgin in 1863. The success of the Borden factory (which produced 240,000 pounds in its first year) inspired other entrepreneurs, and by 1878 there were already between sixty and seventy butter and cheese factories within fifty miles of Elgin. Gould's cheese factory alone was producing almost 500,000 pounds per year, using milk from 1,300 cows.

This great quantity was more than the state could consume, and a brisk trade developed with the eastern states. Between 1877 to 1879 cheese constituted almost 10 percent of all dairy products, but success was already leading to the industry's downfall. Farmers resented the low prices they received from the cheese factories, and retaliated by removing some of the cream from their milk. The producers countered by substituting buttermilk and selling their cheese before it had fully cured. Unsavory cheese is hard to disguise, and the market for the Illinois product turned sour as the reputation of the cheese grew moldier year by year. Filled cheeses were declared illegal in 1896, but by then the industry had already declined to 0.7 percent of all dairy products and Illinois was one of the minor states in cheese production.

By 1900 there were more hogs in Illinois than people, for as one study found, "even cattle feeders preferred to keep a drove of swine, for it was found four cattle would waste enough to feed one hog, and pork secured this way was pure gain."[64] The production of hogs was also connected to other market factors, for when the price of corn dipped, the farmers preferred to feed hogs and sell them. When they withdrew corn from the market, the corn prices tended to rise. When they sold more corn, the production of hogs would tend to go down and their price up.

The transition from razorbacks to purebred swine was a rapid one in Illinois, which ranked first as a "center for pure-blooded swine in the United States"[65] as early as 1870. The Illinois Swine Breeders' Association, founded in 1869 by Thomas Crowder of Springfield, encouraged purebred droves, and by 1880 fully 60 percent of all United States purebred swine breeders lived in Illinois. Berkshires predominated, followed by Poland China, Chester Whites, and Essex.

The presence of the nation's pork-packing capital at Chicago provided an accessible market, and the number of hogs sold increased from 2,000,000 to 3,000,000 between 1870 and 1889. The increase in the number of hogs sold, unfortunately, was not matched by an increase in profit for the farmer. The price per hog declined from $13.62 in 1870 to 1874 to $9.33 in 1885 to 1889, while the price of the corn which the hogs ate did not decline as sharply. A farmer feeding corn could make a gain of $2.75 per hog in the 1870 to 1874 half-decade, but only nine cents in 1885 to 1889. The number of hogs sold declined after 1889, although the gain per hog was back up to $2.39 in 1890 to 1894 on a price of $9.75 per animal, and was seventy cents in 1895 to 1899 on a price of $7.73 per animal. The total number of hogs sold that year was 2,449,320.

The demand for wool occasioned by the Civil War brought a temporary boom to the sheep industry. In 1865 the state recorded its largest wool clip, 12,000,000 pounds, but the end of the war was a deathblow to the wool industry in the state, and the wool clip plunged to 5,739,249 pounds in 1870. A slight revival occurred in the early 1880s, but it quickly died out. The number of sheep in the state had fallen in 1890 to 922,631 from a high of 1,568,286 in 1870, and as wool became less important, sheep breeders turned from merinos to mutton sheep like Leicesters, Cotswolds, and Shropshires. Mutton was not a popular food, however, and the high cost of corn as feed made raising sheep for slaughter unprofitable after 1880. The gain per sheep if fed on corn was never high, reaching a peak of only fifty-four cents in 1875 to 1879. From then on the sheep rancher lost money as the price per sheep declined faster than the cost of feeding corn. The loss per animal was fifty-nine cents in 1880 to 1884; six cents in 1885 to 1889, and seventy-four cents in 1890 to 1894.

The encroachment of civilization was also an important factor in the decline in the Illinois sheep industry. Dogs represented the greatest threat to a flock of sheep, and as more and more people settled in any locale, the number of dogs rose dramatically. As "man's best friend" and part of the family, dogs were not subject to regulations requiring that domestic animals be kept penned, and they inflicted heavy losses on the helpless sheep herders.

The sale of poultry, eggs, and honey and beeswax were minor industries compared to other animal products, although over $1,000,000 worth of poultry products were sold in 1890 to 1894, and more than 4,000,000 pounds of honey were marketed in 1890.

Getting a crop harvested against the onslaught of drought, flood, insects, and disease was harrowing enough, but it was only the beginning of the farmers' struggle. Before that crop could be turned into cash it had to pass through the clutching fingers of railroads and middlemen and reach a market. Hailed at first as the farmers' friend, the railroad soon acquired a far different image. Discriminatory freight rates robbed the farmer of the profit he felt was his due, and as the railroads combined and rationalized their operations, price fixing grew even worse. Canal competition was unreliable, and once the canals were frozen for the winter, the railroads raised their rates still higher. The only alternative to the railroad was wagon hauling, an obviously unsatisfactory option considering the execrable state of prairie roads and the limit in speed and quantity dictated by real horsepower.

The monopolistic abuses of the railroads were matched by similar practices of the warehouses in which the farmer was forced to store his grain. The elevators were often owned or controlled by the railroads, which demanded that farmers pay elevator charges whether their grain was stored or not. Here again, the farmer faced a seemingly unbeatable monopoly. In 1874, for example, it was found that "Chicago had fourteen elevators owned by thirty individuals, but controlled by nine firms who agreed closely on charges. Nearly all the marketed wheat of seven or eight states . . . passed through this monopoly."[66] Farmers complained they found themselves at the mercy of buyer-grading of wheat, and found that if their grain was not quickly sold it had to be stored at ruinous charges. Livestock producers fought high rail rates matched by low prices for their animals set by the beef trust.

Once the corn, hogs, or wheat reached Chicago, it was often shipped again—this time to Europe. Corn was marketed there primarily in the form of animals or dairy products, for "Europe did not appreciate the value of corn as a food for human beings."[67] As the most important outside grainery of western Europe, Illinois exporters reaped fantastic profits—but here again it was the shipper, processor, and commodity merchant who gained.

A problem almost equal to that of marketing was the farmers' ever present battle with credit and monetary devaluation. Capitalists who had purchased bonds during the Civil War were repaid in gold, but the farmer who sold his crop to support the war effort was paid in greenbacks worth approximately forty cents on the gold dollar. Anticipating high agricultural prices, many Illinois farmers had gone deeply into debt during the war in order to expand their tillable holdings, and when prices fell they found themselves caught in a squeeze between plunging prices and a constricted money supply. The money in circulation at the close of the war now had to be spread over the re-admitted South, and between 1865 to 1870 the total circulating declined by one-fourth —from $31.10 per capita to $20.10.

Cash was scarce, and mortgage payments, now made in greenbacks quickly reaching parity with gold, drained off needed reserves. By 1879 the farmer was repaying loans made in cheap money with greenbacks that were increasingly dear. The receipts from his crops were often insufficient to pay the installments on his mortgage in this tight money market, and he then faced a choice between foreclosure and renewal of the loan at a higher interest rate.

Bank loans were hard to come by, and available only at high interest rates. The reason may have been that "too much of the demand on the banks was for greenbacks to settle Eastern accounts . . . every dollar of them withdrawn cancelled to power to lend four other dollars . . . the banks had to keep an extraordinary volume of greenbacks on hand and restrict the amount of business done. Therefore, the bankers had to charge interest up to the limit of the law, and then be careful about the loans."[68] In addition, banks were often located far from the farmer, and were unwilling to take a chance on him. For whatever reason, the farmer found himself dependent on loans from merchants, commission men, and implement dealers, who borrowed the money and passed it on at advanced interest.

The Populists of the 1890s depicted the plight of the cash-pressed farmer in a lament. "The farmer is the man," they sang, "lives on credit till the fall,/ Then they take him by the hand,/ and they lead him from the land,/ And the middleman's the one who gets it all."[69] The answer to the money problem seemed simple: print more. Greenbackism was a popular issue with farmers who saw ever threatening foreclosure blighting their lives because there did not seem to be enough money to go around.

Another drive was toward lowering interest rates. Farmers found it necessary to borrow both for improvements and for even the smallest purchase of new land, as "the increase in farm land values . . . made the mortgage an integral part of most real estate transactions."[70] A maximum interest rate of 10 percent was set by the legislature in 1849, after complaints that a 6 percent limit drove money to other more profitable states. The rate was lowered to 8 percent in 1879, but was generally disregarded. Borrowers were forced to pay commissions and recording fees that boosted the actual rate to 11 and 12 percent. Rates fell in the 1880s and 1890s, until 5 percent was common by the close of the century.

In 1879 the legislature, after refusing to tax mortgages, provided that action "of a court of competent jurisdiction" be required prior to foreclosure sales. Actually creditors preferred extensions anyway, and the number of farms taken in foreclosure was small. Champaign County saw nine farms foreclosed in 1880; only twelve in 1887.

A further drain on the farmer's limited cash resources came in the form of the yearly tax bill. Assessments were based on real and personal property, but invisible wealth in the form of stocks, bonds, and money escaped the assessor's eye. The harder the farmer worked to improve his land, the more the state siphoned off in taxes, while bankers, absentee and alien land owners, the Illinois Central Railroad, insurance men, and money lenders escaped their share of the burden. Tax laws were an ever present and violently disliked reminder of the cozy relationship between government and the combination of interests oppressing the farmer.

Faced with an oppressive tax structure, falling farm prices, rising prices for manufactured products, and discrimination by monopolistic railroad and warehouse corporations, the farmer began looking for ways to fight back. In 1867 Oliver H. Kelley, a clerk in the United States Department of Agriculture, began an organization intended to give the farmer "needed social life . . . and broader social vision."[71] The Order of the Patrons of Husbandry was to be a secret society organized into local units called granges.

The first Illinois grange was organized in the offices of the *Prairie Farmer* in April, 1868. Only eight new chapters were organized until 1872, when sixty-nine were organized in a burst of enthusiasm. The *Chicago Tribune* noted the formation of the state grange in Dixon in March of 1872. At that time there were twenty-seven local units, composed, in the opinion of the *Tribine*, of "the most intelligent class of farmers. The interest is strong," reported the paper, "and the farmers seem determined to apply to their own interest the principles of the organization and the cooperation already made so useful to their enterprise."[72] By 1872 the supposedly nonpartisan grange movement had turned to political activism in its fight against its perceived enemy, the railroad. Hard times and the struggle over railroad legislation swelled the ranks of the grange, and in 1873, 761 new locals were organized. Another 704 were born in 1874.

The organization of the grange recognized the importance of the farm wife, and steered away from the "men only" tenets of some secret societies. Any group of more than nine "but less than thirty" agricultural workers could apply for a charter. Dues and fees were kept low, and were used primarily by the local grange itself. Yearly dues to the national organization fell from 10¢ per month per member to 5¢—and 25 percent of that went to the state organization. After an initial initiation fee ranging from $3 for men and 50¢

for women for charter members and $4 for men and $1 for women
for later members, yearly dues were kept to $1 for men and 50¢ for
women.

Elaborate rituals were borrowed from other secret societies, and
both men and women were eligible for seven degrees. The first
four (laborer, cultivator, harvestor, and husbandman for men;
maid, shepherdess, gleaner, and matron for women) were granted
by the local grange. The more exalted titles, such as Pomona
(hope), were conferred by the state headquarters, and the ultimate
glory of Flora (charity) and Ceres (faith) could be granted only by
the national organization.

Granges served the social functions intended by Kelley, but they
also proved semi-effective pressure groups in the battle against the
railroad giant. And when farmers got together to gripe about
"middlemen," the grange seemed a logical unit for cooperative
activity to free the farmer from their clutches.

Cooperative stores opened to allow the farmer to buy at wholesale rates and get discounts on his large implements by pooling
the purchasing power of a large group. Between 1872 to 1876
farmers' co-op stores were operating in an estimated one-half of the
state's counties. Plans were underway in 1876 for a national grange
co-op, but the plan fell victim to depression. A state buying agency
attempted to coordinate activities, but by 1880 the granger stores
were dying, and all were gone by 1890. The failure of the movement has been laid to "(1) lack of central guiding organization—the
tendency to 'lay the capstone before the foundation'; (2) the consequent lack of knowledge of business administration; (3) undercapitalization; (4) the spirit of isolated independence existing
among the members; (5) benefits to be derived; (6) incompetent
farmer-managers; (7) factionalism; (8) active opposition of competitors, (and) the narrowing of retail margins during the depression of the time."[73]

Putting a farmer behind the counter did not necessarily make
him a businessman, and the grange stores died young as a result.
Their influence, however, did prod other retailers into competing
for the farmer's business with lower prices. The most successful
of these companies was the mail-order house founded by Aaron
Montgomery Ward in 1872. Advertised as "the original grange
supply house," Montgomery Ward cut costs—and prices—by
eliminating salesmen and the overhead of retail outlets and sold
solely by mail—for cash. The cash feature was especially popular to
farmers already suffering at the hands of creditors, and further cut

the mail-order firm's overhead. A further service was selling grain for the farmer on consignment at a charge of one cent per bushel and twenty-five cents per car for inspection.

Most established firms, however, resisted the price-cutting efforts of the grange stores by refusing to sell to them—a move countered by boycotts by the local grange units. A typical boycott resolution appeared in the *Chicago Times* in 1873:

> Plato, [1] . . .
>
> WHEREAS: The manufacturers of agricultural implements have combined in a joint convention, and have passed resolutions not to sell to grangers' or farmers' clubs at retail [sic] prices.
>
> RESOLVED: That we, as Plato grange, do denounce all such proceedings transacted by such manufacturers.
>
> RESOLVED: That we, Plato grange, will repair our old plows and reapers and mowers and use them for the next two or three years to come, before we will patronize any such manufacturers unless they will sell to us at cost and carriage.
>
> RESOLVED: That we, Plato grange, do and all other grangers in this state should, denounce all such proceedings taken by said convention.[74]

As the granger retail outlets died out, however, the farmer, resolutions notwithstanding, was forced back into patronizing the noncompetitive dealers.

Other cooperative movements centered about grain elevators. The first co-op elevator was established in 1884 in Stephenson County. The movement met intense opposition from railroads and grain dealers, and by 1900 only sixteen such elevators were in operation. Dairy and livestock producers attempted to eliminate the middleman also. The Sangamon County Stock and Produce Sale Association was formed in 1874, and in 1889 the American Livestock Commission, a cooperative selling agency, attempted to market members' livestock. The association did not maintain membership in the Chicago Livestock Exchange, however, and quickly went out of business. Farmers' mutual insurance companies also originated during this period, as did farmer-owned telephone companies. A United States Department of Agriculture survey in 1907 showed some 85,000 cooperative societies, with memberships numbering one-half of all farmers in the country. Had all of those farmers been cooperating, the country would have been well on the road to syndicalism. But the cooperative societies did not cooperate with each other. It was common for the individual farmer to cooperate in only one area, such as telephone services, while operating as an individual buyer and seller in all other areas. Lack of sound business ability, undercapitalization, and organized opposition by groups, with the business expertise missing from the farmers' ventures, all combined to render the cooperative movement largely ineffectual.

On the political front, however, the farmers' groups scored some outstanding successes in the early 1870s. Politicians hesitated to oppose the organized wrath of the state's largest voting bloc, and thus Illinois became the first state to enact railroad and warehouse regulations. Spurred by the constitutional provisions of 1870, the grange and other farmers' clubs pressed for rigid enforcement of the Railroad and Warehouse Act. They staged sit-ins on passenger trains, insisting on paying no more than the legal fare. Railroad officials reacted by ejecting them from the trains or leaving their cars stranded on sidings.

Meanwhile, the constitutionality of state regulation of railroads had been questioned in a ruling by Illinois Chief Justice Charles Lawrence. The embattled farmers met the obstacle by organizing the Illinois State Farmers' Association, an avowedly political action group in 1873. A state farmers' convention was held in Springfield in April of that year to "make the governor understand that we *mean business* and are no longer to be trifled with."[75]

The Railroad Law of 1873 answered most of the farmers' demands, although the railroads refused to admit defeat and court battles seemed inevitable. The farmers' association backed its own candidates in the judicial elections of 1873, and scored surprisingly well. Judge Lawrence was defeated, and much of the farm-backed slate was elected. In the county elections in November, the "anti-monopoly" farmers' parties carried fifty-six of the sixty-six counties in which they fielded slates. Hopes were bright for great gains in the state elections of 1874. Success, however, had already begun to destroy the unity of the agrarian movement. *Munn* vs. *Illinois* confirmed the state's right to regulate the railroads, and with the enemy in retreat the members of the farm coalition splintered in competing factions. "Anti-monopoly" lacked central definition, and the confusing and less obvious dragons of tariff and currency reform drew the teeth from the farmers' political momentum. Without the unifying force of a common and perceived enemy, the farmers drifted back into their old parties or flirted with greenbackism or prohibitionism as a cure for the problems of their society. By 1876 the granger movement was no longer viable. It had established the principle of state regulation, then returned to its original role as a social/education body.

The agrarian movement of the 1880s was dominated by Milton George and his National Farmers' Alliance. George began his career as assistant editor of the *Western Rural and Family Farm Paper*, over which he assumed control in 1876. His basic views were that "in a democracy, government should be controlled by the mass of people, rather than by the plutocrats, and that government should use its power to protect those unable to protect themselves. Second, this philosophy was based on a never-changing belief in the innate value and wisdom of the farming class."[76] He believed that "government on all levels was dominated by concentrations of wealth resulting from the unrestricted growth of monopolies, railroads, and other giant corporations," and "agricultural groups should work through the machinery of existing parties and secure the nomination of men favorable to agrarian interests."[77]

The Knights of Labor, open to the farmers, was also at its peak in the 1880s, attempting much the same kind of cooperative ventures as the grange a decade before. The Knights could not resolve, however, the basic conflict between the farmer and the industrial worker, and thus did not succeed in uniting the two in common cause. The farmer needed to sell food at high prices and buy labor cheap. The factory worker needed to sell labor at the highest price and buy food cheap—and those very incompatible aims kept the two groups from uniting. Labor unions and farm movements in the nineteenth century differed in more than aim. The unions prospered in good times and died out when depression made jobs scarce and strikes impossible to win. Farmers banded together during hard times, and returned to individualistic beliefs when times were good and prices high. The two groups were not active at the same times.

The National Farmers' Alliance, however, if it could merge nationally into one political organization, offered the size and power necessary for a real impact on national policy. Unfortunately, basic disagreements threatened the coalition from the start. An attempt in 1889 to unite the factions brought the conclusion that:

> The different elements had too many conflicting interests to do more than adopt similar platforms. The Southern Alliance was secret and excluded Negroes; the Northwestern was just the opposite. The Northwestern Alliance wanted to ban substitutes for lard and butter, but this struck at the cottonseed oil of the South. The Southern Alliance wanted a sub-treasury system, under which the federal government would make loans at one percent interest up to four-fifths of the value of deposited nonperishable farm goods. Because Northern products were more perishable than cotton, the Northwestern Al-

liance would not listen to this. Also, the Northwestern Alliance was the smaller and did not want to be submerged.[78]

In spite of their inner tensions, the alliances made major gains in the elections of 1890, especially in the South, and by 1892 the new Peoples, or Populist, party was ready to enter the presidential lists. By this time silver *vs.* gold had become the central issue, and the Populists had to compete with equally ardent currency reformers within the major parties. The strength of the Populist movement trickled away as dissidents founded their own parties and the major parties co-opted their platforms. By 1896, eleven minor parties were on the ballot in Illinois, each with its own pet solution for the state's problems. And as good times returned, prices rose and interest rates fell; farmers lost interest in the Populist cause and returned to reaping their own prosperous harvests.

All of the elements necessary for an agricultural revolution seemed to be present between 1871 to 1896. Farmers were faced with a sickening downward price spiral for their crops, a series of oppressive, monopolistic practices on the part of the railroads and industry, an inequitable state tax structure, and high interest rates. The national organizations necessary for them to unite to gain power and effect real changes had been made, but the farmers largely abandoned the organizations formed to lead them to victory over the oppressors.

Some of the reason must have lain in the farmer's perception of his role in the American dream. The agrarian mystique of the tiller of the soil whose innate virtue represented the salvation of the republic echoed down from the constitutional debates of 1787 to the philosophy of the farmers' alliances 100 years later. The farmer could not bring himself to seek radical changes in a system whose outward ethic placed him as the keystone of society. No matter how much of his actual position may have eroded as industrialization took over the reins of power, in his mind he still filled the central and most praiseworthy role. To change the system would challenge and possibly destroy that role.

Political parties tended to drain energy away from agrarian organizations instead of building them. They fogged out in the hazy areas of tariff and currency reform—neither clear-cut issues around which all farmers could rally and remain united. Once immediate problems were solved, as in the case of the railroad and warehouse commission, the organized political strength of the farmers evaporated. Farmers may have been angry at the middlemen, but they did not see themselves in the class terms necessary for an agrarian party to radically change things.

State government played a minor role in respect to its largest industry. Farmers tended to be self-sufficient, demanding little in the way of services. They had little time for the game of politics, except for brief bursts of organized energy which quickly died out. Regulation of railroads and warehouses—as well as inspection of livestock—were all initial steps toward government control, but the kind of market control employing subsidies and land banks was still unthinkable, and probably unthought.

The state's major contribution came in the form of agricultural education. The Illinois state fair and county fairs introduced new farming techniques, many of them developed at the University of Illinois. The state department of agriculture was uniformly praised for its noncontroversial work of helping the farmer grow bigger and better crops with improved methods and seeds. Direct state assistance was limited to support of various agricultural associations, such as the state horticultural association, which had the same primarily educational goals.

The wealth of the Illinois soil brought the state great riches between 1865 to 1895. It provided the raw materials for empires built on packing and distilling, and fed the workers who streamed to the cities to work in the factories. Someone was making a fortune from the products of Illinois farms between 1865 to 1890, but the farmer did not think it was he. Even corn, the state's most valuable crop, did not insure the farmer against loss. Migration, especially among the tenant class, took many disillusioned farmers into the factories of the city or the cheaper lands of the new West.

The Illinois climate was often cruel and uncertain, bringing floods, tornadoes, and crop failures time and again. As the new West opened up the products of Iowa, Minnesota, and Kansas, they began to drive Illinois farm products into a corner. Not only were land prices cheaper in the new West, so also were the taxes. And of course national depressions hit the heavily mortgaged farmers especially hard. So what held them on their land?

The Illinois farm in the last half of the nineteenth century was a self-contained unit depending on muscle as well as mechanical labor. The housewife's vegetable garden, chickens, and pigs provided the basics for a healthy, hearty diet. Although the land required capital investment in the form of fencing and drainage, breaking sod, and clearing trees, the farmer was not faced with unbearable cash demands for machinery, fertilizer, and insecticides and herbicides. All of these would have increased the productivity of his farm, but as they were not generally in use he was not hurt competitively for not using them. While cash crises did cause some foreclosures, mainly in the 1870s, even a marginal farmer could feed his family.

Much of the farmer's social life and entertainment was free, centering about church events and patriotic holidays like the Fourth of July. Mass advertising had begun, but had not yet convinced the farmer or his wife they were deprived unless they owned a houseful of appliances, the latest model buggy, or scientific deodorant. Even if the farm did not turn a large cash profit—or any profit at all—it could supply his basic wants.

From a purely economic standpoint, even when he did not make a profit from his crops, the farmer increased his wealth. Increment in land values made his farm worth more each year—giving him the satisfaction of knowing he was prospering even if his bank book did not show it. Farming is also an occupation given to hope. Next year the weather will be fair, the rains gentle, the harvest full. The farmer could take pride in his crop as he saw his year of labor come to fruition under his own hands. The Jeffersonian ideal was a faith accepted on Illinois farms. His days may have been long and his toil hard, but the farmer answered to no man, and his labor in the open air was conducive to robust health and inner satisfaction. And so he stayed.

1. Governor Fifer, *Journal of the House*, Jan. 8, 1891, 25.
2. Fred A. Shannon, *The Farmer's Last Frontier: Agriculture, 1860-1897* (New York, 1945), 369.
3. *Ibid.*
4. *Ibid.*
5. *Ibid.*, 357.
6. *Ibid.*
7. Bogart and Thompson, *Industrial State*, 218.
8. Margaret Beattie Bogue, *Patterns from the Sod: Land Use and Tenure in the Grand Prairie, 1850-1900* (Springfield, Ill., 1959), 172.
9. John O. Bowman, "Trends in Midwestern Farm Land Values, 1860-1890," PhD. dissertation, Yale University, 1964.
10. United States Bureau of Census, *Twelfth Census*, V, *Agriculture*, Pt. 1, Farms, Livestock and Animal Products, 273-274.
11. Bogue, *Patterns from the Sod*, 119.
12. *Chicago Tribune*, Sept. 9, 1871.
13. *Ibid.*, Aug. 22, 1872.
14. Bogart and Thompson, *Industrial State*, 220.
15. Illinois, *Laws*, 1887, 5ff.
16. Paul Gates, "Frontier Landlords and Pioneer Tenants," *Journal of the Illinois State Historical Society* XXXVII (June, 1945). Clyde Walton, ed., *An Illinois Reader* (DeKalb, Ill., 1970), 217.

17. *Ibid.*, 171.
18. *Ibid.*
19. Governor Altgeld, *Journal of the House*, Jan. 12, 1897, 48.
20. Bogue, *Patterns from the Sod*, 180.
21. *Prairie Farmer*, March 21, 1866, 207.
22. Shannon, *Farmer's Last Frontier*, 169.
23. Bogue, *Patterns from the Sod*, 167.
24. *Ibid.*
25. Gates, "Frontier Landlords," 220.
26. Ernest L. Bogart and John M. Matthews, *The Modern Commonwealth, 1893-1918* (Springfield, Ill., 1920), 70.
27. Bogart and Thompson, *Industrial State*, 236.
28. Bowman, "Trends in Midwestern Farm Land Values."
29. Bogart and Thompson, *Industrial State*.
30. *Ibid.*, 237.
31. *Ibid.*, 239.
32. Arthur C. Cole, *The Era of the Civil War, 1848-1870* (Springfield, Ill., 1919), 382.
33. John Stronhm, "Farm Power: From Muscle to Motor," *Prairie Farmer*, Centennial Number, 30.
34. *Chicago Evening Journal*, Oct. 24, 1872.
35. Bogart and Matthews, *Modern Commonwealth*, 61.
36. Shannon, *Farmer's Last Frontier*, 128.
37. *Illinois State Journal*, April 21, 1875.
38. Bogue, *Patterns from the Sod*, 121.
39. Earl W. Hayter, *The Troubled Farmer, 1850-1890: Rural Adjustment to Industrialism* (DeKalb, Ill., 1968).
40. Shannon, *Farmer's Last Frontier*, 145.
41. Bogart and Thompson, *Industrial State*, 258.
42. Hayter, *Troubled Farmer*, 28.
43. *Chicago Inter-Ocean*, Oct. 26, 1875.
44. *Ibid.*, Oct. 23, 1875.
45. Governor Cullom, *Journal of the House*, Jan. 7, 1881, 21.
46. *Ibid.*, Jan. 6, 1887, 37.
47. *Ibid.*, Jan. 10, 1895, 20.
48. *Ibid.*, Jan. 30, 1885, 78.
49. *Ibid.*, 37.
50. *Ibid.*
51. *Ibid.*
52. *Ibid.*, Jan. 10, 1889.
53. *Ibid.*, Jan. 9, 1893, 20.
54. *Ibid.*
55. *Ibid.*, Jan. 5, 1893, 20.
56. *Ibid.*, Jan. 4, 1899.
57. Hayter, *Troubled Farmer*, 45.
58. *Ibid.*, 44.
59. *Journal of the Senate*, Jan. 9, 1901, 24-26.
60. F. Garvin Davinport, "Natural Scientists and the Farmers of Illinois, 1865-1900," *Journal of the Illinois State Historical Society* LI (Winter, 1958), 360.
61. *Ibid.*, 375.
62. Bogart and Thompson, *Industrial State*, 249.
63. Hayter, *Troubled Farmer*, 63.
64. Bogart and Thompson, *Industrial State*.
65. *Ibid.*, 259.
66. Shannon, *Farmer's Last Frontier*, 181.
67. *Ibid.*, 193.

68. *Ibid.*, 304.
69. "Taxes on the Farmers Feeds Us All," *Songs from the Great Depression*, Mike Seegar, vocalist, Folkways FH5264.
70. Bogue, *Patterns from the Sod*, 185.
71. Shannon, *Farmer's Last Frontier*, 329.
72. *Chicago Tribune*, March 5, 1872.
73. Colston Estey Warne, *The Consumers' Co-Operative Movement in Illinois* (Chicago, 1926), 16-17.
74. *Chicago Tribune*, Dec. 26, 1875.
75. Bogart and Thompson, *Industrial State*, 95. *Prairie Farmer*, March 29, 1893.
76. Roy V. Scott, *The Agrarian Movement in Illinois, 1880-1896* (Urbana, Ill., 1962), 23-24.
77. *Ibid.*, 24.
78. Shannon, *Farmer's Last Frontier*, 317-318.

5
Rails, Rivers, and Mud

> By no other agency than that of railroads could the vast
> resources of this State have been developed with such
> wonderful rapidity, and upon no other agent shall we
> continue to be so dependent for future growth and
> prosperity.
>
> Shelby Cullom[1]

To many Americans in April, 1865, the funeral train of
Abraham Lincoln on its mournful way from the nation's capital to
Springfield was a dramatic illustration of the railroad's victory over
great distances. The sad procession traced a magnificent arc westward as it stopped to allow people to say a final thank you and
farewell to the great leader in Baltimore, Harrisburg, Philadelphia,
New York, Albany, Buffalo, Cleveland, Columbus, Indianapolis,
Chicago, and Springfield. The route selected was only one of many
possible among the web of rails connecting the great cities of the
North. The train passed over the tracks of at least seven separate
companies and was relatively untroubled by peculiarities of gauge
or construction. Once in Illinois, Lincoln's train could have continued South to New Orleans or West to the newly opened regions
of Iowa, Wisconsin, or Missouri. At Mrs. Lincoln's request, George
Pullman's sleeping car, the *Pioneer*, completed early in 1865 according to the highest standards of quality and luxury, carried the
mourners during the final portion of the journey. The railroad
system which so recently had played such a necessary role in the
frantic and victorious war effort slowed down for a time and demonstrated its strength in a more quiet and tender fashion than ever
before or subsequently.

Within Illinois, Lincoln's train moved over a rail system which
had appeared within the preceding fifteen years. In 1850, when the
Illinois Central obtained the first federal land grant, Illinois had

111 miles of track concentrated in the northern cross line from Springfield to the Illinois River, and the Galena and Chicago Union Railroad extending westward from Chicago to Elgin, with a branch to Aurora. Construction began in earnest in the 1850s, the banner year being 1856 when the Illinois Central was "completed," and when a standing record of 1,348 miles of rails was spiked down. When gandy dancers became soldiers in 1861, Illinois had 2,790 miles of track, only some 300 miles south of the national road, and ranked second among the states in that category. (The eleven Confederate states had approximately 9,000 miles of track.)

As the Illinois road builders were laying new trackage, so were railroad entrepreneurs across the country. In 1865 railroad mileage in the United States totaled 35,085 miles. The figure increased by approximately 20,000 miles each five-year period, until it reached 166,703 miles in 1890.[2] The Civil War years had interrupted construction, but the pause was healthy, and wartime prosperity provided a springboard for massive postwar expansion. Earnings of most lines in Illinois followed the pattern of the Illinois Central's, which increased from $2,600,000 in 1861 to $7,000,000 in 1865, enabling the road to pay dividends of 8 percent in 1863 and 1864 and 10 percent in 1865. The Chicago, Burlington, and Quincy, whose twenty-seven-mile "airline" (a road as free from curves and grades as possible) into Chicago was among the more significant constructions of the war, nearly doubled its supply of freight cars, mostly of a specialized nature. Increased capital from the swollen passenger and freight traffic, and large amounts of government business, albeit at a reduced rate, permitted other lines to attempt such innovations as the use of coal instead of wood as fuel. The first mail car went into service on August 28, 1864, between Chicago and Clinton, Iowa, on the Chicago and Northwestern Railway.

Between 1865 and the depression of 1873, a remarkable burst of construction and a parallel attempt by the state to regulate the service of railroads occurred, setting the pattern for the generation. By 1870 the state's total of 4,707 miles of track ranked first among the states, a position maintained for forty years, and by 1873 the mileage mounted to 6,589, as nearly 1,200 miles were laid in 1871 alone. Previous attempts at regulation were buttressed by the mandates of the Constitution of 1870, and by 1873 a railroad and warehouse commission was administering a cluster of railroad laws, already amended in accordance with the dictates of the courts.

Everybody wanted to be close to a railroad. It promised wealth to local producers through connection with the national market, wealth to real-estate owners and other businesses through the growth or the creation of urban centers, wealth to those people it might employ; and it was terribly exciting. As a second railroad approached the city, the *Quincy Whig* screamed "we want all the railroads we can get."[3] The *Chicago Times*, whose city had already profited more from its railroads than had any other municipality, bubbled greedily that wealth from the railroads "will so overflow our coffers with gold that our paupers will be millionaires, and our rich men the possessors of pocket money which will put to shame the fortunes of Croesus."[4] The gross earnings of the Chicago rail network had increased from $39,521 in 1864 to $64,758 in 1870, the latter figure totaling receipts from only eight major carriers. The *Chicago Evening Journal* knew why Aurora was "prosperous and wide awake"[5] in February, 1872. The Chicago, Burlington, and Quincy had just paid its 1,985 employees $100,764 in that city. In Charleston just the prospect of the Charleston and Danville Railroad gave the "people new zeal, and several fine buildings, business houses and dwellings [were] in progress."[6] It was no mean achievement for any city to obtain the location of a railroad machine shop, round house, or other service. In November, 1870, "an earnest strife existed between the towns on the new Gilman, Clinton, and Springfield Railroad, over the location of the company's machine shops."[7] At least three cities offered to donate the land, buildings, and "appurtenances" if the Chicago and Alton Railroad would locate their stockyards there.

Driving the first spike (a silver one) on the Paris and Decatur Railroad caused "great rejoicing, bands playing and cannons firing." Hoopeston in Vermillion County did not exist in the summer of 1871, but by January, 1872, it had houses, several stores, a newspaper, and was planning churches and schools. It lay at the junction of the Lafayette, Bloomington, and Mississippi and the Chicago, Danville, and Vincennes railroads. Like Danville Junction and a host of other towns with "junction" appended to their names, Hoopeston was created by and was ready to begin its "romance" with the railroads. Typical of the frenzy was the race for the $30,000 prize to be awarded by the town of Sullivan to the contractor of one of two competing roads striving to be first into the city's limits. (Mount Pulaski offered the victorious workmen in a similar competition sixty barrels of beer.) Isolated prairie dwellers enjoyed reports of the spectacle which occurred in Peoria when four locomotives from the Chicago, Rock Island, and Pacific butted against four from the Peoria and Rock Island in trying to settle a disagreement over the right-of-way on the same track by pure steam power.

Everywhere the trains went, new towns appeared—many of them under the auspices of the railroad company. By 1884 the Illinois Central had directly influenced the naming of thirty-two towns and villages along its route, bringing lasting fame to those wise enough to jump aboard the bustling corporation early. Beginning in Chicago, the Illinois Central chugged south to Grand Crossing which "took its name from the fact that so many railroad tracks crossed each other at that point."[8] Then on to Burnside, named for General Ambrose Burnside, onetime cashier and later treasurer of the company. George Pullman's feudal enclave came next, followed by Riverdale, established when the Pittsburgh, Cincinnati and Southern came through. The next stop was Tucker, immortalizing J. F. Tucker, Illinois Central general superintendent.

Other Illinois Central cities enshrined the memory of George Danforth, purchaser of large blocks of Illinois Central land; Sam Gilman, who built fifty-three miles of track; Buckley, a station agent; Thomas Ludlow and Robert Rantoul, Illinois Central incorporators; Samuel Jarvis Haynes, superintendent of machinery; William Mattoon, a contractor who built the Terre Haute and Alton; George Watson, division superintendent; Colonel Roswell Mason, division engineer; Richard Cobden, a British shareholder; Richard Haldone, station agent; Lawrence Heyworth, British stockholder; Robert Forsyth, general freight agent; S. W. Walker, who got a side track located there; Elia Dunkel, agent; and William Wernon, auditor.

At times the company abandoned the last names of its employees and shareholders and chose more romantic names for budding communities. Neoga, a word meaning "place of the Deity," was named before any thought was given to an actual city. William Ferguson, an Illinois Central agent in London, named Kinmundy after his Scottish birthplace. Nelson Holt, agent and civil engineer, chose the Indian name Tamaroa, and George Watson and R. B. Mason, with future communities already bearing their own names, christened Wautaug and Nora ("a small name for a small place").[9]

Echoes of faraway places came to the Illinois plains with the founding of Polo, named for explorer Marco Polo by an Illinois

Central agent, and Woosung, named by a former sailor-turned-railroad-agent. T. B. Blackstone, president of the Chicago and Alton, named Mendota, and Centralia proved an apt description of a town platted by the Illinois Central as its southern machine shop. The lure of the railroad was strong enough to induce the village of Homo to change its name to Sublette to correspond to the name of the Illinois Central station.

"Prominent businessmen of Carthage spent their leisure time playing marbles on the street,"[10] the *Chicago Times* observed in July, 1872. But there was a more exhilarating way to spend time when the railroads brought famous, and not so famous, dramatic groups, lecturers, and circuses to or through the depots in a rapidly increasing number of towns. Prairie lads were impressed by the big-city drummers the trains brought to town, as much by the supply of lewd pictures the salesmen carried as by the marvelous inventory in their huge trunks. Newspaper readers enjoyed the embarrassment of a Peoria ticket agent whose window bore the great scarlet letters "BIRTHS SECURED HERE." The rumbling locomotives fired the imagination of observers. Walt Whitman expressed his reaction in verse.

> Fierce-throated beauty!
> Roll through my chant with all the lawless music,
>   thy swinging lamps at night,
> Thy madly-whistled laughter, echoing, rumbling, like
>   an earthquake, rousing all,
> Law of thyself complete, thine own track firmly holding,
> (No sweetness debonair of tearful harp or glib piano thine,)
> Thy trills of shrieks by rocks and hills return'd,
> Launch'd o'er the prairies wide, across the lakes,
> To the free skies unpent and glad and strong.[11]

Such intangibles as the opportunity to escape boredom were of undoubted importance in causing Illinoisans to subscribe to more railroad bonds than they could afford.

Since the state government could not grant direct aid to railroads, promoters turned to local government. In 1849 the general railroad incorporation act was amended to provide that any county might, upon vote of its citizens, subscribe for shares in the capital stock of any such corporation to an amount not to exceed $100,000. Later acts raised the amount and extended the power to boards of supervisors where the township organization prevailed and to councils of municipalities. By 1873 it was estimated that local governments had bonded themselves to a total of $2,000,000 (the figure doubled by 1877), in support of railroads. Total support was increased, of course, by contributions of individuals who mortgaged private holdings to produce aid.

Elgin offered the Chicago, Rock Island, and Pacific Railroad $150,000 if it would build through the city; Sycamore offered $100,000 to the Chicago and Pacific for a similar purpose; and the newspapers document hundreds of similar cases. In defense of the "corporate subscription system," the *Quincy Whig* explained that "it is a system which has . . . gridironed our state with improvements; it has encouraged the investment of that in which we are, and will be, as all new sections are deficient, *capital*; it has developed to a wondrous extent our unrivaled natural resources; it has become almost a Western policy, and we cannot afford to go back on it and drive the moneyed sympathy of the nation away from our State."[12] Quincy went to great lengths to demonstrate its faith by voting to subscribe to $500,000 of the bonds of the Quincy, Missouri, and Pacific Railroad, a line chartered and built outside the state. So eager was the city for this venture that its citizens secured a special section in the Constitution of 1870 permitting it, pushed a bill through the General Assembly providing for it, and successfully lobbied to override Governor Palmer's veto.

Construction and business needed little encouragement. At the close of 1870 Litchfield, Illinois, between East St. Louis and Springfield, had fourteen passenger trains per day, seven to St. Louis, three northeast through Decatur, and four east to Indianapolis. By the following year eight railroads had main or trunk lines terminating in East St. Louis, while thirteen railroads had terminals in the broader area opposite St. Louis. In August, 1871, Chicago had 426 trains entering or leaving the city daily. Six railroads were either completed or projected into Springfield. The Illinois River, by June, 1870, was spanned by six railroad bridges, at LaSalle, Peoria, Pekin, Beardstown, Meredosia, and Naples. When the great Eads Bridge opened in 1874 to St. Louis, there were ten bridges crossing the Mississippi from Illinois. As the depression halted construction in 1873, 73 percent of all the land in the state lay within five miles of a railroad; 21.5 percent between five and ten miles; 4 percent between ten and fifteen miles; and only 1.5 percent more than fifteen miles distant.

By 1873 Chicago had won its battle for commercial dominance with St. Louis, and its boomers were already speaking of overtaking New York. "Next to Chicago's matchless geographic position, the network of rails which extended fanshape from the city's center was the most significant of all the factors in her leadership."[13] The obvious importance of Chicago to the railroads themselves was that the city never needed to bond itself to support construction. As it had been the western terminus for the eastern trunk lines, it had become the eastern terminus for the western roads. In 1869 the Chicago, Rock Island, and Pacific connected with the Union Pacific, and trade opened with California. Henry Sienkiewicz summarized Chicago's pre-eminence for a Polish newspaper when he wrote "as the greatest city on the western route of the transcontinental railroad connecting New York with San Francisco, it unites civilization with the Far West. The East sends out the products of its industry, the West its agricultural products and natural resources, and Chicago is the great market place where the exchange takes place."[14] Chicago's admitted dominance stimulated the railroad industry throughout the state. Samuel P. Cummings, delegate to the Constitutional Convention in 1870, regretted the imbalance and wondered whether "every county in the State [were] to be tributary to Chicago?"[15] Statewide building should be encouraged, he continued, because "the interests of the people demand that there shall be competing lines of railroads through this State, and some other termination, to equalize and neutralize the trade in Chicago with that of the balance of the State."[16] It was not to be. Chicago's dominance grew.

Regardless of where they lived in the state, those who expected the railroads to create wealth for them recognized the need for vigilance lest the steaming monsters consume everything they produced, and the desire for regulation existed among railroad managers and shippers from the outset. Having rejected state ownership when the dreams of the internal improvement scheme of 1837 evaporated, the debate over the type of regulation to be employed was between self-regulation imposed by competition or state-regulation through agencies created for that purpose. Both operators and shippers soon rejected untrammeled competition as destructive to profit. Managers sought order by voluntary agreements while shippers turned to legislative solutions. Finally, many Illinoisans felt that increased development of the lake, canal, and river facilities would serve as an effective brake on railroad rates. The history of regulation is second in importance only to the construction of the railroads themselves.

Disorderly competition had been encouraged in 1849 when Illinois enacted an incorporation law whereby charters were issued to promoters who conformed to minimal preliminary conditions in terms of surveys, capitalization, and subscriptions. But even that was avoided because any road organized under its terms still had to obtain from the legislature specific permission to condemn land, thus necessitating a special act for each. Between 1850 and 1870 there was little uniformity among the 322 charters granted in matters of capitalization, increase of stock, indebtedness, the accumulation of a sinking fund, and the location of routes and terminals. Nearly all charters empowered the directors to fix rates without limitation. Free trade in charters resulted in a legislative free-for-all as special advantages were sought.

Illinois had abundant land and labor for building a railroad network, but capital often came from the eastern states or from England, as investors looked westward in search of profits. John Murray Forbes of Boston, head of one group of eastern investors who financed the Chicago, Burlington, and Quincy, exemplified the finance capitalists of the period. Forbes was born in Bordeaux, France, in 1813 of a prominent Boston family, and went into the family countinghouse at the age of fifteen. He represented the family interests in Canton, China, returning at the age of twenty-four with a sizable fortune. Forbes was the prime mover of an investment group which bought and completed the Michigan Central, and then turned to the Chicago, Burlington, and Quincy. His influence was such that the railroad's President James Walker's chief job was to act as a liaison with the Forbes group.[17]

Since the end of the Civil War an undertone of disillusionment with the railroads had qualified the enthusiasm for expansion. Railroads were overbuilt, and there were more facilities than goods to ship. In order to maintain their share of the business, railroads engaged in cutthroat competition. Rates went down at competitive points, but became unreasonably high at noncompetitive places. In January, 1870, the citizens of Geneseo resolved to "subscribe $100,000 to any railroad that would build an opposition line to the present monopoly."[18] On the other hand, when enterprising citizens of Belvidere proposed new railroads to connect the city with the coal fields to the south and Chicago to the east, opponents argued that "the principle of taxing property to build railroads is wrong; that small towns will be started on the new routes a few miles from here which will hack off a large slice of our southern trade, as has been the fact with our northern trade; that competition would soon be destroyed by agreement or consolidation; and that soft coal won't burn worth a cent."[19]

Farmers frequently found themselves paying more to ship

shorter distances than others were charged for longer hauls, and the fact seemed discriminatory regardless of the railroad's complicated explanations of it. Often rates were so high as to wipe out the producer's profits on grain. Fruit growers complained that two-thirds of the price of their product was consumed by transportation costs. Ironically, many of these same farmers had mortgaged their property to buy railroad bonds. Foreclosures were given wide newspaper publicity, especially by the Chicago press. The city had not bonded itself in support of railroads, but the merchants complained of erratic rate schedules and the appropriation of public streets for tracks. Resentment sprang from "the grinding and godless tyranny"[20] of absentee managers who were more concerned about additional expansion or with absorbing competitors than with improving or offering satisfactory service on their roads. Increased revenue from the railroads did not accrue automatically to cover the interest that had to be paid, through higher taxes, on bonds. The frenzied finance of the railroads and the widely publicized activities of buccaneering promoters contributed most to the depression of 1873. A "public-be-damned" attitude on the part of the railroads could be deduced from it all, and the public was not willing to accept it.

The complaints against the railroads centered about "extortionate," "discriminatory," "irregular" rates, and attempts to control them had a history as long as the railroads themselves. The general incorporation act of 1849 had fixed maximum passenger rates for railroads chartered under its terms to three cents a mile, a major reason why no railroads were incorporated under a general law until after 1870. The same act provided that the legislature might alter the rates for roads already chartered on condition that changes did not reduce profits to less than 15 percent of the capital stock. Occasionally the charter of a railroad required uniform rates for both passenger and freight travel, whereas the first act of incorporation of the Illinois Central provided that when the dividends of the company exceeded 12 percent of the investment, the General Assembly might reduce the rates. A long series of measures aimed at punishing rate discrimination, limiting fares, and establishing inspection of railroads and warehouses were doggedly pushed for passage between 1861 and 1869, but even the mild law finally passed in 1869 was never enforced.

Two widely publicized laws passed in 1869, however, concentrated public attention upon the power and greed of the railroads in the state and prepared the way for constitutional and statutory regulation. They were the so-called Tax Grab Law and the Lake Front Act. The first made the promoter's job easier by providing that "whenever any county, township, incorporated city or town shall have created a debt . . . to aid in the construction of any railway . . . whose line shall run to, into or through [them] . . . the state treasurer" was required to place to their credit "all the states taxes," except the state school tax and the two mill taxes, "collected and paid into the state treasury on the increased valuation of the taxable property . . . over and above the amount of the assessment roll of the year 1868 [which] shall be applied . . . to the payment of [their] bonded railroad debt."[21] This act created a false security for small investors who oversubscribed to railroad bonds. The second gave the Illinois Central and the Chicago, Burlington, and Quincy Railway companies a section of the lake front in Chicago, south of the river mouth, for the purpose of constructing dockage and outside harbor facilities, in addition to some valuable land within the city for depots. The city was to receive $800,000 for land worth at least $2,000,000. These laws and the methods used in securing them gave the proponents of railroad regulation a rallying point in the constitutional convention that began at the end of the year and in subsequent general assemblies.

The *Chicago Evening Journal* was quick to point out that since passage of the act, the Illinois Central had "been assiduously buying up . . . the riparian rights" and had secured all the property from 35th to 16th streets. "It appears," continued the *Journal*, "that the railroad company is unusually anxious to pay $800,000 . . . for the submerged lands of the lake which are worth millions."[22]

A general atmosphere of frustration with the railroads had been created throughout the state when the scheduled constitutional convention met in December, 1869. The farmers were the best organized of the aggrieved public, and to stimulate action they convened at Bloomington on April 20, 1870, passing resolutions declaring railroad companies to be public corporations subject to regulation, condemning the practice of railroads of delivering grain to warehouses without the consent of the shipper, denouncing the tendency toward consolidation to influence courts and legislatures, and approving of canals for cheap transportation to furnish competition to the railroads.[23] The new constitution satisfied at least some of these demands by declaring railroads to be "public highways," by instructing the General Assembly to set "reasonable maximum rates" for passenger and freight service, as well as to "pass laws to correct abuses and to prevent unjust discrimination and extortion in the rates of freight and passenger tariffs on the different railroads in this state."[24] Municipal subscription to the capital stock of railroads as well as donations or loans of credit from the same source were forbidden except where already voted by the people.

Governor Palmer told the legislators in January, 1871, that to deny that the state had the power to regulate railroads "is to assert that a power has grown up in the State greater than the State itself, and makes an issue that the representatives of a free people cannot, without the most palpable disregard of their duty, evade."[25] Responding to the mandates of the new constitution and prodded by a group of law makers who united to form the "Legislative Farmers' Club," the first session of the Twenty-Sixth General Assembly enacted a cluster of railroad laws. Separate measures dealt with the regulation of passenger rates, freight charges, the transportation of grain on railroads, warehouses and grain inspection, and the establishment of a board of railroad and warehouse commissioners. The act fixing passenger fares divided the railroads into four classes based upon their gross earnings per mile, an advanced approach at the time, and provided a sliding scale of maximum rates for each which ranged from 2.5¢ to 5¢ a mile. Unjust discriminations and extortions in the freight rates of the various railroads were to be prevented by making any discrimination in rates illegal. Making no provision for occasions when long- and short-haul inequities were justifiable economically, the law made it an offense "to charge *the same* or a greater sum for a shorter distance than is charged for a longer *anywhere on the same road.*"[26] Railroads, as a result of being forced to decrease rates under the terms of an earlier section of the law, were forbidden to increase them on the parts of a system which had been previously charging less than normal. The goal was to reduce tariffs to their lowest competitive level in 1870 since those rates must have been profitable or business would not have been conducted. (Unfortunately, that year was an extremely poor choice as a base period because of the wide fluctuations of rates.) Maximum charges of two cents per bushel for the first thirty days and one-half cent per bushel for each additional fifteen-day period were established for warehousing services. Rates were to be published in the first week in January, were not to be increased during the year, and no discrimination could be made between customers. Discrimination between shippers and warehouses in the handling of grain was forbidden by a separate law. Inspection of grain was to be handled by state inspectors appointed by the governor with the consent of the Senate, as downstaters frowned upon that function being handled by the Chicago Board of Trade, as it had been before 1871.

These laws were to be overseen by the establishment of a board of railroad and warehouse commissioners. The law stipulated that none of the appointees were to be connected with or interested in the stock of any railroad. Accordingly, Governor Palmer named Gustav Koerner of St. Clair County, Richard P. Morgan, Jr., of McLean County, and David S. Hammond of Cook County to form the first board.

Commissioner Koerner was a man of great accomplishment, born in 1809 in Frankfurt-am-Main, Germany, with a Ph.D. from Heidelberg. He was wounded in the Frankfurt revolt of 1833 and fled first to France, then the United States, settling in St. Louis. Koerner was unable to live with slavery, and moved to Belleville, Illinois, the center of an intellectual and cultural colony of German immigrants. He was appointed justice of the Illinois Supreme Court in 1845, but refused nomination after the post became elective. An active Republican, he was appointed minister to Spain in 1862, joined the Liberal Republicans in 1872, and retired from politics in 1876. He devoted the rest of his life to writing, his most famous work being *Das Deutsch Element in den Vereinigten Staten von Nordamerika*.

The commissioners were required to present an annual report to the governor, based upon yearly accounts submitted by every railroad company doing business in the state, which was to contain the information necessary to enforce the laws. Books of the railroad companies could be subpoenaed, and the commission was empowered to investigate any possible violation without the necessity of a complaint. Generally, the goal was to take as firm a hand with the railroads in Illinois as possible, and the commission exemplified the regulative approach to the problem rather than advisory, as taken by its eastern predecessors.

After an initial delay, several important decisions were handed down by the courts on the new legislation. The maximum passenger-fare law was tested by S. H. Moore of Kankakee who, with the support of the board, brought suit against the Illinois Central to recover the $500 penalty for a charge greater than the fixed maximum rate. Judge Wood of the Circuit Court of Kankakee decided for the railroad inasmuch as its charter was a contract and the legislature could neither judge what was a reasonable rate nor fix fares. The Supreme Court upheld the decision, but no statement was made on the constitutionality of the law. A second suit was brought by the commissioners against the Chicago and Alton Railroad in the Circuit Court of McLean County for a violation of the long- and short-haul clause of the act to prevent extortion and unjust discrimination in freight rates. Judge Tipton ruled for the people, holding that the state retained the right to prevent unjust discrimination in spite of the charter of the railroad. But the Supreme Court reversed the decision in that the act violated the state constitution "because it does not prohibit unjust discrimination merely, but discrimination of any character, and because it does not allow the companies to explain the reason for discrimination, but forfeits their franchise upon an arbitrary and conclusive presumption of guilt to be drawn from the proof of an act that might be shown to be perfectly innocent."[27] Judge Lawrence, to be defeated for re-election on the basis of his judgment, suggested the language of an appropriate law when he declared that a greater charge for a short than a long haul should be *prima facie*, not conclusive, evidence of discrimination. Competition at any given point, he continued, was not enough to justify discrimination. The laws had not been observed closely by the railroads since their passage anyway, and in his final message to the General Assembly in January, 1873, Governor Palmer warned that "the people of the State, aware of the refusal of this class of persons to obey the laws, and of the mischiefs their contempt of authority of the State produces, look to the General Assembly to make further and efficient efforts to provide a remedy."[28]

Thirty-five railroad bills were introduced into the House during its session in 1873. Among them was one forbidding legislators to accept free passes, but no legislation outlawing this practice was obtained during the session or the remainder of the century. By 1873 the farmers' political power in Illinois had reached a peak, and their organizations' *raison d'etre* was to strengthen railroad legislation. Under pressure of a meeting of farmers' representatives from seventy-two counties in the state capital the previous month, a bill became law early in May, 1873, which formed the basis of railroad regulation for the remainder of the period. Under its terms any railroad company charging unfair or unreasonable rates or making unjust discriminations was guilty of extortion. Discrimination was minutely defined to cover rate differences for similar service by a railroad for traffic in the same direction, thus modifying the act of 1871. Discriminatory rates were to be viewed as *prima facie* evidence of unjust favoritism, but the existence of competition *per se* was not to constitute sufficient justification for discrimination. The state was empowered to recover not less than $1,000 or more than $5,000 for a first offense, with the fine increasing to $25,000 for the fourth and additional violations, and the injured party was entitled to triple damages, costs, and attorney's fees. The commissioners were to determine whether the act was being observed and were empowered to institute suits against infractions. They were to prepare a schedule of maximum rates for passengers, freight, and cars for each railroad, effective January 18, 1874. The result of the act was to place the burden of proof upon the railroads that rates were reasonable. The act itself was more sophisticated but less stringent than that desired by the organized farmers.

In the midst of the struggle came the panic of 1873, inaugurated by the railroads and followed by six lean years across the nation. The tremendous railroad construction since 1865 had strengthened the economy, but it shrank abruptly when long-term investments were no longer available to support additional expansion. Bankers, such as Jay Cooke, had triggered the panic by the use of short-term credits to support railroad promotions that investors were scorning. Potential investors, foreign and domestic, were frightened by bankruptcies, defaults, and granger rhetoric. According to the *Chicago Tribune*, "the plethora of capital in Germany, consequent upon the prompt payment of the French war indemnity, created a demand for investments. American securities would have been eagerly seized upon had the capitalists not recently suffered from worthless bonds issued by some of our Western roads." Then "the threatening of the Grangers reached Europe, and American railroad bonds became a drug on the market." In Illinois, as a result, "orders were given to suspend all work upon the short line to St. Louis, and half a dozen other projects calculated materially to develop the West fell through. The Milwaukee and St. Paul surrendered the St. Croix land grant from sheer inability to build the required road, and the Northwestern indefinitely postponed the construction of their proposed air line from Milwaukee to Lodi. The Canada Southern, which was confidently expected to run into Chicago next month, dragged slowly along and has now little prospect of connecting Chicago with Buffalo for a year or two to come." Since in prosperous times the railroads "are among the greatest patrons of industry," a decline in production and an increase in unemployment could be expected.[29]

Between 1873 and 1898 the courts upheld the legislation in most of its important particulars, while the commission was able to rationalize its procedures in terms of railroad growth and the demands of the times. By 1887 the railroad problem, national in its implications from the beginning, was being dealt with to some extent by the federal government's Interstate Commerce Commission. The railroad system in Illinois continued to expand, sporadically and more slowly than before, and the railroads resorted to consolidation and pooling agreements in a search for order which still had not been imposed.

In accord with the law of 1873 the railroad commission in Illinois divided the railroads into five classes, and a schedule of rates was set for each. At first little heed was paid to the new rates by the companies which also took the opportunity to raise tolls previously lower than the maximum set by the board. Attacks were made upon the board from the General Assembly, business and industry, and the press in an attempt to discredit the law. Governor Beveridge took the opportunity to defend and to explain the principles of the law in 1873 to the General Assembly when he said it

> does not declare any particular act to be an unjust discrimination, but it declares certain acts to be *prima facie* evidence of unjust discrimination. It does not prescribe any rate to be charged, or declare any rate unreasonable to extortionate, but makes the schedules prepared by the Commissioners *prima facie* evidence of what is a reasonable rate of charges. It does not controvert a single principle of the common law, except to change the rule of evidence, and to throw the burden of proof upon the defendant, and the question whether such an act is an unjust discrimination, or such a charge is extortionate, is to be determined by a court and jury, upon the facts proven under the law.[30]

Should the law be repealed, the only change would be "that the burden of proof would be upon the plaintiff, and there would be no statutory penalties affixed to a verdict of guilty of extortion or unjust discrimination." The governor concluded that "the contest is not one of legal interference—not one of oppression—not one of direct antagonism; it is one for the ascertainment of mutual rights, in which all classes are interested."[31]

In a rush of litigation, the courts upheld the most important aspects of the legislation. They decreed that the rate schedules were necessary to any prosecution for extortion under the act. In January, 1874, the court decided against the Illinois Central for unjust discrimination in delivering grain upon the track, a decision that went far to end the abuse. The most famous case involved the warehouse law of 1871 and resulted from a suit brought by the commission against Munn and Scott, a Chicago warehouse firm, for failure to license themselves according to the law. Both the Circuit Court and the Supreme Court of the state ruled for the people, the latter in September, 1873. Upon appeal to the United States Supreme Court as *Munn* vs. *Illinois*, the first of the so-called "granger cases," Chief Justice Waite ruled in favor of the state on the grounds that when "one devotes his property to a use in which the public has an interest, he, in effect, grants to the public an interest in that use, and must submit to be controlled by the public for the common good."[32] The decision was made in 1877. In 1878 the court sustained the law of 1871, rewritten in 1873, regulating passenger rates in the Neal Ruggles case. The constitutionality of the law of 1873 was not confirmed until June, 1880, in a decision on a suit originally brought by the commissioners five years earlier in the Circuit Court of Douglas County against the Illinois Central for extortion.

Meanwhile the web of rails continued to expand in Illinois after 1873 with 4,262 miles of additional track to be laid by 1898. Growth slowly tapered off, however, as 3,547 miles of track had been laid in the 1870s (499 miles after 1873), 2,251 miles in the 1880s, and 1,043 in the 1890s, with bursts from 1874 to 1876, 1880 to 1883, 1885 to 1888, and in 1890. By 1893 the commission found that 85 percent of all the land in Illinois was within five miles of an operating railroad; 11.5 percent between five to ten miles, 2.5 percent between ten to fifteen miles, 1 percent farther than fifteen miles, and none more than twenty. By 1898 the total mileage had reached a staggering 10,851. (The corresponding figure for 1964 was 10,966, having declined from an all-time high of 12,500 in 1930.) In that year, the commission concluded that "the State of Illinois is so thoroughly covered with a network of railroads that we cannot expect a great increase in the future in the mileage of the main lines in the State. The competition between all main points is now so strong that the construction of new lines would be an unprofitable and reckless adventure."[33] Significantly the southern portion of the state which had been ignored by the promoters before 1870 was now opened to traffic. Between 1871, when the Illinois and Southwestern (to become part of the Baltimore and Ohio system) was completed to Shawneetown, and 1898, Cairo was touched by two railroads in addition to the Illinois Central, and the southeastern part of Illinois between Cairo and Terre Haute found terminals for important roads at Metropolis and Shawneetown on the Ohio River, and Epworth, Grayville, Mt. Carmel, St. Francisville, Vincennes, Indiana, Riverdale, and Hutsonville on or near the Wabash River.

That the railroads provided a pleasant means of transportation for their passengers was attested to by an English traveler in 1878 leaving Aurora for Burlington, Iowa, aboard the Chicago, Burlington, and Quincy.

> This is a very comfortable line to travel upon, as attached to each train are beautiful dining-room cars, where we got our meals with as much regularity and comfort as can be obtained in any first-class hotel, and at no more cost. The tables are of course rather narrow, and you have to guard against your head coming in contact with the person that may be sitting opposite to you. This, with care, is easily avoided, but, altogether, railway travelling in America is made much more comfortable than in the old country, and long journeys are got through with much less fatigue than short ones are with us. In the construction of their cars, too, all the requirements of human nature are amply provided for; every car has a plentiful supply of ice water, and when passengers get tired of sitting they can have a long stroll from one end of the train to the other, and do a little gossiping here and there as they move about. . . . I also observed a good deal of trading being done in the trains, such as in the selling of books and the daily newspapers, also fruits and sweets of every description. I think, however, this trading element is rather overdone, as in a long journey it becomes a bore to be continually asked to buy one thing and another.[34]

The gentleman had the highest praise for the convenience and courtesy with which his luggage was handled.

Along with increased trackage and the use of steel rails, mechanical improvements increased the railroad's speed and efficiency. The Chicago, Burlington, and Quincy installed an improved coupler attachment for air brakes in 1877, and the papers were full of the latest speed records between Chicago and New York. The *Illinois State Journal* reported in 1878 that "W. H. Vanderbilt and party made a run from Chicago to Cleveland, a distance of 357 miles, over the Lake Shore Road on Tuesday, in seven hours, twenty-eight minutes. Vanderbilt expressed objections to riding faster than one mile per minute."[35]

Progress brought such concomitant problems as the "eating house nuisance," as trains were forced to stop in certain stations to allow the passengers to get a meal. This was fine, stated the *Chicago Tribune*, "when railroads were in a primitive state and did not make more than ten or fifteen miles an hour,"[36] but apparently the eating houses had not kept pace with the new era of speed. Attempts were made to serve meals in the sleeper cars, but the exhorbitant prices of $1 and $3 per meal doomed the experiment to failure. In 1876 the Michigan Central installed dining cars on its lines, offering meals for seventy-five cents, and the other lines soon followed suit. The eating house, the *Tribune* was convinced, "would soon be known in history only."[37]

Rate wars and cutthroat competition remained a serious problem for the railroads and the public. Managers attempted to correct the situation by their own devices. Occasionally the railroads sought to control shippers, for example, by purchasing coal lands or by making agreements with sympathetic mine owners to give one railroad their company's business. Coal companies occasionally purchased their own cars, receiving special rates as a result. This activity was supplemented by granting rebates or drawbacks to large shippers which significantly lowered the price of transportation for their products. Pools for the purpose of making a rational division of the traffic among the competing roads quickly evolved. The first large pool had been established in 1870 by the Chicago, Burlington, and Quincy, the Northwestern, and the Rock Island through a voluntary agreement which divided earnings from the Chicago-Council Bluffs business. Each railroad was to retain 50 percent of its freight receipts and 45 percent of its passenger fares, distributing the remainder equally among the members. This "great pool" lasted in one fashion or another until 1885. A second pool was arranged between the Illinois Central, the Wabash, and the Chicago and Alton in 1875. The public did not welcome the pools, and the Daily *Inter-Ocean* voiced public sentiment in 1875 when the new pool was being formed: "For some time past the air which pervades the railway offices of this city has been agitated by pools and rumors of pools. The alleged gigantic and corrupt combinations of the old Eastern trust lines to trample underfoot the long-suffering mercantile public and squeeze the lifeblood out of the hard-working farmer. . . ."[38]

But controls or not, railroad wars continued, and their desultory effects upon shippers were described graphically by Joseph Medill of the *Chicago Tribune* in 1885.

> We will say that the cost of conveying wheat or corn or any agricultural product from Chicago to [New York] is 25 cents per hundred pounds, today. On the strength of that rate our merchants proceed to buy wheat, corn, or oats all over the West . . . and farmers make their bargains based on the cost of transportation from Chicago to tidewater. Suddenly, or with brief notice, the charge goes up to 30 cents. Every merchant who holds that grain, and it may amount altogether to tens of millions of bushels, has instantly lost five cents on each hundred pounds. That five cents is wiped out as completely as if it had

been burned, or sunk without insurance. Then, if there is a fall suddenly of five cents a hundred pounds, that affects not only the grain that was bought by the merchants, but the entire stock of produce remaining in the hands of farmers. At once, of course, there is a natural dissatisfaction throughout the whole farming community at this artificial fall. . . . The first thing you know they are carrying grain to New York from Chicago for 20 cents per hundred pounds instead of 30 to 35 cents. All at once there is a tremendous "boom" in the market. Every man's grain rapidly advances. Then the farmers are all angry because they sold out before the cut in transportation. . . . There is no steadiness, no system, no fixedness for anything, and the whole country is kept in a tremor of expectancy as to whether prices are going up or going down from this unregulated cause.[39]

As early as 1877 delegates appointed by the London shareholders of the Illinois Central to investigate the decline of traffic concluded that "the absorption of the smaller lines into the systems of the larger companies is what must be looked to as the final settlement of the competition between the railroads."[40] The process involved an amazingly intricate combination of bankruptcies, receiverships, name changes, leases, and interlocking directorates. In 1860 there were only four railroads within Illinois controlling over 200 miles of track. (They were the Illinois Central, 705; the Galena and Chicago Union, 261; the Chicago, Alton, and St. Louis, 220; and the Terre Haute, Alton, and St. Louis, 208). By 1898 there were fourteen, and many of the lines with less mileage were controlled by railroads with massive operations outside the state. The largest was the Illinois Central, which had increased its main line from the 705 miles stretching from Cairo northward to Centralia, where it branched by way of Effingham and then to Chicago by way of Decatur and Bloomington to Dunleith, to a total of 1,611 miles of track by absorbing roads in the central and northern parts of the state. The Chicago, Burlington, and Quincy had controlled 400 miles of track in 1865, but by 1898 it operated 1,308 miles within the state, stretching in a maze from Chicago to Clinton, Iowa, in the north, and touching the Mississippi River in at least six separate places southward to St. Louis. The Wabash system connecting St. Louis and Chicago, Keokuk and Danville, with the junction at Decatur, controlled 677 miles of track by 1898. The Chicago and Northwestern had expanded from sixty-six miles of track in 1860 to 594 miles in 1898. The Cleveland, Cincinnati, Chicago, and St. Louis (the Big Four) had branches from Pekin to St. Louis and from Cairo to Danville, totaling some 478 miles of track by 1898. The

Chicago and Alton, which had been one of the most consistently profitable railroads in the state, operated 580 miles of track in 1898. The parent firms of such modern lines as the Milwaukee Road, the Toledo, Peoria, and Western, the Gulf, Mobile, and Ohio, the New York Central, the Pennsylvania, and the Santa Fe experienced the same expansion resulting from their managers' desire to rationalize the business and to make profits as large and predictable as possible.

Regulation of the railroads in the 1880s and 1890s involved the formalization of procedures by the commissioners in Illinois and the adoption of the Interstate Commerce Act by the federal government. Complaints against the railroads in the state had not ceased in 1880, when forty-seven grievances involving extortion, unjust discrimination, or various other violations were registered with the board. The commissioners and the railroads settled each case, with the railroads showing an increasing willingness to arbitrate and to acquiesce in the decisions against them. As a result of the more prosperous roads having absorbed the poorer ones, the board, in 1881, reviewed the earlier rates and reduced the classifications from five to two. Maximum passenger rates were fixed at three cents a mile and freight rates were fixed at 20 to 30 percent lower than those of 1873. In January, 1885, Governor Hamilton remarked that "the authority of this Board, under the law, to regulate railroad charges and prevent discrimination, is now so well established by the decisions of the courts, that nearly all complaints from the people of violations of law are adjusted by the railroads themselves, without litigation, on notice from the Commissioners."[41] In 1893 uniform rules were adopted by the board to govern the method by which complaints were tried.

Until the middle and late 1870s, the federal government had been more concerned with the promotion than the regulation of railroads. Criticism of the industry began in earnest in 1874, with the report of a special senate committee headed by William Windom of Minnesota, but significant regulation was not one of the recommendations. The decision in *Munn* vs. *Illinois* gave the right of regulation, which the states had long held, a federal sanction. In 1876 the first regulatory bill was introduced in the House of Representatives which forbade rebates and rate discriminations, but it died in committee. The Reagan bill, introduced in 1878, contained similar clauses, besides an antipooling agreement. This bill stressed direct court control, and it was the chief competitor to the idea of commission control. That function was not begun by the federal government until the passage of the Interstate Commerce Act in February, 1887, resulting primarily from investigations undertaken by a Senate committee headed by Shelby Cullom, an early participant in the state battle for railroad regulation.

The law applied to railroads engaged in interstate commerce and provided that rates must be reasonable and just, but it did not authorize rate fixing. Pooling operations, discriminatory rates, drawbacks, and rebates were forbidden, as were greater charges for a long haul over the same line. Railroad rates had to be posted and could not be changed without a ten-day notice. The Interstate Commerce Commission was created to investigate the management of roads, with the powers to summon witnesses and compel the production of a company's books. The commission was empowered to require annual reports from the railroads listing details of operations and finances. Although its orders were not binding, it could seek the aid of equity proceedings in the federal courts. Upon Cullom's recommendation, Thomas M. Cooley was appointed chairman of the new commission. Cooley, who identified himself closely with the manager's interests, gave the commission a cautious and conservative caste from the outset. Most important, however, the federal government, basing its actions upon the experience of states like Illinois, had changed its emphasis from promotion to restraint. With the passage of the Sherman Anti-Trust law in 1890, the old problem of consolidation versus competition faced the federal government, but any solutions awaited another century.

In many ways the railroads dominated the postwar generation in Illinois and elsewhere in the nation. The commissioners in Illinois reported that "the total railway capital of the railroads of the State of Illinois at the close of the fiscal year ending June 30, 1898, including capital stock, funded debt, and current liabilities, is $2,736,491,915."[42] Given the qualifications implicit in that figure (such as the fact that it includes nearly ninety miles of elevated street railroads in Chicago capitalized at some $2,000,000 a mile and that much of the latter as well as the total figure represented water), the amount is immensely larger than the state budget, as well as the national debt. The effects of its management upon politics, the economy, and the lives of individual citizens cannot be overemphasized. In addition to the importance of being connected closely with the national market and its fate, Illinoisans found the pace of their lives dramatically increased. Once aboard a train, so close to everyone, an individual left other modes of overland travel that averaged five miles an hour. Riding in a passenger train going fifty miles an hour equaled the speedup experience of a person who compares fifty miles an hour in his automobile with over 500 miles per hour in a jet airplane.

Indisputable, also, is the fact that rates fell and business increased throughout the period. Between July, 1866, and July, 1897, the rate per 100 pounds of wheat shipped from Chicago to New York fell from sixty-five cents to twenty cents. The rate on dressed beef between the two cities declined from ninety cents per 100 pounds in May, 1872, to forty cents in February, 1899. The coal roads in the state experienced a 40 percent decline in rates on their major product during the period. Passenger rates in Illinois declined from an average of four cents per mile in 1870 to an average of 2.07 cents in 1896, and freight rates declined from 2.43 cents per ton-mile in 1870 to .800 (.745) per ton-mile in 1896. The classified companies reporting to the Illinois commissioners in 1873 carried 7,966,502 tons of freight in 1873, increasing to 75,493,330 tons in 1898. The number of passengers carried by railroads in Illinois doubled between 1873 and 1885, doubled again by 1893, and reached a total of 87,696,994 by 1898.

The nature of the railroad and warehouse commission made it the most original contribution of state government during the period. An innovation among the states as a regulative approach, it offered certain advantages to the state which it maintained even after the federal government began its attempts to solve the railroad problem. The commission provided a general supervision over the railroads of the state, and it existed as a permanent body to which the legislature assigned related matters. In spite of attacks upon the commission, it was the only agency which could recommend solutions to problems that would satisfy both management and the public. Its reports constituted an invaluable source of statistical information on the physical conditions of the railroads, their financial situation, and their management. The commission informed the state government about the activities of its counterparts in other states by attending the national conventions of state railway commissioners. In 1889 similar meetings began between the state commissioners and the Interstate Commerce Commission.

During the entire period from 1865 to 1898, water transportation by river, lake, and canal remained important to the state's commerce, but it declined in relative significance when compared with that of the railroads. The Mississippi River, flowing the length of the state and forming its western boundary, continued to support trade in such bulky nonperishable items as coal, sand, stone, and rough lumber. But the magnificent river boats of the 1850s were replaced by tugs, barges, or small packets. The change is best portrayed by one of the river's closest observers, Mark Twain, in his *Life on the Mississippi*:

> Boat used to land—captain on the hurricane roof—might stiff and straight—iron ramrod for a spine—kid gloves, plug hat, hair parted behind—man on shore takes off hat and says:
>
> "Got twenty-eight tons of wheat, cap'n—be great favor if you can take them."
>
> Captain says:
>
> "I'll take two of them"—and don't even condescend to look at him.
>
> But nowadays the captain takes off his old slouch, and smiles all the way around to the back of his ears, and gets off a bow which he hasn't got any ramrod to interfere with, and says:
>
> "Glad to see you, Smith, Glad to see you—you're looking well— haven't seen you looking so well for years—what you got for us?"
>
> "Nuth'n," says Smith; and keeps his hat on, and just turns his back and goes to talking with somebody else.[43]

A continuous waterway through the agricultural heartland of the north central portion of the state from Lake Michigan at Chicago by way of Peoria to the Mississippi at Grafton was formed by the Illinois and Michigan Canal, opened in 1848 and turned over to the state in 1871. The canal ran from a point on the Chicago River about five miles from its mouth to LaSalle, where it connected with the Illinois River southward. Construction of locks on the canal at Henry in 1872 and at Copperas Creek in 1876, as well as a lock and dam at LaGrange in 1890 and another at Kampsville in 1894, greatly improved this route. The river projects were joint federal-state undertakings. Trade declined between Illinois River towns and St. Louis, and after 1878 tolls on the Illinois and Michigan Canal ceased to pay operating and maintenance expenses. Grain, stone, and lumber were the most important commodities carried on this route. Still, hopes for the success of the canal died hard. In 1876, when steam navigation of the Illinois-Michigan Canal proved feasible, the *Chicago Tribune* declared, "its success promised well for an enlarged trade . . . when the river improvements shall be finished. . . . The permanency of water navigation," it continued, "is essential to the great coal mines which lie continuous to the water route."[44]

Lake Michigan traffic, nearly all through Chicago, best weathered the onslaught of the railroads. By 1865 direct shipments to Liverpool, England, were frequent, and in 1871 Congress allowed

Chicago to become a port of entry, thus reducing her dependence on eastern cities. Chicagoans mounted periodic campaigns to improve this route through the enlargement of the Welland Canal at Niagara and by encouraging special treaties with Canada. Although the railroads succeeded in capturing the traffic in perishable goods from the lakes, between 1870 and 1894, depending upon the seasonal accumulation, some two-thirds to three-fourths of the wheat and corn trade east was handled by water. These proportions declined rapidly in the waning years of the century as more grain was kept in Illinois to feed livestock and to be distilled into liquor. Of the major receipts into Chicago, iron ore increased in volume to feed the growing industry in south Chicago, but the once great lumber trade declined because of the decreasing supply to the north. The total number of passengers traveling in and out of the state via the lake route rose from 1,231,000 in 1870 to 1,400,000 in 1878, while six steamers valued at $420,000 and forty-six lives were lost at sea during those years.

Many contemporaries viewed the primary value of the waterways in terms of the natural regulative influence their potential competition exerted upon railroad rates. This outlook was expressed in a *Chicago Times* editorial in early 1878: "With the triumphs of railways, canals have lost their old uses, and many of them their old value. But the railway system of America has itself developed a new use for canals, and given to some of them a new value; a value greater than any they ever possessed before, and one that they can never lose so long as railways are controlled by men, and men by the love of gain. This value is not so much in the low price for which they can carry breadstuffs, as it is in the low price for which they can make the railways carry them."[45]

Agitation for a second canal grew from this sentiment. A convention of some 900 delegates met in Rock Island in 1874, resolving that the construction of a canal from Hennepin on the Illinois River to Rock Island would help solve the transportation problem of the farmers. A second convention, held at Ottawa in 1879, urged the construction of a deep waterway from the Great Lakes to the Mississippi. The National Board of Trade in 1884 endorsed both projects by supporting a resolution expressing the need for them; it was presented by the Chicago Board of Trade. A waterways convention was held at Peoria in 1887 and endorsed plans for the improvement of the Illinois River and the digging of the Hennepin Canal. The decision was finally made, but construction was not completed on the canal until 1907. The entire movement grew from the knowledge that railroad rates were lower where the tracks paralleled a water route.

The most significant conclusion to be drawn is that the amount of goods and number of passengers carried by the waterways declined in both absolute and relative figures when compared with the railroads. Except for the lake, the water courses ran north and south, while since before the Civil War the major flow of goods to and from Illinois had been east and west. At certain periods of the year water traffic was interrupted by ice or low water. Viewing water transportation as an enemy and recognizing that the amount of commerce would not support both ships and railroads, the latter refused to cooperate with the former in the creation of joint facilities or in the trans-shipment of freight. Canal users found themselves faced by rate discriminations from the railroad warehouse complex and by higher costs for rehandling grain shipped by canals. Although railroads did not depend exclusively upon government support for their improvement, waterways did, and this fact explains the lack of interest in river, lake, and canal enlargement by the state government. Although the state was to lay the burden of improvement of the road system upon the local government, the investment of state funds in waterway ventures seemed so unpromising that "national aid" was sought, and Illinoisans in 1882 voted by a large majority to turn the Illinois and Michigan Canal over to the federal government.

While the railroads were connecting the towns and cities of Illinois with one another, as well as with the rest of the nation, in revolutionary fashion, and as intracity travel was being improved by the introduction of the street railway, the condition, if not the mileage, of the roads of the state differed little from that of 1818. Much publicity was given to the intrepid farmers who brought their produce to the larger cities by wagon in order to avoid excessive railroad rates. These adventurers provided good copy for the newspaper reporters, but posed no threat to the railroads or waterways. Rich, undrained prairie soils supported phenomenal crops, but when cleared for roadways, they powdered into choking dust in the summer, became bottomless quagmires in the spring and fall, and froze into devastating ruts in the winter. Impassable during a good part of each year, the roads frequently defeated the best efforts of straining men, animals, and equipment to pass over them, and related limitations were imposed upon rural citizens in terms of social relationships, work life, mail delivery, and school attendance.

The federal government lost interest in road building before completing the national road from Cumberland, Maryland, to Vandalia, Illinois. Although the federal government constructed the bridges, the state paid for construction from the Indiana state line to the old capital. The planned extension of the road to St. Louis never materialized, and on May 9, 1856, the government ceded the road to the state. The once bustling highway fell into disuse after the railroad made it obsolete, and it was not kept repaired. "In 1870 most cities through which the pike passed still referred to their main street as the National Road; 30 years later only the old-timers used the term."[46]

Poets nostalgically summed up the decline of the once-proud road: "We hear no more the clanking hoof/ And the stagecoach rattling by,/ For the Steamking ruleth the travel world,/ And the old pike's left to die."[47]

Financing for public roads was left to the counties, and the *Chicago Evening Journal* reported one method in 1878: "Every male inhabitant of Alexander County, not excepted by the fortunate circumstance that he lives within the corporate limits of Cairo, or by the less fortunate circumstance of his being 50 years of age, will be required to perform five days labor on the public roads of the county during the year 1879, or render to the superintendent of his district a just and fair equivalent in money."[48]

Private enterprise brought toll roads to the state, to the disgust of local citizens. An account of their wrath in 1878 began "a number of citizens of Jefferson and others living on the line of the Elston Tollroad are on the warpath."[49]

However they were built and financed, planked roads could not compete with the Illinois mud. In one common incident livery men in Springfield responded to the muck by refusing to hire out their carriages "until the mud blockade is lifted,"[50] and four days later, the *Chicago Times* reported, "an old citizen of Springfield suggests that the streets of that city be planted with crops. They have ceased to be useful for any other purpose."[51] Sidewalks were not in much better shape than the roads. Pedestrians in Wilmette were warned to avoid walking at night as "every board in ten is loose and is liable to trip you up and leave you for life, and numbers of boards are missing altogether."[52] Intercity transportation improved somewhat with the introduction of cable cars in Chicago in 1882. But a traveler on foot or in a wagon or carriage was not yet able to reap the benefits of mechanization open to the train passenger.

State government's attempts to improve the roads or to awaken the public to the need were few and ineffective. Only three governors devoted space to roads, no more than four short paragraphs, in their messages to the General Assembly. Governor Cullom, in January, 1877, stated that "it is the only disadvantage resulting from our rich and fertile soil, that in many parts of our State the ordinary unworked lanes which serve as public highways are absolutely impassable during a great part of the season when the farmer wants to move his grain and other products to market." The governor suggested "the use of county and municipal credit"[53] to improve the roads, leaving the possibility of state assistance for the legislators to decide. When Governor Fifer brought the matter up again in January, 1893, he undoubtedly expressed the reason why little had been accomplished when he observed "any general system of road improvement will necessitate a large expenditure of money, and if not conducted wisely, it may result in placing upon our people financial burdens heavier than they are able to bear."[54] In his inaugural address five days later, Governor Altgeld completed executive comment when he noted "we are, in this regard, almost where we were half a century ago." Although he suggested that "the state should again take up the matter of internal improvements," he concluded that "wagon roads are to a great extent, a local matter in each county."[55]

Legislation concerning roads reflected this slight interest, and little change was made in the road law of 1841 until 1871, with the appointment of a standing committee of the House on roads, highways, and bridges. Laws in 1872 and 1873 provided for the appointment of county or township commissioners, depending upon local organization. Exceedingly low pay emphasized the fact that these positions were primarily political and ruined any effectiveness these officials might have had in improving roads. Occasionally gold medals and prizes were offered at state fairs for the best road-building machinery, and between 1877 and 1880 a $100 prize was to be given to the township building the greatest mileage of roads each year. Attempts to get something for virtually nothing had little result. However, in 1886 two new laws were passed. The first affected counties under township organization, abandoning the elective overseers provided for in the law of 1873, authorized increased taxes for roads, permitted officials to build permanent roads where possible, and encouraged tile drainage of roadways. The second provided for the construction of "hard roads" by special levy as a result of the vote of the people of any township or county. But the first brick road was not constructed until 1901, and an investigating committee found that by 1900 only twenty-six and one-half miles of macadam road in thirteen counties had been constructed under the "hard roads" law.

To most groups throughout the state, the economic benefits resulting from good roads did not justify the expense involved. This point of view would not change until the automobile definitely replaced the horse as motive power. Farmers' organizations gave little more than lip service to the hard-road idea. Reasoning that their produce eventually reached the railheads, and remembering that they had been burned earlier by purchasing railroad bonds, they refused financial support. Local highway officials were little more than political hacks and opposed a centralized system affecting their jobs. No one of importance suggested an equitable division of the cost between state and local government. And at the end of the period projected electric interurban railroads promised a solution to the problem for the more important rural districts. It remained for another generation to rescue rural travelers from the awesome prairie mud.

1. Shelby Cullom, *Journal of the House*, Jan. 8, 1877, 55.
2. United States Bureau of Census, *Historical Statistics*, 427.
3. *Quincy Whig*, Jan. 8, 1870.
4. *Chicago Times*, Jan. 9, 1870.
5. *Chicago Evening Journal*, May 12, 1872.
6. *Ibid.*
7. *Chicago Evening Post*, Nov. 19, 1870.
8. William K. Ackerman, "Early Illinois Railroads," *Fergus Historical Series*, No. 23 (Chicago, 1884), 109.
9. *Ibid.*
10. *Chicago Times*, July 15, 1872.
11. Walt Whitman, "To a Locomotive in Winter," *Leaves of Grass* (New York, 1931), 475.
12. *Quincy Whig*, March 19, 1870.
13. Pierce, *History of Chicago*, 65.
14. Paul M. Angle and Mary Lynn McCree, eds., *Prairie State: Impressions of Illinois 1673-1967* (Chicago, 1968), 393.
15. *Chicago Evening Post*, May 4, 1870. Illinois Constitutional Convention, *Debates and Proceedings of the Constitutional Convention of the State of Illinois* (Springfield, 1870), 225.
16. *Ibid.*
17. Richard C. Overton, *Burlington Route: A History of the Burlington Lines* (New York, 1965), 117. *Concise Dictionary of American Biography*, V (New York, 1964), 225.
18. *Chicago Evening Post*, March 14, 1870.
19. *Ibid.*
20. *Chicago Times*, March 30, 1870.
21. Illinois, *Laws*, 1869, 316-317.
22. *Chicago Evening Journal*, Dec. 21, 1875.
23. Solon J. Buck, *The Granger Movement: A Study of Agricultural Organization and Its Political, Economic, and Social Manifestations, 1870-1880* (Lincoln, Neb., 1965), 128.

24. *Constitution*, Art. XI, Sec. 15.
25. *Journal of the House*, Jan. 6, 1871, 38.
26. Buck, *Granger Movement*, 133.
27. John Moses, *Illinois, Historical and Statistical*, II (Chicago, 1889-92), 1061.
28. *Journal of the Senate*, Jan. 8, 1873, 15-16.
29. *Chicago Tribune*, Sept. 26, 1873.
30. *Journal of the House*, Jan. 8, 1875, 19-20.
31. *Ibid.*
32. *Munn vs. Illinois*, 94 United States Reports, 113 *et seq.*
33. Illinois Railroad and Warehouse Commission, *Report, 1898* (Springfield, Ill., 1899) iii.
34. J. B. London, *A Tour through Canada and the United States of America* (Coventry, 1879), 72-79.
35. *Illinois State Journal*, July 3, 1878.
36. *Chicago Tribune*, May 18, 1877.
37. *Ibid.*
38. *Chicago Inter-Ocean*, Nov. 16, 1875.
39. Edward C. Kirkland, *Industry Comes of Age: Business, Labor and Public Policy, 1860-1897*, VI (New York, 1962), 80-81.
40. *Railroad Journal*, Vol. 50, 779-781, 811-812.
41. *Journal of the House*, Jan. 30, 1885, 72.
42. Illinois Railroad and Warehouse Commission, *Report, 1898*, iii-iv.
43. Samuel L. Clemens, *Life on the Mississippi* (New York, 1917), 445.
44. *Chicago Tribune*, Dec. 21, 1876.
45. *Chicago Times*, Jan. 31, 1870.
46. Alfred E. Lee, *The National Road* (Indianapolis, 1948), 378.
47. *Ibid.*, 379.
48. *Chicago Evening Journal*, Dec. 10, 1878.
49. *Ibid.*, May 14, 1878.
50. *Chicago Times*, Jan. 12, 1880.
51. *Ibid.*, Jan. 10, 1880.
52. *Ibid.*, Jan. 14, 1880.
53. *Journal of the House*, Jan. 8, 1877, 55.
54. *Ibid.*, Jan. 5, 1893, 34.
55. *Ibid.*, Jan. 10, 1893, 54.

6

Industry: From Chimneys to Smokestacks

Our people are studying more attentively the intimate
and profitable relations between agriculture and
manufactures. To secure the wealth each produces, the
plow, the forge, and the spindle ought to dwell together
on the same prairie. Capital is steadily seeking
investment in our State, and in a few years this new
interest will make us what we ought to be—a
manufacturing as well as an agricultural people.

Richard J. Oglesby[1]

Governor Oglesby's prediction of the industrialization of the prairie state was fulfilled dramatically by the time of his death in 1899. The statistics of industrial growth, if not all of its actual effects, must have been especially satisfying. Between 1870 and 1900, the population of Illinois nearly doubled, while the number of workers in manufacturing quadrupled and the capital invested in industry multiplied over eight times. By 1870, the value of manufactured goods produced in the state nearly equaled that of agricultural commodities, and by 1880 the products of the factories and workshops were valued at more than twice that of the farms. In 1890, the census showed that Illinois ranked third among the states, behind New York and Pennsylvania, as a manufacturing center. In no decade of the period did these states match the industrial growth of Illinois. At the turn of the century, the value of its manufactures had reached a gargantuan $1,260,000,000, more than six times as large as the figure for 1870.

The trend toward factories and heavy industry in Illinois was matched by a national increase in industrial establishments. In 1869 there were 252,148 establishments, including factories and

180

neighborhood and home industries. That number increased to 5,091,490 in 1899.[2] Production in those factories reflected changing economic conditions, as most industries experienced fluctuating productivity.

Between 1865 and 1898 there was no war to distract the state from its obsession with growth. The center of population in the nation moved steadily westward (fifty-eight miles between 1870 and 1880, forty-eight miles the next decade, and fourteen miles in the 1890s) to a point six miles southeast of Columbus, Indiana, by 1900, providing a labor supply and enlarging the midwestern and western markets. The benefits of living at the crossroads of the nation grew with the expansion of the railroad network, and industrially minded people began to exploit the resources for greatness that lay within the borders of the state. Railroads absorbed huge quantities of iron, steel, and coal; they planted cities and connected them to a regional and national market. Chicago, because of its fortuitous location, increased its importance as the marketplace of the area between the Appalachians and the Rockies, supplying the West with mining machinery, boots and shoes, and dry goods, becoming the railroad hub of the nation. Between 1860 and 1900, Chicago's skyrocketing population created an urban market that itself supported continued expansion.

Statistically, downstate Illinois kept pace with the industrial growth of the neighboring state of Indiana. Industrial growth occurred in such cities as Peoria with its massive distilled liquor interests and throughout much of the remainder of the area as the huge coal deposits underlying many counties were opened. St. Louis grew from a population of 160,773 in 1860 to 575,238 people by 1900 and, with a corresponding growth of centers along the Illinois side of the Mississippi River, provided an important market for the products of southern Illinois. Opportunity in both Chicago and downstate attracted ambitious and capable entrepreneurs who won and lost great fortunes to the rise and fall of the business cycle. The General Assembly added its blessing by making the way smooth for independent, unfettered expansion, and in industry there were no attempts at regulation as dramatic or successful as the railroad and warehouse commission. The most significant attempts to impose order, however, came through combination from the industrialists themselves. For interesting data on manufacturing growth see Tables C, D, and E in Appendix.

Before the slowdown caused by the depression of 1873, the elements of the industrial economy emerging from the war were expanded and roughly coordinated. Signs of economic maturity included the creation of the Chicago Clearing House Association in 1865, forming a community of interest, however loose, among the bankers and providing machinery to advance and protect their common interests. The meat-packing industry, boosted by the war, received further impetus and some integration in 1865 when the General Assembly incorporated the Union Stock Yard and Transit Company to manage a cattle yard, a series of branch railroads, a bank, and a hotel. The capital was subscribed by nine railroads. The country's first Bessemer steel rail was made by the Chicago Rolling Mill Company in 1865. In 1869, the North Chicago Rolling Mill Company was incorporated, and it reputedly manufactured one-third of the iron and steel in the nation. One of the first Bessemer converters was built in Joliet in 1873. Coal output in the state increased from 1,078,000 tons in 1865 to 3,920,000 in 1873. Peoria, by 1867, boasted fourteen distilleries and eight breweries, in addition to lesser industries, based on its coal and grain marketing facilities and its supply of unusually fresh and pure water. The National Watch Company, organized in Chicago in 1864, began production in Elgin in 1866. In 1867, the Pullman Palace Car Company was formed with a capital of $1,000,000. And by 1869 Frederick Weyerhauser and C. A. Denkman of Rock Island were operating a lumber mill with an annual capacity of 4,000,000 board feet, and had acquired stumpage (timber but not the land) that was to be the basis of a lumber empire.

During the 1860s, technological innovation, population and market increase, the growth of the factory system at the expense of hand methods of production, and expansion of individual corporations pushed industry in Illinois into a new, modern phase. Industries in which the process of manufacture added most value began to rank in importance with those stressing the simple processing of agricultural products. Governor Oglesby expressed the mood in January, 1867, during his address to the General Assembly. "It is useless to talk of our resources for they are boundless," he said. "Industry, wisely and economically directed, will secure the enjoyment of universal happiness, and our State will become what it was destined to be, the home of the happy."[3]

Economic activity was buoyed by a contagious optimism and faith in industrial growth. Just as they eagerly sought railroads, cities wooed new industries. Cairo was one of many downstate cities that appointed a committee to secure industry from within the United States or abroad by offering free land and a variety of "other encouragements."[4] When the Quincy Improvement Association was organized in 1870, "all the speakers recognized the indispensable necessity of an increase in the number, variety, and extent of our manufacturing establishments, coupled with increased facilities for cheap communication with the sections of the country with which we trade."[5] And four years later, after almost a year of depression, the Quincy Whig observed that "it is a healthy indication that nearly every important town in the State is making extra efforts to secure the location of some manufacturing enterprise."[6] Newspapers proudly printed long lists of patents granted to Illinoisans for a host of gadgetry. The bountifulness of the earth seemed limitless and thrills of excitement, false but typical, spread when silver was reportedly discovered at Rosiclare, gold in Clark County and other places, and copper in Hardin County. When the first rail was turned out of the Union Rolling Mill at Joliet "the event was observed as a gala day."[7] Similar celebrations marked the opening of each coal shaft. Everything seemed possible, and a rural mechanic advertised his ability and willingness, under adequate sponsorship, to bridge the Atlantic. It all seemed justified when the census takers reported manufacturing growth in Illinois in the 1860s showed a 257 percent increase in the value of product, a 243 percent growth in capital, a 261 percent expansion of wage earners, and a 307 percent jump in total wages.

The government, both federal and state, played its greatest role by creating an improved and usable, if somewhat unstable and increasingly inadequate, currency and credit structure. State banks of issue and state bank notes had produced a variety of currency that fluctuated in value and contributed to financial frustration and chaos in the 1850s. In response to the acknowledged weaknesses of state control in an area increasingly sensitive to national pressures and to the need for a uniform currency, the federal government had issued some $450,000,000 in greenbacks under the auspices of the Legal Tender Act of February 25, 1862. State bank notes were eliminated in Chicago by agreement of the city's bankers in 1864, and permanently by a 10 percent tax on them under Section 6 of the Internal Revenue Act of March 3, 1865.

Three types of banks, national, private, and specially chartered state institutions, served the banking needs of Illinois after the war. The National Currency Act of February 25, 1863, established the national banking system. The law required national banks to have one-third of their capital invested in United States securities and empowered them to issue notes up to 90 percent of those holdings.

National banks were given a monopoly of note issue, but the amount in circulation was tied to the national debt instead of more realistic indications of actual wealth. In spite of a brisk political debate over the type and amount of money in circulation, bankers in the large cities and industrialists avoided the problem of limited currency in daily transactions by relying on bank drafts, bills of credit, and various kinds of notes, with little regard to greenbacks, gold, or silver. At the end of the generation, Governor John R. Tanner repeated what everyone knew when he observed that "many times more commercial transactions are based on this kind of currency than on currency authorized by the national government."[8] Outside the big cities, however, business was conducted with bank notes throughout most of the period. By 1865 there were seventy-six national banks in Illinois, and their numbers and influence grew steadily.

The First National Bank of Chicago, the second in the nation to receive its charter, became the leading financial power in the Midwest, and Lymon J. Gage, whose name was synonymous with the bank's, was the most influential banker of the period. He recalled that early in his youth in DeRuyter, New York, "the possibility of earning money appealed to my imagination."[9] Willing to accept any job, he came to Chicago in 1858. In 1868, he began his association with the First National Bank, and by 1871, he was its "Cashier and practically Manager."[10] His judgment and leadership in this position and as an influential member of the Chicago Clearing House Association helped guide the city through the critical periods following the Great Fire of 1871 and the Panics of 1873 and 1893. An excellent judge of men, Gage's loans were based on his evaluation of the character of the borrower rather than his understanding of the enterprise. He was nearly always correct. He backed the high tariff and the gold standard, but he also had the courage to plead for executive clemency for the anarchists convicted of the Haymarket bombing in 1886 and to form the Economic Club, where he exchanged ideas with Socialists and others of less orthodox views. His was as genuine a success story as the city provided; and his prominence grew when he was elected president of the American Bankers Association from 1882 to 1884, founded the Banker's Club in 1883, presided over the group that brought the World's Columbian Exposition to Chicago in 1893, and became president of the First National Bank from 1891 to 1897, when he left Chicago to become Secretary of the Treasury in the McKinley administration.

On the state level in 1865 memories of the 1850s were fresh.

The bankers of Illinois had been tightly enmeshed in politics, unscrupulously maneuvered to benefit a few, and suffered disastrous experiences. The banking system was in transition from that created by the Free Banking Act of 1851, which failed to survive the stress of the war, and that created by the banking law of 1887. Until that year there was no general banking law. Private banks, ephemeral and unregulated, performed a galaxy of functions throughout the state. They constituted the major source of funds for a majority of transactions while the national banks were becoming established. Private banks discounted notes, acted as real estate brokers and financiers, conducted foreign exchange matters, solicited immigrants, engaged in the general banking business, and for a time after the war a few advertised themselves as stockbrokers or dealers in securities. J. Young Scammon and the Marine Bank over which he presided were powers in Chicago financial circles, but many private banks were as temporary as yesterday. They operated in Illinois well into the twentieth century.

Specially chartered state banks were the third variety. Foreseeing the elimination of special legislation by the impending Constitutional Convention of 1869, the General Assembly organized twenty-five banking institutions, two loan and trust companies, and seventy-two insurance companies by special charter in 1867, and sixty-seven banks, fourteen loan and trust companies, and fifty-six insurance companies in 1869. Some of the banks were commercial, some had savings and trust features, some of the insurance companies were empowered to borrow and loan money and become banks, and none of the charters required reports to a state officer. Illinois witnessed the development of a plethora of small banks, even under the national system, with no legal relationship to one another.

The least secure pieces were certain to fall from such a loose and uncoordinated system when it was bumped. The shock came September 13, 1873, with the failure of the Philadelphia banking firm of Jay Cooke and Company, considered the most powerful in the country. When foreign investors rejected bonds supporting the development of railroads and heavy industry, bankers were forced to issue short-term credits while the interest on previously issued securities drained remaining surpluses. Investors in speculative securities went under. On September 24, the Chicago Clearing House Association agreed that its members could suspend payments on large demands, after which only the First National and two other banks continued to meet calls. But on September 26 five national banks, led by the Union National, went into temporary suspension. The liquidation of the latter institution four days later shattered confidence throughout the region. Bank loans were contracted on an average of 25 percent. Heavy industry girded for what turned out to be six lean years, and farm prices spiraled downward.

By the 1880s, state banking institutions had discovered that they could operate profitably despite the federal prohibition on note issue, and there was a demand that the government facilitate their creation. At the same time, it had become necessary for the state to regulate the institutions already created. As a result, the General Assembly passed a general banking law in 1887 which provided that the state auditor receive applications to organize banks and issue a certificate for business after investigation. The auditor had to make annual examinations and receive reports every three months. Stockholders were subject to double liability; the bank was to own no real estate except its own establishment; no more than one-tenth of its capital could be loaned to one borrower; and minimum amounts of capital stock were established for towns of various populations. All banks of special charter were subject to the provision. In 1887, there were twenty-six banks of this sort operating in the state. Acts regulating savings banks and providing for the creation of trust companies were passed in the same year, and together these three laws provided the nucleus of banking legislation well into the twentieth century. Regardless of these efforts, national banks had established a wide margin of dominance by 1900.

The effects of the Panic of 1873 were not disastrous in Illinois. The basis of an industrial economy already existed and commercial interests exploited it as it consolidated. The railroad network, its major outline laid in Illinois, expanded at a more measured pace. The volume of freight increased with each reduction of rates, upholding income. Coal production continued to rise. Technological innovation and mechanization permitted industrialists to lower costs more rapidly than prices fell so that profits were still large enough to create substantial fortunes for many. But failures, although unnerving, were no longer surprising, and they marked the decade. The "savings bank crash," which occurred late in 1877, followed a run on the Union National Bank precipitated by the suicide of its president, William Coolbaugh, on November 14 in front of the Douglas Monument. The event was a shock but accepted as grim reality. Some of the optimism, the automatic happiness, was gone. Yet the decade prepared a firm foundation for future expansion and witnessed impressive economic achievements in spite of hard times.

Although industry and manufacturing showed spectacular increases, the agricultural nature of the state remained a common bond. In 1880, the only enterprise carried on in every county of the state was flouring and grist mill products, and in Scott, Platt, and Menard counties it was the only enterprise. Wages varied widely in this trade, with Scott County's ten employees earning $260 per year, Menard County's twenty-six earning $308 per year, and flourers in Cook County taking home $534 annually. Cook County did not lead the state, however, for Madison County workers averaged $573 per year.

In such selected areas as slaughtering and meat packing and the production of iron and steel, substantial industrial growth was recorded in Illinois in the 1870s. Because of the banking problems and tightness of credit, total capital increased by only 49 percent, the smallest for any decade of the generation. But the value of products grew 102 percent, to a total of $414,864,673, for the state by 1880. Most significant, Chicago began to assert its industrial dominance over downstate in the 1870s. In 1870 approximately 44 percent of the state's value of product came from Chicago, but by 1880 the lake city was producing nearly 60 percent of the total. And, once established, Chicago continued to expand its margin of dominance throughout the generation. In 1870 three of every eight workers in manufacturing were employed there, and by 1900 nearly two of every three worked in Chicago. They earned more on the average in the lake city than downstate. By 1890 more than $2 were invested in manufacturing in Chicago for each $1 downstate (although the figures had been almost even in 1880), the value of products were nearly three times greater in Chicago than the remainder of the state, and the value added by manufacturing was twice as large.

The dominance of Chicago by 1880 shows clearly in the census figures.[11] Cook County boasted 155 separate industries, with tobacco, cigar, and cigarette manufacturers the most numerous with 300 establishments employing 1,512 men, 135 women, and 101 children. Slaughtering employed the most men (7,180), but the women's clothing field remained the county's biggest employer, giving work to 4,118 men, 4,001 women, and 374 children.

Two stamped-ware manufacturers, with a product valued at $20,000, generated the smallest amount of capital, according to the

1880 census figures for Chicago. Other minor industries included one corset firm, two explosive and fireworks plants, two fire extinguisher firms, and two companies for regalia, society banners, and emblems.

Chicago not only dominated the state, it was also fast becoming a recognized national center for industry, ranking third (behind New York and Philadelphia) in gross product, $249,022,948 in 1880. It ranked first in slaughtering, sash doors and blinds, and planed lumber; second in agricultural implements, brick and tile, furniture, iron and steel, and tanned leather; and third in printing and publishing, distilled liquor, foundry and machine shop products, and men's clothing.

By nearly all indexes the premier industry in Illinois was slaughtering and meat packing, with Chicago the most important center in the nation. In 1868 Benjamin P. Hutchinson, whose fortune came from the grain trade, pork packing, banking, and speculation in high wines and whiskey, consolidated several small companies into the Chicago Packing and Provision Company. This company dominated output until the season of 1878-79. The industry in Illinois grew phenomenally during the 1870s from $19,000,000 in 1870 to nearly $98,000,000 for the state by 1880. Nearly 85 percent of this was in Chicago, included beef and related products, and accounted for 34 percent of that city's total value of manufactured product. The census of 1880 recorded that "the concentration of this industry is startling, the single state of Illinois contributing almost one-third of the [nation's] whole, the single city of Chicago producing $85,324,371."[12]

The iron and steel industry, concentrated in the Chicago area, expanded so rapidly that Illinois rose in rank among the states according to production from fifteenth in 1870 to fourth in 1880. Chicago benefited from the cheapness and ease with which the ores from the iron mines of the Lake Superior region were landed at its docks, from the availability of limestone deposits around Lemont, from the low price at which huge supplies of coal from Pennsylvania, Indiana, and downstate Illinois, were available, and from its situation at the center of the great market for rails and other iron and steel products in Illinois and the nation. Although production was not always regular, the capacity of Illinois mills was huge. In the month of April, 1875, for example, the Joliet Iron and Steel Company produced 5,368 tons of steel. According to the *Joliet Signal*, "this immense production surpasses the boasted work of the Troy, New York, Johnstown, Pa., and North-Chi. Mills for the same time by nearly 1,000 tons."[13] In 1880, there were thirteen rolling mills and steelworks in Illinois, three of which were Bessemer steelworks—two at Chicago and one at Joliet—and one was an open-hearth steelworks at Springfield. Seven of the state's ten blast furnaces in that year were in Chicago. By 1880 twenty-one establishments throughout the state turned out a product valued at $20,500,000; eleven of the plants were in Chicago and their products totaled $10,400,000.

Closely related to this basic industry were at least two others that contributed heavily to the total production and character of the entire period. They were agricultural implements and railroad rolling stock. Among the important manufacturers of agricultural implements were the David Bradley Manufacturing Company, the Crover, Steele and Austin Company, William A. Deering and Company, and the F. C. Austin Manufacturing Company, all of Chicago. John Deere, developer of better steel plows, created the Deere Company in 1886 and guided it for fifty years. The company controlled subsidiaries throughout the Midwest, especially the Deere and Manser of Moline, which made corn planters and disk harrows; the Moline Wagon Company, which made farm wagons; and the Union Malleable Iron Company of Moline, which made castings.

Such relatively simple implements as plows, harrows, and rakes could be and were produced in many locations throughout the state, but the quantity manufactured of the more complex harvesters and separators required larger factories, a specialized division of labor, and the production of uniform, interchangeable parts. These establishments clustered in the larger cities, especially Chicago.

The giant of the harvester industry, headquartered in Chicago, was the firm of C. H. and L. J. McCormick. By 1875 the firm was capitalized at $4,000,000 and produced an annual product valued at $2,000,000. The McCormick Harvester cost $175 cash or $185 on time; and the Improved Prize Mower cost $95 cash or $105 on time.[14] In January, 1876, the *Chicago Post and Mail* reported that "the McCormick reaper factory of Chicago turns out on average a complete machine every 12 minutes—five machines every working hour during the year; and more than one-half of them are combined reapers and mowers."[15] The market was huge, and the next spring the same paper observed that "it is cheering the Chicago interest to know that the Texas wheat crop has just been cut with Illinois reapers, and that much of the grain will seek our elevators."[16] In 1879 the company became the McCormick Harvesting Machine Company, controlled by Cyrus Hall McCormick.

As the Chicago area was closely identified with railroads, it was also an important center for the production of railroad cars. Synonymous with the city and the industry was the name of George M. Pullman. He had come to Chicago as a street contractor and won fame in 1858 when with 5,000 jackscrews he rescued the Tremont House, a famous hotel, from sinking in a bottomless pit of mud. Pullman was the complete businessman—inventor, strategist, executive. He directed his energies to producing a sleeping car with maximum comfort for the passenger. Building his cars around the hinged upper berth, he decorated them lavishly at a total cost of $20,000 per car. Others built theirs for $5,000. He made them a foot wider and two and one-half feet higher than other cars, forcing railroads using them to alter bridges and platforms. In response to huge orders, he founded the Pullman Palace Car Company in 1867, and in the 1870s he was shipping cars to England and had opened a shop in Italy. After 1881 the town of Pullman, "the most extensive and perfect industrial undertaking in the country,"[17] embodying the qualities of its namesake—efficiency, economy, control—was made the center of his production. Every aspect of the town, from its parks, lakes, and recreation island to a sewage farm which was fertilized at the rate of one acre to every 100 people, was planned and directed by Pullman and his executive staff. Shops, a hotel, library, and theater lined the well-kept streets, and a magnificent gothic "Green Stone Church" supposedly met the spiritual needs of the workers. Unfortunately, Pullman expected every aspect of his model city to show a profit, and congregations which wished to use the church found themselves unable to pay the $1,200 yearly rental. The savings bank which encouraged thrift also deducted exhorbitant rental on the city's houses and apartments from the paychecks it cashed, and rentals were not lowered when the depression of 1893 brought sharp wage reductions and layoffs.

All kinds of railroad cars, including sleeping, dining, and chair cars as well as freight cars, were built, and great quantities of steel axles and drawbars were supplied to the western roads. The Pullman Company in combination with others in the industry totaled $24,000,000 value of product by 1900.

Chicago demonstrated its versatility and aggressiveness in other areas of production. In this age of iron and steel, foundry and machine shops abounded, producing a variety of products: plumbing fixtures, stoves, and tools for an industrial society. Each city of any size possessed shops of this type. They increased in importance, and by the end of the period their products ranked second in total value in Chicago and in the state itself. Although flour milling remained important to the city, its production failed to match advances made by Minneapolis and St. Louis as the area of wheat production moved west, or to downstate areas closer to output. Chicago remained an important grain distributing center, however. A more profitable industrial use for grain was its distillation into alcohol, and between 1870 and 1890 the value of that product rose from $6,000,000 to over $22,000,000. Although Peoria overshadowed Chicago as a distilling center, Chicago's prominence in the brewing industry grew. Its citizens reportedly consumed forty-nine gallons of malt liquor per capita in1890, and in that year Chicago ranked sixth in the nation among brewing cities.

As a lumber market, Chicago led the cities of the nation. A tremendous expansion in the local market, encouraged by the rebuilding after the fire of 1871, made up for the city's loss of leadership in countrywide sales. More than 98,000 buildings were constructed between 1871 and the depression of 1893, as the forests surrounding the Great Lakes and those of the South and West became dwellings and places of business. Related to the lumber industry were wagon and carriage making. Nine-tenths of the total national production reportedly took place within a 250-mile radius of Chicago in 1879, with a value of products growing to $4,500,000 in 1890, including lumber and planing mill products, baseball bats (turned out in greater numbers by A. G. Spaulding and Brothers than any other firm), and furniture. The printing and publishing business led by the firms of R. R. Donnelly and Sons, Rand McNally and Company, and A. C. McClurg and Company, turned out a product valued at over $29,000,000, which ranked it fourth in the cities in that category. One hundred and forty-nine establishments manufacturing men's ready-to-wear clothing ranked second in the city in value of product, $36,000,000 by 1890. Hides from the slaughterhouses meant that Chicago was a leader in the manufacture of leather goods, and by 1890 it ranked fifth among the shoe manufacturing cities.

Concentration upon sales as well as production was necessary, and Chicago was the center for commercial drummers who hawked their wares in cities and towns throughout the state and region. Twelve thousand of them from forty-four states and six foreign countries paraded in Chicago in July of 1893. The parade may have proved an embarrassment to the *Chicago Times* which had forecast their extinction in 1874. The *Times*'s gloomy warnings came from the discriminatory taxes and clerks' fees charged peddlers by municipalities. "Who now thinks of the rights of the peddlers?," asked the *Times*. "No one."[18] Advertising, flamboyant and aggressive, competed with the knights of the trunk in the period. One enterprising advertiser released thousands of cats with the name of his product attached to their backs, while newspapers were filled with such pronouncements as that explaining the civilized demeanor of Japanese children: "Their discipline is perfect, their manners graceful, and their complexions and general appearance greatly improved by the use of B. T. Babbit's best soap."[19]

New inventions and gadgets seemed limitless in quantity and use. Edison's phonograph ("too startling for the contemplation of any being but God"),[20] condensed milk, aluminum cookware, and James Bryan's "Practicable typewriting machine"[21] which "appeared to [him] in a dream" all came to Illinois, along with Bryon Brothers Coal Hole Cover, Doty Washer and Universal Wringer ("Get them if you have to live on one meal a day"),[22] Baragwanath Steam Jacket Feed-Water Heater and Purifier, and McGee's Hipless Corsets.

Revolutionary in its eventual impact was the introduction in the 1870s of instant communications via the telephone. Reception of the new instrument was often lukewarm at best. In October, 1877, the *Chicago Times* reprinted an article from the *New York Times* entitled "The Dangers which Lurk in an Apparently Harmless and Useful Invention Pointed Out."

> When this notorious instrument was first introduced, it was pretended that its purpose was an innocent one. We were told that the telephone would enable a man in New York to hear what a man in Philadelphia might say; and though it was difficult to understand why anybody would ever want to listen to a Philadelphian's remark . . . there was nothing necessarily immoral in this possible use. . . .
>
> If any telephonic miscreant connects a telephone with one of the countless telegraphic wires that pass over the roofs of this city there will be an immediate end of all privacy. . . . An invention which thus mentally makes silence the sole condition of safety cannot too severely be denounced, and while violence even in self-defense is always to be deprecated there can be little doubt that the death of the inventors and manufacturers of the telephone would do much toward creating that feeling of confidence which financiers tell us must precede any revival of business.[23]

Heedless to the warning, farsighted Illinoisans continued to install the "notorious instrument." In November, 1877, Grier and Company of Peoria installed the city's first business phone, connecting their office with the union elevator. They paid M. M. Buck and Company of St. Louis, western manufacturers of the Bell Telephone, $50-per-year rental. When the first call was made, "the gentlemen in the elevator . . . whistled and sang 'the Battle-cry of Freedom.' There wasn't a dry eye in the entire Board of Trade building when the music was finished."[24]

As the telephone industry continued to connect business to business, city to city, the *Chicago Evening Journal* commented: "The telephone is superseding the telegraph . . . in the central and western portions of Illinois connection is already established between the cities of Urbana and Champaign, Bloomington and Normal, and projected between Rock Island and Moline . . . the use of the telephone for short distances is likely to become general."[25]

The Atlantic and Pacific Telephone Company set up its first line in Chicago in 1877, connecting its main office with the home of John N. Hills in Ravenswood. Hymns from the Moody and Sanky revival proved a spectacular success over the often noisy line. In May, 1878, work was begun on the city's first telephone exchange, and service began on June 26. Within six months 450 businesses and five homes had subscribed to the service. The Bell Telephone Company of Illinois was incorporated in 1878. In 1881 the Chicago Telephone Company bought the Bell company and the American District Telephone Company. (The Chicago Telephone Company would become Illinois Bell in 1936.) By 1882 the system had 2,610 telephones in Chicago and 392 in the suburbs.

Governmental regulation of the burgeoning industry seemed likely, and in 1881 a bill was introduced in the Senate seeking to prohibit telephone companies from consolidating. The *Chicago Tribune* acidly commented, "Senator Tanner proceeded to lock the doors after the horse had been stolen."[26] Private enterprise flourished in the telephone business, however, with massive consolidation not to come until well into the twentieth century. Bell was not yet in control, as evidenced by this ad in the *Illinois Gazeteer* in 1886: "Horbert's Telephone takes the place of Bell telephone on all lines less than two miles in length. Over 2,000 lines in successful operation."[27]

A copper, metallic circuit, private-branch exchange was established in Chicago in 1891. The *Chicago Times* estimated in 1893

"8,500 telephones [are] now in practical use within the city limits. Estimating the population of Chicago to be 1,500,000, this would mean a telephone to every 175 inhabitants."[28]

Telephone company historians present a more sanguine picture:[29]

Year	Number of Phones	Number of Phones Per Capita
1870	499	1 to 1,094
1880	2,971	1 to 169
1890	7,766	1 to 141
1900	34,414	1 to 49

The first downstate exchange opened in Peoria in 1879, and by the end of the year Jacksonville, Quincy, Bloomington, Pekin, Springfield, Moline, Rock Island, Decatur, and Danville all had exchanges. If company statistics are accurate, Illinois was considerably better supplied with telephones than the rest of the United States. Census figures show 3,000 telephones in use in 1876, or 0.1 per 1,000 persons. By 1900 there were 1,356,000 telephones in use, or 17.6 per 1,000 persons.[30]

Long distance calling began in 1881, and by 1886, sixty-three "toll stations" in nine Chicago suburbs enabled callers to talk to the big city. Most toll stations were located in drugstores, with the druggist computing the charge for the call. Alexander Graham Bell himself made the first New York-Chicago call in 1892. The toll came to $9. Lincoln's son, Robert Todd Lincoln, served as director of the Chicago Telephone Company from 1889 to 1919, and held a brief term as president pro tem of the company in 1897.

In 1880 the United States census listed one Illinois telephone enterprise among the forty in the country. Capitalized at $2,000, the firm employed sixteen men producing a product valued at $5,700. Under occupations, the 1890 census listed 3,785 men and 548 women as telephone and telegraph operators, and 667 men and 84 women as telephone and telegraph linemen and electric light and power company employees. Growth in the 1890s compelled the census takers to separate telephone and telegraph operators into separate categories. By 1900 male telephone operators were fast becoming anachronisms, and were outnumbered 463 to 1,401.

Coinciding with the introduction of the telephone and telegraph was the introduction of electric lights. In 1877 the electric arc light was hailed by the *Chicago Tribune* as "the only light that will be used in large rooms, public places and manufactories." The *Tribune* quoted a German paper as saying, "we are evidently on the eve of a great revolution in lighting as when gas superseded oil lamps and tallow."[31]

In 1880, the *Chicago Times* facetiously announced the solution not only to the high cost of generating electricity, but to the racial problem as well. Noting the electric sparks produced by the "action of the whip on the natives' naked skin," Mr. R. W. Hitchinson brought a discovery back from Central Africa. His theory was that "a very light touch, repeated several times, under certain conditions of bodily excitement, and in certain states of the atmosphere would produce a succession of sparks from the bodies of natives." Hitchinson concludes, "the using of the nigger for the purpose of producing cheap electricity comes like a happy inspiration. It supplies one of the most urgent wants of the period, and at the same time, it wholly relieves the country of consideration as to what shall be done with the negro to prevent him from [*sic*] undergoing extermination."[32]

Mr. Hitchinson's theory, despite its exposure in the *Times*, did not perceptively hurt the Edison Light Company. A holder of 200 shares in 1879 disdainfully turned down an offer of $800,000, refusing to sell for less than $1,000,000. "These shares," remarked the *Chicago Times*, "cost him a few months ago $6,600."[33] The Supreme Court confirmed the Edison Patent in 1893, with consequent battles with such competing companies as Westinghouse and Sunbeam.

In 1890 electric company linemen and employees were lumped with telephone and telegraph linemen in the census returns. By 1900 they had gained a separate listing, with 446 men and 46 women employed.

Shoppers in Chicago had a choice of numerous palatial stores. By 1890 the list included John V. Farwell and Company, rated as the third wholesale drygoods house in the country by volume of business, Carson, Pirie and Company (they added Scott in 1891), which advertised a line of the finest products from foreign countries, or Mandell Brothers, which since 1874 offered its growing selection of goods to mail-order purchasers. But the two merchants whose fame was most widespread were Marshall Field and Aaron Montgomery Ward. Field began his career in Chicago as a dry goods clerk in 1856, became general manager of the store in 1861, a partner the next year, and in 1865 started a wholesale-retail firm in partnership with Potter Palmer and Levi Leiter. Temporary setbacks occurred with the loss of the store in the Great Fire of 1871, and the destruction by fire of the retail store in 1877. In rebuilding, under Field's guidance, the firm established a policy which became its trademark throughout the nation, "the customer is always right." Quality goods were obtained as cheaply as possible through buyers residing abroad or from the firm's own factories, and transactions were strictly cash. The wholesale and retail business totaled $24,700,000 in 1881 when the firm on the withdrawal of Leiter became Marshall Field and Company. In 1893 the company opened a splendid new store on Wabash Avenue, and did a $3,500,000 business. Field, silent and single-minded, a force unto himself in the city, was the personification of economic success and power.

Aaron Montgomery Ward had been a clerk with Field and Leiter for two years and a traveling salesman after the war. In this capacity he became alert to farmers' complaints about low prices for their produce and high prices for retail goods. In 1872 Ward and George R. Thorne began a business, capitalized at $2,400, based on the idea of purchasing goods in large quantities directly from the manufacturer and selling, on approval, for cash directly to the farmer. In 1873 to 1874 the Grange began stocking their cooperative stores with goods from Wards, and the name became a byword to farmers. By 1886 his famous *Buyer's Guide* totaled 304 pages of salable articles, and by 1888 the firm was doing over $1,000,000 of business annually.

Technological improvements affected almost every aspect of life in Illinois—including the newspapers published and read through the state. The introduction of stereotype plates in 1861 meant that single-column rules were no longer necessary to hold the type onto the press cylinders. White-space and double-column ads began appearing after 1871, but news headlines clung to the traditional one column, with several decks, often with a dozen different type faces, roman, boldface, capitals, lower case, and italics, with the last deck sometimes reading simply, "etc., etc., etc."[34] Probably the most notorious of the multiple deck heads appeared in the *Chicago Times* over a story telling of two executions:

JERKED TO JESUS

FOUR SENEGAMBAIN BUTCHERS WERE
WAFTED TO HEAVEN ON YESTERDAY
FROM SCAFFOLDS

TWO OF THEM, IN LOUISIANA, DIED
WITH THE SWEET CONFIDENCE
OF PIOUS PEOPLE

WHILE YET TWO OTHERS, IN MISSISSIPPI
EXPIRED EXHORTING THE PUBLIC TO
BEWARE OF SISTERS-IN-LAW[35]

In 1863 William Bulluck introduced the first web-perfecting press. It printed (perfected) both sides of the paper simultaneously, with the paper coming from a continuous roll which was cut and folded into pages after printing. R. Hoc Company developed a more efficient web press in 1871, and Mergenthaler introduced the Linotype in 1887.

More important to individual subscribers was the introduction of an efficient method of turning wood pulp into paper to replace the rag paper then in use. Prices of newspaper stock dropped from twenty-two cents per pound in 1863 for 100 percent rag paper to eight and one-half cents per pound for a rag-pulp mixture in 1874. By the 1880s rag stock was virtually eliminated from newspaper use. The savings was passed to the reader, with the *Chicago Daily News* becoming the first midwestern paper to sell for one cent in 1876. The *Chicago Tribune* gradually dropped its price from five cents to one cent in 1895.

In 1880 Illinois listed 243 printing and publishing establishments employing 3,650 men, 531 women, and 531 children, with a total value of product of $7,114,939. Only New York, Pennsylvania, and Massachusetts exceeded these figures. Figures in 1900 showed a healthy increase, with 2,450 men and 240 women listed as journalists, 653 men and 9 women as newspaper carriers, and 13,653 men and 1,210 women as printers, lithographers, and pressmen.

After 1880 the slaughtering and meat-packing industry in Chicago grew in importance and was dominated by "the Big Three" of packing: Philip D. Armour, Gustavus Swift, and Nelson Morris. These giants of enterprise pioneered in technological advances and were master tacticians on the grand scale, concentrating more upon growth and integration than coordination. In addition to unquestioned economic and commercial ability and acumen, these men shared the luck of being at the right place at the appropriate time. Chicago happened to be between the huge supply of western livestock only recently tapped by the railroads and the great hungry markets of the eastern United States and of Europe. As Louis F. Swift observed of his father, he appeared "at a time and place which made his every stroke count for two or ten thousand times the strokes of men who came before or will come after."[36]

Nelson Morris, Gustavus Swift, and Philip Armour succeeded quickly in Chicago. Morris parlayed a five-dollar-a-month job in the stockyards in the 1850s and a trade in dead and disabled stock into his own business by 1859. Army contracts during the Civil War made him a millionaire by 1865, and in 1890 his personal fortune was estimated at $8,000,000. Philip D. Armour rose from a day laborer in California before the war to Milwaukee, where he became a partner in the Plankington and Armour packing plant, to Chicago in 1875, from where he soon dominated packing and grain storage interests in most of the urban centers of the nation. Armour's wealth was estimated at $25,000,000 in 1890 and his net worth at $12,000,000 by the depression of 1893. By that year his business, in which his son, J. Ogden, had become a partner in 1884, employed over 20,000 men in Chicago, Omaha, and Kansas City, and the packer declared that the wages he paid fed more people than any other man. Gustavus F. Swift, the "Yankee of the Yards," also appeared in Chicago in 1874, having risen from employment in a butcher shop to independent meat dealer, to wholesaler in cattle, with wide experience and respectable trade in meats. Building from the profits from a pioneering trade in dressed beef to the East after 1877 and upon his tremendous desire to expand, Swift incorporated in 1885 with a capitalization of $300,000, recapitalized in 1886 at $3,000,000, and by 1893 the concern boasted capital of $15,000,000.

The packers in a fashion typical of industry during the period borrowed heavily to finance their enterprise. They approached banks throughout the Midwest and the East, and on the basis of character and general reputation secured funds, often in exchange for nothing more than a promissory note. According to Louis Swift there was "hardly a bank east of Ohio and north of Virginia which did not have a Swift note or two—whether it was a large bank with five hundred thousand dollars or a small bank with fifteen hundred. But in the widely-scattered indebtedness lay an unlikelihood of its all being called in at the same time."[37] Armour borrowed heavily and reinvested the great majority of his profits into his business. He added to his resources by speculating in grain and conducting successful corners on the pork market in 1879, 1880, and 1884, the latter two deals earning him a profit of over $10,000,000.

When Swift began shipping dressed beef eastward by re-frigerator car in 1877, the *Chicago Tribune* noted: "A new staple is added to the American market, for the handling of which Chicago will be the center, as for breadstuffs, and lumber, and packed meats. The industry of stock raising will be increased to an extent that will virtually constitute a new industry. . . . For the people of Great Britain the supply of fresh meats at prices which will enable the laboring classes to use them almost as freely as the laboring classes of our own country will prove an inestimable blessing."[38]

By the mid-1880s, four businesses, Swift, Armour, Morris, and George H. Hammand and Company, who made the "Big Three" the "Big Four," used some 1,500 refrigerator cars. The plants themselves, however, remained large consumers of ice cut from the rivers and lakes and stored until summer. In six weeks at the close of the year 1880 Armour and Company alone "put away in their ice house four thousand one hundred car loads of ice, in all fifty-eight thousand tons."[39]

Markets were sought aggressively if not systematically. It was enough for the packers to realize they existed. Agents sold meat or were replaced. In opening the New York market, Swift simply sent a salesman to the city with instructions to sell the meat that would follow him in increasing carloads each week. He sold it. When wholesalers of meat were not successful enough in moving his products, Armour set up forty branch offices to sell directly to retailers. Swift always gave a dealer handling competitors' products a chance to join him. "If you'll handle my beef," he remarked, "we'll be partners. If you won't handle my beef, I'll put it in against you."[40] It was an offer they could not refuse.

Nelson Morris owned the distinction of opening trade in live cattle and dressed beef with the British Isles in 1868. In 1877 the London correspondent of the *Chicago Evening Journal* reported that American beef was selling at three pence per pound cheaper than the English product, and that it was "greedily bought by housekeepers."[41] By the mid-1880s, all the major packers were in the exporting business, and in 1885 Armour alone exported some 2,500,000 pounds of compressed beef to the British government for its Nile expedition. The abundance of the product in the Sudan seemed to have turned the tide of battle and elicited the observation that while "The prophet had a host of Khans,/ And some were brave and able;/ But then you see, they couldn't win—/ They lacked the Armour Label."[42]

Technological innovations and the packers' abhorrence of waste led them to find uses for the whole animal and to develop related industries turning waste products into by-products. At the end of the period the census takers noted that:

> The flesh is sold as meat, the blood is dried and sold for clarifying purposes, the entrails are cleaned and made into sausage casings, the hoofs are turned into neats-foot oil, the parings of the hoofs, hides, and bones are converted into glue, the finest of the fats are turned into butterine, lard, oils, and the finest tallow, the cruder fats are made into soap grease, the hides are marketed for the manufacture of leather, the horns are sold to comb makers, the larger bones are used for the making of knife handles and for other purposes, the switches and tail ends are sold to hair mattress makers, and the short hair which cannot be dried and curled for sale is sold to felt works.[43]

Swift's "long suit," according to his son, "was keeping expenses down. Next in his interest, perhaps, came developing by-products—which is another form of the same thing."[44] Waste through carelessness was enough to cost any worker or manager his job, and under the sleepless vigilance of the packers little waste occurred.

This tremendous source of wealth and growth could not escape criticism and controversy. The packers consumed everything that entered their places of business except the smell and filth of their raw materials which sullied the air and the Chicago River to the constant annoyance of the Chicagoans. Content to leave the packers to their gargantuan struggles, ordinary citizens could not escape the stink of the yards and packinghouses, and the *Chicago Tribune* on April 7, 1877, underlined the obvious when it wrote "that the entire drainage from all the stockyard establishments is carried into a fork of the South Branch of the city limits and there it accumulates, has accumulated, stinks, and will stink until such time as removed."[45] In winter a mountain of fat collected on the ice, occasionally caught fire, and floated majestically away to the hazard of riverside establishments. Employment tended to be seasonal, and at best the packers shared the dominant attitude among employers that labor was simply a factor of production. Safety measures in the plants were virtually unknown, and horrible accidents were too frequent. Labor trouble around the yards was common. Among their products, oleomargarine, called butterine, suine, or oleo, faced constant attack.

Because some packers marketed an unsavory product, the General Assembly passed an act on May 31, 1879, requiring both the manufacturer and the seller to label the product specifically according to content. Additional legislation in 1881 prohibited food adulteration generally, and required that oleo and related products be labeled with their true names and proportion of ingredients. Foreign exports, especially pork, fell off to Germany, France, and England in the early 1880s because of the reputed inferiority of the product.[46] A commission appointed by President Chester A. Arthur in 1883 to investigate conditions in the packing industry reported that the attacks on American pork from abroad were slanderous, but exports did not show marked increase until after inspection began in the Chicago plants in 1891. Yet as the final decade of the period opened, the industry concentrated in Chicago clearly had established a national and international dominance. By 1900 the industry "gave employment to 27,861 wage-earners, or 7.1 percent of the wage earners employed in the state, and the products were valued at $287,922,277, or 22.9 percent of the total value of the products of the state."[47]

No state had two such cities as Chicago, and yet even without Chicago, downstate Illinois compared favorably with the entire neighboring state of Indiana in industrial output. A marked advantage appeared in per capita value, illustrating the relatively greater size and mechanization of industry west of the Wabash. By 1870 the leading downstate counties in gross value of products were Peoria ($8,000,000), St. Clair ($7,000,000), Adams ($5,000,000), Rock Island ($5,000,000), Madison ($5,000,000), and Kane ($4,000,000). Flouring mill products led in value in each of the counties mentioned, except Kane and Rock Island, where they ranked second. In Rock Island the production of agricultural implements was most important, and in Kane County the manufacture of freight cars led. Each county produced machinery, iron products, castings, or forged and rolled iron in significant quantity. Carriage and wagon building were important to each county. Distilled liquor production ranked second in Peoria County, fifth in Rock Island County, and the brewing of malt liquors ranked fifth in St. Clair County. The production of watches earned third rank in Kane County.

By 1900 the ten leading counties outside Cook in gross value of product in millions of dollars were Peoria ($49,700,000), St. Clair ($41,900,000), Will ($20,800,000), Kane ($21,400,000), Madison ($18,500,000), Rock Island ($15,900,000), Winnebago ($13,600,000), LaSalle ($13,000,000), Tazewell ($12,500,000), and Adams ($9,600,000). Totals for each county came, for the most part, from one or two manufacturing cities within its borders. In Peoria County, the city of Peoria, ranking second only to Chicago as a trading center, accounted for $48,800,000 of the total value of products, and of this $26,700,000 came from the distilled liquor industry. (The total value of distilled liquors for Peoria in 1870 had been $2,100,000, all of this accomplished with a work force averaging 213 persons.) The city was ideally located for this industry in the center of the corn belt, over a rich bed of coal, and near an abundant supply of excellent water of a uniform temperature for cooling mash. High excise taxes, as much as $2.00 per gallon in 1866, 70¢ in 1872, and to $1.10 in 1894, encouraged concentration of the industry in a few large distilleries. (Federal revenue collected from the "Whiskey Trust" in 1890 on a ninety-cents-a-gallon tax totaled $23,126,589.20). A heavy export trade to Europe had developed in the 1870s, but this market dried up by 1880 because of increased European output and discriminatory duties against the American product. High taxes and overproduction led to the formation of a pool in 1881 and the Distillers and Cattle Feeders Trust in 1887 to limit output and maintain prices. As a result of Peoria's capacity, Illinois led the nation in the manufacture of distilled liquors by 1890, producing one-quarter of the world's supply. Cooperage or barrel making was a related industry, with a product valued over $1,300,000, and thousands of cattle fed from the cooled mash after distillation. In addition Peoria ranked fourth in the nation as a center of production of malt liquors. The production of agricultural implements in Peoria was a $2,300,000 industry in 1900.

The two Illinois counties opposite St. Louis, St. Clair, with industry centering about the cities of Belleville and East St. Louis, and Madison, with manufacturing primarily in the cities of Alton, Edwardsville, and Granite City, supported an industrial complex by 1900. The area contributed a large production in foundry and machine shop products, a growing iron and steel industry, slaughtering and meat packing (the National Stock Yards at East St. Louis was sending 240,000 head of cattle east yearly by 1876), glass making, brewing, and the manufacture of wood pulp. Much of this production was due to the proximity of the St. Louis market and the region's abundant supply of coal.

Joliet accounted for nearly the entire manufacturing output of Will County, and $13,000,000 of that was concentrated in the iron and steel industry, which began to grow in the city in the mid-1870s. In Kane County, Elgin was an important center of dairy products, printing and publishing, and watch making, while Aurora had a large foundry and machine shop concentration and was important for the repair of railroad cars. Rock Island had long been a center of the lumber industry, developed primarily through the efforts of Frederick Weyerhauser and C. A. Denkman who, until they moved their offices to St. Paul in 1891, based a lumber empire in the city. By 1893 the firm owned "more standing pine than any other body or corporation in the northwest."[48] Moline had produced agricultural implements in significant quantity since the John Deere and Company plow works moved there from Grand Detour in 1847; the Barnard and Lease Manufacturing Company had opened a farm machine works at Moline in 1860; and the Moline Plow Company was formed in 1865. Rockford in Winnebago County had a varied industrial output, including furniture, hosiery and clothing, and agricultural implements.

Many towns had at least one industry that gave them some prominence. For example, DeKalb was the home of the Barbed Fence Company, established by the inventor of barbed wire, Joseph Glidden. According to the daily *Inter-Ocean*, on December 15, 1875, "they are working up a fine trade on the Pacific slope and have an order today from one point in Texas for 200 spools. This fence can be made for about 60¢ per rod of wire, and marvelously cheap. It is astonishing what fresh impetus this one manufactory has given to business in DeKalb."[49] (The *Inter-Ocean* sent a reporter, who signed his many articles "The Rambler," to dozens of communities downstate in 1875 to report on their industrial progress.)

Downstate Illinois contributed two broad categories of materials that in many ways influenced the state's industrial character. The first was its agricultural products, valued at some $285,000,000 in 1900, which were produced by commercial farmers, and helped supply the industries of milling, slaughtering and meat packing, distilling and brewing. Farmers provided a market for agricultural implements and many of the other products of the factories.

The utilization of the almost limitless supply of bituminous coal underlying downstate counties provided the power for many of the industries of the state. Coal mining developed rapidly in the 1860s as the railroads provided necessary means to tap interior fields, as the locomotives began to burn coal, and as factories and homes increased their demand for the product. The establishment of the Bessemer process of steel manufacture in the 1870s permitted Illinois coal, chemically unsuited for blast-furnace fuel, to be used in the steel industry. The potential of the vast amounts of coal in Illinois led the state geologist to observe in 1886 that the abundance of Illinois' coal would inevitably propel the state to the forefront in commerce and industry now that the steam engine had become indispensable. Production first reached 1,000,000 tons in 1864, 5,000,000 by the end of the 1870s, 15,000,000 by 1890, and the high for the period was 20,072,758 in 1897. From 1880 the five counties of St. Clair, Sangamon, Madison, Macoupin, and Vermillion were consistently among the ten leading coal-producing counties. By 1898 there were five counties producing over 1,000,000 tons a year. They were Sangamon (1,700,000), St. Clair (1,600,000), Vermillion (1,500,000), LaSalle (1,600,000), and Macoupin (1,200,000). The total value of this product was $14,500,000.

Each new vein of coal opened seemed to promise new wealth and life to areas otherwise passed over by the industrial revolution. Cannons were fired, bands played, and general celebrations were held. The event meant jobs for immigrants who had been miners in Europe, and it meant the possibility of bringing over additional members of the family to find employment in the mines.

Until 1870, coal mining centered about such cities as Alton, Peoria, Rock Island, and Springfield, primarily to supply the local market. Immediately following the war, St. Clair County was the traditional leader in output because of its proximity to the St. Louis market, while the Chicago market received its coal by water from the east. Coal-burning locomotives consumed much of the total produced in the state. But with the extension of the railroad network, and the lowering of rates in the 1880s, the mining industry began to move into the central and southern counties. These areas could now compete for the St. Louis and Chicago markets, which consistently consumed some two-thirds of the total coal mined in the state. These ready supplies of coal attracted additional industries to the cities. In 1870, for example, the ten counties supplying St. Louis and Chicago produced 65.5 percent of the coal mined in a total of thirty-seven counties.

Large shipping mines operated on a small margin of profit but a tremendous volume replaced local enterprises in importance. By 1890, they comprised only one-third of the total number of mines, but produced 93 percent of the state's coal. The Chicago, Wilmington, and Vermillion Coal Company's mines in the Streator district were responsible for LaSalle County's importance in the northern field. The Wilmington District in the northern field extended through portions of Will, Grundy, and Kankakee counties and centered about Braidwood and Braceville, sixty to seventy miles from the Chicago market; it was developed by the Chicago, Wilmington and St. Paul Railroad Company. In Vermillion County, with mining operations concentrated around Danville, and the

Chicago market, opened by the Chicago, Danville, and Vincennes Railroad, production was dominated by the Ellsworth Coal Company, the Grape Creek Coal Company, and after 1890, the Consolidated Coal Company of St. Louis.

Mining in the central field, served by increasing numbers of railroads, expanded dramatically in the counties of Sangamon, Macoupin, and Madison because of the quality of the coal and because they were tributaries to the St. Louis market. The mines of Mt. Olive-Staunton area originally under the control of the Ellsworth Coal Company dominated production. St. Clair County continued to lead the southern field, supplying St. Louis with fuel for heating homes and with a coal of low sulfur content to reduce the iron ore of Pilot Knob and Iron Mountain, Missouri, to pig metal. Mining activities had begun in Perry, Randolph, and Jackson counties, but the southern field had not yet gained the prominence it would in the twentieth century.

Coal formed at least 10 percent of the volume of freight of railroads in Illinois, and on many of the lines over one-half of the freight was coal. In its annual report for 1871, the St. Louis, Alton and Terre Haute Railroad Company noted the increasing demand for coal, both for manufacturing and fuel, and planned to foster this potential source of important railroad revenue. By the mid-1880s, bituminous coal from Illinois had replaced the eastern product in the big-city markets. Chicago and St. Louis became important centers of trans-shipment of coal supplies to the west and northwest.

By the end of the period, the industry had virtually assumed the pattern it was to retain in the twentieth century. Overproduction had led to the formation of large companies whose directors reported from the market centers of St. Louis and Chicago. Mechanization, the undercutting machine, for example, which could do the work of six men, had been introduced to cut costs and increase efficiency. The central and southern fields were contesting for the Chicago market, as well as that of St. Louis. Coal had established itself as third in volume of product behind manufactures and agriculture, insuring a supply of fuel for the industrial expansion. And towns with names of Coal City, Coalton, Coal Valley, Glen Carbon, and Kingston Mines hinted that a unique way of life, more important to miners than managers, existed in Illinois.

With the expansion of production that took place in the 1880s came sharp competition for markets among the manufacturers. Endless attempts were made to reduce the effects of this constant struggle within the various industries by controlling production and maintaining prices. Illinois firms experimented with each of the classic sequence of devices meant to abandon clawing competition. Informal gentlemen's agreements proved unworkable even for short terms. Illinois firms then became members of exact, but legally unenforceable, divisions of business called pools, including the Western Pig Iron Association, the Western Wagon Makers Association, and the Chicago and Milwaukee Breweries Association. When these proved ineffective, industrialists resorted to trusts or contracts that placed the voting stock of several companies in the hands of "trustees." Holding companies, paper corporations absorbing the legal identities of several companies, followed in the succession of integrating devices. The most significant movement toward economic order was finance capitalism. This phenomenon resulted from the accumulation of capital in the hands of a few American and European financiers, enabling them to dominate their own investment markets, and the industrialists' willingness to accept outside or banker leadership in the 1890s when their credit needs increased just as the economy was entering a period of depression.

In a bewildering rush, often changing from one form of incorporation and integration to another overnight, the important industries in Illinois consolidated. Peoria was the location of the offices and the majority of the production of the Distillers and Cattle Feeders Trust organized on May 10, 1887, to control American production. Capitalized at $30,000,000, three-fourths of which was water, the trust originally included twenty-four distilleries in Illinois: twelve in Peoria, five in Chicago, three in Pekin, and one in each of the cities of Sterling, Lebanon, Canton, and Riverton. (By 1889 the number of distilleries was down to twelve, six of which were in Peoria.) Joseph B. Greenhut, a former stablehand, was elected president of trustees and headed the combination until its demise in 1898. Prominent industrialists were connected with the business throughout its history, including such men as Nelson Morris, a trustee for a time, who also had thousands of cattle feeding on the wet corn mash after the process of distillation had taken place. Pressure was put on independent distillers to join the trust, and there was strong evidence that the combine was connected to the bombing of the distillery of H. H. Shufeldt and Company of Chicago on December 10, 1888, because of that firm's aloofness from the organization.

Because the word "trust" had acquired an unfortunate onus, the

"Whiskey Trust" incorporated under Illinois law as the Distilling and Cattle Feeding Company in 1890. But because the organization continued to utilize some of the more unfortunate practices in its power, such as granting rebates to those who purchased its product, it came under widespread suspicion in the state and nation. In 1893 the Illinois General Assembly authorized a sweeping inquiry into the company's activities, and a similar investigation was conducted by the House of Representatives. The committee of the latter group decided that the practices of the company were beyond federal authority, while the General Assembly's committee recommended dropping all charges against the company and resting the state's case on *quo warranto* proceedings filed by the Attorney General of Illinois, M. T. Maloney, on May 13, 1893, in the Circuit Court of Cook County. The state asked authority to cancel the company's certificate of incorporation, charging that it had exceeded its powers under the charter, that it destroyed competition, that it was generally repugnant to public policy, and that it was illegal. The state's case was sustained by the circuit court and upheld by the Illinois Supreme Court in June, 1895. Because of its loose financial practices, the company had gone into receivership earlier in the year. In August, 1895, the remains of the shattered empire were put together under the name of the American Spirits Manufacturing Company.

On May 1, 1889, the Illinois Steel Company was formed, combining the North Chicago Rolling Mill Company, the Union Iron and Steel Company, and Joliet Steel Company, including blast furnaces on the south branch of the Chicago River. At its formation, it was believed to have the largest steel production capacity in the world. The company was capitalized at $50,000,000 in 1891, owned ore and coal deposits, stone quarries, and transportation facilities. In 1892 its net earnings were $2,019,268. (By 1890 the value of product of the iron and steel industry in Illinois surpassed $39,000,000.) At the close of the period in 1898, and typical of the consolidation of the 1890s, Elbert H. Gary, a former county judge, formed the Federal Steel Company, made up of the Illinois Steel Company, Minnesota Iron Company, Lorraine Steel Company of Lorraine, Ohio, and Johnstown, Pennsylvania, and the Chicago Outer Belt Railroad. This huge undertaking, capitalized at $200,000,000, marked the way of the new century and controlled much of the production in the West.

In 1886 the Consolidated Coal Company of St. Louis was formed, uniting seventy-one mines in the five counties of Vermil-

lion, Madison, Clinton, Macoupin, and St. Clair. Combination occurred in the production of harvesters in 1890 when the leading
manufacturers led by Cyrus McCormick, William Deering, and
others formed the National American Harvester Company, with a
capital of $35,000,000, employing 50,000 men, and producing
350,000 machines a year. The Elgin Watch Company reportedly
was purchased by an English syndicate in 1890, and in the same
year the Chicago Junction Railways and Urban Stockyards Company, a New Jersey corporation, took control of the Union Stock
Yard and Transit Company by acquiring 98 percent of the stock.
Five of the ten directors were from the East, four from London,
and one from Chicago.

Consolidation was evident not only in industry in the 1890s, but
also in banking, with the organization of the Illinois State Bankers
Association in 1890, the Private Bankers Association in 1891, and
their unification in 1894 under the previous name. The largest
banks, such as the First National of Chicago, increased dramatically
in size and influence. These efforts did not evolve smoothly, however, and competition and jagged fluctuation in the business cycle
continued into the twentieth century.

As industry grew and attempted to replace competition with
order by forming larger and larger combinations, pools, and trusts,
the government encouraged growth by attempting to assure order
in the banking and financial community, by failing to enforce the
property tax equitably, and by passing unenforceable antitrust laws
aimed at placating those who saw abuses in the huge industrial
complexes.

In 1891, Illinois followed the example of the federal government
by enacting an antitrust law which prohibited corporations, part-
nerships, individuals, or any association of persons from entering
into any pool, trust, or agreement to regulate prices or to fix limits
on the quantity of any article manufactured, mined, produced, or
sold in Illinois. Although the courts held that any corporation
doing business in Illinois, whether chartered in the state or elsewhere, was subject to the law, it was no more effective than its
national counterpart before 1898.

For example, in 1893, when a customer refused to pay his bill to
the Milk Shippers Association, a body incorporated under the laws
of Illinois which controlled the distribution of milk in the Chicago
area (and thereby raised its price), the appellate court in the
Chicago district held "that individuals have a right to combine by
forming corporations, that being in fact the main purpose of cor-

poration laws. To such a case, therefore, the anti-trust act was inapplicable."[50] The law did, however, express the increasing concern in the state with the problems of monopoly and price fixing. Yet the state was ineffective in regulation, and through its inaction in such areas as the equitable collection of taxes encouraged expansion. Governor Altgeld pointed out in 1897 that the Pullman Company was assessed at $1,500,000 instead of $8,000,000, at great savings to the company and expense to the citizens.

In his inaugural address in January, 1893, Governor Altgeld summarized the general prosperity of Illinois in the previous twenty years. "The richness of our soil has attracted husbandmen from all quarters of the globe. Our great mineral resources and central location have drawn the manufacturers of almost every kind of goods; great railroads transverse nearly all parts of the state; while, owing to the push and enterprise of our people, our commercial interests are scarcely rivaled in the world."[51] The tremendous growth of the 1880s, the greatest of the entire period, certainly justified his statement. But within months of Altgeld's inauguration, the nation was stricken by the worst depression in two decades, the full effects of which in Illinois were delayed and then multiplied by the closing of the World's Columbian Exposition at the end of October. As in 1873, the stability and optimism of the economy in 1893 was reflected in the activities and fate of the banks.

On the evening of Monday, May 8, the Chemical National Bank of Chicago, holding the deposits of the World's Columbian Exposition exhibitors, suddenly suspended operations. Confidence was restored somewhat when wealthy citizens, George M. Pullman and Martin A. Ryerson, among others, gave guarantees against losses. But within less than a week, the Columbia National Bank and its affiliate, the United States Loan and Trust Company, the nucleus of an unstable empire daringly managed by Zimri Dwiggins, died as recklessly as they had lived.[52] This "ugly blow to confidence" was followed on June 3 by the failure of the financial house of Herman Schaffner and Company which had made large loans to speculators in street-railway stocks for which the market had disappeared. Schaffner hired a boat and rowed out into Lake Michigan to his death. When a run began on the Illinois Trust and Savings Bank, Marshall Field and P. D. Armour announced that their offices would provide full payment for depositors. The extent of the jitters caused by these events was reflected in the order by the Chicago Police Department to arrest newsboys shouting about bank failures.

But the failures continued in spite of the Chicago banks under the leadership of Gage and the First National who imported gold directly from London and called in loans. Between May 4 and October 4, 1893, Chicago banks reduced loans nearly 27 percent, some 12 percent more than the national average. Chicago bankers reduced their balances in New York and refused to purchase New York exchange, but by the end of July, the large banks in the city, weakened by country banks having withdrawn their deposits, authorized their representatives in the Chicago Clearing House Association to issue clearing house certificates for the first time in Illinois history. But this device, evidence of ultimate disaster to many, was never used. By August, twenty-four banks other than national institutions had failed throughout the state. On the first day of the month, the wheat corner engineered by Michael Cudahy collapsed, and the bottom fell out of the market as eight of the most influential operators on the Board of Trade joined Cudahy in bankruptcy. Business failures were up 30 percent over 1892, and liabilities rose from $2,600,000 in 1892 to $18,700,000 in 1893. This index was to remain discouragingly high throughout the decade, even though the general level of assets in Illinois was higher than the nation's average.

Although crop yields in Illinois were consistently good and production figures in major industries rose during the decade, ruinously low prices led to business failures, increased consolidation, and high rates of unemployment. Per capita wages were down 5 percent in the 1890s compared with the previous decade. And the overall growth rate in every index slowed drastically over the 1880s.

By 1893, it was obvious that the state of Illinois was no longer immune from the economic and financial fate of the entire nation. It was equally certain that the government in Springfield was incapable of solving the problems which a majority of citizens concluded were at the base of difficulties. Those were the maintenance of the gold standard, related to the total supply of money, and the tariff. To many, the depression was clearly a political matter, the result of electing Democrats to govern the state and nation in 1892. "In these good old times the manufacturers of luxuries are the first to suffer, but the people thrown out of employment need not worry or go hungry," observed the *Mendota Bulletin* in a burst of sarcasm. "They have always got those roosters [symbol of the Democratic party] to fall back on. They can have them fried for breakfast, boiled for dinner, and fricasseed for supper."[53] The "breakup of the Whiskey Trust" was the exception rather than the rule, and it was not accomplished under the antitrust law. Efforts were made, it will be seen, by the government to alleviate the suffering of workmen caught in the inexorable process of economic growth.

But any questions about "the system" were forgotten with the return of general prosperity by 1897. The generation was to end in confidence much as it had begun in unparalleled optimism. As the new century approached, the mood of expectancy, of opportunity burst out on every side, fed by victories for sound money, good crops, unprecedented exports, and a successful foreign war. In his address to the General Assembly in January, 1899, Governor Tanner spoke of "the return of confidence and prosperity, in consequence of the overthrow of those twin political heresies—free trade and free silver" as having been "almost as instantaneous as though the country had been touched and healed of its plague by the rod of Aaron."[54] Whatever the cause, it was obvious to all close observers that the magic necessary to heal depressions or control great industrial complexes was beyond the congeries of the government of the state.

Among other changes, the generation of great Illinois entrepreneurs who had built giant industrial complexes and left family dynasties to rule them was dying out. Cyrus Hall McCormick died in 1884, George Pullman in 1897, Philip Danforth Armour in 1901, Gustavus Swift in 1903, Nelson Morris in 1907, and Marshall Field in 1907. They were buried in Graceland Cemetery, and their magnificent monuments are reminders of the wealth they created. Lyman Gage had left Chicago and the First National Bank in 1897. Through constant vigilance, unparalleled shrewdness and acumen of the marketplace, battling to survive competition and depression, these men had built empires. But they were builders and expansionists instead of integrators, and it is doubtful that any of them really understood what was happening economically. The market expanded so rapidly that the strongest men were bound to take advantage of it, producing as much as possible, selling it, and producing more. They were granted loans because they made the system work; they were good bets, and the bankers provided them money because they had been successful. The bankers themselves were unable to stay abreast of the growth. It was not until the end of the period that centralized authority was achieved by anyone. That phenomenon came as a result of finance capitalism imposed by bankers and managers who in the 1890s, for the first time, had money in a depression to build combinations and central direction. The new generation of McCormicks, Armours, and Fields were more sophisticated, less worried about competition and depression, and more willing to cooperate with one another and the community of industry and banking than their fathers. Since they were centered in Chicago, they would be partially responsible for increasing its dominance in the state in the twentieth century.

By the end of the century, Illinois had assumed a definite business and industrial complexion. Typewriters and telephones had replaced pencils and messenger boys in the offices across the state. Many cities had boards of trade, established during the generation. The number of bankers and brokers had increased from 1,096 in 1870 to 6,591 by 1900. Of the latter group, some 571 were commercial brokers. Industrial fairs and exhibits were increasingly popular throughout the period, important ones being held in Chicago in 1873, 1876, and culminating in the World's Columbian Exposition in 1893. If for no other reasons than it was large, mechanized, and awarded to the city with the most aggressive business community, it was appropriate that Chicago was its location. Although most industries showed significant increases during the 1890s, the two that grew at the greatest rate mark the growing sophistication of Illinois industry.

Manufacture of electrical apparatus grew from eleven establishments producing products valued at $486,730 in 1890 to eighty-two establishments with a value of product of $12,169,425, or an increase of 2,400.2 percent by 1900. More uses were found for agricultural products, especially corn. In 1890, there were four establishments producing glucose, with a product valued at $4,370,322. By 1900, the glucose plants were making thirty-five distinct products from corn and numerous related items, consuming 22 percent of the crop, and six establishments were manufacturing products worth $18,122,814, representing a growth of 314.7 percent in the decade. And the increasingly complex machinery which the industrialists produced changed the lives of the people. Labor suffered from the impersonal nature of increasingly large factories whose absentee owners treated their workers as a feature of production.

To farmers modern agricultural implements meant many things, among the most important being that individuals unable to adjust to the business and commercial farming demanded by widespread use of sophisticated tools could not survive. At the same time, the increasingly efficient mechanisms emancipated the farmer from the back-breaking labor for a limited return to which he had been timelessly tied by the ox-plow, the hoe, the spade, the scythe, the cradle, the hand rake, the hay fork, the flail, and the hand fan. It had indeed become an industrial era, and the great wealth created a basis of confidence in the status quo, if not general happiness, that would be extremely difficult for reformers to breach.

1. Governor Oglesby, *Journal of the House*, Jan. 4, 1869, 11-12.
2. United States Bureau of Census, *Historical Statistics*, 340.
3. *Journal of the House*, Jan. 7, 1867.
4. *Chicago Tribune*, Jan. 21, 1870.
5. *Quincy Daily Whig*, Dec. 7, 1870.
6. *Quincy Whig*, March 8, 1874.
7. *Chicago Evening Post*, July 13, 1870.
8. *Journal of the House*, Jan. 4, 1899, 30.
9. Lyman J. Gage, *Memoirs of Lyman J. Gage* (New York, 1937), 17.
10. *Ibid.*, 47.
11. United States Bureau of Census, *Tenth Census, 1880. Manufactures*, xviii.
12. *Ibid.*, 1180.
13. *Joliet Signal*, May 1, 1875.
14. *Chicago Tribune*, Aug. 21, 1875.
15. *Chicago Post and Mail*, Jan. 5, 1876.
16. *Chicago Post*, June 27, 1876.
17. *Chicago Tribune*, April 2, 1881.
18. *Chicago Times*, Feb. 2, 1874.
19. *Chicago Evening Journal*, Sept. 20, 1876.
20. *Ibid.*, March 22, 1878.
21. *Chicago Times*, Aug. 26, 1873.
22. *Chicago Evening Post*, Oct. 1, 1870.
23. *Chicago Times*, Oct. 20, 1877.
24. *Peoria Transcript*, Nov. 8, 1877.
25. *Chicago Evening Journal*, May 7, 1881.
26. *Chicago Tribune*, Feb. 1, 1881.
27. *Illinois Gazetteer*, 1886 (NI), 315.
28. *Chicago Times*, Jan. 1, 1893.
29. Ralph Mahon, *A Golden Anniversary, 1878-1928: The Story of Fifty Years of the Bell Telephone in Chicago* (Chicago, 1928), 14.
30. United States Bureau of Census, *Historical Statistics*, 481.
31. *Chicago Tribune*, March 19, 1877.
32. *Chicago Times*, Dec. 10, 1880.
33. *Ibid.*, Dec. 30, 1879.
34. Frank Luther Mott, *American Journalism, a History, 1690-1960*, 3rd ed. (New York, 1962), 400.
35. Sidney Kobre, *Development of American Journalism* (Dubuque, Iowa, 1969), 447.
36. Louis Swift, with Arthur Van Vlissingen, Jr., *Yankee of the Yards: A Biography of Gustavus Franklin Swift* (Chicago and New York, 1927), iii.
37. *Ibid.*, 43-44.
38. *Chicago Tribune*, Feb. 18, 1877.
39. *Chicago Times*, Jan. 16, 1881.
40. Swift, *Yankee of the Yards*, 71.
41. *Chicago Evening Journal*, Feb. 3, 1877.
42. Pierce, *History of Chicago*, 132.
43. United States Bureau of Census, *Twelfth Census, 1900. Manufactures*, viii, pt. 11, 164.
44. Swift, *Yankee of the Yards*, 4.
45. *Chicago Tribune*, April 1, 1877.

46. Pierce, *History of Chicago*, 132-134.
47. United States Bureau of Census, *Twelfth Census, 1900. Manufactures*, pt. 11, 163-164.
48. *Rock Island Argus*, Jan. 31, 1893.
49. Chicago *Inter-Ocean*, Dec. 15, 1875.
50. *Chicago Evening Journal*, Jan. 25, 1893.
51. *Journal of the House*, Jan. 19, 1893, 49.
52. F. Cyril James, *The Growth of Chicago Banks*, I, *The Formative Years, 1816-1896* (New York and London, 1938).
53. *Mendota Bulletin*, July 8, 1893.
54. *Journal of the House*, Jan. 4, 1899, 15.

7
Labor Struggles for Power

> When capital aggregates itself and forms vast
> combinations, surely labor has a right to do the same
> thing, and all legitimate efforts of the wage-earners of
> our country to better their conditions should receive
> both moral and legal encouragement. This is particularly
> true for the reason that it is much more difficult for
> laborers to combine for industrial and moral ends that it
> is for capital.
>
> John R. Tanner, 1897[1]

Wage workers steadily increased in Illinois in response to the demands of industry. In all some 259,092 Illinoisans, or 15 percent of the total population, served in the Civil War and by their absence contributed a favorable labor market in those years. Over 72,000 soldier-consumers became potential producers by mustering out in 1865. They swelled the number of paid laborers to 742,015 by 1870, or 29 percent of the total population. By 1880 some 32 percent of all Illinoisans were gainfully employed; in 1890 the figure was 35.4 percent of a total population of 4,821,550.

Approximately two-thirds of the workers in the entire state were American-born, and they led in every broad occupational field except mining. Native-born workers dominated desirable job classifications, scattered throughout the state, and escaped the work force whenever possible. Reaping the rewards of the second generation, three of every four professional, clerical, and agricultural workers were American-born. While native-born Americans in 1890, for example, formed 78 percent of the total population of the state, they made up 70 percent of the entire work force, and constituted only 45 percent of the workers in Chicago. Native Americans did not dominate the skilled trades, however. In July, 1880, the *Tribune* observed that "the skilled trades are almost en-

215

tirely in hands of foreigners, principally Germans and Scandinavians," even in Irish and American neighborhoods. The Irish
found employment in "plumbing, horseshoeing, and work in the
rolling-mills, packing houses, and glue factories," while "the only
trade where Americans have a majority is printing."[2] The Illinois
Bureau of Labor Statistics' Report for 1886 contained this
explanation:

> The American mechanic's boy is born to no condition in life from
> which he may not rise, or hope to rise, or which at least he may not
> abandon for better or worse. All the precepts of the schools and
> teachings of observation suggest other ways of making a living, or at
> least other avenues in life, than those of his father. Add to this the time
> and toil required to learn a trade, and the frequent objections to his
> being admitted to the shops, the encroachments of machinery upon
> intelligent skill in all industries, the lack of technical training in the
> public schools, and it is not difficult to understand why the
> American-bred youth seek clerkships, and swell the ranks of non-
> producers who live by their wits rather than by manual industry.[3]

Addressing the General Assembly in 1889, Governor Fifer noted
"that our country offers far better opportunities for the laboring
man than any other."[4] Widely heralded possibilities for workers in
Illinois already had led to an influx of immigrants in manufacturing and mining centers. Foreign-born workers made up approximately one-third of the work force throughout the period, and by
1900 57 percent of the work force had at least one parent born
abroad. Throughout the generation, the Germans formed the
largest group of immigrants who worked, and they were followed
closely by those from the British Isles, of whom the Irish were most
numerous. Then came the Scandinavians and British Americans.
The censuses of 1890 and 1900 indicate that eastern Europeans
toiled in industrial Illinois in increasing numbers, and following
the northern Europeans came the Bohemians and Austro-
Hungarians, Polish, Russians, and Italians. Immigrant workers
concentrated in Chicago, where they formed 55 percent of the
work force in 1890, and in the mining towns of southern Illinois.
   The nature of employment changed in the generation. Agriculture accounted for 50 percent of the gainfully employed in 1870,
but only 25 percent by 1900. Manufacturing and mechanical industries producing, among other things, the farm machinery which
allowed greater production from relatively fewer farmers grew
from employing 23 percent of the work force to 32 percent in 1900.
Of these, 63 percent performed unskilled labor in 1870, declining

to 28 percent in 1900, and the majority of unskilled by 1900 were of foreign parentage. Those who worked in trade, including merchants, salesmen, and related activities, grew from 8 percent of the total work force in 1870 to 14 percent in 1900, and two-thirds of these were American born. The mining industry employed 7,760 people in 1870 and 38,184 in 1900, and made up 2.1 percent of the toilers, but they produced a product valued much greater than their numbers indicate. The foreign-born element among the miners formed the majority throughout the period—coming primarily from the British Isles, especially Wales, where they had gained previous experience in the industry.

By 1900 over 100,000 men and women served the transportation and communications industry. More than 40,000 worked on the railroads in Illinois, which led the states of the nation in miles of track, and nearly an equal number labored as draymen, hackmen, or teamsters. Some 6,000 workers served the telegraph and telephone industry. As a result of the clerical demands of business, typists, stenographers, and bookkeepers increased from .04 percent of the workers in 1870 to 5.7 percent in 1900. Professional workers, teachers, doctors, lawyers, clergymen, and others grew from 2.8 percent of the work force in 1870 to over 5 percent in 1900, and in 1890 more than 86 percent of these were American born. Those engaged in public services expanded from 4,771 in 1870 to 18,912 by 1900, or 1.05 percent of all workers, indicating that the administrative state was not yet an important employer. For interesting statistics on employment see Tables F and G in Appendix.

Women began to play a greater role in the work force as the economy of the state shifted from a rural and agricultural to an urban and industrial basis. In the cities, economic pressures demanded that they supplement family income by becoming wage earners. In 1870 women constituted over 8 percent of the workers of the state, and increased to 16 percent by 1900. Discriminated against politically and economically, more than half of the working women in 1880 found only the work of domestic servants open to them. Rather than accept this form of employment, many women, especially in Chicago, worked in sweatshops in the garment industry, where they received approximately one-half of the salary paid to males for similar jobs. This fact led the Bureau of Labor Statistics to state in 1880 that "35 to 90 cents a dozen for making shirts, certainly calls for a change in the policy of merchants who are passing the lives of women over their counters in every package of this illy-paid work they sell."[5] Aside from preventing their employment in the mines, the hours and conditions of labor for women in industry did not receive the slightest attention from the legislature until late in the period. Of the 295,000 working women in 1900, there were 80,000 domestic servants, 23,000 teachers (women outnumbered men three to one, but only thirty-one taught on the college or university level), 12,000 clerks, and 11,000 stenographers.

Economic pressure forced some 44,000 children between the ages of ten and fifteen to seek employment in 1880. Sixty-four percent of these worked on farms, while many of the remainder toiled in sweatshops, coal mines, and before the days of the pneumatic tube, as "cash boys" or "cash girls" in the large department stores in Chicago. For most of the period the employment of children of any age for any hours was legal in Illinois, except that children under fourteen could not work in the mines, and their employment on the stage or in acrobatics was regulated. Late in the 1880s the percentage of child labor to adult labor was greater in Illinois than in the more completely industrialized state of Massachusetts. The problem of child labor was reduced but not eliminated by 1898.

Negroes played a minor role in the work force. In 1890 some 24,000, or 1.75 percent, of the paid laborers were black men and women. Over 6,800 were domestic servants, nearly as many were unskilled laborers, and the only other categories claiming over 1,000 were agricultural laborers, farmers, and laundresses. They filled few positions in the professions or in skilled labor. The census of 1890 lists eleven "colored" (includes Negroes, Chinese, Japanese, and "civilized" Indians) lawyers, eighteen physicians and surgeons, nineteen salesmen and saleswomen, and twenty-two apprentices. The black workers found themselves unaccepted as a regular part of the work force. Occasionally duped by employers into becoming strikebreakers, they became more willing to take a white man's job as labor organization excluded them.

The Civil War boom collapsed late in 1865, and unemployment stalked the workers until the spring of 1870. Unemployment, technological, seasonal, or cyclical, meant hardship and deprivation for the laborer. The winter of 1869 and 1870 found nearly one-half of Chicago's workers unemployed, the highest level for a decade. On January 18, 1870, the *Joliet Signal* observed that "never before was the complaint in regards to the scarcity of money and the hard times so prevalent as at present. The laborers and their families are the greatest sufferers."[6] Private charitable organizations attempted to meet the problem but rapidly exhausted their funds. In Chicago the employment bureau of the YMCA encouraged the unemployed "to obtain work in the warm climate of the Southern States."[7] Many observers credited the worker with more mobility than he had, and the *Chicago Tribune*, typically, suggested that "Chicago servant girls, out of employment, should go to New York City, where the demand for their labor is great, and where high wages are paid."[8] And in March, 1870, the Chicago Relief and Aid Society announced that they had "placed in the hands of every such laboring man as we have aided during the past of previous winters, and whose age, health and condition of family were such as to offer no valid objection to his going to the country, a carefully prepared circular, setting forth the advantages to himself and his family of a removal from the city to the country, offering to aid him in such removal, and notifying him that if he declines to, this society can do no more for him in the future."[9]

Business revived in the summer of 1870 and remained vigorous until the fall of 1873. Rapid expansion in heavy industry accounted for much of the prosperity, and many jobs sprang from the need to rebuild the large area of Chicago destroyed by the great fire of 1871. The cyclical economic situation impelled workers to explore a spectrum of organizational activities, including trade unionism, local and national federation, an eight-hour crusade, and Marxism, in their search for a semblance of order and security in their lives.

A firm nucleus of trade unions existed in Illinois by 1865, in spite of the anti-union LaSalle Black Law passed two years before. The National Typographical Union had locals in Chicago and Peoria in the 1850s, and the railroad brotherhoods appeared in a number of cities in the 1860s.

In addition to the railroad brotherhoods, Illinois, outside Chicago, became familiar with unions from the coal miners. A unique, inbred type, they found it hard to leave the mines because of economic and social barriers and because mining got into a man's blood. A *Tribune* reporter was amazed to discover that "these laborers are the most devoted to their business of any class I ever met; and this struck me as being peculiar, as it is black and grimy enough; but they say with a peculiar accent of their own, 'Na, na, mon,—we ha no wish fur any ther work, and we could na live at a' wi out our black diamonds.'"[10] Working under conditions and with tools only beginning to change after 500 years,[11] the majority of miners were immigrants whose families dug coal in the old country.

They took pride in the fact that the black diamonds they raised
were a necessity of life, without which furnaces in locomotives,
foundries, mills, and homes would die. Although the temperatures
in mine shafts were comfortable all year, choking and explosive
dust and gas, especially in the shafts of the southernmost counties,
presented work hazards. Frequently, the miner in the northern
shafts worked on his knees in water.

Every occupation counted its dangers, and a first-class miner
knew how to limit them. Still miners worked in darkness illumi-
nated only by the flickering oil or carbide lamps on their caps. In
spite of the skill and precautions of an individual, carelessness, or
inexperienced miners, or owners unwilling to construct sound and
safe shafts made violent and sudden death too common.

From 1882 to 1913 individual fatalities averaged sixty-one per
year, and "234,317 tons were mined and 392 employed to one man
killed."[12] The disaster at Braidwood, Illinois, in 1883 contained all
of the elements on a grand scale which led those sixty-one miners to
their deaths each year one by one: unsafe conditions in the mines,
capricious nature, unheeded warning, and individual bravery. The
Diamond Mine in Braidwood was located on a level, marshy tract of
land with no natural drainage to keep water from seeping into the
mine. The mine itself was only fifty-four feet below the surface, and
for several days prior to February 16, 1883, that surface had been
drenched with water from a thaw and rains so that water stood from
one to three feet deep "like a sea over the entire face of the
country."[13] The superintendent of an adjacent mine ordered his
men out of the shaft, but Diamond Mine continued to work.

At 11 o'clock in the morning the "cager" noticed an unusually
large amount of water flowing to the bottom of the shaft, and after
investigating, sent out an alarm. Water had broken through on the
eastern boundary and was rapidly flooding the mine. At this point,
flaws in the mine's construction acted to trap the miners. The
roadway leading to the escapement shaft contained a dip about
fifteen yards in length at a point where the roof also rose. This
pocket filled with water, and those miners who could not hold their
breaths and force their way through the water had no other escape.
Another problem was created by ventilation doors used to control
the air currents. As the water backed up behind them, the doors
sealed the miners off from the escapement shaft. Sixty-nine miners
died. A survivor, William Dennison, describes that morning:

> I was working at the face when the alarm was given by one of the
> drivers. . . . We had not gone far before we met the water. . . . I heard
> someone shouting to the others that they had gone the wrong way,

and hurrying after them as if to bring them back, but I never saw any of them afterwards. When we got to the door leading to the escapement it took seven of us to get it open. The water was surging against it in great waves and rising with every wave. When we had forced our way through the door, we found about fifteen men in there ahead of us, and up to their chins in water, and the dip ahead of them filled to the roof. . . . Then Smith called out that it was death to stay there, and he would rather die trying to get through. Six of us plunged after him into the water tunnel. I got down on my hands and knees and began to grope my way, through the dark, hurrying and trying to hold my breath. Just as I thought I must be nearly through I found my way obstructed by a fall of rock against which I struck my head with such force as to be almost stunned, but I rallied again and made my way over it, and then encountered two men struggling wildly in the passage. Fortunately I escaped their dying clutches, for another moment's delay could have been fatal to me.[14]

Rescue efforts were "as brief as they were futile," but two miners bravely attempted to re-enter the mine through the escapement shaft. The bodies of Harmon Unger and Blazius Shatzel were found with twenty others at the bottom of the shaft. Among those others were John Pearson and Matthew Redmond, both thirteen years old, and Robert Stewart and William McQuinston, both fourteen.

Violence followed miners out of the pits. They clashed with the private guards of employers, with the police, and with the militia in their fight for better conditions. And they fought among themselves because there were always more miners than jobs and because drunkenness and brawling relieved the pressures and drabness of life. The *Inter-Ocean* reported without compassion an illustrative incident of coal-miner life in Centralia in the mid 1870s. The city "was taken possession of on Saturday night by a mob of unruly miners, who made themselves a terror to all peaceable citizens. This kind of behavior appears to be peculiar to miners. Periodically, at other places as well as Centralia, they indulge in mammoth sprees, on which occasions they parade the streets in a body, fight among themselves and with whomever they chance to meet, and make night hideous with their drunken revelry."[15] Revelry caught the attention of Chicago reporters, but unemployment, low wages, gruesome accidents, and frustrating attempts to organize, followed by bitter strikes, were more typical of the generation.

St. Clair County, where coal mining began in 1842 to supply St. Louis with fuel, was the birthplace of the first national miners' union. The American Miners' Association, organized in West Belleville on January 28, 1861, extended its influence throughout

Illinois and into other coal-producing areas. The association based its existence on the resolve that it would "not submit to any reduction of the present prices of mining, under any circumstances whatever, in any of the mines that came under [its] jurisdiction."[16] An industrial union, its historian boasted that it "may justly claim to have initiated the modern labor movement in the United States."[17] John Hinchcliffe of the association edited the *Weekly Miner*, until a libel suit forced its removal from the state in 1865. Hinchcliffe, with the support of the miners, served in the General Assembly in the early 1870s and sought protective legislation for his constituents. But the association he once served succumbed to the recession in 1869 and 1870, and the miners broke up into local protective and benevolent associations.

Following the pattern of craft unionism, the Iron Molders organized in Chicago, Quincy, Bloomington, and Springfield. City-wide Local 23 of the National Union of Iron Molders was chartered in Chicago in March, 1860. Bargaining relationships between the local and the huge McCormick reaper company were constant and effective from 1862 to 1886, and although the union made up only 10 percent of the work force, bargaining gains were shortly passed down to the unskilled workers. Wage settlements were oral, of no set duration, and bargaining began by unilateral action—an announced wage cut followed by a strict ultimatum from the union.

The building trades began to unite in Chicago, tailors unionized in the lake city and in Springfield, and a cigar makers' local appeared in Jacksonville by 1873. Reacting to the ruinous effects of automation in their trade, the Chicago Shoemakers Union joined the Order of the Knights of St. Crispin in 1868. These efforts at organization resulted in an impressive nucleus of trade unions in Illinois in the early 1870s.

To increase their strength, the unions experimented with city and national federation. The General Trades Assembly, a city central organization, was established in Chicago in 1864 to educate the workers in political action and to coordinate the economic efforts of the locals. Claiming to represent 8,500 workers from twenty-four unions in 1865, it advocated the formation of a labor party, the control of war profits, the lowering of the cost of living, the equalization of taxes, the increase of wages, and the shortening of hours. This first effort at a city-controlled organization disappeared with the hard times in 1869 and 1870.

Illinois unionists also participated in the formation of the National Labor Union or Congress at Baltimore on August 20, 1866, and in its subsequent activities. John Hinchcliffe represented the Miners' Lodge of Illinois and chaired the convention, while Andrew Cameron represented the General Trades Assembly and the Illinois Eight Hour League. The convention endorsed arbitration over strikes in settling economic disputes and adopted a report written by Cameron to form an independent labor party to lead the fight for an eight-hour law.

The National Labor Union thus joined with the Illinois workers in their fight for the eight-hour day. Eight-hour leagues existed among the workers in Chicago, and in the spring of 1867 they wrested an eight-hour ordinance from the city council. Numerous candidates for the General Assembly in 1866 pledged to support the cause on the state level, and on March 5, 1867, Illinois became the first state to boast eight-hour legislation. The law applied to "all mechanical trades, arts, and employments, and other cases of labor and service by the day, except in farm employments," and where contracts did not provide otherwise. The act did not "affect labor or service by the year, month, or week,"[18] or overtime. Richard Trevellick, an orator-organizer from the National Labor Union, led a movement to breathe life into the harmless law, and the General Trades Assembly threatened strikes if employers refused compliance after the date it was to become effective, May 1, 1867. Throughout that day, despite employer opposition, 10,000 trade unionists representing forty-four unions participated in what the *Chicago Times* called the "largest procession ever seen on the street of Chicago."[19] The parade may be cited as the original May Day labor demonstration, nineteen years before the generally accepted May Day, 1886. But after a week of strikes and threatened violence, labor's resistance was overcome, the law became a dead letter, and the issue receded until it contributed to the violent explosion at Haymarket Square in 1886.

In August, 1867, the second convention of the National Labor Union met in Chicago. Hinchcliffe chaired the meeting, greenbackism and political action occupied the delegates' time, and Cameron set the tone as he blamed the "money monopoly" for labor's troubles. Alex Campbell represented Miners Union 6, LaSalle, and Illinois workers in general at the federation's conventions in 1868 and 1869. The organization turned toward political action exclusively, and it became the National Labor and Reform party in February, 1872. The organization disbanded when Judge David Davis of Illinois, the party's presidential nominee, deserted it. During its last years it earned one historian's judgment that it "was a typical American politico-reform organization, led by labor leaders without organizations, politicians without parties, women without husbands, and cranks, visionaries, and agitators without jobs."[20]

Marxism presented an alternative solution to those workers dissatisfied with the limited goals and successes of trade unions. A small but vigorous group of Marxists had operated among the German workers in Chicago since the 1850s. At first they believed in trade-union action as the way to power. But by the 1870s the disciples of Ferdinand LaSalle, led by Edward Schlager and Andrew Cameron, assumed leadership, and to them trade unionism alone implied debilitating cooperation between laborers and employers. Direct political action was their answer. They preferred arbitration to strikes in settling labor disputes, and they rejected the destruction of private property. These became the general goals of *Der Sozial-Politische Arbeiterverein* formed in 1871.

The organization was both available and willing to lead worker protest against the unemployment and depression following the failure of the Philadelphia banking house of the buccaneering Jay Cooke on September 18, 1873. Over-expansion and speculation in railroads required a re-adjustment in the economy which threatened to take years. Laborers in other heavy industries, retrenching for lack of credit, found themselves without work. By the end of the year over 40 percent of Chicago's work force was jobless. The *Chicago Times* predicted a winter of suffering for the working man, and took the opportunity to point out that "the man who fritters away time in a strike is an idiot, with reference to himself, and a criminal in reference to those dependent upon him. He should make the most of every remaining moment." Wages declined an average of 8 percent over the following four years, but more than 50 percent on some jobs. When workers for the Chicago, Burlington, and Quincy at Aurora protested a one-hour reduction in work and a 7 percent cut in pay, the *Chicago Evening Journal* termed it the work of "demagogue communists and hayseed politicians." Grievances were compounded, especially in Chicago, by bogus employment agencies whose sole purpose was to relieve the workers of any remaining funds.

On December 21 over 5,000 Chicagoans responded to *Der Sozial-Politische Arbeiterverein*'s call to a mass meeting where resolutions were passed to demand work or credit assistance from the city to help overcome the effects of the depression. The following day, 10,000 workers paraded to city hall to present their demands. Rebuffed, the leaders formed the Workingmen's party of the state of Illinois on January 12, 1874. Its platform included promises to abolish monopoly, to institute public ownership of transportation and communication facilities, to inaugurate stricter state control of banks, fire insurance companies, prison and child labor, and education. Failure to win the anticipated assistance of the farmers or meaningful voter support turned the party to more revolutionary Marxism. In the following months speakers at mass meetings fulminated against "arrogant capitalism" and predicted a proletarian revolution within a generation if labor was not freed from its bonds. The Illinois party affiliated with the Workingmen's party of the United States in July, 1876, and the new group experienced some success in the fall elections.

By the spring of 1877 the nation was entering its fourth year of the depression. Preceding years had seen labor disturbances, but June, 1877, was darkened by the ominous news that ten members of Molly Maguires, a secret organization of coal miners that promoted violence in eastern Pennsylvania, were hanged for murder. According to the *Chicago Tribune*, this brand of justice must surely continue, "until order is restored in the coal mines, or the last Molly Maguire has been remorselessly choked to death."[21]

But hanging was not the answer to hunger and unemployment. A brief notice in the *Tribune* indicated the depth of those problems. "Neil Sievers, a Norwegian residing at 179 W. Huron Street, finding himself unable to procure employment, and his wife and children sick a-bed with this long continued fasting, plunged a knife into his left breast at 11 o'clock yesterday morning." According to the medical report, the family was "starving to death."[22]

Only a few workers surrendered totally to despondency. Some became tramps, and the Cairo correspondent of the *Chicago Evening Journal* observed that "they are becoming as thick as flies and as noxious as the plagues of Egypt."[23] The situation resulted in the passing, by the General Assembly, of a stringent vagrancy law, to become effective in July.

On the other hand, workers were considering strikes and direct action. Unions remained weak with small memberships, and strikes were local and uncoordinated. Hard times, however, encouraged militancy and provided a common ground for laborers throughout the state and nation. Observers feared that trouble would begin among the railroad workers. The railroads were the advance agents of industrialism, opening a national market for the first time and themselves providing a market for iron, steel, coal, and the products of related industries. They were the leading industry of the period. According to *The Railway Age*, "204,732 persons derived their support directly from the wages paid employees of Illinois railroads."[24]

Any benefits unionism offered had not yet reached large numbers of ordinary maintenance or track workers. The low-paid work itself produced rough, economically marginal men. Maxwell Bodenheim portrayed their life when he wrote:

> The rails you carry cut into your hands
> Like the sharp lips of an unsought lover.
> As you stumble over the ties
> Sunlight is clinging, yellow spit
> Raining down upon your faces.
> You are the living cuspidors of day.
> Dirt, its teasing ghost, dust,
> and passionless kicks of steel, fill you.[25]

And Carl Sandburg described the lot of his father, a blacksmith who became a virtual hunchback from a knot of muscle, the result of unceasing toil at the Chicago, Burlington, and Quincy shops in Galesburg. The son wrote:[26]

> From 1876 to 1904 August Sandburg walked from his home to the same Q. blacksmith shop six days a week for a ten-hour workday. On an eight-hour day he would have had in those years many days amounting to two or three years of time for work of his own choice, for rest, for play and talk with his children and friends, for his accordion and his Bible. In those added two hours a day across those years his personality would have reached out and down and up, would have struck deeper roots in the good earth and sent higher branches toward the blue sky.[27]

The toil was difficult enough, but it was all these men had and unemployment was unbearable.

If labor trouble should begin on the railroads, Illinois could not escape it. By 1877 it had a total mileage of 7,334, more than any other state, and Chicago was the railroad center of the nation. Premonitions of things to come had caused the state to awaken its military forces from their postwar lethargy. A "military code" had been approved by the General Assembly in May, 1877. Although complete implementation of the law was impossible immediately, the militia officially became known as the Illinois National Guard, and the troops were armed with efficient weapons and trained in modern methods.

In order to control the situation on the railroads, the General Assembly passed a law effective July 1, 1877, providing a fine and a jail sentence for engineers who abandoned their locomotives at unscheduled places or in the event that "two or more persons shall willfully and maliciously combine or conspire together to obstruct or impede by any act, or by means of intimidation, the regular operation and conduct of the business of any railroad company."[28]

As the summer of 1877 began, Illinois was ready to blow up because of depression, poverty, and unemployment. The entire package was bound together by the long and twisted fuse of the railroad managers, who made the situation worse by agreeing that wage slashes were to cushion the shock of declining business. The Pennsylvania Railroad led the way by announcing a 10 percent cut in wages on June 1. The next month the New York Central, the Baltimore and Ohio, the Lake Shore and Michigan, the Michigan Central, and others within the state followed with their own reductions. When the Chicago, Burlington, and Quincy was forced to declare a cut from a 10 percent to an 8 percent dividend to their stockholders, one director wrote that the logical solution was "to adopt the same plan that the Penn. Central has done, namely a reduction of ten percent on all salaries that average over one dollar per day."[29]

The fuse was lighted in the East when labor halted traffic in Martinsburg, West Virginia, and a strike, spreading in violence and intensity, moved west. Nine persons were killed before the strike reached Pittsburgh. There, on July 21, after resisting militia, a mob tore up railroad tracks and burned down machine shops, the Union Depot, and other property, with damage estimated between $5,000,000 and $10,000,000. Twenty-six people were killed in Pittsburgh.

Action in Illinois began in East St. Louis, where the strike was loosely coordinated with one in St. Louis. Most of the railroads in the area, having participated in the general wage cut in the spring, were manned by resentful workers. Unemployed men in other occupations, especially coal miners, contributed to the unrest. On July 21, an enthusiastic meeting, with a Wabash brakeman presiding, was held in East St. Louis for the purpose of deciding on a course of action.

The meeting was joined by a large delegation of the Marxist Workingmen's party of the United States from St. Louis and addressed by its leaders, including Henry F. Allan, Laurence Gronlund, and Albert Currlin. A railroad strike was voted for midnight and amidst much excitement, but little violence, freight traffic was halted. Mail trains and passenger service ran as usual. As the strike spread, however, reaction on the part of police, strikers, and the press led to violence. Passion ran especially high in Chicago, where Bohemians and German slum dwellers clashed with police and six companies of United States infantry sent by Governor Cullom at the request of Mayor Monroe Heath. In all the city lost $2,000,000 in unshipped goods, $3,000,000 of various wholesale businesses, and $1,750,000 of products which had failed to be produced by idle factories. Peoria and East St. Louis saw bitter confrontations, while railroad workers walked out at Aurora, Effingham, Peoria, Galesburg, Monmouth, Decatur, Urbana, Carbondale, and other railroad centers. Coal miners in LaSalle, Springfield, Carbondale, and elsewhere throughout the state struck in sympathy with the railroad men.

A much grimmer struggle, in terms of human suffering, took place between the coal miners and the mine operators at Braidwood, one of many towns in Illinois with little but the presence of a seam of coal to explain its existence. The miners made up the majority of the population, were influential in local politics, and found that the small group of middle-class people in the town sympathized with their difficulties—perhaps because their businesses depended upon the ability of the miners to pay. But ownership of the mines was absentee, and the company had little understanding of the plight of the community. The miners worked twelve- to fourteen-hour days, but averaged less than three-days' work each week. They were paid monthly, and half of that reward was in scrip usable only at the company-owned "truck" store. The "pluck-me" system, as the miners called it, was a major reason why most of them sank deeper and irretrievably into debt. Wages were cut from $1.20 a ton for coal mined to ninety-five cents a ton in 1876, and further in 1877 to seventy cents in summer and eighty cents in winter.

On April 1, 1,500 coal miners had struck for $1.05 a ton. They had been met by an announcement from the operators that they would not receive their last month's pay. Negro strikebreakers had been imported. On July 27 the events of the great railroad strike encouraged the miners to force the Negroes out of town. The third regiment and the tenth battalion of infantry, Illinois National Guard, arrived the same day. The Negro strikebreakers were returned to the mines two days later. The strike dragged on until November 8, when a few hundred miners went back to work on the company's terms. The remainder were left to their own devices, and the weak union that had been organized in 1872 disappeared.

There was general agreement among Illinois leaders on the causes of the disturbances of July, 1877. Fear of foreigners was a factor, and whenever possible, violence was blamed upon German and Bohemian agitators. (The only Negroes involved in the Great Strike were as strikebreakers at Braidwood, and racism of the modern sort was not important.)

In those days the most negative characteristic of a man was being idle. Governor Cullom singled out what most believed to have been the reason for violence. "The vagrant, the willfully idle was the chief element in all these disturbances, and we have to recognize the fact that we have among us a class which is ready, at all times, to join in any movement looking to a disturbance of the peace and an opportunity to plunder."[30]

The dominant view was that the individual bore entire responsibility for his economic condition. If a man was unemployed it was felt that it was because he did not want a job rather than that there were no jobs available. The governor summarized the majority sentiment as follows: "The fact is, that there was, at no time in this state, any widespread or organized strike among the laboring classes. There was a great deal of dissatisfaction at what the employed, in certain lines of industry, regarded as an oppressive reduction of wages. When trouble broke out in the Eastern States, a very few turbulent spirits among the laboring men, joined by the idlers, tramps, and generally those who make up what is known as the 'dangerous classes,' taking advantage of the general alarm, were enabled, for a few days only, to paralyze the industry of the state."[31]

Most people believed that the striker-rioters should have been dealt with harshly. According to the *Chicago Times*, "proclamations only excite ridicule; clubs may hurt, but incite anger and revenge; bullets, however, when well directed, exercise a soothing influence."[32] The National Guard, not investigatory or regulative bureaus or relief agencies, was the branch of government to handle the problem. Governor Cullom was well pleased with "the agencies for the preservation of peace which the state has at its command, and the lawless classes have learned that there is power enough to thwart and punish any attempt to override the law, disregard civil authority, and interfere with the rights of peaceable citizens in the use of their property or the disposal of their labor."[33]

The National Guard had been dispatched to Chicago, Peoria, Galesburg, Decatur, East St. Louis, Braidwood, and LaSalle in the hot July of 1877. According to the adjutant general's reports, the National Guard was used in Illinois at least thirty times between 1877 and 1898, including eight times in labor disputes on the railroads and fourteen times in miners' strikes. Most of the remaining eight call-ups involved labor trouble in other industries. According to the *National Guardsmen*, the official magazine of the organization, "the future historian of the National Guard will write of A.D. 1877, 'In this year began the Era of Appreciation.'"[34]

Conspiracy-minded editors who knew better and the public which tended to believe what they read attributed the Great Strike to Marxist influence. Certainly it was true that by mid-July radicals were both shouting and acting in East St. Louis and Chicago. In Chicago, Philip Van Patten, the national secretary of the Workingmen's party of the United States, and Albert Parsons, a socialist whose ancestors had arrived in North America on the Mayflower, a typesetter, and a Chicagoan since 1871, railed against "unjust" employers. Other prominent radicals, including John McAuliffe, Laurityz Thorsmark, William Jeffers, and August Spies, joined them.

For a few days the Workingmen's party was of some importance in the railroad strike, if for no other reason than it had a program and leadership on the scene. But the extent of its influence was limited. Parsons was advising caution and nonviolence as late as July 22. On July 24, the Workingmen's party published an announcement in the Chicago papers which read: "Under any circumstances keep quiet until we have given the present crisis due consideration."[35] Van Patten, as a national leader and the coordinator of the party's strike efforts, received $4.61 for additional expenses incurred during the strike—this in addition to his modest salary of $10 a week. Frank Norbock, leader of the Bohemian section of the party, was killed.

According to the *Chicago Times*, Charles Tessman, another leader, "was a conspicuous and influential leader in the viaduct fights, and he fell shot through the head, pistol in hand, after having fired twice upon the police."[36] Parsons was intimidated with the threat of hanging, and his effectiveness as a leader was ruined for some years. By the end of the strike, the Workingmen's party in St. Louis and its representatives in East St. Louis had lost confidence in themselves and had broken their contact with the people. One of the leaders even secured permission for the St. Louis police to arrest non-Marxist speakers for giving incendiary talks.

The public concluded that public demonstrations, such as workers marching from shop to shop, should be judged by actions of the worst elements taking part in them rather than by the most responsible participants. The daily *Inter-Ocean* warned that "the authorities cannot discriminate between the honest and the dishonest workingmen when both are found marching together, and the former must suffer with the latter if worst comes to worst."[37] The *East St. Louis Gazette* published a poem that emphasized how mob action affected the honest workmen.

> To the angry mob 'twas nothing—a little house or two
> And when they fired the depot, sir, my house near by
>   went, too.
> My eyes are opened wider now—I see the sad mistake.
> When thrifty men with shiftless ones a common cause
>   do make.
> The scamps with nothing they can loose, but everything
>   to gain.
> Are they that benefit by strikes, not honest men, that's
>   plain.
> May I be blamed if ever I go on a strike again.[38]

When unionists attempted to cooperate with the authorities to maintain or to restore order, their efforts were rejected. Railroad men in Galesburg offered their services to the mayor to help preserve the peace, but they were refused. In East St. Louis and in Braidwood the mayors worked with the strikers. The East St. Louis strikers' police were arrested by the National Guard and the mayor was vilified, while the mayor of Braidwood was arrested for his efforts.

Throughout it all there was little sympathy for trade unions. The Reverend Dr. Charles Fowler, editor of the *Christian Advocate*, published his opinion of unions in the *Chicago Post* on July 28, 1877. "Trade unions," he said, "are foreign to our institutions. They are chiefly composed of foreigners. They have brought with them infidelity, and disregard for the sanctity of the Sabbath, and for the rights of others. They have perverted and overstated notions of liberty."[39]

The Chicago police refused to allow unionists in that city to meet on July 29 in spite of the leaders' pleas that this was the best way to get men back to work. The president of the Industrial University (the University of Illinois) stated that "strikers have never helped the cause of the laboring man."[40] Judge Drummond, summing up the case against the strikers arrested for contempt of court said, "We all acknowledge the rights of labor. It is simply the right of a man who performs labor to obtain the best price he can from his employer; not by an agreement among employees or by a statement or order, or from the dictation of one man to another."[41]

The *Illinois State Journal* wrote that where trade unions "originated laborers are a class—doomed to remain so; in this country the laborer of today—this week—this month—expects to be an employer mingling the fruits of his toil with those whom he may hire."[42] The workers did not join unions in great numbers. This complacency was due to the fact that the tremendous wealth of the state, as inequitably divided as it might have been, was sufficient to satisfy enough people to prevent effective worker organization. Other workers reacted by forming fighting groups of their own, drilled, and prepared to protect the workers against the state troops and the police. The *Lehr und Wehr Verein*, the Irish Labor Guards, the Bohemian Sharpshooters, and the *Jaeger Verein* marched the streets of Chicago with fixed bayonets. These impotent and ineffective games frightened other citizens, and the activities were forbidden by law in 1879.

Recovery from the depression occurred in 1878 and lasted until 1893, with recession between 1883 and 1885. The cost of living continued to climb, and in the winter of 1881 and 1882, for example, prices in Chicago jumped an average of 60 percent on flour, meat, potatoes, butter, and milk. Examining the wage record of 114 different occupations in 1882 and 1886, the Bureau of Labor Statistics found that wages decreased in seventy-one, did not change in twenty, and showed minor increases in twenty-three. The continued expansion of the rail network, the development of the coal and steel industries, and the tremendous growth of the farm-related, meat-packing industry meant that Illinois was a semi-agricultural, semi-industrial state unlike any other in the nation. The uniqueness was sharpened by the tremendous growth of Chicago and lesser urban centers in the midst of the prairie. Steel worker and corn farmer worked within sight of one another, and in some towns only the railroad tracks separated the residences of coal miners with heavy foreign accents from those farmers who traced their ancestry to colonial Virginia.

In such an amalgam, the Knights of Labor had a natural appeal. Sired by Uriah Stephens, the organization was born among the Philadelphia garment cutters in 1869. Secret and ritualistic at first, the Knights emphasized one idea that seemed reasonable to the heterogeneous work force in Illinois. Solidarity, cooperation of the various callings and crafts, inclusiveness rather than exclusiveness, expressed in their motto, "An injury to one is the concern of all," was the Knights' goal. Here was a chance, it seemed, for the Chicago iron worker, the Peoria cooper, the Belleville miner, and the Cairo merchant and farmer to unite for economic improvement. In fact, only liquor dealers, lawyers, doctors (later admitted), bankers, professional gamblers, and stockholders were barred from a membership which could be skilled or unskilled, male or female, white or black.

The basic unit in the order was the local assembly, which might be either a trade assembly consisting of workers in a single craft or mixed assembly made up of several trades and callings, and might even include employers. Five local assemblies could form a district assembly, the jurisdiction of which remained ill-defined, and District Assembly 13 was organized August 1, 1877, at Springfield, with local assemblies from Springfield, Hollis, Kingston Mines, Limestone, and Peoria. The next year a General Assembly was created which provided a superficial national direction.

From 1879 to 1893, during the entire active career of the Knights, its nominal leader was Terence V. Powderly. A sensitive and vain introvert in the van of rough, boisterous followers, Powderly stood out like "Queen Victoria at a Democratic convention."[43] But he was an excellent speaker whose moralistic banalities and tireless pen somehow preserved his leadership. Antistrike and touting land reform, temperance, and the cooperative movement, he personified the fluid form, function, and philosophy of the Knights. As the leader expressed it, "The right to strike is undoubted; the policy and wisdom of exercising the right are doubtful. When the grand aims of the Order are fulfilled, and cooperation becomes the rule of distribution, strikes will be unnecessary. . . . The suicidal policy of strikes is a relic of barbarism, nourished and fostered by capital as a means of enslaving labor."[44]

Growth of the Knights was steady in the late 1870s and early 1880s. On August 19, 1877, Local Assembly 400 organized in Chicago, and its sojourners spread the influence of the order. District Assembly 24 appeared in the city in 1879. In the southern part of the state, miners joined in increasing numbers. In 1877 H. W. Smith organized thirty assemblies among the miners. And many small towns with no industry to speak of embraced local assemblies. These "represented not wage-earners solely but the last frontier of semi-itinerant craftsmen and small shopkeepers, who had no interest in the mass movements of the newly-mobilized regiments of the wage-earning East."[45] Local Assembly 2,361 in Washington County, for example, was organized in 1882, and reported sixty members representing twenty separate occupations.

Membership in labor organizations, the Knights, and the trade unions spurted upward in 1885 and 1886. The order won apparent victories in strikes against the Union Pacific, the Missouri Pacific, and the Wabash railroads, creating the illusion of effectiveness. On May 1, 1886, the employees of the Chicago stockyards, skilled and unskilled, struck and apparently won the eight-hour day. At that time, 176 unions, one-half of which organized in the previous eighteen months, boasted a membership of 45,000. Some 306 local assemblies of the Knights claimed a membership of 52,400. In addition, the Miners and Mine Laborers' Protective Associations numbered fifty-six, with a total membership of 7,000, while ninety-six organizations of railroad employees had 9,000 affiliates. Accounting for dual membership by some workers, 634 organizations in Illinois counted a total enrollment of 103,843, or nearly 8.8 percent of the entire work force.

The ethnic attraction of the organizations differed. Seventy-nine percent of the trade unionists were foreign born, but only 55 percent of the Knights were recent immigrants. The Bureau of Labor Statistics explained the more balanced appeal of the Knights by the fact that it originated as a totally American organization, appealing in its democratic, inclusive, and reformist ways. Chicago claimed 76 percent of the trade unionists, but only 53 percent of the Knights. The latter group scattered throughout fifty counties outside Cook. Organized coal miners, all outside Chicago, made up 13 percent of the trade unionists and 10 percent of the Knights.

What these workers wanted varied somewhat with individual organizations, but their shared purpose was expressed best perhaps in the program of the recently formed state federation. On invitation from the Chicago Trades and Labor Assembly to convene for four days during the last week of March, 1884, 104 delegates had appeared to form a statewide labor organization. Sixty-one representatives came from Chicago and forty-three from downstate. Forty-seven came from trades' unions and forty-five from assemblies of the Knights. Five delegates representing farmers' organizations also appeared, but indicated their displeasure by withdrawing the first day. The remainder of the delegates agreed on sixteen demands detailing their complaints against and hopes for the economic and industrial system in Illinois.

Immediate and unanimous agreement was reached on the demand to abolish the practice in Illinois of letting the labor of convicts in penitentiaries by contract to the highest bidder. Notices to the effect regularly appeared in the papers.

Proposal.
Convict Labor to Let.

Illinois State Penitentiary,
Joliet, Ill., June 24, 1881.

Sealed proposals will be received by the undersigned up to 1 o'clock p.m., Thursday, July 28, 1881, for the labor of from 125 to 150 convicts.

One hundred of these men are able-bodied and adapted to most any and all kinds of labor. From 25 to 50 men, more or less, are not fully able-bodied and have heretofore been employed manufacturing cigars and other light work.

Contractors will, in addition to the price of convict labor, be charged from ½ to five cents per man per day according to the nature of their business for the use of teams in hauling, on the prison grounds, raw and manufactured material to and from their work shops.

Contracts to run not more than eight years.

No bid will be received for able-bodied men for less than 60 cents per man, per day.

Commissioners of Illinois State Penitentiary.[46]

Rates of pay varying from fifty to eighty cents a day allowed a contractor to place his products on the market at prices injurious to labor and manufacturers alike. As a result of concentrated effort by the representatives of workmen, a constitutional amendment was adopted in 1886 making the practice illegal. The problem remained for many years, however, because many contracts still had many years to run and others had been extended to the legal maximum of eight years just before the amendment passed.

Other demands of the state federation included the establishment of boards of arbitration to settle labor-management disputes, an eight-hour law for all but agricultural workers, employer liability for injuries suffered on the job, an efficient apprenticeship law, prohibition of child labor under age fourteen, compulsory education, rigid enforcement of mine safety and ventilation laws, abolition of the LaSalle Black Law, and the statutory rejection of iron-clad (yellow-dog) contracts. The demands continued with a request for the relief of taxpayers on mortgaged real estate, for weekly paychecks, and for the abolition of the truck system of payment through company stores. They included also "abolition of land monopoly by non-resident holders," criminal punishment for those speculators who gambled in or created "corners on the necessaries of life," the right of labor organizations to hold property and conduct cooperatives, more complete control of water and rail transportation by the state, and regular inspection of workshops, dwellings, food, drink, and drugs.[47] Andrew C. Cameron briefly headed the new organization known as the Illinois State Labor Convention until 1886, the Illinois State Labor Association until 1888, and the Illinois State Federation Labor thereafter, when it regrouped and joined the American Federation of Labor. The sixteen-point platform expressed organized labor's goals for the remainder of the century and into the next.

With increasing membership and an appealing statewide program, organized labor seemed to be coming of age in 1886. But internal struggles between the trade unions and the Knights already had weakened the crusade, and external pressures released by the anarchists and the Haymarket bomb brought it limping to a halt. Jurisdictional problems seemed especially pronounced among the cigar makers and the coal miners. Within the Cigarmakers International Union, opposition developed to trade unionism where workers organized by craft. Reaction to the "new unionism," advocated by international president Adolph Strasser, as well as personality conflicts among the local leaders, led some workers to desert in favor of the Knights. In Chicago, dissatisfied members of Cigarmakers Local 14 withdrew and formed the Progressive Cigarmakers Union. Openly radical, the new group urged extremist measures to redirect society. The dissidents issued a white label to compete with the well-known blue label that appeared on the products of workers affiliated with the older union. In June, 1884, the Progressive Cigarmakers Union joined four other unions to form the radical Central Labor Union in competition with the Trade and Labor Assembly.

Dualism drained organized power among the coal miners. Daniel McLaughlin, president of the loosely coordinated state miners' organization, in September, 1885, at Indianapolis helped launch the National Federation of Miners and Mine Laborers. As a result of the initiative of the new federation, two joint conferences of miners and operators were held at the end of the year. The second, held in Pittsburgh in December, was attended by miners and operators from Illinois and four other states who worked out the first interstate agreement in the bituminous coal industry, a method followed, with interruptions, for the next fifty years. A formal wage scale was the key to the Pittsburgh agreement. Encouraged by this hint of success, 8,000 union miners sent delegates to the convention of the Illinois miners in Springfield in February, 1886, where the state was formed into districts, the union incorporated under state law, and officers elected.

Almost simultaneously, on May 20, 1886, Mine and Mine Laborers National District Assembly No. 135, Knights of Labor, was organized at St. Louis to coordinate the efforts of the local assemblies. In Illinois, south of East St. Louis, most organized miners affiliated with the Knights, while those in the northern section joined the national federation. Mine operators who had agreed to the Pittsburgh wage scale of the national federation complained that they could not compete with the cheaper Knights-produced coal from the south. The bitterness between the rival organizations of miners caused by the wage differential erupted in a strike at Grape Creek in the summer, 1886. When the operator refused to pay the Pittsburgh scale, the national federation miners quit work while the Knights stayed on the job and became scabs in the eyes of the strikers. Negro strikebreakers were introduced, and all semblance of effective worker-organization collapsed.

Meanwhile, on May 4, 1886, the Haymarket bomb exploded the dreams of progress, identified the labor movement in the public mind with anarchistic radicalism, and forced organized labor to pause and deal with yet another peripheral problem. The bomb resulted from a combination of events: the re-emergence of the eight-hour ideal among the workers, the tension engendered when a handful of wild-talking and only half-serious anarchists adopted the eight-hour cause as their own and began exchanging irresponsible threats with the Chicago press, the eagerness of some elements of the Chicago police to crack skulls, and the insane desire of a still unknown and demented bomber to have his revenge upon society.

Johann Most's appearance in the United States in 1882 had given the radicals an apostle of violence around whom they could rally. Most was primarily responsible for the Pittsburgh congress of revolutionary Socialists which formed the International Working People's Association in October, 1883. The majority of his followers were Germans, not yet attuned to the American labor problem. Anarchist strength centered about Chicago where the *Arbeiter Zeitung, Verbote, Fackel*, and the English *Alarm* were published. The primarily German radical unions formed the major strength of the Central Labor Union.

In the same period, in what became its most significant action, the Federation of Organized Trades and Labor Unions, the predecessor of the American Federation of Labor, passed a resolution in 1884 dedicating the organization and its affiliates to the establishment of the eight-hour day after May 1, 1886. With its endorsement by the anarchist-tinged Central Labor Union, the formation of an Eight-Hour Association with a broad base of support, and the threat of strikes if employers did not comply, the eight-hour crusade mushroomed.

Chicago lived in growing apprehension as the appointed day approached. The first two days of May were peaceful enough, but on May 3 violence broke out between 6,000 members of the Lumber Shovers' Union holding an eight-hour–day mass meeting and the police on the Black Road, a block from the always tense McCormick Harvesting Machine Company's works. August Spies, German-born and the leading intellectual of the Chicago anarchists, witnessed, but did not incite, the affair and rushed to the *Arbeiter-Zeitung* office to pen his inflammatory "Revenge Circular." He urged the workers "to rise in your might . . . and destroy the hideous monster that seeks to destroy you. To arms we call you, to arms."[48] A meeting to protest police brutality was called at Haymarket Square for the night of Tuesday, May 4.

Because the crowd was disappointingly small, the meeting was held near a passageway called Crane's Alley, one-half block north of the square. For some thirty minutes, the assembly was addressed by Spies, whose remarks were followed by more from Samuel Fielden, an English-born teamster turned anarchist because of his frustrations and hardships as a worker. Both speakers were quite moderate. However, the police department, anticipating trouble, had assembled 180 men at the Des Plaines Street station under the command of Inspector John Bonfield and Captain William Ward. Fielden was unable to hold the crowd and many scattered. Mayor Carter Harrison, in attendance for a time, stopped at the station on his way home to inform the police that little trouble could be expected from the meeting. But the police failed to take the mayor at his word, and Bonfield and Ward at the head of a column of police suddenly interrupted Fielden's peroration by an order to disperse. At that moment a wild scream was heard, followed by the explosion of a bomb among the police. One policeman, Mathias J. Degan, was killed instantly, and six others died later. In a wild exchange of shots, some sixty-six officers and twelve other persons were wounded.

Chicago erupted with antiforeign and antiradical sentiment and action. As one historian summarized it, "Police and private opera-tives were engaged in feverish activity. People were thrown into jail without warrants, and freedom of speech and assembly seemed in danger of extinction. The color red became a sign of dishonor, and to be known as a socialist was to be classed among the outcasts."[49] On June 3, indictments were returned against Albert Parsons, August Spies, Samuel Fielden, Adolphe Fischer, Michael Schwab, Oscar Neebe, George Engel, Louis Lingg, Rudolph Schnaubelt (arrested, released, and never found again), and William Seliger, who turned state's evidence. The men were charged with killing Officer Degan and with conspiring with an unknown person to commit murder. After a change of venue had been granted, the spectacular trial of the defendants began in July in the court of Judge Joseph E. Gary.

Parsons, who had eluded police, electrified the courtroom on the first day of the trial by turning himself in to stand trial with his comrades. His attorney, Captain William Black, had assured Parsons he would be acquitted.[50] Of the 981 veniremen called for the jury, 757 were dismissed, but after the defense had used all of its 160 peremptory challenges, Judge Gary refused to dismiss for cause two of the finally selected jurors. Both admitted having already formed the opinion that the defendants were guilty from reading press stories, but said their minds could be changed.

In an atmosphere of unparalleled prejudice against the accused from the press, the pulpit, and the city's leaders in the form of the Chicago Citizens' Association, the prosecution created the impression of a lurid conspiratorial threat led by the accused against the city. It did not seem to matter that no one knew who threw the bomb, that it was quite obvious that the accused did not, and that to link them directly with the deed was impossible.

In fact, State's Attorney Julius S. Grinnel ironically summed up the defendant's real crime in his opening statement: "Gentlemen, for the first time in the history of our country, people are on trial for endeavoring to make anarchy the rule."[51]

On August 19 the jury reached its verdict, and the following day the court pronounced the death sentence for Spies, Schwab, Fielden, Parsons, Fischer, Engel, and Lingg, and a fifteen-year prison term for Neebe. Later historians would attribute that sentence to the hysteria of Chicago, the bias of the jury, errors and prejudice on the part of the judge, perjured evidence, and the willingness of all to accept an extraordinary theory of conspiracy. The sentence for murder was considered just, and although the indictment never mentioned it, most people were more relieved that anarchism was to be strangled by the hangman's noose than they were about the destruction of convicted murderers. It was unquestionably "a case of Society against Anarchy with revenge as the motive."[52]

The Illinois Supreme Court upheld the verdict, even though Justice John M. Mulkey admitted, "I do not wish to be understood as holding that the record is free from error, for I do not think it is."[53] Defense council carried the case to the Supreme Court on a Writ of Error, but the high court was unable to claim jurisdiction and the decision stood. Many courageous people protested the decision, but such leading citizens as Marshall Field demanded that the sentence be carried out. On November 10, 1887, Governor Oglesby commuted Fielden's and Schwab's sentences to life imprisonment. Lingg took his own life. The following day Spies, Parsons, Fischer, and Engel were hanged for their alleged crimes.

Related public sympathy for the condemned men was organized by George Schilling into an amnesty association which soon numbered 100,000 members. Conservatives joined on the grounds that the prisoners had suffered enough. Their ranks included bankers Lyman Gage, Chicago *Inter-Ocean* publisher William Nixon, Judge Samuel P. McConnell, Edward Osgood Brown, Clarence Darrow, Judge Murray F. Tuley, Lyman Trumbull, Edward Dunne, and William Goudy.[54]

The inauguration of John Peter Altgeld as governor brought hope to this group, for Altgeld was known to be friendly to labor and passionate about justice. The governor agreed to review the case, and his decision was fortified by a Supreme Court decision on January 10, 1893, in which the court reversed its stand in the Haymarket case and held that a juror who had read about a trial in the press and decided on the defendant's guilt was ineligible to serve. *The People* vs. *Coughlin* gave the governor a strong legal basis on which to base his pardon message.

The Haymarket trial touched the consciences of thoughtful men throughout the country, and greatly influenced the later literary works of men like Vachel Lindsay and William Dean Howells. Howells wrote a stirring letter to the *New York Tribune* on behalf of the convicted anarchists, and continued to champion their cause in the face of what he felt to be public censure of his own career. Echoes of the controversy returned in his books, *The Quality of Mercy*, *The World of Chance*, and *A Traveller from Altruria*.[55]

The Haymarket bomb eliminated the possibilities of anarchism or extremism of any sort as the guidelines for the labor movement. By this time, however, the main elements of the movement, the unions and the Knights, had rejected these approaches and were not directly involved in the incident. Protests against the execution came from labor leaders, but their indignation was only a part of a widespread horror among elements in every area of society at this miscarriage of justice, and the events triggered a further readjustment in the labor movement. The eight-hour campaign, which had been successful for a time, had weakened to the extent that, by the end of 1886, fewer laborers were working that schedule. Labor entered politics with the formation of the United Labor party on August 21, 1886, but formal organization collapsed after the municipal elections in Chicago in 1887. The Knights of Labor began to decline in influence. Workers came to consider Terrence Powderly as much too utopian, and he was blamed by many for bungling what might have been a successful strike among the packinghouse workers in Chicago in 1886. Trade unions affiliated with the American Federation of Labor (AFL) seemed to be performing basic functions in a better fashion.

In response to the demands of the press and business leaders, who out of ignorance or a desire for personal gain failed to discriminate among labor unionists, socialists, and anarchists, the instruments of social control were strengthened by the government. State troops had been sent to Joliet and Lemont in April, 1885, to quell disturbances among the quarrymen, to East St. Louis in April, 1886, as a result of a switchmen's strike in the railroads, and to Chicago in November of that year because of violence in the union stockyards. The antilabor mood of the times and the obvious desire of certain employers to use the state government as an ally in strengthening their control of society led Governor Oglesby, no great friend of labor, to remark that "strikes in every instance led to what seemed a necessity to resort to the military in aid of the civil powers of the State." He continued that "the many signs of willingness of a large portion of our people, especially of incorporated wealth, to impatiently demand the use of the militia in all cases of threatened or real violence, without an effort to secure the protection of the law through the civil forms and procedure provided by law, is an unpleasant augury, and one to be constantly watched by the ardent friends of constitutional liberty."[56] The Merritt Conspiracy Law of 1887 stated that anyone conspiring with or inciting others to do violence was liable whether or not he was the actual perpetrator of the deed.[57] This was to apply if a man's actions consciously contributed to a crime, even if he had never met the criminal.

In the same year the state reacted by moving against the weapon of the boycott. The device had been used successfully, although not always wisely, by both the Knights and the trade unions in more than half of the fifty cases investigated by the Bureau of Labor Statistics in 1886. Thus, employers helped to form the Cole Anti-Boycott Law, which provided a maximum penalty of two-years' imprisonment and/or a fine not to exceed $2,000 for anyone conspiring to institute a boycott or a blacklist or the officer of any organization that required his members to take such a stand.

The workers in Illinois experienced relatively good times between 1887 and 1892, but the period was marked by dissatisfaction among the railroad workers and by a widespread strike in 1888 on the Chicago, Burlington, and Quincy Railroad. During the first week the strike, which began on February 27, was amazingly successful in halting operations, but soon the company found men, including many unemployed Knights, who were willing to take the strikers' jobs. In retaliation, a boycott of Burlington rolling stock was applied by the two unions to prevent connecting railroads from handling the cars of the struck carrier. By March 21, judges in federal districts in Nebraska, Illinois, and Iowa ruled that the boycott was illegal and that "in cases of the Union Pacific, a land grant road chartered by Congress, of the Wabash, a road in the hands of a receiver, and of the Belt Line and the B. C. R. and N., which were neither . . . an injunction was the proper remedy."[58] Important precedents were set in the reasons for breaking the boycott, the willingness of the courts to grant injunctions (this method had been used five times in Chicago in 1886), and by the conclusive evidence in the minds of Eugene Victor Debs and other workers that unless the railroaders cooperated in a single union, jurisdictional divisions would continue to prevent victory. These opposing ideas would emerge dramatically in Chicago during the Pullman Strike of 1894. Management, which had lost some $3,000,000 as a result of the strike, began discussions among various roads to prevent future disasters—a precedent for the founding of the General Managers' Association in 1892.

On the other hand, the government made attempts to satisfy at least three longstanding grievances of organized labor. For years it had protested the government's acceptance of the police power exercised by management, using private detectives and industrial police as guards and strikebreakers. This situation had deteriorated since 1870 when Governor Palmer had told the General Assembly that;

The employment of detectives in aid of the enforcement of the laws, is painfully suggestive of a rapid approach to the condition of social and political helplessness, where the people, without confidence in the laws of the land, or in the agents appointed to execute and enforce them, surround themselves with spies, and eagerly await the coming of a master, who, by his own vigor, will give protection to their persons, self-appointed, who take no oaths and give no bonds to secure their fidelity to the laws, or to indemnify parties they may injure, whose authority to pursue, watch and arrest, seem undefined, and whose jurisdiction is without boundary, is an anomaly in a land of law.[59]

Based partially on this reasoning and partially on the knowledge that an ineffective law denouncing the practice but still permitting it reduced the effectiveness of protests, a law was passed in 1887 reserving the police power for public officials. The law was strengthened in 1893 when authorities were forbidden to appoint individuals as special police if they were not citizens of the United States and residents of the county the year before the dispute. Abuses continued, however, and detectives from the Pinkerton agency became symbols to the workers of the alleged alliance between industry and government.

Governor Fifer outlined another grievance of the workers when he said that "a great wrong, doubtless, is committed against the rights of laboring men of this country by the importation of foreign cheap labor. Men who pay no taxes, who are not in sympathy with our institutions and laws, and who do not intend to become citizens, but on the contrary expect to return at some convenient time to the country whence they came, are permitted to come here and compete with our own citizens in the labor market for employment."[60] Nothing was done regarding the situation in private employment, where it was the greatest threat, but a law was passed in 1889 prohibiting the employment in public service or on public contracts of aliens who refused to declare their intention of becoming citizens. Finally, a law was passed in 1891 protecting the use of the union label, a practice which had been widely adopted in the 1880s, from counterfeit manufacture and use by nonunion employees.

A more significant political victory, although of a different nature from anything that had happened before, occurred in 1892. George Schilling, a prominent member of the Socialist Labor party in Chicago during their slight successes in 1876 and 1878, resembled modern labor leaders in that he forsook his radical, socialist past when he discovered a sympathetic champion of labor in a major party. The little cooper mustered labor's forces for the Democrats and his friend Judge John Peter Altgeld, candidate for governor, in 1892. Schilling organized the Anti-Contract Convict

Labor League, incorporated under Illinois law, ostensibly to invalidate contracts providing for prison labor, but which was an indirect movement for Altgeld all along. He rallied the Illinois State Federation of Labor to the cause, and the labor vote was instrumental in the Democrats' success.[61] The election of Altgeld as Governor of Illinois and Grover Cleveland as President of the United States were expressions in part of dissatisfaction with deteriorating economic conditions and Republican extravagance nationally.

In his inaugural address to the General Assembly, Altgeld observed that "the increasing density of population in our large cities, and the establishment of what has been called the 'sweating system,' whereby many people are made to work amid unsanitary conditions which constantly imperil the health of the community, and the employment of children in factories and shops, where they become stunted in both body and mind, and unfit for citizenship, call for more thorough legislation."[62] Mrs. Thomas J. Morgan and the Illinois Bureau of Labor Statistics, under the direction of Florence Kelley, conducted investigations of the miserable sweatshops, and their evidence, support from organized labor, and the governor's commitments led to the passage of the Sweatshop Act in 1893. It set standards for the protection of the health of women workers, and it provided for the eight-hour day and a six-day work week, along with the inspection of the products of sweatshops to prevent the spread of disease.

The Sweatshop Act also dealt with child labor. The laws of 1872, 1877, and 1891 on the subject had failed to correct abuses because of loopholes and lack of specific provisions for enforcement. Under the terms of the new law, children under fourteen were forbidden employment in any manufacturing establishment, workshop, or factory in Illinois. Children between fourteen and sixteen were denied work unless the parent or guardian provided an affidavit of the child's age and birthplace to be filed by the employer and to be made available to factory inspectors upon demand. Certificates of physical fitness from regular physicians could be required by the inspectors for any child who appeared physically unable to perform assigned duties.

Evasions were still possible when children who were discovered in places of employment denied that they worked there, or when affidavits of age and physicians' certificates were falsified. The law allowed child labor in unpleasant places other than those specified, and it failed to provide for safety measures. Provisions for educational requirements and for adequate enforcement were also omitted. Unfortunately, too, the eight-hour provision was held to be unconstitutional after it had come under attack by the Manufacturers' Protective Association (to become the Illinois Association of Manufacturers in 1895). Yet through the efforts of Florence Kelley, who insisted on conscientious inspection, prosecutions increased, conditions improved, and Altgeld was justified in 1895 when he told the General Assembly that the law "has accomplished much for humanity."[63] A new law of 1897 made corrections in each of the shortcomings of the previous legislation.

A special grievance involved the common practice among employers of compelling their prospective workers to sign "ironclad," (later "yellow-dog") contracts by which they promised to withdraw from unions if they belonged and not to join while under contract. After considerable protest from organized labor, an act was passed in 1893 guaranteeing the right of employees to join labor organizations. An employer discharging a worker because of his membership in a union was subject to a fine not to exceed $100 and to a prison sentence no longer than six months, or both. This law was declared unconstitutional in 1900 as a violation of the due process clause of the constitution and because it was, in the opinion of the court, special legislation favoring union over nonunion workers. In its decision, the Illinois Supreme Court included the revealing phrase "labor is property."[64]

Workers were faced with new problems when within a few months after Cleveland's inauguration in March, 1893, the "panic of 1893" triggered a four-year depression. As a result of bank closings, business and industry in Illinois ground into a lower gear. A nationwide crop shortage, in conjunction with a record low price for wheat (forty-nine cents a bushel), affected railroads, warehouses, and producers. An uncertainty toward federal financial and monetary policy contributed to the collapse. The inflated prosperity connected with the World's Columbian Exposition from May through October delayed the effects in Illinois, but when the "white city" was deserted on October 30, the realities of the depression were brought home to the enlarged work force in Chicago and throughout the state. Some indication of the severity of the situation was indicated when the usually stable Elgin National Watch Company announced it would dismiss one-half of its 3,200 employees on August 1, 1893. Over 200,000 jobless were reported in Chicago in the winter of 1893 and 1894. In September, on Labor Day, Governor Altgeld informed the workers of Chicago that "there seems to be a long dark day ahead of you. It will be a day of suffering and distress, and I must say to you that there seems to be no way of escaping it."[65] He cautioned them against the "mistaken policies" of violence and anarchism, assured them of the support of the state government, and encouraged them to organize to be better able to help themselves. The following winter wages plummeted, unemployment rose, and the spring of 1894 brought little relief. Illinois workers joined Jacob Selcher Coxey when he led his ragged "army" to Washington to seek government help for the unemployed, only to be arrested for walking on the grass.

The miners in Illinois faced a particularly acute situation. One consolation was that the problem of dual unionism had been solved in 1890 when an agreement between the National Progressive Union and District Assembly 135 formed the United Mine Workers of America (UMWA). But the new organization was small and unproven. The state union boasted only 500 members in 1893. Still the miners' lot had become so desperate that the United Mine Workers of America called a national strike on April 21, 1894. Illinois miners, union or not, responded in large numbers as 125,000 coal miners left the pits across the nation. Their attitude was expressed by Spring Valley miners when a county official suggested that they capitulate to the reduction in wages and let the county help them. Their reply, in the *Mine Workers Journal*, indicated their bitterness:

> If after toiling and moiling, sweating and fuming, digging, backing, shoveling, sawing, smothering, gasping, scraping, in water, mud, bad air, foul stenches, dangerous caves, treacherous rocks, pushing, heaving, twisting, hammering, lifting, prying, boring, wedging, sometimes in spaces not sufficient for full-grown rats, sometimes where the earth is open like a vast toothed dome whose teeth are hanging in the shape of jagged stones and ready at any minute to crash down and kill—this man, Lovejoy, a public officer, tells those men that if they, after doing all this from ten to thirteen hours a day, and after having exhausted every nerve and muscle and vein in their body, have not earned enough to pay for supper, the county will help them—that is, they will sup poorhouse fare after toiling like galley slaves.[66]

Miners in Illinois averaged $12 a month and had reached a low point for laborers in the industry. On Independence Day 300 Spring Valley miners offered to go into voluntary slavery in return for adequate shelter, food, and clothing. A settlement of the strike, June 9, proved to be unenforceable by the bankrupt union. The militia had been sent out on nine different occasions in May and June, 1894, to control trouble around the mines. The bitterness and excitement of the period crackled through impassioned editorials. The *Chicago Tribune* labeled Governor Altgeld as a "demagogue" and excoriated him for being "socialistic" and "anarchistic," insisting that "it is time for him to teach these anarchistic aliens a lesson on the ability of the people to maintain and protect their rights and enforce the laws which those of them who may survive their attempt to subvert them will remember as long as they stay in this country and for some time after they have gone back to their own—and the sooner they go back the better."[67]

Governor Altgeld reported that "we have had so many calls for arms and ammunition that our supply has been exhausted and we find we have not enough to supply the demand."[68]

The final incident involving the militia occurred at Mt. Olive. Miners at Mt. Olive halted the trains to prevent shipment of nonunion coal. Since some of the trains were carrying United States mail, the federal court for the southern district of Illinois at Springfield issued an injunction forbidding interference with railroads in federal receiverships or with any trains carrying United States mail. The federal authorities appealed to Governor Altgeld to use state troops to keep the mails on schedule. When these troops appeared on June 17, the trains began to move. If this pattern of enforcement of the law by the state had been maintained, one of the most serious issues arising out of the Pullman strike would not have occurred.

Nine years earlier representatives from various bureaus of labor statistics throughout the United States, led by Carroll D. Wright of the Massachusetts bureau, had written a highly complimentary report about living and working conditions at the "model city" of Pullman, Illinois. During its early years, the city was known as the most extensive and perfect industrial undertaking in the country. It was completely owned and operated by George Pullman to provide a home for his labor force, and to make money. He did both. Presbyterian ministers seeking to pay the rental and the gas and heat bill at Pullman's church complained that "the word 'monopoly' seemed to be written across the pulpit and cushioned seats."[69] The investigators concluded that "if the workman at Pullman lives in a 'gilded cage,' we must congratulate him on its being so handsomely gilded; the average workman does not have his cage gilded."[70] By the spring of 1894, however, the "cage" appeared drab and oppressive to the workers, a place of monotony and surveillance. Estimates of wage reductions from 1893 to May, 1894, ranged from 19 percent (the company's), 25 percent (a federal commission's), 33.33 percent (a private study), and 70 to 85 percent (the iron machinists at Pullman). In addition, the 5,500 man work force of July, 1893, had been reduced to 3,300 by May, 1894. Rents for Pullman's housing and prices at Pullman's stores remained nearly 20 percent higher than in Chicago. Under these conditions, the longer a man worked and lived in Pullman the greater his debt became. In desperation the grim workers joined the American Railway Union (ARU).

The ARU had been formed in Chicago on June 30, 1893, by Eugene Victor Debs of Terre Haute, Indiana. It was an industrial union, open to all "white" railway employees, and was Debs's answer to the debilitating aloofness and selfishness of the railroad brotherhoods in the face of managerial cutbacks. Fresh from a victorious strike against the Great Northern Railroad (the only significant victory for labor in a strike-torn year), the 140,000-man ARU had its first convention at Chicago in June, 1894. The Pullman contingent of the ARU, having unsuccessfully attempted to negotiate with their employer, had struck on May 11. The leaders were discharged the following morning. After the situation was brought to his attention, Debs visited Pullman on May 14, and was deeply moved by the plight of the workers. Rejected in its attempts to restore wage cuts, the convention, against Debs's better judgment, voted to boycott the Pullman company on June 26. Within a few days, the boycott had been answered by more than 124,000 workers, and the railroads were paralyzed.

The General Managers' Association, a voluntary, unincorporated, and, later, illegal society made up of the twenty-four railroads that served Chicago, announced its opposition. Formed to encourage efficient operation and cooperation of the railroads, the managers were strongly antiunion. They had decided the previous year, for example, to dismiss all union men, including engineers, conductors, and firemen, in case the switchmen struck, and to replace them with nonunion workers. Under the direction of John M. Eagan, the managers sent guards to protect property and recommended the appointment of deputy United States marshals. As a result, over 2,000 of them were appointed. At first, violence in Chicago was minimal because Debs insisted upon peaceful action by the strikers and because the police managed affairs so efficiently that no one thought it necessary to request the state militia.

Federal intervention, so vigorously protested by Governor Altgeld as being both unnecessary and unconstitutional, was the decisive factor. Seeking federal intervention, the *Chicago Tribune* hissed venomously about Altgeld, "This lying, hypocritical, demagogical, sniveling Governor of Illinois does not want the law enforced. He is a sympathizer with riot, violence, with lawlessness, and with anarchy. He should be impeached."[71] Under the direction of the attorney general of the United States, Richard Olney, a sweeping injunction was issued against the union. It ordered the ARU "to desist and refrain from in any way or manner interfering with, hindering, obstructing, or stopping any of the following named railroads."[72] The basis of the order was that the union was interfering with the United States mails. The ARU decided to ignore the injunction.

Violence, not perpetuated by the strikers, broke out, and on July 4, President Cleveland ordered federal troops to Chicago. A general strike was called for July 10, but it met with poor response from the workers. Mobs of hoodlums attacked and destroyed railroad property. The Springfield *Register* was typical of the majority of the newspapers in Illinois when it blamed this destruction upon undesirable new immigrants and when it failed to mention the paucity of ARU men involved. "The names of most of the men wounded in the Chicago riots are Polish puzzles. It is safe to say that not one of them has sufficient intelligence to run a railroad."[73] On July 17, Debs and a number of other leaders were charged with contempt of court for disobeying the injunction. In spite of the work of Clarence Darrow, and later Lyman Trumbull, as defense councils, Debs was sentenced to six months in jail at the McHenry County Jail in Woodstock. The strike was called off on August 5.

The Pullman strike was based upon the best principles of unionism. But it was poor tactics and it marked the end of the ARU and the adoption of industrial unionism by a significant number of workers for another generation. Debs's term in the Woodstock jail gave him time to reject traditional approaches to political problems and to become a socialist. He would shortly become the long-term head of that movement. Government by injunction was to be the way of the future in labor-management relations; "a machine gun on paper," according to Debs. President Cleveland and Richard Olney had demonstrated that the attitude of federal government constituted the supreme power of the land, overriding the objections of the state at will. As one cartoonist expressed it: "Says Governor Altgeld to President Cleveland: 'You das'ent knock this chip off my shoulder.' Says President Cleveland to Governor Altgeld: 'Don't bother me; I'm busy.'" Unfortunately for workers, the attitude of the federal government was antilabor. George Pullman suffered also, for Altgeld saw to it that tax assessment on his properties was made more equitable, and the state brought suit which ended in a judgment that Pullman's "model" town had been an illegal transgression of authority from the beginning.

In an attempt to salvage some of their losses, Illinois workers turned to politics in 1894, hoping to amalgamate the labor forces for independent political action with the Populists in the off-year elections. But vigorous internal dissension between the socialist and nonsocialist elements weakened the effort, and the election resulted in an overwhelming Republican victory. Those who were left of the group of laborers advocating independent political action and those who had leaned toward the People's party moved to the Democrats and began planning to elect William Jennings Bryan in 1896.

The events of the mid-1890s caused a shake down in the labor movement in Illinois, ending its formative period. The American Federation of Labor, cautious in its support of such unwise campaigns as that of the ARU in 1894, demonstrated by the simple fact of its survival until 1897, and by expanding its membership for the next seven years, that it offered a semblance of unity and protection for weak unions. Because it concentrated on economic matters, higher wages, and shorter hours, and because it minimized internal disputes by adopting the principle of craft unionism, the AFL demonstrated that it could provide job security to workers better than could other more ambitious organizations. The Illinois Federation of Labor, the AFL's representative on the state level, continued its gradual growth, and in 1895, downstate delegates purged the federation of William C. Pomeroy and the corrupt Chicago labor "skates." It was an increasingly loud voice supporting labor legislation in Illinois. The ninety-six delegates at its 1898 convention would increase to almost 600 in fifteen years.

The trade agreement was a mark of the increasing power and stability of the trade unions which enabled them to cooperate with management to insure orderly coexistence. The Chicago bricklayers had established one in 1887, and the National Association of Stove Manufacturers had set up on a national level in 1891. Another, the most significant one, was established in the coal fields.

However, before the United Mine Workers of America could become permanently established and hold the allegiance of the miners, it needed to win concessions from the operators in more direct confrontation. In 1897 business conditions improved and increased the demand for coal. When the miners asked for increased rates, the operators responded with a reduction. A walkout was called for July 4, and by August some 40,000 Illinois miners had walked off their jobs under the leadership of William D. Ryan, John Hunter, and the rapidly rising John Mitchell. For once the public supported the miners, and even Governor Tanner praised their self-control and emphasis on law and order. In September a compromise settlement was worked out. The operators had been forced to make real concessions for the first time. Still, the miners were placated only by Mitchell's conciliatory efforts and the provision for a joint interstate conference of operators and miners scheduled to meet in Chicago, January, 1898, to decide on a new scale.

At the January meeting, which was to produce the Central Competitive Field Agreement, the operators from Illinois, Indiana, Ohio, and Pennsylvania discovered that thirty years of strife had forced the miners to agree on a number of basic principles. They had learned that local strikes were futile attempts that benefited the employers. They recognized that since the four central states produced only one-third of the nation's coal, they had to stand solidly among themselves to prevent the expansion of nonunion coal fields. The continued importation of immigrant miners and the opening of every seam of newly discovered coal had resulted in an industry nearly 50 percent over developed, and this situation called for shorter hours for the purpose of spreading the work to increased numbers of miners. The possibility that owners might engage in technical manipulations of screens and scales in order to cut down the amount of coal actually credited as mined to each worker called for payment for "run of mine" coal, or all the coal produced by the miners. The agreement of January, 1898, the pattern to be followed for thirty years, laid the basis for gains in each of these areas. The fundamental principle behind the agreement was to allow each district to produce coal at costs that were competitive and that would allow it to retain its share of the market.

The agreement was a major victory over the chaos that had caused losses to both the miners and the operators. It meant that the fate of the Illinois miners lay with the strength of District 12, UMWA, which coincided with the state's boundaries. The strength of the miners was tested almost immediately by the operators who controlled the mines at Virden and Pana along the Chicago and Alton Railroad south of Springfield. The operators felt they could not profit under the terms of the agreement. Unsuspecting Negro labor was imported to both places, and pitched battles at Virden resulted in the death of seven miners and five guards. (The device of using Negro miners as strikebreakers had been used before, and it contributed to the incipient racism of the mining towns.) But with public support on the side of the miners and with Governor Tanner's use of the militia to prevent the importation of more strikebreakers, the mine owners capitulated and the wage increases were restored. It was a major victory, and the miners' union had established itself.

Since the time the legislature had been instructed by the Constitution of 1870 to do so, it had slowly developed a mining code. A law in 1872 provided general safety measures and inspection. County mine inspectors were provided for in 1877, and a general revision and elaboration of the law was made in 1879. Virtually every session of the General Assembly thereafter dealt with miners' problems. Miners were authorized to employ check weighmen to verify the amount of coal mined. The truck system of wage payment was forbidden, and weekly wage payment in lawful money was required. In 1895 alien law was passed, giving miners a claim of mine property for the total amount of work performed. In 1899 a general revision of mining laws was passed, making the mining code of Illinois comparable to that of any other state in the nation. In spite of the gains, however, the laws were inadequately enforced, and work in the coal mines of Illinois continued to be unrewarding and dangerous.

Another organization that promised to contribute order and some degree of coordination to the labor movement was reborn in Chicago. The Chicago Trades Assembly, weakened by factionalism, met in January, 1895, and reorganized itself into the Chicago Trade and Labor Congress. The AFL decided that the new organization was more of a political party than a city central group, and refused recognition. Both the assembly and the remnants of the labor congress dissolved themselves to form an amalgamated organization called the Chicago Federation of Labor (CFL). It was to be the political wing of the Chicago unions, but as a city central affiliated with the AFL, it was to assist in the organization and to regulate the relations between the trade unions of the city. The city central, and especially the CFL, was organized labor's way of meeting the particular needs of the workers in the several trades. By 1898 there was no question that Chicago posed labor problems unique from those faced in the rest of the state.

The history of the working men and women of Illinois between 1865 and 1898 featured a labor force which was growing rapidly, changing in nature, and being tossed constantly by the sharp peaks and deep trough of the business cycle. Chimneys of small, intimate, frontier enterprises with a close identification of the interests of owners and workers gave way to the modern smokestacks of huge, impersonal factories and mines with absentee owners. Management viewed labor as a necessary factor of production to be obtained as inexpensively as possible, while the workers sought a greater share of the vastly increased wealth which they helped produce. Labor-management relations revealed the frustrations of the present and the uncertainty of the future, contributed to an undertone of bitterness, and erupted in episodes of deadly violence. Accepting the tension between them as permanent, labor and capital experimented in organization to increase their relative power.

Workers eventually embraced the trade union which emphasized economic rather than political action, and employed the weapons of the strike, the picket and the boycott. Newly formed managerial associations geared to destroy the unions with strikebreakers, private guards, yellow-dog contracts, and the blacklist. As not all businessmen organized into huge corporations, only a minority of workers, fewer than one in ten, joined unions from 1865 to 1898. But spokesmen for the most well-organized groups on both sides best articulated general conditions in their areas at any given time as well as pointing the way for future development. Seeming worker apathy toward unions resulted from a number of considerations, including job competition encouraged by management between the ethnic and racial groups of the heterogeneous work force, periodic and crushing depression, conflicting and new collectivist ideologies bidding for the allegiances of workers in the midst of a farmer and individualist-oriented society, and the actual, grievance-eliminating increase in worker well-being over a generation in a prosperous state. The two most important roadblocks to unionism themselves constituted significant recognition of its importance: firm opposition from management and the attitudes and actions of an unsympathetic government.

The state government insisted that violence and the destruction of property be avoided, but it actually encouraged mayhem by legalizing the anti-union activities of management while declaring the weapons of organized labor to be criminal acts. By 1898 organization itself could be termed as illegal conspiracy. The boycott was forbidden. Striking, picketing, and the peaceful spreading of propaganda could be halted by the injunction. Governors were encouraged to wield the National Guard against strikers more vigorously than they did. On the other hand, except for the years between 1893 and 1900, employers could legally cripple unions by the use of the yellow-dog contract. There were no limitations on the discharge of employees, and the use of the blacklist was widespread. Lockouts were frequent. Strikebreakers were widely employed, whether they be from the industrial departments of private detective agencies or special deputies employed by local law enforcement bodies. Negro scabs were imported from the South.

The government did adopt some pioneer social legislation to alleviate the increasingly publicized sufferings of individual members of the work force. Problems of hours and pay, of safeguarding health, life, and limb within the factories and mines, of sweatshops and child labor, among others, received legislative attention. The laws were impressive in number, especially since before 1865 there were none, but the provision of insufficient funds and personnel weakened the application and supervision of the laws, and the problems proved greater than the solutions.

1. Governor Tanner, *Journal of the House,* Jan. 11, 1897.
2. *Chicago Tribune,* July 11, 1880.
3. Illinois Bureau of Labor Statistics, *Report,* 1886, 228.
4. Governor Fifer, *Journal of the House,* Jan. 14, 1889, 216.
5. Illinois Bureau of Labor Statistics, *Report,* 1881, 285.
6. *Joliet Signal,* Jan. 18, 1870.
7. *Chicago Evening Journal,* Jan. 8, 1870.
8. *Chicago Tribune,* Jan. 15, 1871.
9. *Chicago Times,* March 24, 1870.
10. *Chicago Tribune,* May 5, 1881.
11. Edward A. Wieck, *The American Miners' Union* (New York, 1940), 143.
12. John J. Milhouse, Director, Illinois Department of Mines and Minerals, *A Compilation of the Coal Reports of Illinois, 1882-1930* (Springfield, Ill., 1931), 44.
13. *Ibid.,* 69.
14. *Ibid.,* 72.
15. Chicago *Inter-Ocean,* Dec. 20, 1875.
16. Wieck, *The American Miners' Union,* 91.
17. *Ibid.,* 21.
18. Illinois, *Laws,* 1867, 101-102.
19. *Chicago Times,* May 2, 1867.
20. Norman J. Ware, *The Labor Movement in the United States, 1860-1895: A Study in Democracy* (New York, 1929), 11.
21. *Chicago Tribune,* June 22, 1877.
22. *Ibid.,* June 23, 1877.
23. *Chicago Evening Journal,* July 2, 1877.
24. *East St. Louis Gazette,* July 21, 1877.
25. Maxwell Bodenheim, "Track Workers," *Illinois Poets: A Selection,* E. Earl Stibitz, ed. (Carbondale, Ill., 1968), 83.
26. In this, or any other task, of course, workmen's compensation laws were still unknown.
27. Sandburg, *Always the Young Strangers,* 97.
28. Illinois, *Laws,* 1877, 168.
29. Robert V. Bruce, *1877: Year of Violence* (Indianapolis, Ind., 1959), 55.

30. *Journal of the Senate,* Jan. 10, 1877, 18.
31. *Ibid.*
32. *Chicago Times,* July 27, 1877.
33. *Journal of the Senate,* Jan. 10, 1877, 18.
34. *National Guardsman* I (Vol. 1, 1871), 70.
35. *Chicago Times,* July 24, 1877.
36. *Ibid.,* July 30, 1870.
37. Chicago *Inter-Ocean,* July 27, 1877.
38. *East St. Louis Gazette,* Sept. 1, 1877.
39. *Chicago Post,* July 28, 1877.
40. Chicago *Inter-Ocean,* July 30, 1877.
41. *Ibid.,* Aug. 1, 1877.
42. *Illinois State Journal,* Aug. 1, 1877.
43. Ware, *Labor Movement,* 85.
44. *Journal of United Labor,* May 15, 1880.
45. Ware, *Labor Movement,* 120.
46. Chicago *Inter-Ocean,* July 4, 1881.
47. Eugene Staley, *History of the Illinois State Federation of Labor* (Chicago, 1930), 33-34.
48. Pierce, *History of Chicago,* 277.
49. *Ibid.,* 281.
50. Francis X. Bush, "The Haymarket Riot and the Trial of the Anarchists," *Journal of the Illinois State Historical Society* XLVIII (Autumn, 1955).
51. *Ibid.,* 293.
52. Ware, *Labor Movement,* 375.
53. Bush, "Haymarket Riot," 302.
54. Harvey Wish, "Governor Altgeld Pardons the Anarchists," *Journal of the Illinois State Historical Society* XXXI (Dec., 1938).
55. Howard A. Wilson, "William Dean Howells' Unpublished Letters about the Haymarket Affair," *Journal of the Illinois State Historical Society* LVI (Spring, 1963).
56. *Journal of the House,* Jan. 6, 1877, 24.
57. Illinois, *Laws,* 1891, 100. The law, never enforced, was repealed in 1891.
58. Donald L. McMurry, *The Great Burlington Strike of 1888: A Case History in Labor Relations* (Cambridge, Mass., 1966), 135.
59. *Journal of the House,* Jan. 6, 1871, 43.
60. *Ibid.,* 44.
61. Staley, *History of State Federation,* 101.
62. *Journal of the House,* Jan. 10, 1893, 53-54.
63. *Ibid.,* Jan. 10, 1895, 19.
64. *Gillespie* vs. *People,* 58 *Northeastern Reporter,* 1900, 1007.
65. Altgeld, *Live Questions,* 298-302.
66. Elsie Gluck, *John Mitchell, Miner: Labor's Bargain with the Gilded Age* (New York, 1929), 23.
67. *Chicago Tribune,* May 29, 1894.
68. *Chicago Times,* June 8, 1894.
69. Altmont Lindsey, *The Pullman Strike* (Chicago, 1967), 53-54.
70. Illinois Bureau of Labor Statistics, *Report,* 1888, 653.
71. Lindsey, *Pullman Strike,* 192.
72. *The Federal Reporter* LXIV, 726-727.
73. *Illinois State Register,* July 12, 1894.

8
Chicago: The Ultimate City

I will harden your heart
or break it,
If you will abide in me.
Ernest McGaffey[1]

The word "Illinois" conjures an image of fields of corn, of soybean mash, and soot-faced miners. It also evokes the equally vivid image of the ultimate city—Chicago. By 1860 Chicago was the largest city in the state, but by the turn of the century it would stand, a robust and ribald giant, unequaled in the Midwest in size, wealth, railroads, and production. Industry and transportation flourished there, drawn by the city's fortuitous location and nourished by an endless supply of immigrant labor. Not even the devastating fire of 1871 could choke the headlong rush to grow, expand, build, thrive. The city merely coughed, then proceeded to rebuild bigger, if not better, than before. Chicago was not a city in love with the past. The future was all.

Beneath the bright optimism for the future, however, lay a dark seam of violence and primal savagery which forever linked the metropolis to its frontier past. Crime was always prevalent—and was put down violently. Policemen who shot suspects, even in error, were commended rather than reproved. Crimes without victims (gambling and prostitution) were pandemic and made mockery of the Puritan ethic the city preached but did not practice. Less visible but more harmful were the corporate crimes—tax evasion, sweatshops, traction frauds, consumer fraud, and stock-watering, which allowed the wealthy to place the burden for payment for city services onto the struggling middle class at the same time they were profiting mightily from city concessions. It was not a compassionate age, and the ruthless tycoons who built large fortunes and indulged in lesser philanthropies did so by exploiting the labor of hungry immigrants, bone-weary women, and full-eyed children. Not until the 1890s did a force arise primarily committed to challenge the brutality of the inner city, and that force was the gentle but determined power of women reformers united in determination to make the struggle for city survival bearable for the weak.

Every aspect of city life grew and changed during the period, requiring an enormous increase in city services. Pure water remained a problem throughout, as did the need for adequate sewage disposal. Gas and electricity replaced tallow and wood for heat and light, and provided opportunities for fortunes to be made or lost. Regulation of utilities kept aldermen busy and rich, and reformers in despair. Political fortunes were tied closely to party—but also to the needs of differing ethnic groups and classes, and personal charisma often canceled out the demands of either.

The era ended as it began, in a stupendous blaze, but this time it was a blaze of glory. Beautiful, gaudy, bursting with life, with material success, with glorification of industry and wealth, the World's Columbian Exposition was both vulgar and magnificent. The fake stucco fronts of the white city covered girders of steel, strong and enduring like the city which built it. And as the century closed, it was an appropriate tribute to the city which had turned mud flats into a twentieth-century metropolis.

Chicago was a latecomer to the state's (and the nation's) population explosion. Residents of the capital at Vandalia saw little chance for the future growth of the scraggly area around old Fort Dearborn. But a flood tide of immigration carried to the lake city on the burgeoning rail system convinced the scoffers once and for all time. The great fire of 1871 swept through a city of 298,000; 1888 saw 503,185 Chicagoans bustling about the "Windy City"; by 1890, 1,000,000 called the metropolis home, and in 1900 the figure rose to 1,685,575.

The total population grew by a phenomenal 268 percent in twenty years, and the proportion of women became almost equal to that of the men—indicating that the city's frontier days were permanently past. In 1870, 56.98 percent of the native born were from Illinois; by 1890 that figure had increased to 67.23 percent. Migrants from the old Northwest Territory continued to dominate the native-born population, and easterners often kept their "true" home memories alive with such clubs as the "Sons of Vermont."

It was not only the native born, however, who gave Chicago its throbbing vitality, its zesty flavor. By 1890, 77.9 percent of the city's population was of foreign parentage.[2] The immigrant groups clustered in self-imposed ghettos, each group moving out to more prosperous areas as newcomers moved into the mudsill of the social and economic strata—as well as the abandoned slums of the seventeenth ward.

Railroad promoters and confidence men clustered about the New York harbor in the 1850s touting the wonders of Chicago and shipping off carloads of often bewildered immigrants in ships and trains deemed "little better than hog pens."[3] Their success is evidenced by the fact that foreigners outnumbered native-born residents by 54 to 46 percent in 1858. Many of the city's new citizens then were Germans, fleeing the chaos of their own country. The sturdy burghers dominated Chicago's immigrant population both in numbers and in influence by the 1870s, and that power continued into the twentieth century. The embargo of the war years slowed the stream, and by 1870 native born outnumbered immigrants in the city, a position they would continue to hold.

In 1850 the Irish numbered 20 percent of the city's population and 31 percent of the foreign born. By 1870 their influence was overshadowed by the Germans, who now made up 41 percent of the foreign born and 20 percent of the city's population. Scandinavians, with 15.9 percent of the foreign-born population by 1890, and English, with 10 percent, were also identity groups with which to reckon. Beginning in the 1870s and 1880s, the immigrant tide shifted its base to southern, central, and eastern European countries, and by the mid-1890s, Chicago was the leading population center for "Poles, Bohemians, Croatians, Slovakians, Lithuanians, and Greeks."[4]

Czechs settled from Halsted to Ashland and south to Sixteenth Street in an area known as Pilson. Thrifty homeowners, the Bohemians worked in the lumber yards and furniture factories. The Poles tended to cluster about such Catholic churches as St. Stanislaus Koska, where 30,000 lived by 1892, but the Poles disdained fellow Poles if they were Jewish. "The Poles," said M. Osach, president of the Polish National Alliance, "are one thing. The Polish Jews are another."[5] The Poles also disliked the Irish, but "the insistence of the papacy that all Catholics in America be one people operated in favor of eventual Americanization."[6]

The city's Jews were of thirteen different nationalities, the largest group being almost all the city's 2 percent Russian population. They lived in the seventh, eighth, and nineteenth wards, and a 100 percent increase in population between 1880 and 1890 still meant a grand total of only 20,000, a minute percentage of the 450,066 foreign born. Many lived in the "poor Jews quarter" at the west end of the Tenth Street bridge. The poorest became fruit peddlers, others went into sweated tailoring, rising to the control of sweat-shops of their own by the 1880s. They were especially successful in the cloak industry, and bankers Henry Greenebaum and Emanuel Mandel became prominent citizens. Those who became wealthy sponsored night schools, where English, United States history, and government were taught to new arrivals. The German Jews were active in the reform movement, but the orthodox Talmud schools continued to cling to old-country traditions.

The poorest of the large nationality groups were the Italians. They moved into the slums vacated by the Germans, Irish, and Scandinavians in the seventeenth, twenty-second, first, and nineteenth wards. Working in menial, low-paying jobs, the Italians' frequently small stature and swarthy complexions made them all the more noticeable as they scavenged through the city as ragpick-ers. Rumors of Mafia entanglements in "Little Sicily" did not en-dear them to their neighbors any more than did their hesitance to become naturalized citizens. "Of the 31.27 percent of all foreign-born males twenty-one years-of-age or older still not naturalized, the Italians by 1890 made up 46.19 percent,"[7] reports one source.

In 1879 fewer than 3,600 Negroes had migrated north to Chicago. The number grew to 14,271 in 1890, most of whom lived along Clark and Dearborn streets in the south division. Although their chief employment remained unskilled menial labor and domestic service, they organized a fire company in 1872, were served by two newspapers, and participated in a variety of clubs from the Colored Men's Library Association or the Daughters of Labor to the fourteenth ward Republican club.

Within the culture of the city as a whole, the diverse nationality groups developed thriving subcultures as they attempted to ap-proximate their native lands in the New World. A thriving foreign-language press kept each group informed, and foreign-language theaters and musical groups catered to their homesick souls. Each group maintained active, and sometimes competing, civic and so-cial clubs, such as the Order of Hagugari, the Svithoid Society, and the Clan-na-Gael. Conflict among differing Irish societies was especially bitter, and was blamed for more than one murder. Both the Irish and the Germans were active in politics, and the impor-tance of German influence is seen in the decision of the city to teach the language in the public schools. By 1890, 34,547 pupils were

receiving German instruction. Brewing and banking proved especially profitable for the Germans, whose endless thirst for ale was a
constant source of dismay to the native-born temperance fanatics.

An off mix, Chicago's population: hairy-chested frontiersmen,
anemic-sweated tailors—a roaring combination of language and
culture, hatreds and passion. Sometime pious, often scandalous,
frequently violent, Chicago's wildly, improbably mixed population
elbowed its way to dominance in the Midwest.

The city's growth in population required expansion, and the
Chicago corporate limits grew from thirty-five to 185 square miles.
The population density of 14,314.5 per square mile in 1880 fell to
6,343.4 in 1890 as more and more land was annexed. Land was
vital, but so was housing, and Chicago's answer was to crowd more
and more people into the central-core slums. In spite of the chance
to rebuild after the fire, sanitary conditions in the rebuilt area
deteriorated as increasing numbers of people were crammed into
tiny rooms. The Board of Health began urging regulation in 1874,
but the City Council did not act on its advice until 1880, when the
board was allowed to inspect sanitary conditions in places of employment. A state law to that effect was passed in 1881, but by 1886
over one-third of the city was still without indoor toilet facilities.
The slum population was estimated at 162,000 in 1893, when "over
49 percent of the population lived in dwellings housing more than
ten occupants."[8]

Amid those slums, Chicago during the 1860s was busy earning its
reputation as the "wickedest on earth."[9] On the "Sands" north of
the river, saloons, gambling dens, and bawdy houses were torn
down in 1857, but were quickly replaced by Robert Blant's "Under
the Willows" at Wells and Monroe. "Conley's Patch" at Adams and
Franklin catered to sailors, while young men of fashion frequented
Lou Harper's at 219 Monroe. Office buildings with vacant (and
nonelevatored) floors were let to "businesses" of a suspicious nature. Carrie Watson set up shop at 441 Clark Street during the Civil
War, and her establishment was still going strong during the fair in
1893. For those whose tastes ran to gambling, Randolph Street,
between State and Clark, and along Clark to Monroe was the place
to go. In spite of heavy losses in the great fire, Chicago's "Entrepreneurs of Sin" rebuilt, so that when visitors came for the fair they
were not disappointed: over 2,000 gambling houses greeted them;
"there were whole avenues lined with brothels; at the approaches of
every railroad station lurked street walkers."[10] Chicago earned its
reputation.

Chicago in the 1860s was a town in a hurry. McCormick's harvesters were winning the war for the North, actually *increasing* wheat production despite the shortage of manpower. Too far from the front to be endangered by southern armies, Chicago's increasing dominance in rails, shipping, meat packing, and manufacturing was matched only by New York City itself.

Such a rapid burst of energy and prosperity demanded buildings—and the city's burgeoning lumber and construction trade met the demand. The major building thrust, of course, went into commercial buildings, but workers also had to find shelter, and wooden tenements were thrown up to meet the demand. In March, 1870, the *Chicago Tribune* noted that "our builders have always run into one of two extremes, and have built rows of marble fronts that cost from $10,000 to $18,000 for each tenement . . . or else have erected frail wooden houses that cost from $2,500 to $3,500."[11] Pine tinderboxes with pitch or tar-paper roofs lined the wooden sidewalks. The minimal fire and safety codes served as a lever in the payoff game, but not much else.

Fires, of course, were pandemic, but for the bustling city the clanging of the fire bell was usually an event mourned only by individual sufferers and their insurance companies. A few fires seemed a small price to pay for the rapid expansion and prosperity symbolized by the acres of new wooden structures. In 1870 the *Tribune* bemoaned the loss of a commercial block by fire, and hoped "the community will find in it reasons for demanding the enactment of a more rigid system of public supervision over architects and buildings."[12] Such supervision was not forthcoming.

During that year, 669 fires (an increase of sixty-nine over the preceding year) burned $2,447,000 worth of property—an average per fire of $3,659. Seventeen firemen were injured. Going into the summer of 1871, the Chicago fire department consisted of "16 steam fire-engines and one extra engine. To each belongs a hose wagon . . . the chief, three assistant fire-marshalls, one clerk, three wardens, five drivers, one hose-cleaner, two City Hall watchmen and two hundred and ten men."[13]

All during that summer the sun shone on Chicago, and only one inch of rain fell between July and October. In Peoria, the people watched "in wild amazement"[14] as the Illinois River sank into the sand. On October 7, a fire broke out on Chicago's west side, and before it was under control it had done $1,000,000 damage. The exhausted firemen returned to their stations to rest and celebrate their victory over the blaze.

The next day, Sunday, October 8, 1871, at 9:30 in the evening, the fire bell rang again; the watchman directed the still-weary crews to the west, approximately one mile from 137 DeKoven Street, home of the Patrick O'Leary family (and the O'Leary family cow). By the time the fire trucks discovered the mistake and arrived at the true location of the fire, it was out of control. Winds of twenty miles per hour tossed flaming firebrands along before the main fire, spreading the flames in all directions. In spite of its intensity, the blaze did not alarm the city, accustomed as it was to frequent fires. The massive area burned over the previous night was a natural fire wall, and the Chicago River seemed a natural boundary, confining the destruction to a limited area.

At midnight, however, the wind blew a burning ember one-third mile ahead of the blaze. It floated over the river into a wooden shanty—and the conflagration roared on. Conley's Patch went up in flames, scattering prostitutes into the night. The county jail caught, freeing 250 prisoners who promptly looted a nearby jewelry store. The Chicago Historical Society disappeared, along with its priceless collection of early city records and Lincoln's original copy of the Emancipation Proclamation. Everywhere the streets were crowded with families carrying what precious items they could to safety. A too-great attachment to material belongings proved fatal to some, as it did to a banker, who failed to return from "one last trip" back into his home safe. As each area of safety was threatened, the tide of people moved again, seeking the lake's cool waters as a haven from the choking smoke, the flying cinders. Lambert Tree remembers the scene at the lake shore this way:

> When we arrived on the Lake Shore we found thousands of men, women and children, and hundreds of horses and dogs, who had already fled there for refuge. The grounds were dotted all over at short intervals with piles of trunks, chairs, tables, beds and household furniture of every description. . . . It seemed as if this great open space, with nothing but the broad lake on the east of us, ought to be safe; and yet there, a few hours later, and for the second time that morning, we nearly perished from suffocation.
>
> Here and there a mother lay upon the ground clinging to her infant. . . . A poor woman, extremely ill, who had been brought down on a mattress, died in the midst of a mixed crowd of men, women and children; and, although the fact that she had died was understood in the vicinity of where she lay . . . a knowledge of the fact seemed to be received with comparative indifference.[15]

All Monday and Monday night the fire raged, and when it was finally over, 250 people were known dead—2,000 acres of city homes and businesses were scorched wastelands; 18,000 buildings were gone; and 90,000 of the city's 298,000 people were homeless. A few Jeremiahs declared the city dead forever, but even before the smoke had cleared William ("Deacon") Bross was heading East to drum up investments in the "new" Chicago.

Public reaction to the crisis was immediate and practical. Wagon-loads of food and medical supplies poured into the stricken city. Cincinnati, for example, distributed eleven carloads of supplies from a soup kitchen which served 4,000 gallons of soup per day. Actors and athletes staged benefits; Canada, England, Germany, and France all sent aid; and the Illinois General Assembly met in special session to authorize aid and public-buildings projects. In all, $4,820,148.16 was donated for relief of the city, $900,000 of it from foreign donors. A Congressional attempt to aid the city by exempting building materials from the high protective tariff met stiff opposition from midwestern lumber barons, including some from Chicago, and the final bill was largely ineffective. The federal government did restore United States court records lost in the blaze, built a new post office and customhouse, and repaid the city taxes on liquor distilled in bond.

Perhaps the hardest hit industry in the city was insurance. Only $96,553,720.94 of the $196,000,000 lost in the fire was covered by insurance, but that was enough to bankrupt fifty-eight firms, many from out of state. Hardest hit were those which had invested heavily in Chicago real estate and Chicago and Cook County securities, and by 1872, only 39.36 percent of all claims had been paid. Compounding the problem was the widespread loss of records due to the fire, and such companies as the Knickerbocker Fire Insurance Company went into bankruptcy proceedings with the handicap that it "has lost all its books, list of policy-holders, etc. during the Big Fire and is, therefore, unable to give an account of its liabilities."[16] Losses by Illinois companies because of the fire came to $31,706,632.81, of which $6,320,000 was finally paid.

Blame for the fire itself was a subject of sermons and speculation for years. Was it really Mrs. O'Leary's cow which kicked over a lantern that fateful night? Whose icy hands at the milking caused that dire kick? Or was it a divine hand which punished wicked Chicago? For its sins of the flesh? For the City Council's vote against Sunday saloon closing? In retribution for the havoc wreaked on the South during the Civil War?

In the days immediately following the fire, however, there was not time for speculation because whatever the cause, the city lay in ashes and relief was needed at once. Mayor Mason immediately called for Lt. General Philip Sheridan's army forces to keep order and to help prevent looting. A seven-man General Relief Committee was formed, and on October 14 direction of the massive relief effort was given to the Chicago Relief and Aid Society. Composed of such pillars of the community as George Pullman and Marshall Field, the society commanded sufficient prestige and public confidence to handle the glut of money and supplies without fear of scandals. Emergency food and coal rations were set immediately, with each family of five qualifying for one ton of coal per month, and a weekly food allotment of 3 lbs. of pork, 6 lbs. beef, 14 lbs. of flour, 1⅛ pecks of potatoes, ¼ lbs. tea, 1½ lbs. sugar, 1½ lbs. rice or 3½ lbs. beans, 1¼ lbs. soap, 1½ lbs. dried apples, and 3 lbs. fresh beef. The society oversaw the building of 8,000 homes (none measuring more than 18′ by 24′) which sheltered 40,000 homeless. By November 18, 5,497 temporary structures were up and 200 permanent ones were in progress. Many were of wood, in spite of the obvious drawbacks of that material. The Common Council also acted, setting prices on necessities to avoid profiteering and closing all saloons at 9 P.M. for one week. Public buildings were set up as relief centers.

The loss to the city was not total. Only 24 percent of the city's grain in 21 percent of the grain storage areas was affected. The stockyards were untouched, and doubled production in 1872. Rolling mills on the north and south sides remained, as did 600 manufacturing plants and workshops on the west side. Total loss in stock, machinery, and products came to $13,255,000, but that was from a total of $102,350,000.

After an initial panic in securities and railroad stock, investors' faith in the city returned and J. Young Scammon was cited as "most energetic of them all." *The Illinois Staats Zeitung* commended Scammon for the zeal with which he set about rebuilding, as by January he had "completed five handsome brick buildings, has five under construction, and closed contracts for fourteen more." Scammon completed his first building within two weeks after the fire, beginning "while the bricks were still smoking with heat."[17]

Scammon was not alone in his zeal to rebuild. While Bross urged easterners to hurry to Chicago to make their fortunes, the *Tribune* was trumpeting "all is not lost . . . let the watchword be: Chicago Shall Rise Again."[18] In that same issue, the *Tribune* commended the building of "Barracks for the Poor" and the employment of "our unfortunate sufferers"[19] as builders, to be paid with relief funds. By October 20, it could report "the vast magnitude of the work of clearing away the ruins and rebuilding Chicago is of itself proving an immediate means of relief to the mechanic and laboring men, who are finding plenty of employment at remunerative wages."[20] Laborers were placed through the relief and aid society's labor bureau at the courthouse, "at which all able-bodied men out of employment and asking relief from the society's agents are required to report."[21] The city had learned at least one lesson from the fire. On November 1, the Common Council "passed a resolution that asphalt pavement be adopted instead of wood, both for streets and sidewalks."[22] Over 122 miles of sidewalks had burned in the fire (from a total of 680 miles), and it was replaced by iron and stone squares, covered with cement.

Just as the packers managed to turn a profit from every unsavory part of the pig, so did enterprising Chicagoans profit from the fire. On December 5, the *Joliet Signal* noted there were "already prospects for fifteen complete histories of the Great Chicago Fire . . . and there are nine hundred lecturers in the field. It is an ill wind that blows nobody good."[23] In January, a magazine offered to the first three subscribers "a nail from the barn in which the O'Leary cow was stalled."[24] Loads of slag "artistically reshaped"[25] were sold as decorative mementos in cities across the country, and to the benefit of many, debris from the fire was shoveled into the lake —providing additional land on which the city could build.

As the first year since the fire drew to a close, Chicagoans could attend discussions on "The Merits of the Chicago Fire" or light their cigars on the still smoldering embers in the ruins of the national elevator.[26] On October 20, 1872, a cornerstone was laid in Central Park for a monument to the fire, in June, 1873, a week-long jubilee celebrated it, and from September 25 to November 12, 1873, more than 60,000 people visited the Inter-State Industrial Exposition commemorating the holocaust. It would take more than a little fire to daunt the Windy City.

Need for drastic and immediate relief and reconstruction after the fire led to a movement to strengthen the executive branch of city government. Under the leadership of Mayor Joseph Medill, elected on the "Fireproof Ticket," pressure in the state legislature resulted in the "Mayor's Bill" on March 9, 1872. The bill expired in two years, however, and the city reverted to the charter of 1863 which limited the authority of the mayor. The Common Council had been empowered by the state in 1872 to seek incorporation, but stalled an election until the citizens' association exerted sufficient pressure in 1875. Voter turnout, blamed on confusion of the issues by the sudden reversal of the association's support, was very light, but on April 23, 1875, Chicago was incorporated by a vote of 11,714 to 10,218.

The Common Council now became the City Council, and the mayor's role was strengthened, although he could not vote, except to break a tie in the council. The council's powers extended over ninety separate areas, ranging from finance to regulation of kite-flying. Aldermen served two-year terms, without pay. Salaries were provided in 1881, and the city was redistricted into thirty-four wards in 1889.

The Constitution of 1870 set aside a separate judicial circuit to meet the legal needs of Cook County, but most of those who met the law did so in the person of the politically appointed Justice of the Peace. The J.P.'s fee system was open to abuse, and reformers like Governor Altgeld sought in vain to change it.

As the needs of the city grew more complex, the mayor's power increased. He appointed commissioners, answerable to himself, to replace cumbersome boards heading the city's various departments, and the most noticeable of those departments was the Chicago Police. Salaries for the minions of the law remained very low, an undoubted factor in the reputed graft within the department, and by 1892 salaries ranged from $720 to $1,000 per year. Crime rates kept pace with the increase in population, with the result that one out of every eleven citizens was arrested in 1892, and the ratio in some areas of the city was one in four. The vigilante toughness of a frontier outpost continued despite the city's size and growing sophistication, so much so that some felt that "all of Chicago in the eyes of even her most ardent partisans was ever in the shadow of the dominance of the criminal elements."[27]

Disorderly conduct was the greatest cause for arrest, and a total of 55,427 disorderly persons were hauled before a J.P. on that charge in 1892, an increase of 6 percent over a fifteen-year period. Although far fewer in number, the cases involving assault increased 30 percent in that period of time, as violent reactions to frustrations of city life became more common. To the public, however, the most serious criminal problem was gambling, which flourished under the kindly eyes of city officials throughout the period. Al Smith and Harry Varnell ran large-scale operations, but none was more successful or cozy with the authorities than Mike McDonald's, "The Store." Driven temporarily underground during the administration of Mayor John Roche in 1887, McDonald and his cohorts were sometimes credited with originating P. T. Barnum's adage, "There's a sucker born every minute."

Carter Harrison's efforts to supervise the gambling operators and keep them honest were no more successful than was his attempt to keep the "ladies of the evening" under control. "An unofficial policy of confining vice to a small area and maintaining as high a degree of order as possible . . . appeared to be about the best that could be done."[28] Criminals of all description, including first offenders and persons waiting trial, were herded into the House of Corrections, where some attempts to improve conditions were made in the 1890s. The efficiency of the police force was increased through the use of telegraph alarms and municipal pensions for disabled policemen, and those with twenty years of service were set up in 1887.

The city's fire limits were extended after the 1871 fire, but conditions leading to the fire were not corrected. Another disastrous fire in 1874 led to the formation of a citizens' association which worked for civic improvement, while a further result was an embargo on the city by fire underwriters. The embargo was not lifted until a department of fire inspectors was established in 1875. It was not until 1876 that the fire department was separated from the police department. The department was placed under a separate municipal pension system in 1887. The fire department's personnel increased to over 1,000 by the 1890s, and telegraph alarms increased speed and efficiency.

In terms of money, the most active city department was the Department of Public Works, and the chief headache of the department was water—how to get enough to drink and how to dispense of it once it was befouled. At first glance the problem seemed simple. Lake Michigan surely contained more than enough water for the thirstiest city, and as for sewage, Garlic Creek, now known as the Chicago River, was an obvious depository.

Unfortunately, the river carried its increasingly noxious burden into the lake—and ultimately into the city's drinking water. The Chicago stockyards fed its animals pure water from deep artesian wells, then dumped its refuse into the odiferous river for the city to drink. As the *Chicago Times* noted one March, "the accumulated fat and grease of the winter appeared to be floating down the river yesterday."[29] The *Chicago Tribune* described the water as "a nuisance that has made Chicago scarcely endurable."[30] The crib pumping water into the city stood only 600 feet from the mouth of the river which daily spewed forth its load of wastes. "At times," pointed out the *Tribune*, "the stench in dwellings from the fearful water was intolerable. It was not only black, with a shocking odor, it was greasy to the touch."[31] In March, 1867, the city's first attempt at a remedy was the opening of a tunnel running two miles under the lake, and water usage promptly increased by 3,000,000 gallons a day.

An event typical of Chicago occurred in 1871 when the Chicago River was forced to run backwards.[32] In theory, a deep cut in the Illinois-Michigan Canal would send the river (and the city's sewage) into the Illinois River, thus polluting river towns instead of Lake Michigan. Problems developed immediately. William Ogden and John Wentworth had improved their own property by cutting a ditch from the Des Plaines River into a tributary of the Chicago. The increased flow not only backed up the canal; it also filled it with silt. An agreement with Ogden and Wentworth was finally reached in 1877, and the Des Plaines was dammed. But as the *Tribune* complained, "something is necessary to be done to cleanse the Chicago river. The stench arising from the filthy stagnant slush is not only injurious to the health of the sailors, but the water is really injuring and discoloring the vessels to such an extent that when they get to some other port they are actually ashamed to show themselves."[33]

Other projects of the Department of Public Works included the construction of tunnels under the river. In 1871 the *Illinois Staats Zeitung* commended the contractors on the completion of the La Salle Street tunnel, but unfortunately, as the paper pointed out, "it cannot be used, because LaSalle Street is, for men or wagons, impassable. From the River to Chicago Avenue it is neither graded, nor filled out; there are no gutters and no sidewalks. All the garbage from the neighborhood is dumped there. Piles of dirt, old pots and crinolines litter the place, where chickens run around. . . . It looks to us like so much nonsense, to put $700,000 as frozen capital into a tunnel that cannot be used."[34]

The sidewalks were not in much better shape, as the *Chicago Times* was quick to point out: "The city attorney thinks that if the board of public works would expend $1000 in good, stout planks and tenpenny nails and the manual labor necessary to insert the former into the latter on some of our sidewalks, they would save the city of Chicago at least $100,000 which it will have occasion to redistribute among the victims of the casualties resulting from the present foot snares that are tripping so many of the unwary."[35]

More controversial than the streets themselves was what went under and over them in the form of utility lines and mass transit facilities. The 1870 constitution forbade the state to grant franchises to street railroads, leaving Chicago City Council an open hand. The state had already, however, granted three railroad companies twenty-five-to-ninety-year franchises in the city, and in 1874 the state restricted franchises to twenty years, which the city got around by confirming in 1883 all existing franchises. Attempts to get license fees from the companies were resisted until 1883, when they were set at $50 per car. A new method of assessment, however, canceled out the gain, and in 1886 dog licenses at $29,948 were running neck and neck with the immensely profitable streetcar companies, which paid only $30,530.85 on their assets.

Chief of Chicago traction magnates was Charles Tyson Yerkes. Yerkes was born into a Philadelphia banking family, and soon became a leading broker there. Caught short in the panic of 1871, Yerkes was convicted of embezzlement and served a short jail term. Backed by Philadelphia bankers, he came to Chicago on his release, obtained an option on the North Chicago street railway, and soon became traction king of the city. Yerkes's motto was "buy old junk, fix it up a little, unload it on the other fellow,"[36] but he did build 500 miles of new track, electrify another 250, and was working on completing the downtown loop at the time of his downfall. His specialty was subsidiary companies and heavily watered stock, and his influence in the city was unequaled by any other robber baron. The lines under his control increased their capitalization from $11,437,000 in 1886 to $54,705,536 in 1898—most of that increase being water.

Yerkes was not well liked, and when he ran short of cash in 1892 his credit plunged. Yerkes then went to William Rainey Harper at the University of Chicago and offered the gift of a million dollar telescope and observatory provided Harper would announce the gift immediately, but give Yerkes several months to actually come up with the money. Harper agreed, and Yerkes's apparent affluence gave him the credit he needed to borrow ready cash.

It was his high-handed use of power that led to his eventual finish in Chicago. In 1895 his men introduced into the state legislature the Humphrey bills, which renewed all of his franchises for 100 years with no payment to the city. Governor Altgeld refused to be bought, however, and he vetoed the steal. Yerkes removed that obstacle by massively publicizing Altgeld's supposed radicalism, especially his pardon of the Haymarket martyrs, and in 1897 a more pliant Governor John Tanner signed the measure, now known as the Allen bill.

Yerkes's stockholdings skyrocketed on the exchange, but public outrage was this time too strong even for him. Mass meetings and parades denounced the bill, and an angry mob with guns and nooses surrounded city hall as the aldermen deliberated authorization for the city. Estimates that Yerkes had spent $1,000,000 on bribes for the measure were extra ammunition, and the council defeated the bill.

Yerkes's downfall also brought down every legislator who had voted for the measure, all were defeated in the following election, and in 1899 the Allen bill was repealed. The episode also led to increasing agitation for public ownership of municipal traction systems. Yerkes, now a social outcast, sold out his holdings for $20,000,000 and sought greener pastures in London, replaced by an equally rapacious figure at the turn of the century, Samuel Insull.

Yerkes figured prominently in another business loosely regulated by Chicago's eminently corruptible aldermen. Until 1882 the city's gas needs were supplied by the Chicago Gas Light and Coke Company in the north and south and People's Gas Light and Coke Company on the west side. In 1886 the Yerkes's backed Consumers' Gas Company joined the Equitable Gas Light and Fuel Company in a rate-cutting war with the old companies. None of the gas companies were happy with competition, however, so on April 28, 1887, they consolidated into the Chicago Gas Trust, and prices leaped from $1.00 to $1.50 per thousand feet of gas. The increase prompted legal action on the part of the citizens' association, and on November 26, 1889, the state Supreme Court declared the gas trust illegal. Five months later the trust changed its name to the Chicago Gas Company and attempted a revival, but continued legal pressure forced it to dissolve.

Gas, however, was too big a money maker to yield easily to mere courts. In 1890 gas illuminating and heating ranked first in the city in capital investment at $40,851,246. Although not formally united, the old gas trust continued as separate companies with many of the same people involved in each. In 1896 the Bureau of Labor Statistics suggested that "this combination is greater than the State of Illinois."[37] The gas trust backers were quick to see the potential of electric lighting, and incorporated in 1887 as Chicago Arc Light and Power Company, making it mandatory that if a Chicagoan wanted to heat or illuminate his home by 1890, he most likely paid the gas trust for the privilege—at its rate. The city itself got its electricity, however, from four city-owned electric plants which were used to light street and bridges. They first began supplying power in 1888.

One of the busiest of the city agencies was the Chicago Board of Health. Reorganized in 1876, it consisted of a commissioner and a staff which nearly tripled in twenty years, from thirty-four to ninety-two. The board consisted of medical, meat and stockyards, burial, milk, tenement and factory inspectors and fumigators. One of the board's chief headaches was garbage. Everyone wanted it dumped—someplace else—and responsibility for disposing of the city's trash and leftovers was shifted from place to place, with no satisfactory solution. The board's efforts to cut the smell from the rendering plants resulted in a city ordinance regulating slaughtering, packing and rendering, soap factories, and tanneries. The ordinance was actively supported by the civic association and approved by the Illinois Supreme Court. Chicago also claimed the distinction of passing the first antismoke ordinance of any large city.

The board turned up massive evidence of the light regard for humanity of the city. In 1880 teams of tenement inspectors found 85 percent of those dwellings defective, and food inspectors seized between 85,000 and 1,991,164 pounds of unfit meat per year. But in spite of the roughness of Chicago life and the primitive state of medical care, Chicago's health showed improvements through the city's vital statistics. The death rate of children under five fell from 59 percent of all deaths to 45 percent, even though deaths from heart disease and pneumonia increased. Typhoid and enteritis continued to plague the city until completion of the sanitary district canal in 1900, when the death rate from typhoid dropped from 173.8 per 100,000 in 1891 to 29.1 per 100,000 in 1901.

In 1865, Chicago's Lincoln Park was described by the *Chicago Republican* as "a sandy and savage strip, part jungle and part graveyard lying between the lake shore and what is called the Green Bay Road. . . . Its denizens are mostly crawfish, sand flies and the smouldering bodies of those who died contributing to the growth and prosperity of Chicago."[38] The state authorized park districts in 1869, and Chicago's park enthusiasts began planning an elaborate park system. Lincoln Park purchased a bear cub for $10 in 1874, bought more animals from Barnum and Bailey in the 1880s, and the Lincoln Park zoo was launched.

Chicago did nothing on a small scale. Plans were laid for a thirty-five-mile strip of parks and boulevards along the lake and encircling the city. By 1892, the Lincoln Park Commission, South Park Commission, and West Side Park Commission had developed eight large and twenty-nine small parks at a cost of $24,000,000.

The project was delayed by litigation as the park district attempted to regain custody of valuable lake frontage given the Illinois Central in the infamous Lake Front Steal of 1869. Although the act was repealed in 1873, the road fought for the land in the courts until the United States Supreme Court ruled in 1892 that the state could not divest the city of submerged lands "as great as that embraced by all the merchandise docks along the Thames in London."[39]

Another city function which involved most of the citizenry was the public school system. The fifteen-member school board increased to twenty-one in 1891. They supervised a staff of teachers which increased from 476 in 1872 to 3,520 in 1891 to 1892. Men teachers were used primarily in the secondary schools, and their salaries averaged four times greater than those of their female colleagues. In hard times, the board paid the teachers in scrip, and suspended their salaries altogether in the bleak days of 1877 to 1878.

The number of pupils increased from 38,035 in 1872 to 166,895 in 1892. School building attempted to keep pace, but by 1892 the city had 14,000 more students than seats. The schools received a 5 percent personal property tax, three-fifths of which went for buildings, and derived a second important source of revenue from the rental of school-owned property, much of it valuable downtown real estate. The property was a source of continuing court battles, as the board attempted to raise and the lessees to lower the rent. The state also contributed to Chicago schools with a two-mill levy on the state property tax, interest on money given the state by Congress in 1837, and money from the sale of public land. The bulk of the financing, however, remained local.

The state supported the development of the Chicago Public Library—authorizing tax levees for support of public libraries in 1872, and the possible assessment was increased by the General Assembly in 1881 and again in 1891. The foundation of the Chicago library was an 8,000-book collection received from the English after the great fire destroyed the library founded by the Young Men's Christian Association under Louis Newberry. In 1874 the City Council spent only $25,000 of the $60,000 levied for the library, but by 1897, the expanding service was moved into a spacious new building.

Care of the city's poor was left to Cook County authorities, although 92 percent of the county's population resided in the city. Fines on prostitutes and the proceeds of liquor licenses supported homes for "erring women" and alcoholics, but most relief work was left to private charities. By the 1890s, Cook County was spending slightly more than $600,000 per year on welfare.

The cost of underwriting the city's expenses was borne chiefly by the general property tax. Unfortunately, this proved another golden opportunity for the "grey wolves" of the City Council to line their pockets. John Powers, of the nineteenth ward, specialized in fixing assessments for such men as Yerkes, who paid taxes on an assessment of $1,337, which covered his stable of race horses, mansion, private museum and library, and an art collection which sold after his death for $769,000. With such generous assistance to the wealthy from the aldermen, it is no wonder that Chicago's assessed valuation actually declined from a high of $312,072,995 in 1873 to $256,599,574 twenty years later!

A complicated system of town, county, and state equalization boards further increased the difficulty of a just tax base sufficient to operate the growing city. The state legislature in 1873 limited the tax levy to 3 percent of assessed valuation, and this was lowered further to 2 percent in 1879. The vast difference between the value of county land and the value of city property increased the problem of an equitable tax base. It took 253,077 acres of farm land to equal one acre of downtown business property, and it was the farmers who were sitting in Springfield making the rules. The state, for example, deprived Chicago of the taxes on one of its largest industries, railroad capital stock and rights-of-way. In addition, the tax was often uncollectible and that which was collected was squabbled over by a myriad of overlapping state, county, and local taxing bodies. In the vital area of finance, Chicago was at the mercy of the often anti-urban biases of downstate legislators. In an effort to make up its deficit, the city resorted to *ad hoc* assessments for such items as streetlights and sewerage. These assessments increased fifteen times while proceeds from property taxes doubled. License fees also swelled the city coffers to the extent that the state allowed the city to require them.

Other expedients, such as interest-bearing scrip and time warrants, were declared invalid in the courts. Noninterest warrants on uncollected appropriations were issued to pay city employees, who often had to accept 15 percent discounts from those willing to cash them. The state also kept the city from going into debt greater than 5 percent of assessed valuation of taxable property until a constitutional amendment in 1890 authorized the bonds to finance the Columbian Exposition.

All of the city's structural functions operated by statute, but behind those statutes, pulling the levers that made things go, was a colorful and transient cast of political figures. Republicans and Democrats vied for the mayor's chair, aldermanic seats, and county offices, although numerous minor parties also played a role. Chicago's consummate politician was "our Carter," Carter H. Harrison. Beloved of the immigrants, with a black slouch hat and white horse his trademarks, Harrison, a Democrat, claimed blood lineage to the Irish, Swedes, and Germans while he campaigned among the Italians as the "23rd Duke del Piazza in disguise and to the Chinese Laundry man as a descendant of Confucious."[40] He lost in his first bid for Congress in 1872, coming back in 1874 to defeat the same opponent, Jasper Ward, by five votes. Harrison remained in the House until 1878, then concentrated his energies on city politics. First elected mayor in 1879 (defeating Republican Abner Wright and Socialist Laborite Ernst Schmidt), Harrison served five terms. When the ebullient mayor attempted to gain a state office, Chicago loyally backed him, but his bid for governorship failed and he learned that downstate Illinois was a frosty climate for Democrats. As the newspaper sage Mr. Dooley said, "Charter Haitch? What wud a man that's been mayor iv Chicago do with an infeeyor job like the presidence?"[41]

The civic reform drive resulting from the "Great Steal" election of 1884 almost ousted Harrison from the mayor's chair. Fraud was exposed in 165 of 171 precincts in every stage of the electoral process. Republican reformers swept into office in 1885, but Harrison hung on by 375 votes. His only defeat for mayor came in 1889 when he ran as an independent Democrat in a field of five. Hampstead Washburne (Republican) defeated DeWitt Cregier (Democrat), Harrison, Elmer Washburn (Citizens), and Thomas Morgan (Socialist). Returning to the straight Democratic fold in 1893, however, Harrison was granted his desire to be World's Fair mayor by an 11,000 vote plurality and fell victim to an assassin the same year.

The complex national mix of the city made Chicago politics more baffling as voters were subject to inter- and intra-national intrigues, as well as to the pressures of economic class which manifested themselves in numerous worker-socialist coalitions. Local issues caused the city to differ strongly from the rest of the state in voting trends, as downstate backed the Republican nominee for president in four out of five races; Chicago in only two. Only three of ten mayors elected between the fire and the fair were Republicans, as more and more immigrants and workmen sought a congenial home within the Democratic party.

People outside the city thought of Harrison, Marshall Field, or

John Altgeld when they thought of Chicago politics. In the political world in microcosm that made up each city ward, however, the *real* politicians were the ward aldermen. Dispensers of patronage jobs, they held tremendous power to make life sweeter for their constituents and for themselves as well. Chicago's first ward, for example, was a polyglot of wealthy businesses and slums. Michigan Avenue, with its mansions and skyscrapers like the Monadnock building, stood side by side with the levee, squalid slums, warehouses, department stores, fine hotels, and flop houses. The levee was itself a mixture: Carrie Watson's fashionable brothel for the rich, flea-infested cribs for the poor, elegant gambling houses, and dime peep shows and bucket shops. It was a teeming, vibrant, smelly place to live, and it gave birth to strong-willed, flamboyant, gutsy politicians. If a man survived in the first ward, he had to be a realist, accepting life's seamy side, and not holding his nose at every strange odor.

Two of Chicago's most colorful figures were products of the first ward's boisterous milieu. John Coughlin and Michael Kenna, better known as "Bathhouse" and "Hinky Dink," became prototypes of the big city boss as they played the political game, making up new rules as they needed them. The Bath was born in Conley's Patch, son of an Irish grocery owner. The store was lost in the great fire, and young John grew up wealthy only in his abundance of friends. He was a large, bluff man, gregarious, if not overly bright, and at nineteen he began his political career as a rubber in a bathhouse, where he hobnobbed with jockeys and gamblers, fighters and businessmen, and learned that "the most prominent citizen shucked down to the skin, is much like everyone else."[42] Coughlin was ambitious, and soon owned his own bathhouse, where he met the first ward's political chieftains, including Joe Mackin, the man who introduced the free lunch to Chicago's saloons. He became a Democratic precinct captain, and in 1883 was elected to his first office—president of the first ward Democratic club.

Bathhouse was known by all as he strolled through the levee, but he was not a patron of the assortment of pleasures offered there. As he put it, "I wear good clothes, and you can't wear good clothes unless you're clean on the inside."[43] With King Mike McDonald's power slipping, Garfield race-track backers looked to the faithful Bathhouse to protect their interests on the City Council. The ward convention was duly rigged against Billy Skakel, would-be ward boss, and John Coughlin became the Democratic candidate. It was 1892.

During the preceding thirty years, boodling had become an art form in Chicago. The council had "disposed of twenty-five percent of the streets to various railroads. Sixty companies, including department stores, junk shops, foundries, laundries and factories had taken possession of 175 of the Ward's thoroughfares."[44] Boodle, or kickback payments, ranged from $100 to $25,000 per ordinance, the highest known being $100,000 plus two pieces of city property. The art was further improved by Johnny Powers of the nineteenth ward, who instituted the practice of granting franchises one block at a time. Powers was the epitome of the city boss: he maintained a close, personal relationship with his ward constituents, visited the sick, and never missed a funeral. Paying off the council's boodlers, which included most of the honorable aldermen (the few incorruptibles like John O'Neil and Martin Madden standing out like heroes in comparison), was cheap compared with the potential cost of honest franchises, for the city literally gave away its valuable property, both over and under the streets and alleys. No councilman, proposing another franchise for Charles Yerkes, was foolish enough to ask that the traction tycoon pay the city a just sum for the rights he was receiving—rights from which he would reap vast profits for years to come.

It was into this council, dominated by "Prince of Boodlers" Johnny Powers, that Coughlin took his seat. Bathhouse joined the city's other Democratic leaders at their daily lunch at Billy Boy's Chophouse, where he was readily accepted, but his failure to save the Garfield track lost him the support of his original backers, and his seat on the council was saved only by his political partnership with Hinky Dink Kenna.

Kenna was a tiny man, terse in his speech, but a whirlwind of activity. The pair made a cartoonist's dream: big loquacious Bathhouse and diminutive, laconic Hinky Dink. Between them, they ran the first ward until more sinister forces of the Capone era left them merely shadow bosses. The basis of their support lay in a loyal cadre recruited from the toughest elements of the ward, and in return for "protection" money, Coughlin and Kenna offered an extensive benefit program. Two defense lawyers (including future judge John Coverly) were put on full-time retainer to "spring" any member of the organization "busted" by the police, and tubercular prostitutes were sent to Denver for the cure—courtesy of the organization. One of the city's periodic reform drives was underway when Coughlin and Kenna set up their organization, and the gambling dens in the ward were suffering from frequent raids. Downtown, Mayor Harrison was feeling the pressure from the tourists coming for the fair who considered the first ward's many attractions a vital part of their trip to Chicago. The raids stopped; Coughlin and Kenna were on their way!

Hinky Dink was a gambler, running an honest game from his saloon, and during the bleak days of the crash of 1893 to 1895, he turned his bar into a relief station, providing food, ale, and shelter to the desperate unemployed. No matter how far down a man fell, he could always get a lift from Coughlin and Kenna. The pair did not dispense pious homilies or seek utopian solutions to the economic chaos around them; they dispensed hot food and sleeping rooms in the loft.

Kenna was also, however, canny enough to see the political benefits to be gained from his benevolence. All he asked in return was a vote, and he got it. Kenna's loyal floaters, combined with the assistance of the tough Quincy Street gang and the selective eyes of the police, gave Coughlin his second aldermanic victory in 1894. When the totals were in, forty supporters of opponent Billy Skakel were wounded, two critically, and hundreds were in jail. Coughlin forces lost nine injured, none arrested.

The next year it was Hinky Dink's turn to run, but fate conspired against the little boss. On February 25, 1895, blanket fifty-year franchises were granted by the council to Ogden Gas and Cosmopolitan Electric Companies for heat, power, telephone, and telegraph service. The fictitious companies were an obvious move to sandbag the gas trust and force it to buy out the potential competitors. The civic federation screamed in outrage, and in the tide of moral indignation Hinky Dink's aldermanic hopes foundered. The nefarious Skakel helped sabotage Kenna by backing the Republicans and revealing to them the names of all of Kenna's "Tombstone" voters, while the Democratic campaign fund was depleted to buy the votes needed for the Ogden ordinance.

In spite of the city's demands for reform, the new council boodled on as before, and Yerkes got franchise after franchise, including the union electric ordinance which allowed four traction lines making up the downtown loop a fifty-year franchise at a payment to the city of only 3 percent of gross revenues. Coughlin then did some sandbagging of his own, presenting a General Electric ordinance authorizing a second loop system in competition with Yerkes. It was his biggest business coup. As usual, the civic federation was up in arms at the blatant steals of the council, and a Municipal Reform party turned into the Municipal Voters' League to oust the boodlers—especially Johnny Powers and Bathhouse John. The league's president, George E. Cole, was given $10,000 and a free hand. He published a scathing attack on them, listing the boodle ordinances for which they had voted.

According to Cole, "of sixty-eight aldermen holding office in 1895, fifty-seven were known grafters."[45] Bathhouse was outraged—Cole had listed his birthplace as Waukegan instead of Chicago! Eighteen of the league's targets, including the mayor, fell in the election, but Powers and Coughlin sailed in victorious. Although the Municipal Voters' League failed to oust Bathhouse, its influence in the rest of the city was pervasive enough to change the makeup of the city council. By 1900, only seven members of the old boodle gang were left in office.[46]

To add insult to injury, Hinky Dink and the Bath then staged the ward's first annual benefit ball (for the benefit of persons unnamed). The whole ward was invited to the all-night bacchanal held in an armory decorated by Bathhouse like a "freshly painted nightmare from Johnny Wong's hop house."[47] Bathhouse was resplendent in green and lavender, and Hinky Dink toted up the profits—$25,000. The newspapers expressed horrified dismay at the alleged orgy, but the first ward apparently did not read the *Tribune*, because the balls became a high point of the season for years to come. Coughlin improved his public image somewhat by sponsoring an anticigarette campaign, and Michael Kenna eventually joined him in the City Council. They scandalized the pious, but remained true to their credo: "Never take anything big."

Bathhouse and Hinky Dink *were* of, by, and for the first ward, and that was the basis of their strength, the reason the righteous wrath of civic reformers fell on deaf ears at election time. They were not outside mobsters coming in to oppress the helpless and unwilling citizens of the ward; they lived there, they were part of the life-style. They knew the people, and they stood ready to help them whenever they could. It did not matter that those citizens ran keno games or brothels, or that the manner of the ward offended the sensibilities of Chicago's bluebloods. Coughlin and Kenna were true to their roots, and if they raked in a little honest boodle, if they collected a little "protection" money, in the eyes of the first ward they were entitled. Bathhouse and Hinky Dink had charisma, they made the people of the first ward feel a brightening pride when they saw "their" aldermen up there on the front pages, hobnobbing with the tycoons. The liberals could point accusing fingers and shake their knowing heads, but they could not make the first ward turn its back on its own.

The first-ward balls represented one social milieu, but it was not the only one within the diversity of the city. Chicago's business tycoons rapidly accumulated the kind of money necessary to ape the polish and social customs of the East. Wives of the pork barons and railroad czars, the lumber tycoons and real estate lords bought status, and an exclusive society with all the trappings paid them due homage. Finishing school, the Grand Tour, dancing lessons from Augustus Bournique and J. Edward Martine were *de rigueur* for Chicago's young debutants and their beaux. "The Cinders," a social set formed after the fire, led to "an exclusive Assembly patterned after its predecessors in Philadelphia and other eastern points."[48] The suffocating smells of the slums seldom reached Prairie Avenue, where Marshall Field, Philip Armour, George Pullman, and their friends resided in a wildly eclectic array of mansions. Scattered in select pockets about the city, the leaders of Chicago society visited each other's homes, exclaiming over Mrs. Potter Palmer's "castle" on Lake Shore Drive and lumberman Joseph Ryerson's Rush Street brownstone. Industrial giants demanded homes worthy of their success, and an impressive array of pseudo-Tudor palaces, French chalets, and Greek-renaissance–rococo gingerbread houses were erected in the 1870s and 1880s.

Bertha (Mrs. Potter) Palmer, "The Queen," ruled the social roost. Her multiturreted pseudo-Tudor brownstone had no outside doorknobs, and visitors' cards, pushed through a slot, passed through the hands of twenty-seven servants before the fortunate guest was ushered into The Presence. Even her most intimate friends wrote for appointments. Mrs. Harold McCormick, of the reaper family, surpassed Mrs. Palmer in grandeur and eventually replaced her as society leader. Four servants waited table when Mr. and Mrs. McCormick dined alone, and even breakfast required printed menus—in French. Protocol conformed to the Victorian ideal so that New Year's Day meant "At Homes" and calling cards. Charities were supported from the proceeds of elegant balls, and in 1887 the Grand Charity Ball distributed its after-expenses largess among several Chicago institutions. Unfortunately, as the balls grew more and more elaborate, the funds actually reaching the city's poor diminished proportionately.

Hefty, multicourse, sit-down dinners were the ultimate test of a hostess's elan, and as society grew, these events overflowed even the sumptuous (and often pretentious) homes of the city's 200 millionaires. When that occurred, the would-be aristocrats held their parties at one of the "Big Four" hotels: the Tremont House, the

Grand Pacific, the Palmer House, and the Sherman House. The Palmer House, rebuilt after the fire, was one of the city's wonders, complete with a barbershop floor paved with silver dollars.

Women's clubs took the time of most of the society matrons, while others combined their club work with varying degrees of attention to reform movements. Ellen Henrotin, wife of a broker, was influential both as national president of the Federated Women's Clubs and also in the Consumers' League, which attempted to improve working conditions for women and children by boycotts of exploiters—a tactic that proved less than successful.

The 1871 citizens' association was a male-dominated group which yielded in 1893 to the civic federation, headed by banker Lyman Gage and Mrs. Palmer, among others. In its first year, the federation donated $135,000 to various agencies and led to the founding of the bureau of associated charities. An attempt to arbitrate the Pullman strike failed, but heat was put on the gambling industry by federation zealots who marched in and burned its equipment. Opposition to the boodlers and the gas trust led to the city's first civil service ordinance, loosely enforced at best. In 1896 the federation organized Chicago's first vacation schools, taking slum children to the country for fresh air, a successful project which the various women's clubs continued. The federation strongly believed in private charity, and avoided any actual city involvement in its activities, for "to have done otherwise," says Ray Ginger, "would have violated one of its cardinal aims: economical government and tax reduction."[49] However, the "grey wolves" were forced to economize on street cleaning after the federation budgeted $30,000 to take on the job, cleaned the streets for $10 per mile, and caused more than a few eyebrows to lift over the $18.50 the city had been paying private contractors. The next city street-cleaning contract was for $10.50 per mile.

A primary target of the federation was election reform, and its off-shoot, the Municipal Voters' League, successfully ousted several of the worst of the wolves. In 1898, Governor Tanner, at the federation's behest, called a special session of the legislature which passed some of the redistricting and election reforms demanded by the group. The reforms proved ineffective in important instances, however, as "Bathhouse," "Hinky Dink," and Johnny Powers still sailed into office.

When it came to trusts and the sins of big business, the federation straddled the fence, pointing up a major weakness of such groups. As Bert Leston Taylor put it:

There was a man in our Town
   And Jimson was his name,
Who cried, "Our civic government
   Is honeycombed with shame,"
He called us neighbors in and said,
   "By Graft we're overrun
Let's have a general cleaning up,
   As other towns have done."

The experts came to Our Town
   And told us how 'twas done.
"Begin with Gas and Traction,
   And half your fight is won.
Begin with Gas and Traction
   The rest will follow soon."
We looked at one another
   And hummed a different tune.

Said Smith, "Saloons in Our Town
   Are palaces of shame."
Said Jones, "Police corruption
   Has hurt the town's fair name.
Said Brown, "Our lawless children
   Pitch pennies as they please,"
Now would it not be wiser
   To start Reform with these?

The men who came to Our Town
   Replied, "No haste with these:
Begin with Gas—or Water—
   The roots of the disease.
We looked at one another
   And hemmed and hawed a bit;
Enthusiasm faded then
   From every single cit.

The men who came to Our Town
   Expressed a mild surprise,
Then they too at each other
   Looked "with a wild surmise."
Jimson had stock in Traction,
   And Jones had stock in Gas,
And Smith and Brown in this and that,
   So—nothing came to pass.[50]

Or, as Finley Peter Dunne's Mr. Dooley so aptly put it, "A man that'd expict to thrain lobsters to fly in a year is called a loonytic; but a man that thinks men can be tur-rned into angels be an iliction is called a rayformer an' remains at large."[51]

Not all of Chicago's gently bred women were content with charity balls and part-time reform work, and into the city in the 1890s came one of the most dedicated and influential groups of women in the city's history, the ladies of Hull House. Few careers were open to a well-educated woman in 1889, and it took a courageous, dedicated woman to break out of the Victorian stereotype into a meaningful life of her own. One such woman was Jane Addams. Born in 1860 in Cedarville, she was a sickly child, overwhelmed by conscience and greatly influenced by her father, a man who knew Lincoln. A trip to Europe and the world's first settlement house, Toynbee Hall, stirred in her a commitment to the poor that would express itself in physical work instead of preaching and homilies. In September, 1889, Jane Addams purchased a house on Halsted Street in the heart of the nineteenth ward, renovation took a year, and in 1890 Hull House began its mission in Chicago when the owner was twenty-nine years old.

She was joined by several equally dedicated women, including Ellen Gates Starr. Julia Lathrop, also of Illinois, daughter of the first man to plead emotional insanity as a defense for murder and a friend of Lincoln; Florence Kelley, reared in Philadelphia, impressed by poverty on a tour of Europe, divorced with two small children; Dr. Alice Hamilton, pathologist and specialist in industrial medicine; Alzina Stevens, Grace and Edith Abbot all came to work at Hull House. These were remarkable women, concerned with the plight of the oppressed, willing to dedicate their lives to the hard, sometimes dirty work of bringing them hope.

Jane Addams's Hull House cohorts tackled some of the city's most persistent and difficult problems. Convinced that much of the filth in the nineteenth ward resulted from inadequate garbage collection by patronage collectors, the women of Hull House stubbornly fought for better service. "During two months of 1892," for example, "the Hull House groups filed more than one thousand complaints with city hall,"[52] which responded with irritation by appointing Miss Addams garbage inspector for the ward—a job she took quite seriously, rising early each morning to walk the streets in search of uncollected garbage. An attempt to clean up the politics of the ward was less successful, but the publicity generated by that action and the other projects of the settlement began to have an impact on the life of all Chicago as "settlement residents helped inform the public about the consequences of unemployment, low wages, inadequate education, bad housing, shocking health and sanitary conditions, and exploitation by landlords and merchants to make the poor pay more."[53]

The activities of Hull House set an American precedent for urban settlements across the country, as other reformers began looking to Halsted Street for solutions to the problems plaguing urban centers. The very existence of such a project, staffed by women, broke with more than one stereotype. The first physician on the Hull House staff, for example, was not only female, she was also black.[54]

It was not only settlement workers from other cities who were touched by the Hull House experience, for Governor Altgeld, Henry George, and John Dewey all visited and were impressed by the work being done there. And in 1896, fledgling historian Charles A. Beard was amazed to discover that "in Chicago, experiments in social democracy were actually in motion." According to his wife, Beard "was impressed by the class divisions between aristocrats and laborers: it made a deep and lasting imprint on his mind and influenced his future activities."[55] That impression of the importance of class divisions underlies the thesis of Beard's most important work, *An Economic Interpretation of the Constitution*.

Hull House was first and foremost dedicated to families, to the welfare of women and children unable to cope with the brutality of the city. Its first program was a kindergarten, quickly followed by reading clubs, penny savings banks, a day nursery, employment bureau, lectures on architecture, arts, and crafts, a Plato club, a Jane club. Attempts by Miss Addams to break the power of the ward boss, Johnny Powers, were frustrated by Powers's control of city jobs in the ward, jobs needed by the voters more than they needed an honest alderman. All denominations were welcome to offer their services at the settlement, but some of the more strait-laced were put off by Hull House emphasis on fun as well as "enlightenment."

Although most of the women who lived and worked at Hull House came from comfortably fixed families, the settlement's work depended on outside contributions. Miss Addams spent each summer in Bar Harbor, Maine, where the socialites gave generously for the cause, but contributions from the employers who were exploiting the nineteenth ward's people were not accepted.

By happy coincidence, the period's only Democratic governor, John Peter Altgeld, took office as Hull House was beginning its work. When the Chicago Trades and Labor Assembly demanded an investigation into sweatshops, Florence Kelley made the study, the first sociological survey of an American urban center. When the state's first meaningful factory inspection law passed in the legislature, Altgeld appointed Mrs. Kelley to head the staff of twelve inspectors. Portions of the law setting an eight-hour day for women and regulating child labor were thrown out by the courts, but a start had been made. Altgeld also appointed the first woman trustee of the University of Illinois. When Altgeld was replaced in 1896 by John Tanner, Tanner promptly dismissed Mrs. Kelley and replaced her with a representative of Illinois Glass Company, one of the worst child-labor offenders.

Julia Lathrop went from Hull House to become the first director of the State Board of Charities and the first director of the United States Children's Bureau. Grace Abbott followed her as second director of the state board, and her sister Edith, Dean of the School of Social Science Administration at the University of Chicago, was superintendent of the League for the Protection of Immigrants and supervised the policing of employment agencies following state legislation providing for regulation. When the state's first juvenile court was established in 1899, it was the women of Hull House who gave it direction and Sophonisba Breckenridge whose study of 13,000 juvenile delinquents provided the first real research into the problem of juvenile offenders. Unlike the civic federation, Jane Addams expected the city or state to take over her successful projects once they were underway, and economy in government meant less to her than feeding the hungry in body and soul.

Miss Addams explained the Hull House philosophy for the Illinois State Historical Society in 1906. "We initiate such things as seem needful," she said, "but we hold our activities in the hollow of our hand, ready to give them up at a proper opportunity."[56] She was anxious to establish the differences between missions and settlements, two activities which were often confused in the minds of the public.

The purpose of a mission, she said, was to "go into a neighborhood, and try to persuade the people who live there to believe as they believe, and to this end . . . they have classes, clubs and many of the things a settlement has, but it is all secondary. . . .

A settlement on the other hand, is a group of people who go into an industrial neighborhood . . . to find out . . . what the social and civic needs of that neighborhood are, to awaken in a neighborhood a sense of responsibility that they may demand and work for better civic, educational and industrial conditions.[57]

The fashionable leisure of Bertha Palmer and the fervid activity of the Hull House ladies was available to the select few, the women whose financial security made their reaction to the sordid facts of urban life a matter of choice. The majority of Chicago's women had to adjust to the city as best they could. By the turn of the century one out of every four Chicago women was employed, many of them in sweated industries. Settlement worker Mary E. McDowell worked in the stockyards district attempting to improve the working conditions of women. After one tour of the yards, she relates, "I visited a room colder than your ice box—a veritable cold storage box, where pork was prepared for shipping long distances. 'Here nothing is wasted,' the superintendent told the visitor. But the immigrant girls worked in mid-winter wrappings—while cold sweat ran down the walls of the enclosed room."[58]

For those with the time and/or money to enjoy it, Chicago's "high culture" was largely the work of millionaire philanthropists. Charles Hutchinson, president of the corn exchange, and lumber king Martin Ryerson collected masterpieces for the Chicago Art Institute, designed by John Wellborn Root. In 1886, Ferdinand Peck, merchant and real estate tycoon, hired Adler and Sullivan to design the Chicago Auditorium, proclaimed "the greatest room for opera in the world."[59] When the building opened in 1890, McCormick, Pullman, and Armour were influential in bringing Theodore Thomas to Chicago to conduct the symphony orchestra.

Thomas was at first discouraged by Chicago's tastes, which ran more to the popular music of McVickers' Theater than high opera, but he persevered, gradually introducing more and more classical music into the symphony's repertoire. Hired to conduct at the World's Fair, Thomas planned two concert series: one popular, one classical. The noontime "pop" concerts were jammed, but the symphonies were canceled as a financial disaster and Thomas quit the fair in disgust. The spaciousness of the auditorium made advance tickets for regular concerts unnecessary, and the symphony suffered a lack of season subscribers. Eventually, months before Thomas's death, the Chicago symphony moved into its own home.

Chicago produced an abundance of writers, artists, musicians. Henry Blake Fuller's *The Cliff-Dwellers* first showed the world the insides of the city in 1883. It was followed by *With the Procession* in 1895, a book about the social struggles of Chicago's merchant elite. Upton Sinclair, Robert Merrick, and Theodore Dreiser all gained literary fame writing about the city. Eugene Field wrote poetry, but the city's poet laureate in the 1890s was a woman, Harriet Monroe.

A real focus of intellectual endeavor existed on the mud flat outside the city on which the University of Chicago was rising.

Aided by generous contributions from J. D. Rockefeller and Marshall Field, President William Rainey Harper set out in 1892 on an academic scavenger hunt. He offered $7,000 per year to full professors (compared with Princeton's $3,500 offer to Frederick Jackson Turner), and he got the very best. As one historian put it, "Yerkes bought legislatures, Ryerson bought paintings, Harper bought scholars, for cash on the line."[60] In the humanities he hired constitutional historian Herman Eduard von Holst and renaissance expert Ferdinand Schevill; in science he hired Henry Donaldson, John Ulric Nef, Otis Whitman, and Albert Michaelson. Donaldson brought with him his pupil, behaviorist John Watson. (Michaelson won America's first Nobel prize in physics.)

Physiologist Jacques Loet, biologist John Coulter, geologists T. C. Chamberlin and J. Lawrence Laughlin, sociologist Albion Small, a veritable "who's who" of academia, signed up to enlighten the Midwest at Harper's new school. More widely known to the lay public were Thorstein Veblen, author of the *Theory of the Leisure Class,* football coach Amos Alonzo Stagg, and educational philosopher John Dewey. Other schools cried "Rape!," but the University of Chicago got its faculty.

Just as the great fire marked the beginning of a new era in the city's history, so did the Columbian Exposition mark the ultimate in that era. It was a fair bounded by superlatives, dedicated to success, to the deification of business and industry. To later historians, while the fair showed "incredible abilities to deliver the goods, it also revealed that almost nobody in Chicago knew what sort of goods should be delivered."[61] But to the city in 1893, the white city was the final horselaugh at the effete easterners who had scoffed at the Midwest's cultural and industrial pretentions.

Congressional approval of Chicago as the site of the 400th anniversary party of Columbus's voyage was a major victory over eastern competitors. The World Exposition of 1892 subscribed $5,000,000 in stock to build the fair, and the city pledged $5,000,000 more. Constitutional limits were easily surmounted with a hastily passed amendment, and the fair was underway.

The architectural firm of Burnham and Root was selected by the forty-five-man board of directors to plan the grounds and buildings, which were to take shape in Jackson Park. Burnham was the executive of the firm, living at the park and directing the 7,000 workmen until the work was completed. Root, designer of the Monadnock building, took over the creative design for the twelve major and 200 minor buildings. Root was well acquainted with the new styles in architecture being developed for use with steel cage construction, but given this ultimate challenge, he froze in the past. Preliminary sketches utilized everything from "mosques and pagodas to Romanesque towers."[62] Root summoned the nation's leading architects and artists to Chicago to plan the buildings, but died a few days later, and the architects took off in all directions. Steel construction was carefully hidden under layers of gingerbread and phony Greek columns, and over all was poured a layer of stucco which was painted white and trimmed with gold. Only Louis Sullivan's Transportation Building remained true to its age, a stunning example of what architecture could be in the future.

Opening day saw the grounds thronged with spectators, and President Cleveland, Governor Altgeld, and Mayor Harrison all appeared. Jane Addams came, and her purse was stolen! All during the fair a stream of American and foreign dignitaries poured into Chicago. The Spanish Infanta Eulalla punctured the pride of Mrs. Palmer by refusing her invitation to tea, saying "I prefer not to meet this innkeeper's wife."[63] Most of the wealthy visitors were not quite so finicky, and the Union League Club was kept busy supplying champagne in glasses, in watermelons, and in ice.

For the not-so-wealthy the fair offered freak shows and excitement on the midway: a map of the United States made entirely of pickles, a 250-foot ferris wheel, and 9,000 paintings, "nearly all of them mediocre."[64] Major attractions were the Palace of Fine Art (which would house both the Field Columbian Museum and the Museum of Science and Industry in the years ahead); the curious Fisheries Building; the Women's Building, with its model kitchen; the Children's Building, where demonstrations of the teaching of deaf mutes and manual training were staged; and the Horticulture Building, with its two sculpture groups by Lorado Taft. The heart of the fair was its Court of Honor, where the wonders of mines and electricity were on display. The Administration Building boasted a dome higher than that of the national capitol. If not quality, the fair certainly had quantity.

The town was "wide open" during the fair, as Tom O'Brien, "King of Bunko," netted $500,000 from luckless gamblers, and Carrie Watson and Vina Fields had to run their girls in double shifts to meet the demand. The most shocking crime of the fair, of course, was the murder of Mayor Harrison on American Cities Day. His assassin, Patrick Prendergast, was speedily tried and hung, despite the heroic efforts of defense attorney Clarence Darrow. Darrow's parade of fourteen physicians testifying to Prendergast's insanity during appeal previewed the technique he would perfect during the Leopold-Loeb case years later, but Prendergast was the only client Darrow ever lost to the executioner.

A more imaginative crime was thwarted before the fair began. Alderman Johnny Powers, ever alert to chances for boodle, proposed that water for the fair be piped in from the crystal springs of Waukesha, Wisconsin, eighty miles distant. Snide comments, such as "How many men supporting this ordinance ever drink water?,"[65] failed to detract the grey wolves who eagerly passed it. Lobbyists in the Wisconsin legislature secured the same results there, only to meet defeat at the hands of Wisconsin's governor, who vetoed the measure, as did Mayor Washburne. Fair visitors would have to take their chances on the Lake Michigan water supply, like the rest of the city.

The Panic of May, 1893, proved a minor setback to the fair, but as depression gripped the rest of the country, visitors and their cash continued to pour into Chicago. By the last day, 27,000,000 visitors had visited the white city, and investors received 10 percent return on their investment. Among the visitors were many reform congresses which met at the grounds, ranging from suffragettes to a labor congress. Largest was the Parliament of Religions, and an interdenominational, interreligious affair. The fair also had other sobering moments when Henry Adams deplored the lack of national purpose exposed by the exposition; Louis Sullivan bemoaned its effect on architecture, predicting dourly: "The damage wrought by the World's Fair will last for half a century from its date, if not longer."[66] And speaking to the American Historical Association, Frederick Jackson Turner pointed out the inevitable changes which had to occur since the American frontier was gone forever.

Gone forever, also, was the frontier settlement that had once been Chicago, and in its place stood a metropolis in which over 1,000,000 people struggled for the almighty dollar. For Chicago, now bristling with skyscrapers and awash in the fumes of heavy industry, was above all a city devoted to building and making, to buying and selling. A cultural and linguistic polyglot, the city absorbed the energy and labor of wave after wave of immigrants, using their sweat to create a "second city" capable of challenging New York herself.

Location was key to the city's growth. Without the agricultural and mineral resources which arrived daily by freighter and rail, and which left by the same routes as furniture and reapers, engines and potted hams, the city would have withered away. This state of dependence-independence was especially true of the city's relationship to the state of Illinois. Chicago needed the coal, corn, and hogs produced downstate. It needed the freight trains that carried those products, and the farmers whose "wish books" were the basis of the city's prosperous mail-order business. And the state needed Chicago, as well, an outlet for its produce, a supplier for its wants. Chicago's taxes flowed into the state treasury, and its prosperity brought both prestige and cultural resources not drawn to states like Indiana or Iowa.

The relationship was mutually beneficial, but it was also a breeding ground for jealousy and ill-feelings. Farmers and miners saw the products of their back-breaking labor returned to them from the city in other forms, and costing far more than they had been paid for the raw materials. As both producer and consumer, downstate was perpetually the victim of the greedy middleman, Chicago. "City slicker" became a small-town pejorative, reflecting also a defensive inferiority complex as small-town dreams of glory faded before Chicago's success. Chicagoans added fuel to the fire with self-confident smugness, and a righteous indignation at the folly of the rural-dominated state legislature.

Nowhere was the tension more evident than in the matter of state control of many of the city's important functions. The population of the city had grown from 12 percent of the state's population in 1870 to 35 percent in 1900, without an increase in formal power. Apportionment always left the city underrepresented, and the state legislature was indifferent, frequently hostile, to the unique problems of the state's only major urban center. Politicians both venal and honest depended on the whims of Springfield when faced with any new crisis of city government. Every aspect of city life was controlled in some measure by laws passed in Springfield to apply primarily to rural communities. Often this outside influence was both beneficial and necessary, for certainly factory owners and slumlords were not about to police their own shoddy practices without a legal prod from the state. In other areas, however, the state's influence complicated rather than solved problems. Overlapping governmental and taxing bodies made an efficient and equitable tax structure impossible. Township government overlapped the city, and the Cook County sheriff was in the ludicrous position of policing the Chicago chief of police. As Bessie Pierce pointed out, "This hydra-headed system of county, city and town government ... with its innumerable clerks, commissioners and other officials, opened the way for professional politicians to spread their influence."[67] It was also damnably inefficient.

In spite of its problems with the state, Chicago continued to grow, virtually a state within a state. Life was special there. It could be cruel as the winter wind off the lake, but it was never dull. It had a smell, a taste, an excitement all its own. An excitement forever captured by Illinois poet Carl Sandburg:

> Come and show me another city with lifted head singing so proud
> to be alive and coarse and strong and cunning.
> Flinging magnetic curses amid the toil of piling job on job, here
> is a tall bold slugger set vivid against the little soft cities'
> Fierce as a dog with a tongue lapping for action, cunning as a
> savage pitted against the wilderness,
> Bareheaded,
> Shovelling,
> Wrecking,
> Planning,
> Building, breaking, rebuilding
> Under the smoke, dust all over his mouth, laughing with white teeth
> Under the terrible burden of destiny laughing as a young man
> laughs,
> Laughing even as an ignorant fighter laughs who has never lost
> a battle,
> Bragging and laughing that under his wrist is the pulse, and
> under his ribs the heart of the people,
> Laughing!
> Laughing the stormy, gusty, brawling laughter of Youth, half-naked
> sweating, proud to be Hog Butcher, Tool Maker, Stacker of
> Wheat, Player with Railroads and Freight Handler to the
> Nation.[68]

1. Ernest McGaffey, "Message of the Town," *Illinois Poets: A Selection,* E. Earle Stibitz, ed. (Carbondale, Ill., 1968), 38.
2. Pierce, *History of Chicago,* 22. Pierce's classic study of Chicago is the most important source for this chapter.
3. *Workingmen's Advocate,* June 11, 1870.
4. Pierce, *History of Chicago,* 32.
5. *Zgoda,* Oct. 31, 1881.
6. Pierce, *History of Chicago,* 38.
7. *Ibid.,* 45.
8. *Ibid.,* 56.
9. Lloyd Lewis and Henry Justin Smith, *Chicago: The History of Its Reputation* (New York, 1929), 117.
10. *Ibid.,* 197.
11. *Chicago Tribune,* March 19, 1870.
12. *Ibid.,* Sept. 4, 1870.
13. *Illinois Staats-Zeitung,* Jan. 10, 1871.

14. *Illinois State Journal,* Oct. 4, 1871.
15. Lambert Tree, "The Fire," *Illinois Prose Writers: A Selection,* Howard Webb, ed. (Carbondale, Ill., 1968), 76-77.
16. *Illinois Staats-Zeitung,* Jan. 10, 1872.
17. *Ibid.*
18. *Chicago Tribune,* Oct. 12, 1871.
19. *Ibid.*
20. *Ibid.,* Oct. 20, 1871.
21. *Ibid.,* Dec. 14, 1871.
22. *Illinois State Journal,* Nov. 1, 1871.
23. *Joliet Signal,* Dec. 5, 1871.
24. *Chicago Times,* Jan. 13, 1872.
25. *Illinois Staats-Zeitung,* March 11, 1872.
26. *Chicago Evening Journal,* Jan. 11, 1872.
27. Pierce, *History of Chicago,* 304.
28. *Ibid.,* 306.
29. *Chicago Times,* March 2, 1871.
30. Lewis and Smith, *Chicago,* 74.
31. *Ibid.,* 96.
32. Pierce, *History of Chicago,* 304.
33. *Chicago Tribune,* Sept. 18, 1875.
34. *Illinois Staats-Zeitung,* March 8, 1871.
35. *Chicago Times,* June 20, 1875.
36. Lloyd Wendt and Herman Kogan, *Bosses in Lusty Chicago: The Story of Bathhouse John and Hinky Dink* (Bloomington, Ind., 1967), 37. Originally published in hard cover as *Lords of the Levee,* Wendt and Kogan's spritely description of Chicago underworld politics is another valuable source for this chapter.
37. Illinois, Bureau of Labor Statistics, *9th Biennial Report,* 1896, 239-320. Pierce, *History of Chicago,* 229.
38. *Chicago Republican,* June 15, 1865.
39. *ICRR* vs. *Ill.* 146 U.S. 387, 1892.
40. Pierce, *History of Chicago,* 356.
41. Finley Peter Dunne, *The World of Mr. Dooley,* Louis Filler, ed. (New York, 1962), 57.
42. Wendt and Kogan, *Bosses in Lusty Chicago,* 17.
43. *Ibid.,* 21.
44. *Ibid.,* 34.
45. Sidney A. Roberts, "The Municipal Voters' League and Chicago's Boodlers," *Journal of the Illinois State Historical Society* LIII (Summer, 1960), 118.
46. *Ibid.,* 145.
47. Wendt and Kogan, *Bosses in Lusty Chicago,* 155.
48. Pierce, *History of Chicago,* 468.
49. Ray Ginger, *Altgeld's America: The Lincoln Ideal Versus Changing Realities* (New York, 1958), 251.
50. Bert Leston Taylor, "Reform in Our Town," in Stibitz, *Illinois Poets,* 48.
51. Dunne, *World of Mr. Dooley,* 72.
52. Louise C. Wade, "The Heritage from Chicago's Early Settlement Houses," *Journal of the Illinois State Historical Society* LX (Winter, 1967), 433.
53. *Ibid.*
54. Irving Dilliard, "Civil Liberties of Negroes in Illinois since 1865," *Journal of the Illinois State Historical Society* LVI (Autumn, 1963).
55. Peter A. Soderbergh, "Charles A. Beard in Chicago, 1896," *Journal of the Illinois State Historical Society* LXIII (Summer, 1970), 129. Mary Ritter Beard, *The Making of Charles A. Beard: An Interpretation* (New York, 1955), 14-15.
56. Jane Addams, "Social Settlements in Illinois," *Transactions of the Illinois State Historical Society for 1906,* 331.
57. *Ibid.,* 332.

58. Mary E. McDowell, "A Quarter of a Century in the Stockyards District," *Transactions of the Illinois State Historical Society for 1920*, 230.

59. Ginger, *Altgeld's America*, 305.

60. *Ibid.*, 309.

61. *Ibid.*, 8.

62. *Ibid.*, 15.

63. *Ibid.*, 19.

64. *Ibid.*, 20.

65. Wendt and Kogan, *Bosses in Lusty Chicago*, 70.

66. Ginger, *Altgeld's America*, 22.

67. Pierce, *History of Chicago*, 339.

68. Carl Sandburg, "Chicago," in Stibitz, *Illinois Poets*, 138-139.

9
Prairie Culture

The children now growing up should become devout
gardeners or architects or park architects or teachers of
dancing in the Greek spirit or musicians or novelists or
poets or story-writers or craftsmen or woodcarvers or
dramatists or actors or singers. They should find their
talent and nurse it industriously.

N. Vachel Lindsay[1]

Vachel Lindsay's vision of a state devoted to the arts was
an impossible dream for the post–Civil War generation. For the
new immigrant, the miner, the sweated factory worker, life was a
dawn to dusk struggle for a grey survival. The farmer at work in the
free air lacked both the labor-saving machinery to grant him leisure
and the easy access to metropolitan centers to use any free time to
expand his cultural horizons. For most others it was a time of hard
work, twelve-hour days, endless work weeks, with the leisure to
indulge in cultural pursuits a priceless luxury afforded to the very
few. The creative genius within the state's population embodied by
such men as Gustavus Swift and Aaron Montgomery Ward was
directed not toward the arts but toward business, manufacture,
empire building.

This is not to say, however, that all forms of literature, art,
religion, and education in Illinois were stagnant. The newspaper
business saw tremendous change and expansion, serving as an
introduction to America for the immigrant, the colorful and often
vituperative voice of political factions, and a forum and training
ground for new writers. Although no Illinois writers produced
masterpieces during the period, the works of outside writers were
increasingly circulated as immigrant and women's groups combined with government and philanthropists to sponsor free public
libraries. Artistically, perhaps, it was the architects who won the

most lasting success, as the Chicago school of building transformed the nation's urban centers. It was the state's churches which exerted the most pervasive and immediate influence on the daily life and attitudes of the people. That influence was augmented by the state, as the common schools were expanded and joined by the beginnings of a high school system and by new state universities.

Home-grown writing reached great numbers of readers in the state through the newspapers. The political influence of newspapers had been important since territorial days, and it continued to grow. There were more newspaper readers than ever before, as national circulation jumped by 222 percent against a population increase of 63 percent between 1870 and 1890. Part of the rise in readership came with a decrease in the illiteracy rate from 20 to 13 percent. The rest came from a general lowering of the literary pretensions of the papers themselves to the lowest possible point. Immigrants able to read no other English could learn the language, and often did, from the simplified prose of the press.

Chicago was a thriving publishing center, boasting eleven daily, twenty-two weekly, and a larger indeterminate number of monthly papers in 1860. Many were part of the foreign language press, exerting great influence over their immigrant readership. The most important paper in Chicago, and perhaps the state, however, was the *Chicago Tribune*, under the leadership of Joseph Medill. Taking a conservative Republican stance, the *Tribune* was antilabor and a vigorous defender of the status quo. Medill's style prompted a rival paper to state in mock disbelief, "Yes, it was the editor of the *Chicago Tribune* who recently lectured in Ohio on journalistic decency and propriety. You wouldn't suspect it on reading his own humbug and blackguard paper, but it is nevertheless a fact."[2]

The *Tribune* took a more independent and liberal stance during the years 1865 to 1874, when it was edited by Horace White and financially controlled by White and Alfred Cowles. The paper backed the liberal Republican slate in the election of 1872 and was "read out of the Republican party" for its heresy,[3] but Medill regained control on November 4, 1874. With ever expanding interest, the *Tribune* opened a London bureau in 1877, sent reporters to cover both sides of the Russo-Turkish war, and in 1891 assigned a reporter to accompany Admiral Perry's trip to Greenland. The paper's chief advertisers were the patent medicine companies, and while Lydia Pinkham ministered to the readers' ills, George Uptmas, writing as Peregrine Pickles, reviewed music for high society. During the period sports and women's pages were added and amply illustrated with pictures.

To counter the *Tribune's* Republican line, Chicago Democrats turned to the *Chicago Daily Times.* Copperhead during the war, the paper supported Democratic candidates and was prolabor—so long as labor did not try to organize the *Daily Times.* The paper specialized in racy, human interest stories, always taking a super-pious stance. Editor William Story was bombarded with libel suits—and attacked physically in the street by a troupe of British burlesque artists whom he had labeled "bawds."

Story introduced the city's first Sunday entertainment section, and sent a foreign correspondent to London in 1881. At his death in 1884 the paper foundered, in spite of the presence of the brilliant, young Finley Peter Dunne. It was absorbed by the *Chicago Herald*, a more literary paper, where Dunne was given the opportunity to develop as an editorial-feature writer and originator of the Irish political sage, Mr. Dooley.

The Chicago *Inter-Ocean,* led by J. Young Scammon, compensated for the *Tribune's* temporary political lapse in 1872. With the motto, "Republican in everything; independent in Nothing,"[4] the *Inter-Ocean* sang Republican praises and gained readers by its support of civic, religious, and philanthropic causes. However, the chief competitor of the *Tribune* was the *Chicago Daily News.* Founded in 1876, it followed the Pulitzer pattern of exposé and spectacular detective work. Usually Republican, it was moderate on labor issues, and labeled the *Tribune,* "The Chicago Daily *Nuisance."* The *Daily News* opposed traction magnate Charles Yerkes, and introduced the colorful style of sports reporting—originating the baseball term "southpaw," for instance. A morning edition began publication in 1881, and in 1892 the combined *Chicago Daily News* was the only Illinois paper among the top ten circulation papers in the country.[5]

Chicago did not have a monopoly on newspaper activity. The Springfield papers—the Republican *Journal* and Democratic *Register*—exerted great influence from their vantage point in the state capital. By 1900, 1,250 publishing companies were printing newspapers and periodicals in the state. Wood-pulp paper, the web-perfecting press, and the Linotype all freed small-town editors from total dependence on boiler-plate copy, and almost every town had its *Argus* or *Gazette* or *Republican.* The small-town editor attracted readers with his flamboyant style, and guarded his community's morals against the drunkard, the philanderer, and the nonconformist.

Newspapers in downstate Illinois were often family enterprises, personal and close to their readers' lives and problems. Country readers turned to the *Monmouth Atlas* or the *Galesburg Press and People* to find out "who had Sunday dinner with whom, or what married son in Kansas or Colorado was visiting the home folks."[6] The insides might still be boiler plate, but the rural papers carried all the local news on page one. "Railroad wrecks were always good reading," recalls one reader, "especially when a local citizen was one of the passengers involved."[7]

In an age when the only means of mass communication was the print media, the colorful descriptive prose of the press was the sole means of giving the audience an at-the-scenes feel for a story. Although colorful description served a necessary purpose, it frequently gave a dangerously biased slant to the news. The Chicago press adopted no doctrine of fairness, for example, in its reportage of the great strike of 1877. "BLOOD," screamed the headlines. "TERROR'S REIGN, THE STREETS OF CHICAGO GIVEN OVER TO HOWLING MOBS OF THIEVES AND CUT THROATS." The stories under the headlines ran in the same vein. "Rake the mob with grape shot from the artillery," urged one paper, "and follow the thing up with a bayonet charge." A list of the strikers killed and wounded was followed by the extraneous observation that "many others have been wounded, and no doubt some others killed whose names cannot be obtained immediately, their relatives and friends desiring for good reasons to keep such names a secret." The reader followed the story of street fighting in an area described in this way: "All around this section (South Canal Street) are massed some of the vilest dregs of the city's population. In the Bohemian district flourish two low dives called Bohemian halls and within their reeking and filthy precincts commune societies, foreign labor companies, foreign trade unions, and low-lived political associations hatch communism and treason." The action itself was described in equally vivid style:

> The pale air was streaked with blood. Huge, bloated women at the windows yelled encouragement and defiance. Pistol balls shrieked as they flew. The clash of sabers and shouts of maddened men made the hot air hideous. Horses were spurred into the job, and swords rose and fell with cruel significance. Alleys were gutted of molten masses of enraged humanity. Great massive blows fell on their passion-stained faces, and tore the rage out of them. Shrinking figures darted behind boxes and fired upon the cavalry. The prisoners shrieked for rescue and sank quivering in the wagons under the cut of clubs. Stones rattled on the streets and from the windows came showers of missiles.[8]

Some editors may have been as cynical as Edgar Lee Masters's Editor Wheden, whose goal was "to be able to see every side of every question, to be on every side, to be everything, to be nothing long; to use great feelings and passions of the human family for base designs, for cunning ends."[9] More probably his goal was to reflect the beliefs of his readers—readers steeped in a puritanism in which financial success was proof of virtue.

Big city newspapers were not yet faceless corporate entities, and the chain makers were still tentatively grasping at their empires. Competition among papers was a deadly earnest game pursued by flamboyant personalities. And the readers got to watch the fun. "Journalism is the profession without jealousy," wrote a bemused cynic on the *Burlington Hawkeye* in 1878. The *Chicago Evening Journal* reprinted his praise of the profession in a time of mounting competition and rising vituperation:

I don't believe there is a profession in the world so free from jealousy as this. We love each other. And when . . . we feel constrained to call a contemporary a "measureless liar," he knows we mean business, and if he is a man who will get mad at a little trivial thing like that, he comes over with a club and mashes us and that is the end of it. We may have occasion to denounce him, in the heat of the conflict, as a "moral hyena . . . and destroyer of the truth, upon whose lips the dear, pure truth, if ever it could spring from a heart so blackened and stained with crime, turns to ashes and bitterness before it can be uttered." We may feel it our duty to call an esteemed contemporary a "pattering slave to a gang of petty tyrants," an unprincipled scoundrel whose groveling carcass, wallowing in the cesspool of corruption steeped to its thieving eyes in abhorrent partisan infamy, pursues its nefarious traffic to the very shadow of the mocking gallows it has cheated too long. We get mad at these things sometimes, dreadful mad, awful mad. But we get over it, especially if the other man is the biggest.[10]

While their elders read the news, schoolchildren were learning about virtue and success from the Horatio Alger series and the Elsie Dinsmore books. Mr. Coffin's *Old Times in the Colonies* and *The Story of Liberty* told "what went on over in Europe that sent people heading across the ocean to America." As Carl Sandburg remembers, "You learned about 'tyrants' and 'tyranny' and people slaughtered in fights and wars about religion, how your head came off if they caught you for 'heresy' which was where you didn't see God and Jesus the same way as those who cut your head off."[11]

Coffin also wrote *The Boys of '76* and *The Boys of '61*, the latter a washout among Sandburg's friends. "It was a bigger war in '61 than '76," Sandburg thought, "and maybe so big he couldn't get his head around it." Tom Sawyer and Huckleberry Finn were available, but "they seemed to be for a later time." Instead, "Every boy except the dumbest read . . . *Toby Tyler: Or, Ten Weeks with a Circus* and *Tim and Tip: Or the Adventures of a Boy and a Dog.*"[12]

When they finished the daily papers, the grown-ups turned to the family Bible for reading, or to "how-to" books like *American Plumbing* and *The Amateur Printer: Or Type-Setting at Home.* For "literature" lovers, Sears Roebuck's advance series offered Emerson's *Essays* and *The Autocrat of the Breakfast Table,* along with a host of romantic novels. Bertha M. Clay had no fewer than eighteen titles of the 125 available from Sears in 1897. Mrs. Clay's less than immortal *A Mad Love, Only One Sin* and *Dark Marriage Morn* spiced life in the Calvinist prairie state[13] and provided an emotional release. As one writer remembers it, "The purpose of literature was the cultivation of noble sentiments, and grief was evidence of refinement, especially if it were vicarious. It was bad form to weep over the hardships of everyday, which were many, but tears over the sad fate of a character in a book provided a needed and safe emotional outlet."[14]

Literary and debating societies flourished in the small towns of downstate, because "if we wanted intellectual entertainment we must provide it ourselves."[15] Debates centered about such age-old questions as "resolved, that the pen is mightier than the sword." One debater remembers: "We seemed never to debate contemporary problems, tariff, civil service, reform, the waste of public lands and dwindling farm incomes . . . we had not become politically awake and articulate in National affairs. The stormy decade of the nineties was still to come."[16]

Reading was a luxury in those days. Only those with time to spare during the long work day could sit idly reading, for as the pre-electric shadows closed in, Illinois families had little choice but to go early to bed. Further, free public libraries as a source of books were in short supply. The great Chicago fire of 1871 consumed between 2,000,000 and 3,000,000 books, and instigated a worldwide public outpouring of donated books into the smoldering city. More important, it provided the public support necessary for the passage of the state's first library law, on March 7, 1872. Municipalities could now support public libraries out of tax funds, and nine cities took advantage of the law the first year: Elgin, Rockford, Chicago, Earlville, East St. Louis, Moline, Rock Island, Oregon, and Warsaw. In the next seven years, seventeen more public libraries opened their doors across the state, and by 1906, 112 of 146 city libraries in the state were tax-supported.[17]

Much of the support for the library movement came from such private groups as the St. Clair Library Association. A society of

German immigrants, living in and near Belleville, donated its own books for a library and organized under a constitution written by Gustavus Koerner in 1860. A German singing society, the *Belleville Saengerbund*, merged with the library group. Both dissolved in 1883, giving their entire collection to the free Belleville Public Library. In the same period school district libraries and subscription libraries formed a precedent for the tax-supported system.

A public library did not spring into being with the wave of a governor's pen or a mayor's decree. Moline, for example, was one of the first cities to levy a tax for a library, but the city library board soon found the $800 city levy totally insufficient and appealed for private aid. Civic groups raised $5,864.38 in a subscription drive; women's groups raised money from lectures and banquets; and the Greeley-Brown political club donated its leftover campaign funds—$11.80. The library opened with a fund-raising strawberry festival on May 10, 1873, and moved into new rooms donated by a wealthy benefactor in 1877. By the turn of the century, however, the Moline Library had outgrown its home, and the city asked Andrew Carnegie for a library grant. He offered $38,000, providing the city donated the land, and agreed to maintain the library at a cost of no less than $3,800 per year—a sum well within the enlarged city library tax levy.

By 1906 the state boasted forty-eight Carnegie-financed library buildings and a statewide circulation of more than 2,000,000 volumes per year. Carnegie was neither alone in his belief in the power of the printed word nor in his quest for immortality through endowment. In 1887 wealthy merchant John Newberry endowed a private research library to be located in Chicago. The Newberry Library concentrated on the humanities, but was joined in 1897 by the John Crerar Library, a research facility devoted to science and technology—stretching somewhat its founder's decree that it "create and sustain a healthy and moral Christian sentiment in the community."[18] Generally, libraries were a goal on which all segments of society could agree, and cooperation between the state, immigrant groups, women's groups, and wealthy benefactors made the food for intellectual growth available throughout the state.

Illinois poets in the pre–Civil War years railed against slavery, but a more constant theme was life on the "beautiful Prairie Land, flecked with white cottages, like the fair lilybells nestled in green."[19] Lincoln's Secretary John Hay captured the awe of the settler as he surveyed the endless acres of prairie land in an 1858 poem:

> No accent wounds the reverent air,
> No footprint dints the sod,

> Lone in the light the prairie lies,
> Rapt in a dream of God.[20]

That dream of solitude and peace had vanished from the prairie of 1895 as smoke-belching trains and telegraph wires brought even the most rural farmers into the bustling hurly-burly of city life. The sentimentality of the rural poets was slowly replaced by the brusque realism of the urbanites—but not without a struggle. Ernest McGaffey, lawyer and literary critic of the *Chicago American,* embodied both styles: wistfully yearning for the "mournful piercing notes that mark the whistle of the Meadow-Lark," in the same volume that spoke the bitter "Message of the Town":

> Look up to the stony arches
> Where art and mammon meet,
> There's a sound where Traffic marches
> A call in the City street,
> For a voice is ever ringing
> 'Gird up your loins and flee
> I will harden your heart or break it
> If you will abide in me.'[21]

Neither reality nor irony was as popular as dreams. Eugene Field's *Chicago Daily* column, "Sharps and Flats," poked not-so-gentle fun at Chicago's pretensions in such poems as "When Stedman Comes to Town," which included the verse:

> And Mrs. Hamm, a faded belle,
> And one no longer young.—
> She speaks the native quite as well
> As any foreign tongue,—
> At Mr. Hamm's reception she
> Will wear a gorgeous gown
> That show all else but modesty,
> When Stedman comes to town.[22]

But it was not Field's wit which inspired teachers to proclaim, "England might have Shakespeare and Milton, New England might have Longfellow and Holmes, but Illinois and the corn belt had Eugene Field." It was a slightly maudlin ballad entitled "Little Boy Blue" which brought him fame. No wonder he could wryly note: "No, Nature reserved this tender bard/For the kindlier age of Pork and Lard."[23]

While the problems of city life were finding expression in poetry, the daily lives of rural Illinois continued to influence future city poets. In 1914 Edgar Lee Masters, a Chicago attorney, brought out a scandalous volume of epitaphs, voices of the dead of Spoon River. Collecting names from Spoon River and Sangamon County cemeteries, he gave a vivid picture of small-town Illinois in the decades after the Civil War. Temperance forces were in full sway, driving the pious to "slip behind the prescription partition in Trainers drug store"[24] for a drink, and forbidding divorce to the most miserable couples. Murder and desertion could free an unhappy spouse, but rural Illinois recognized no other escape.

Not all Illinois writers remained in their home state, and not all used the state as a topic of their writings, but their early lives in the prairie state nonetheless carried over into their later work. One nationally known sociologist, geologist, and botanist, Lester H. Ward, was born in Joliet in 1841. His later works reflect the years he spent in the "backward region" of Illinois.[25]

Among other Illinoisans making their way in the world was Francis Grierson, pianist-essayist. His *Modern Mysticism* appeared in 1899, and his *Valley of Shadows,* published in 1909, contained reminiscences of life in Illinois and Missouri, and dealt with the theme, "Lincoln the mystic."[26]

Although Illinois was not a mecca for writers in the years before the turn of the century, the growth of Chicago into a worldly and fascinating urban center, second only to New York, destined that city for future literary greatness. As Masters, Sandburg, Theodore Dreiser, and Harriet Monroe sought the literary congeniality of the city in the early years of the twentieth century, a tradition was being born. Vachel Lindsay, another Illinois poet nurtured in downstate Illinois in those turbulent years of the 1880s and 1890s, for example, would remain in his hometown of Springfield but receive his first public renown in the pages of Monroe's *Poetry Magazine,* published in Chicago.

The only Illinois artist to emerge from obscurity during the period was sculptor Lorado Taft. Born in the same month as the Civil War, April 29, 1860, Lorado Taft became one of the most influential figures in American sculpture. An early graduate of the University of Illinois, Taft began his career as a teacher at the Chicago Art Institute in 1886. His most famous works were portraits and allegorical groups such as the *Fountain of the Great Lakes* at the Art Institute. He also earned fame as an art historian and author, publishing *The History of American Sculpture* in 1903 and *Modern Tendencies in Sculpture* in 1921. Robert Marshall Root acquired some fame for his painting of the Lincoln-Douglas debate at Charleston, but was better known as a designer of Tiffany glass.

The cities of Anna and Chester contributed two artists to the popular scene, Frank Willard, creator of Moon Mullins, and Elgiar Segar, creator of Popeye.[27]

Illinois' greatest contributions to art were its buildings, most of them commissioned by the state's new business aristocracy. For their homes, the new rich ordered rococo, with gables and cornices, gingerbread castles whose value was judged by their size. Notable exceptions were two homes designed by the young Frank Lloyd Wright: Charnley House (1892) and Winslow House (1893). Winslow House in River Forest was Wright's first acknowledged independent work after leaving the office of Adler and Sullivan, and although he was influenced by Sullivan's cut stone facades and plaster friezes, the house predicts the prairie house Wright would perfect in later years. Its sheltering roof and low massing marked a turn toward human dimensions in architecture. The real architectural genius of the state, however, drew its inspiration not from homes, but from business. Grand enterprises demanded grand edifices, and the titans of business commanded that they be built.

In 1885, Marshall Field sent to Boston for Henry Hobson Richardson to design a wholesale store worthy of his thriving business. Comprising 500,000 square feet of floor space, the building's very size was impressive—although Field doubted that he could profitably use that much space. Field's pessimism proved unfounded, and the massive sandstone structure greatly influenced both Field's customers and Chicago architect Louis Sullivan. Its simplicity and stone arches broke the bonds of the gilded age and pointed to the obvious design necessary for a tall building.

The well-bred and new rich could get along in a modest three-story plus attic home, but rising costs of city land demanded that business and industry build up, not out. Two developments made that possible: the introduction and improvement of elevators and of structural steel. Without steel to support the building, a sixteen-story structure like John Wellborn Root's Monadnock building required walls fifteen feet thick at the base, wasted space, and had no large display windows. The Monadnock, however, avoided decorative frills, to the disappointment of the pigeons and the future inspiration of students of the new style of architecture.

Structural steel was adapted to building in the mid-1880s, and buildings like the Chicago Rookery, designed in 1886 by Burnham and Root, combined both masonry wall-bearing construction and a skeletal frame. The first all steel frame building in the world was William LeBaron Jenney's Home Insurance Building, completed in 1885, and followed by Holabird and Roche's Tacoma building in 1888. The technique of "Chicago construction" was quickly copied in New York and other big cities. Louis Sullivan took the steel frame, added horizontal windows, and heralded a new age in architectural design: the era of the skyscraper.[28]

Just as big business gave needed impetus and funding to revolutionary trends in architecture, so did the wealthy as they began commissioning libraries, museums, and auditoriums. Dankmer, Adler, and Sullivan combined a hotel, office building, and auditorium into an acoustic masterpiece in the Chicago Auditorium building in 1893. The endowment for the Newberry Library in 1887 resulted in 1893 in a five-unit renaissance-like structure designed by Henry Ives Cobb.

Dreams of glory found their way into buildings built to accommodate future greatness. When dreams fell through, those hopeful structures looked mockingly down at dusty villages whose hopes had gone sour. The most notorious example of overbuilding plunged Macoupin County into debt for forty-three years to pay for the state's most magnificent courthouse. Originally budgeted for $50,000, cost overruns eventually totalled $1,380,000. Although the building was solidly built, and glorious in its execution, it cost twice its worth and was completed amid charges of mismanagement and litigation to stop completion. Begun in 1867 and completed in 1870, it was not paid for until 1910 and remained a magnificent if sometimes embarrassing heritage.

Illinois architecture, its sources as varied as its population, made strides toward a rational, functional style which attempted to unite beauty with simplicity and function. All styles, from classic Greek to the colonial Georgian of Allerton House in Monticello, and the French Empire styling of the Huffman House in Quincy to renaissance-romanesque combinations like Cairo's customhouse and post office, sprouted on the corn fields and in the growing cities. And amid the cheerful clutter of it all, Frank Lloyd Wright's quiet revolution was taking shape.

In Illinois, as in the rest of the Midwest, the little brown church in the vale remained the most important influence on the cultural and intellectual life of the state prior to 1900. For the native born, that influence was usually a hardy protestantism, fundamental in doctrine, puritanical in tradition, and capitalistic in economic dogma.

The impact of immigration from central and eastern Europe can be especially seen in the makeup of the major church denominations during the period. Roman Catholics were not included among the major denominations until 1900—and they then had the largest membership of any church group in the country. In the United States, church membership stood at:

Year[29]	Catholic	Presbyterian	Methodist	S. Baptist
1870		445,000	1,822,000	
1880		573,000	2,694,000	1,673,000
1890		761,000	3,442,000	1,236,000
1900	10,130,000	983,000	4,226,000	1,656,000

Choice of denomination was vital. Albert Britt remembers, "it seems not to have occurred that an active connection with any church could be avoided. Church membership was almost as much a part of citizenship as choice of a party and exercise of the right of suffrage. . . . Only the landless and drifting could ignore it."[30] Minor differences in dogma loomed large as salvation hung by the slender thread of total immersion or foot washing. Nontheological hair-splitting aside, however, Illinois Protestant churches were remarkably similar as they led onward their Christian soldiers.

Country churches were built by their parishioners as a material gesture of devotion. Four walls and a roof and floor, an unadorned rectangle innocent of altar or ecclesiastical symbols and trappings, held the wooden pews and pulpit. In the cities, congregations adopted the eclectic styles of an architecture prominent in other areas of endeavor and put up a variety of edifices. Typical of the grandiose style was the Methodist building in Springfield, a three-story yellow stone structure seating 500, built in 1884. Its lofty steeple and minaret tower proclaimed a staunch faith in the perpetual growth of the congregation.

Services followed a ritualized order: "prayer, song, Scripture, exposition, exhortation, collection and benediction."[31] High point of any service was the call to repentant sinners to come forward. Sermons were based on a literal belief in the Bible, and if the tempests of a changing society were raging all around, within those four solid walls the social problems of the world vanished before the all-consuming importance of personal salvation.

The camp meetings popular in the state's frontier days continued to draw "seekers" who camped out at Clear Creek and Watseka, Macomb and Streator. In the cities, traveling evangelists held mass revivals, with Dwight L. Moody and Ira O. Sankey holding a celebrated meeting in Chicago in 1876. They were rivaled on the circuit by Thomas Harrison, the "boy evangelist," in the 1880s and Georgia evangelist Sam Small, who claimed attendance of 260,000 during a five-week meeting in Chicago in 1886. In 1889, former baseball player William "Billy" Sunday fell short of Small's record in his first public appearance as an evangelist. He "converted" forty-eight youths.

A revival was serious business, and violent emotional reactions were expected as sinners heard the call. One evangelist recalls: "When seekers were invited forward, again Mr. Teeters' friend rose to get away; but he could not. In about twenty minutes he lay perfectly helpless and apparently unconscious. He remained thus . . . perhaps in all, three hours. Then he came out, one of the happiest of men."[32] The emotional uplift of a "protracted meeting" highlighted the ever present battle against personal sin that marked Illinois protestantism. Corporate sin was considered none of the church's business.

Census figures hardly do justice to the schisms and controversies covered under the title "Methodist" or "Lutheran." The Illinois Baptists included by 1890, 95,237 Regular Baptists (North), 350 Seven-Day Baptists, 6,096 Free Will Baptists, 2,605 General Baptists, 5,301 Primitive Baptists, and 51 Old Two-Seed-in-the-Spirit Predestinarian Baptists. The most numerous protestant group, the Methodists, claimed twelve separate subgroups, and the Presbyterians, ten. Smaller denominations like the Dunkards were equally divided, splitting into Old Order, Conservative, and Brethren Progressives. Differences between competing sects within a denomination were as fierce as those between two different denominations, as each group claimed the "Keys to the Kingdom."[33]

Immigrants during this period were mainly Lutheran and Catholic as Germans and Irishmen settled in ethnic groups around the state. The church provided cultural continuity with the Old Country and eased the transition into American society. In many cases, however, it also hampered assimilation of the immigrant into the cultural mainstream as first-generation immigrants clung to native-tongue services and refused to venture into the alien society.

French Catholic missionaries were among the state's first white settlers, and Catholic communions in the Cahokia-Kaskaskia area remained strong. In 1868 the Alton diocese had 100 priests, 123 parishes, fifty-six parochial schools, two colleges for boys, three academies for girls, and three hospitals. The diocese was divided in 1887, and a new Belleville diocese established. The country's only Negro priest carried the cross at the consecration of the new diocesan bishop in 1898, and the church's new area had grown to sixty-three priests, eighty-two churches, five chapels, fifty-three parochial schools (including nineteen public schools staffed by nuns), one orphanage, and three hospitals. Swelling immigration into Chicago by 1890 saw 267,795 of the state's 473,324 Roman Catholics living in Cook County. All 150 Reformed Catholics lived there, as did all 155 Catholic Apostolics and all 2,000 Greek Uniate Catholics, making Chicago the second largest Catholic center in the United States. More than 205,500 Roman Catholics lived in downstate Illinois, 12,000 in Williamson County, and 15,000 in Jo Davies.[34]

Although some Germans joined Evangelical churches, the home of the Reformation was still a stalwart bastion of the Lutheran church. The General Synod of the Lutheran church was organized in St. Clair County in 1836 with the encouragement that "St. Clair County . . . contains more Germans than any county in the state."[35] A theology school established by the group in Hillsboro in 1846 was moved to Springfield in 1852 as Illinois State University. Doctrinal differences soon split the group, with the German record going to one faction, the English record to another. Illinois State was sold to the Missouri Synod in 1870, and the new central Illinois Synod set up its own seminary at Carthage College. By 1890 Illinois Lutherans were divided into twelve synods, with 2,501 communicants belonging to independent Lutheran churches.

Just as people turned to new political parties when they disagreed with a policy of an old one, so did they turn to new churches as arguments over doctrine split denominations into proliferating splinters of the "true church." For those who could not reconcile their beliefs within any of the established sects, "new" religious groups opened their doors. The Salvation Army claimed 922 militants in 1890, the Social Brethren, 839, the Society of Ethical Change, 175, the Spiritualists, 1,314, the Theosophical Society, 68, the Unitarians, 1,932, and the Universalists, 3,434. As the century closed, Mary Baker Eddy began drawing converts to Christian Science, and John Alex Dowie led the faith healers from his Christian Catholic tabernacle across from the world's fair.

Claiming that "DOCTORS AS A PROFESSION are Directly Inspired by the Devil," Dowie railed against "those poisoners general and surgical butchers" who had persuaded the legislature to require antidiphtheria innoculations. "By the time these gentlemen have got through," he warned, "they will have the legislature hand the children over to them at birth and keep the whole population in their hands from the cradle to the grave." Dowie claimed harassment by the "infamous State Board of Health" and the "infamous City Board of Health"[36] in his crusade against medicine.

The state's Jewish population was also divided, with 4,405 Orthodox upholding traditions abandoned by 5,766 Reformed. Almost all of the Jewish population lived in Chicago, with 4,345 of the Orthodox and 4,872 of the Reformed congregants living in Cook County. In 1889 Chicago counted one Protestant edifice to every 315 Protestants, one Roman Catholic church to every 2,202 Roman Catholic communicants, and one synogogue to every 919 of the Jewish faith."[37]

The publication of Darwin's *On the Origin of Species* and the increasing importance of scientific thought and methods posed a threat to churches which based their legitimacy on a literal interpretation of the Holy Scriptures. Adam and Eve and Jonah and the Whale were hard to reconcile with evolutionary theory and the proofs required by scientific thought. The church responded to the crisis by closing its doors to the controversy and tossing out ministers who attempted a new interpretation of the scriptures. The most famous heresy trial of the 1870s occurred in Chicago when Dr. David Swing was charged with "using equivocal language in respect to fundamental doctrines, rejecting a literal interpretation of the Bible or its plenary inspiration and not sincerely receiving and adopting the confession of Faith of the Presbyterian Church."[38] Acquitted by the Chicago presbytery, Swing was removed from his church by the synod of Illinois (North), which reversed the local decision. The *Chicago Times* regretted the verdict, pointing out that "those bespeaking toleration for Swing's point of view represented three-fourths of all the brains, courage and progress of the City of Chicago."[39] The Methodists soon followed suit, ejecting Dr. Hiram Thompson from his Chicago pulpit and finally completely out of the church when exile to Aurora failed to close his mind and mouth to new ideas. Orthodox Jews were equally zealous, and the *Chicago Times* reported the expulsion of a rabbi who "did not conduct the services in accordance with the ancient forms of the sect."[40] Both Swing and Thompson formed their own independent churches, where they continued to preach their "heresies."

Robert Ingersoll took a more extreme view, maintaining that religion and liberty were antithetical. Although excoriated as "the blasphemer, the filth dispenser, the willful falsifier of facts,"[41] "Pope Bob's" agnosticism won many adherents as radical free thinkers organized into liberal leagues to insure the total separation of church and state.

Churches were intimately involved in almost every aspect of community life and were not unwilling to take on the "evils" of the day. In 1881 Dr. Herrick Johnson, a Chicago Protestant, launched an attack on the theater, "because of its demoralizing influence and because it was an institution which could not be recognized by those who professed Christianity."[42] Chicago's four major theaters, McVickers, the Opera House, Hooleys, and Haverly's were accused of exposing the public to such "filth" as *Camille, Phadre,* and *The Pirates of Penzance.* The controversy raged in press and pulpit throughout the next year, as Dr. David Swing, acquitted of heresy by the Presbyterians, led the anti-Johnson forces. Chicagoans continued to attend the theater, and the antitheater campaign eventually fizzled out with no appreciable effect.

By the mid-1880s, movements toward cooperation between church groups were underway. In Chicago the Methodist churches joined a combined Chicago Home Missionary and Church Extension Society incorporated in 1885. In 1886, a convention of Christian workers from around the state discussed their mutual problems and resolved "to promote union among the various city evangelization agencies" and "cooperate with the churches without regard to denomination."[43] A Bible and Prophecy Conference debated the "second coming," and in 1890 a Conference on the Past, Present, and Future of Israel attempted to harmonize Jewish-Christian relationships. Cooperation did not extend, however, to the Catholic churches, which were a prime target for bigoted groups like the American Protective Association.

Ecumenical action in the 1880s and 1890s was a tenuous movement as tentative efforts at joint action brought rival groups into cooperative ventures. Internal organization and doctrine remained inviolate, but efforts at cooperation in the social mission of the church had some success. That success was vital, as the church faced a massive new challenge.

Protestant doctrine emphasized hard work, with financial success translated into evidence of spiritual blessings. Ministers sided with employers in strikes, and the situation reached the point where it could be said, "there is no place in the average Chicago church for the poor man . . . surrounded by individuals who not only regard poverty as a disgrace, but by their vulgar display endeavor to perpetually remind the poor man of his poverty."[44] Understandably, church membership and support by the working class declined, and by the 1890s church building was no longer keeping pace with the increase in population.

The Chicago Methodist Ministerial Alliance attempted to respond in 1878 by opening its sessions to leading socialists. The program had no tangible results, however, and it remained for individual clergymen to awaken their congregations to the social needs of the world outside the cloister. Baptist George C. Loxmer was an early advocate of the new viewpoint of Christian concern for the living and working conditions of the poor. Concerned clergymen opened missions on "Bum Boulevard," like Colonel George Clarke's Pacific Garden Mission, established in 1877. From 1883 to 1890 the Chicago Missionary Society organized twenty-four churches, and the Congregational City Missionary Society enlarged its activities to include kindergarten, an industrial school for girls, mothers' meetings, and recreation and reading rooms. In 1886 the Armour Mission, a philanthropic project, began providing social services and a nonsectarian gospel.

The Salvation Army arrived in the late 1880s and moved into the void left by Chicago's Protestant rejection of the plight of the working class. In June of 1892 the army launched a general social service drive in the Chicago slums. The social gospel drew individual adherents among Protestants, but it was a personal thing. Protestant humanism was not yet recognized by the official voices of Illinois Protestant denominations.

For Illinois Catholics, the situation was quite different. The church had always been actively involved in social welfare work, especially in the establishment of schools, hospitals, and orphanages. In 1891 Pope Leo XII, in the encyclical *Rerum Novarum,* gave his approval to labor unions and endorsed a broad social program. Cardinal Gibbons insisted on a sympathetic approach to the problem of the working man, and thus preserved for the church the loyalty of this vast part of the American population.

The Reformed Jewish congregations also responded to social needs in the 1880s. On November 4, 1880, the cornerstone was laid for Michael Reese Hospital, the best equipped medical facility in the Midwest. The hospital opened in 1889, joining an employment bureau, United Hebrew Charities, Young Men's Hebrew Charity Association, and Young Ladies Aid Society as Jewish enterprises.

The church's role in the lives of its youth was most evident in the Sunday schools, which often drew greater attendance than did morning worship. Lessons came from carefully prepared teachers' manuals and stuck strictly to biblical exposition. Youth groups like the Methodist Epworth League channeled the enthusiasms of adolescents into virtuous channels.

In addition to their Sunday school manuals, such denominational publications as the *Congregational Advance, Methodist Episcopal Christian Advocate,* and *Baptist Standard* spread the "good word."

Liberal Christians, including Swing, published the *Alliance* in 1873. It merged with the *Weekly Magazine* in 1882 and died in bankruptcy two years later.

A degree in theology was not necessary for a man with a "call" to begin preaching, but most denominations did maintain seminaries for training their clergy. Chicago was home of the Garrett Biblical Institute (Methodist), Chicago Theological Seminary (Congregational), McCormick Theological Seminary (Presbyterian), Baptist Union Theological Seminary (Lutheran), and the Norwegian Theological Seminary (Evangelical Lutheran). Carthage College downstate trained Lutheran ministers.

The seminaries were continually hard-pressed for funds, unless bailed out by philanthropists like John D. Rockefeller and Cyrus McCormick. Rockefeller rescued the Baptist school which merged in 1892 with the University of Chicago, and McCormick salvaged the Presbyterian institution which then adopted the name. The theology schools were in the vanguard of the social gospel movement, inspiring students who gradually spread the word to older pastors as they began their active ministry.

Reflecting a new concern, the state's first department of sociology was established in the Chicago Theological Seminary in 1890, and was greatly enhanced by the arrival of Graham Sumner in 1892. Sociological instruction had begun supplementing theological lessons after 1880, and the movement toward a stress on sociology spread to the University of Chicago, which set up a department of sociology in 1892. Church influence in education extended far beyond the seminaries, however. Catholics and Lutherans developed a thriving system of parochial grade schools, and the vast majority of the early colleges in the state were church-related.

Private schools were still the best and most widely available type of education by the close of the Civil War, although the Illinois School Law of 1855 provided for tax-supported local schools. Newton Bateman, secretary and traveling agent of the Illinois State Teachers Association, organized in 1853, served as Civil War school superintendent and is credited with inclusion in the 1870 state constitution of the section requiring the General Assembly to "provide a thorough and efficient system of free schools, whereby all children of this state may receive a good common school education."[45] Gradually a system of free public education covered the state.

Nationally, only 57 percent of the population between the ages of five and seventeen was enrolled in public day schools in 1870. That figure slowly increased until 72 percent of all school-age children were enrolled by 1900. Enrollment did not always mean attendance, however. When the national average length of school term was 132.2 days in 1879, the average number of days attended per pupil was only 78.4. As in Illinois, the average length of the school term increased nationally—to 144.3 days. Pupil attendance also increased, but only to 99 average days per year in 1900. Obviously, not all states had Illinois' compulsory attendance laws—or if they did, they were not rigorously enforced.[46]

The free school, however, did not dampen the enthusiasm of private school advocates, especially as the public schools often did not extend to high school, and the state university system was still in its infancy. Illinois College in Jacksonville, a Presbyterian-Congregationalist venture, and McKendree College, a Methodist institution in Lebanon, vied for honors as the state's oldest colleges. The DuQuoin Female Seminary, established by the Presbyterians in 1855, was the first girls' school in Egypt, although it did not grant degrees. Private schools were not always church related. In 1884 Clay and Grace Brown Murah opened the Creal Springs Academy, a coeducational school begun with fifty-nine students, twelve "on the collegiate level, whatever that may have meant,"[47] and other private school entrepreneurs did likewise.

Although tax-supported common schools were mandatory after 1870, attendance was not. Advocates of compulsory attendance contended with vocal forces opposed to the idea. A *Chicago Times* editorial branded the idea "another instance of the growth of fanaticism in this country which supposes that it has the best of self-government to legislate people into morality." The *Times* saw the problem as a constitutional one, stating, "the law has no more right to compel children to attend school than it has to compel them to attend church." A less noble cause for sentiment against compulsory attendance was the fact "that a poor man who may need his children at home to help earn bread, shall be compelled to send them to school."[48]

The compulsory attendance controversy continued to ferment until 1883, when the state's first attendance law required children between eight and fourteen to attend school for twelve weeks a year. A stricter law in 1889 required attendance for those between seven and fourteen for sixteen weeks, eight of which had to be continuous. These laws inspired powerful opposition, especially among immigrant groups, and were considered partially responsible for the backlash election in 1892 of the state's first Democratic governor since the war, John Peter Altgeld. One of Governor Altgeld's first acts was to declare the compulsory attendance law "violates the fundamental principals of free government," but he asked for an acceptable substitute, since "the State cannot permit children to grow up on the street learning nothing but the rudiments of crime."[49]

Those who attended the state's rural schools faced a Spartan life, with long hikes through the snow to arrive at a sparsely and uncomfortably furnished plain rectangular building. Pictures and decorations were as unheard of as contoured chairs, for "life was not only real and earnest, but it was also taught, and school was part of our apprenticeship."[50] Once at school, eager (and not so eager) scholars set about learning by rote the three R's, plus geography. In the late 1880s popular fear of radicals and anarchists inspired a spate of civics courses which were added to the curriculum. Students memorized the state and federal constitutions, but were left on their own to interpret them. In Chicago the *Daily News* invested $19,000 for prizes and awards for patriotic essays, and in 1889, the *Youth's Companion* offered prizes to the best essay in each state on "the influence of the United States Flag When Floated Over a Public School Building." "Miss Lizzie Hazard of the Galesburg High School won for the State of Illinois."[51]

Geography was a standard subject, taught by the same rote method as the three R's. What did the budding geographers learn? "Facts, my dear sir, facts: names of capitals, rivers, cities, mountains, lakes, chief products of, countries bounded by."[52] But if the country schools excelled at anything, it was spelling. Classroom spelldowns and interschool spelling "schools" gave a competitive sparkle to the mundane subject, and years later tricksters like "phthisic" and "assessable" were child's play to the spelldown graduate. Those spelling words were painfully written in Spencerian script, named for the penmanship teacher who developed the school. Handwriting "experts" traveled from school to school teaching students the art.

Teachers were certified at week-long county superintendents' "institutes" where they were required to pass examinations in elementary subjects. Often "the examination proved little more than that the applicant knew more than his pupils."[53] Teachers' salaries were low, with men teachers earning more than schoolmarms. As one school board member put it, "a woman just ain't worth thirty dollars a month."[54]

The Illinois State Normal School was chartered in 1857 in Bloomington, and the Southern Illinois Normal University opened in 1870. The establishment of the Southern Normal in Carbondale killed off the Christian church's thriving Southern Illinois College. With a peak enrollment of 370 in 1869, the school closed in 1870 and its grounds were sold to the city to be included in Carbondale's bonus to the state to secure the Normal. Normal schools stressed thorough grounding in classical subjects, believing "methods" would come naturally once the would-be teacher knew his material. Pedology had not yet superseded knowledge as the teacher's key need, although at the close of the century, the "science" of education was receiving wide attention through the work of University of Chicago professor John Dewey.

An early attempt to found a state agricultural university resulted in the chartering of Illinois Agricultural College in Irventon in 1861. The school was to run on the proceeds of seminary land sales, and was headed for success until a bank failure wiped out its funds. The state recovered its investment by selling the school's assets. The $9,000 left after the state was repaid was turned over to the Normal school.[55]

A more successful state effort was launched in 1867. Under the leadership of Illinois College's Jonathan Baldwin Turner, Congress passed the Morrill Land Grant College Act in 1862. This bonanza granted 30,000 acres of federal land for each senator and representative to be used as an endowment for industrial and agricultural education. The war, of course, delayed implementation in Illinois. The state's existing schools were eager to divide the pie among themselves, but Turner and Illinois College President Julian Sturtevant overcame their pleading. The General Assembly authorized the Illinois Industrial University in 1867.

Competition for the state school centered about McLean, Logan, Morgan, and Champaign counties. Bids of $285,000 (Champaign); $470,000 (McLean); $385,000 (Logan); and $491,000 (Morgan) were received. Champaign County's bid, when combined with its political influence, won the school for Champaign. Classes opened for 110 scholars in 1868 and the first permanent building was begun in 1871.

No sooner had the university been chartered than a conflict arose over the direction it should take. Leading the group dedicated to keeping the new facility strictly an agricultural school was Matthias L. Dunlap of Champaign, a member of the board of trustees. He was strongly opposed to regent John M. Gregory, who "tried . . . establishing a comprehensive university designed to extend the sphere and multiply the advantages of the old education for the benefit of others besides the learned professions and fix work related to agriculture and the mechanic arts upon basic underlying sciences."[56] Acrimonious debate was largely kept from the public by carefully edited public statements from the board, but the tug-of-war continued.

Gregory faced another immediate problem—securing public support and prospective students for a new school with as yet no academic reputation. The first regent took a four-fold approach to the·problem of advertising the new school. He placed heavy reliance on the printed media, including catalogs and announcements in newspapers and magazines; he set up an active visitors program, which brought in guests to tour the new facility in the hopes they would spread the word after their visit; he entered the new university in expositions such as the International Exhibition in Philadelphia in 1876; and he made numerous public speeches—all with wide press coverage.

Gregory's hectic schedule got the new university successfully launched, but it left him physically exhausted, and in 1880 Selim Peabody replaced Gregory as university regent. Peabody lacked Gregory's dynamic speaking style, and during his administration it was the faculty which took to the field with speeches and lectures. This aspect of their university commitment sometimes overshadowed their teaching duties, and the school found it advantageous to hire assistants to actually teach classes for men like George Morrow while the famed agriculturist was out recruiting new students.

By the time the Illinois Industrial University became the University of Illinois in 1885, Dunlap's hopes for an agricultural emphasis had been smashed. Engineering was now the dominant program. The need to publicize the school, however, continued. Governor John P. Altgeld secured funds during his administration to advertise the advantages of the University of Illinois to all male schoolteachers in the state,[57] and trustee Napolean Morrison utilized architecture for public relations by insisting that the new engineering building be placed on a hill in prominent view from the railroad so that train passengers would all be impressed by the grandeur of the new building.

Thomas J. Burill became the university's third regent in 1891, and under his auspices the school began offering a range of free services to the state—all of which, of course, would stimulate favorable comment. Individuals and communities were urged to send samples of their water supplies to Champaign to be tested for potability, and as the range of services increased so did the clientele to whom the University of Illinois was considered important and necessary. The public relations drive also underlay administration pressure on faculty members to publish and to form an intercollegiate sports program.

TABLE 5. STATE-SUPPORTED COLLEGES AND UNIVERSITIES

Institution	Location	Date Authorized
Illinois State Normal	Bloomington	1857
University of Illinois	Champaign	1867
Southern Illinois Normal	Carbondale	1869
Eastern Illinois Normal	Charleston	1895
Northern Illinois Normal	DeKalb	1895
Western Illinois Normal	Macomb	1899

Carving a major university out of the prairie proved a major task, and all of the nineteenth-century regents showed keen awareness for the need to publicize and create a favorable image for the university—a need founded on a "dearth of students, the hunger for funds, the need to capture or disarm critics and the deep desire to overcome a gnawing inferiority."[58] The regents looked to the success model of business, and adopted business techniques to sell the new school to the public. Such a technique ran the obvious risks that publicity might become an end in itself, and that the public might come to judge the university solely on the basis of its utilitarian functions. Its success, however, in creating a favorable public image, an increasing student body, and funding from the state legislature proved the public relations efforts more than worthwhile.

Regent Gregory should not have been surprised at the difficulty of attracting students to his new university. Nationally, only 9,372 degrees were conferred in 1870. That figure increased to 29,375 in 1900. Women increased their proportion among college graduates slightly. In 1870, a total of 7,993 men and 1,378 women received baccalaureate degrees, and by 1900, 27,410 men and 5,563 women completed college and advanced degree studies.[59]

Agricultural education was often misunderstood by farmers who had learned their trade from their fathers or by trial and error. The *Hillsboro Journal* heaped scorn on the new university in 1875, noting: "They take the young men out in the spring of the year and compel them to sit on a fence with kid gloves on their hands, umbrellas over their heads, and fifteen cent cigars in their mouths. ... This is hard on the young gentlemen, but they learn to farm, you know, and that is what the institution is for. ... They actually spent $15,000 in one year in determining the various points of difference between a gnat and a mosquito. ... The gnats and mosquitos will rejoice to learn that so much difference exists."[60]

Criticism from another angle resulted in a legislative committee which investigated charges in 1870 of "too much time being given to Greek and Latin." The committee found "194 students from Illinois, twelve from other states as well as fourteen young ladies. Fifty are studying agriculture and horticulture, fifty-four mechanics and civil engineering, sixty-five chemistry, fifteen comparative anatomy, 138 mathematics, twenty-one military tactics, ninety-two English, sixty-three German, twenty-five French, twenty-five Latin and none Greek."[61]

Social fraternities had begun replacing literary societies on campuses by 1870. Although seven national fraternities had organized sixteen chapters by that year, regent John Gregory termed them an "anachronism" and urged Illini to "discard this tattered toggery of the college lads of the older states."[62]

In its early years, Illinois Industrial University was resolutely set apart from the traditional collegiate mode. It had no song, no colors, no fraternities, and gave no degrees. Its motto "Labor and Learning" was in English instead of Latin. In 1877 Professor of Agriculture G. E. Morrow reiterated the school's pledge "to secure a wider and better education for the industrial classes."[63] The following spring Morrow planted what would become America's oldest experimental corn plot.

Students were not content with their innovative education, however, and activists persuaded the General Assembly to allow degrees in 1877. University colors were adopted in 1879 and a school song in 1880. By 1884 the *Illini* bitterly commented, "our school will succumb to the fashion and become the proud owner of a college shout."[64] They were right.

Student complaints centered about the grading system and lack of relevance of the curriculum. "The truth is," complained one, "we become superficialists and let other men do our thinking for us." Lorado Taft, who would one day sculpt works for his alma mater, deplored the shallowness that meant, "the least premonition that anything bearing a tinge of thought is to be expressed is viewed with horror from afar."[65]

Students began a campaign to change the name of the school, and alumni took up the cause in 1884. "We want it understood," they said, "that this is not a home for the feeble-minded, that homeless reprobates are not received in charge, and that the dairy on the farm is not to supply milk for orphans."[66] On June 19, 1885, the legislature approved the name change.

The fraternity ban continued into the 1880s, although political clubs were active. Hair styles were a source of debate, as the *Illini* complained in 1883, "the dude hair mania is almost monopolizing our boys."[67] Compulsory chapel attendance and military training caused administrative headaches as radical students and faculty challenged these institutions.

Two other state-supported colleges were authorized during the 1890's—Northern Illinois and Eastern Illinois Normal schools at Dekalb and Charleston. Governor John Peter Altgeld was the driving force behind the formation of these two teacher-training institutions. The bills authorizing the new schools were lobbied through the legislature by a coalition of politicians and businessmen like Joseph Glidden from the two areas of the state which got the Normals. Although by twentieth-century standards the Normal schools were not much more than glorified high schools, they did much to upgrade the educational level of the common schoolteachers past the then-prevalent eighth-grade level.

Illinois education by 1900 had assumed somewhat the shape it would take in the next century. A strong system of parochial elementary schools and colleges supplemented a statewide system of free public schools. The commercial genius of the state had inspired a growth of "practical" education, and vocational and technical schools such as Chicago's Armour Institute were founded. Classical subjects like Greek and Latin were being replaced by typing in the high schools, but the grammar schools continued to stick with traditional methods and subjects. In areas with large immigrant populations, like Chicago, German was being taught in the public schools, and such "frills" as physical education and home economics were also gaining ground. Beginnings were made for a system of state-supported universities, and once again church, state, immigrants, and wealthy, who endowed private education, were working in parallel harness to provide a needed service. Only the high schools had not yet received attention and organization. More important, the years following the Civil War were a seedbed time, a time in which the writers, poets, and artists who would bring Illinois fame in the new century received their nurture. In cultural activities, as in governmental and economic activities, the growth and development of the late nineteenth century would be organized and focused in the opening decades of the twentieth century.

1. N. Vachel Lindsay, "A Gospel of Beauty," broadside in Lindsay home, Springfield, Illinois. Elizabeth Graham, Curator.
2. *Chicago Evening Journal*, Nov. 16, 1877.
3. Harris L. Dante, "The *Chicago Tribune*'s 'Lost Years,' 1865-1874," *Journal of the Illinois State Historical Society* LVIII (Summer, 1965), 140.
4. Masthead, *Chicago Inter-Ocean*, July 1, 1877.
5. Kobre, *Development of American Journalism*.
6. Britt, *America That Was*, 92.
7. *Ibid.*
8. *Chicago Evening Journal*, July 23, 1877. *Chicago Times*, July 24, 1877; July 25, 1877; July 27, 1877. *Chicago Post*, July 26, 1877. *The Inter-Ocean* (Chicago), July 28, 1877.
9. Edgar Lee Masters, "Editor Wheden," *Spoon River Anthology* (New York, 1962), 132.
10. *Chicago Evening Journal*, July 15, 1878.
11. Sandburg, *Always the Young Strangers*, 116.
12. *Ibid.*, 117.
13. Israel, ed., *1897 Sears Roebuck Catalogue*, 340.
14. Britt, *An America That Was*, 69.
15. *Ibid.*, 152.
16. *Ibid.*, 153.
17. DeLafayette Reid, "Our State's Public Libraries," *Illinois History*, XIX:VIII (May, 1966), 173-175.
18. *Ibid.*, 181.
19. M. Josephine Bassett, "Noble Illinois," in Stibitz, *Illinois Poets*, 25.
20. John Hay, "The Prairie," in Stibitz, *Illinois Poets*, 30.
21. Ernest McGaffey, "Message of the Town," in Stibitz, *Illinois Poets*, 38.
22. Eugene Field, "When Stedman Comes to Town," in Stibitz, *Illinois Poets*, 45.
23. Eugene Field, "Extinct Monsters," in Stibitz, *Illinois Poets*, 46.
24. Masters, "Deacon Taylor," *Spoon River*, 80.
25. Andrew Sorenson, "Lester Frank Ward: The 'American Aristotle' in Illinois," *Journal of the Illinois State Historical Society* LXIII (Summer, 1970), 63.
26. Harold P. Simonson, "Francis Grierson—A Biographical Sketch and Bibliography," *Journal of the Illinois State Historical Society* LIV (Summer, 1961), 201.
27. Esther Mary Ayers, "Art in Southern Illinois, 1865-1914," *Journal of the Illinois State Historical Society* XXXVI (1943).
28. Frederick Koepper, ed., *Illinois Architecture: A Selective Guide from Territorial Times to the Present* (Chicago and London, 1968).
29. United States Bureau of Census, *Historical Statistics*, 228-229.
30. Britt, *America That Was*, 79.
31. *Ibid.*
32. Chauncey Hobart, *Recollections of My Life: Fifty Years of Itinerancy in the Northwest* (Red Wing, Minn., 1885), 363-364.
33. United States Bureau of Census, *Report on Statistics of Churches in the United States at the Eleventh Census: 1890* (Washington, D.C., 1894), 38-40.
34. *Ibid.*
35. Rev. P. C. Croll, D.D., *History of the Evangelical Lutheran Church in Illinois and the Middle West* (NI, 1916).
36. Rev. John Alex Dowie, *Doctors, Drugs & Devils . . . or . . . the Foes of Christ the Healer* (Chicago, 1894), 4-5.

37. Pierce, *History of Chicago*, 423.
38. *Ibid.*, 430. *Chicago Times*, Feb. 24, 1874; March 3, 1874; April 14, 1874.
39. Pierce, *History of Chicago*, 430.
40. *Chicago Times*, Aug. 16, 1871.
41. Pierce, *History of Chicago*, 434. See also Eva Ingersoll Wakefield, ed., *The Letters of Robert G. Ingersoll* (New York, 1951).
42. Harold Schiffler, "The Chicago Church-Theater Controversy of 1881-1882," *Journal of the Illinois State Historical Society* LII (Winter, 1960), 363.
43. Pierce, *History of Chicago*, 451.
44. *Ibid.*, 438.
45. *Constitution*, Art. VIII, Sec. 1.
46. United States Bureau of Census, *Historical Statistics*, 207.
47. John Allen, *Legends and Lore of Southern Illinois* (Carbondale, Ill., 1963), 201.
48. *Chicago Times*, Jan. 21, 1871.
49. Governor Altgeld, *Journal of the House*, Jan. 10, 1893.
50. Britt, *America That Was*, 70.
51. Sandburg, *Always the Young Strangers*, 127.
52. Britt, *America That Was*, 63.
53. *Ibid.*
54. *Ibid.*, 52.
55. Ernest G. Hildner, "Higher Education in Transition, 1850-1870," *Journal of the Illinois State Historical Society* LVI (Spring, 1963).
56. Winston N. Solberg, "The University of Illinois Struggles for Public Recognition, 1867-1894," *Journal of the Illinois State Historical Society* LIX (Spring, 1966), 7.
57. *Ibid.*, 24.
58. *Ibid.*, 28.
59. United States Bureau of Census, *Historical Statistics*, 212.
60. Ebert, *Illini Century*, 8.
61. *Chicago Tribune*, Oct. 1, 1870.
62. Ebert, *Illini Century*, 13.
63. *Ibid.*, 17.
64. *Ibid.*, 19.
65. *Ibid.*, 20, 21.
66. *Ibid.*, 23.
67. *Ibid.*, 33.

Conclusion

"Let us build for the centuries. . . ."

John Peter Altgeld

Governor John Peter Altgeld was usually a man ahead of his time. In this one statement, however, he gave voice to the dominant credo of Illinoisans at the close of the nineteenth century. The man who in 1865 dreamed of owning his own prosperous farm or general store or canning factory expanded his vision by the turn of the century to dreams of numerous farms worked by tenants, to schemes for welding together a mighty chain of stores, to plans for pooling the management of all canning factories in order to eliminate competition from individual owners. Illinois was building for the centuries, forging empires in lumber and pork, in steel and coal.

Abraham Lincoln would not have recognized Illinois had he returned as the calendar turned over for the twentieth century. He could see his name everywhere: on multivolume biographies, annual celebrations, street signs, monuments, and sales gimmicks —but the substance and the spirit had changed. The cities dominated the countryside in many ways, the values and thrust of organization replaced the individualism of Lincoln's era, and industrialization was the most potent and expanding force of the day.

The population of Illinois had more than doubled in the thirty-five years since the assassination. Now 4,821,550 persons lived in the state ranked third among the states in the union. Almost 1,000,000 of that total was foreign born, with immigrants from southeastern Europe, Russia, and Asia gaining in numbers. Over half of those millions lived in communities of more than 2,500. Many cities were lighted by electricity and connected to their neighbors by telephone.

320

Women had ventured out of the kitchen and could now vote for trustees of the new University of Illinois and be elected to school boards. They served on state boards and held key roles in state agencies. Women doctors, lawyers, and settlement workers functioned successfully in the man's world, and well-organized social and philanthropic clubs kept more traditional ladies busy. Women were now a major part of the work force in all cities, and on all jobs. They were attending coeducational colleges, writing poetry, and forming effective lobbies against "demon rum." Many had the temerity to demand the vote and equal pay for equal work.

Springfield remained the state capital, but a new constitution was in effect and the number of legislators had doubled. They met in a new $4,000,000 capitol building. The common schools now cost all citizens $12,000,000 per year, and total state government expenditure had skyrocketed to $13,000,000, with a state payroll of 18,900 workers. Springfield was now also the home of the permanent state fair and the new attorney general's office.

In sharp contrast with the simple functions performed by state agencies in 1865, the needs of an increasingly complex state by 1900 had called forth a confused jumble of boards and agencies. A state board of charities oversaw fifteen institutions, and almost every area of human endeavor had acquired its own bureau or board to supervise, license, and inspect—although none were notably efficient. One new agency had achieved some remarkable results—especially in the field of labor relations! The Illinois National Guard stood ready at the drop of a strike vote to do battle for the forces of big business. The state's prison population was no longer leased by private contractors, and an attempt had been made to rationalize the pardon process. The state's judiciary had expanded to include seven Supreme Court districts, and there was a new appellate court and juvenile court system.

The romance of the rail had gone sour by the turn of the century. No longer seen as bearers of wealth, the railroads were blamed for economic hardship suffered by farmers subjected to monopolistic freight rates as well as for the financial panics which hit when overcapitalized roads collapsed. Determined efforts had resulted in state regulation of the railroad and warehouse industries on both the state and local—as well as national—levels.

Farming continued to be an individual enterprise in the main, and in the dawning corporate age the individual farmer could not compete. Disastrous price squeezes and extortionate freight rates robbed them of their profits, although diversified crops and increment in land values kept the agricultural depressions from driving

the farmers from the land. In actual number, however, farm workers had declined from 50 percent to 25 percent of the population
since 1865.

Industrial workers were in much less enviable, although in many
ways similar, position. The miners, railroad workers, the unskilled
laborers, iron molders, and teamsters faced an industrial system
which could and did squeeze out more and more work for less and
less pay. Women now made up 16 percent of the work force.
Unions were still neither prevalent nor powerful, but in 1900
strikes were no longer strangers to the state. The idealistic reform
labor groups had been replaced by the businesslike approach of the
American Federation of Labor. Organized labor had not yet won a
firm foothold, but it had settled its internal conflicts for the time
being and was ready to march into the twentieth century, bloody
but unbowed.

One promise of the war years had more than been fulfilled.
Industrial output reached an annual value of more than
$1,250,000,000. Illinois had become the nation's third-ranked in-
dustrial state, and its industrial products doubled in value those of
its farms. Of all its industries, meat packing had come most to
symbolize the new Illinois. Chicago produced 84 percent of the
state's total, and the state produced one-third of the nation's total
output. When a banker in Pittsburgh or a miner in Minnesota sat
down to a canned ham, it was probably canned in Chicago. Iron and
steel foundries, agricultural implement plants, railroad car manufacturers, and mail-order sales firms all took the spotlight once
reserved for the sturdy and virtuous individual farmer.

Astride the new economic empires came the empire builders
—the Swifts, Pullmans, Armours—men whose credo was the an-
tithesis of the Lincoln mystique. These were the new titans, the men
who made things run. Their wealth was fabled, their power unlimited, their influence as models of success untold. As they struggled for control of the economy for their own profit, these giants
organized and centralized, eliminated competition, and devised
new modes of business behavior. The new world they built,
however, was not always a brave one. Disastrous business failure
plunged businesses into bankruptcy, railroads into receivership,
and workers into breadlines.

By 1900 the czars of the new age were old men, ready to turn over
their fiefdoms to their heirs. The old men could identify with
Lincoln's humble background. They were also self-made and as
lacking in the formal educational and social graces as Lincoln

himself. Their own rapacious energy brought them power, and while Lincoln used his power to reinforce the old values, the new industrial giants used theirs to change them. Their sons were born to wealth, educated at the most expensive prestige schools, and imbued with the corporate mentality. American life would never again be as simple as it was in 1865.

Culturally, the state was ready to blossom in 1900. A circle of young realistic writers had gathered in Chicago, the nest of the Robin's Egg Renaissance. A new school of architecture, the first truly American school, had evolved in the Windy City. Art museums and libraries dotted the prairie. Common schools were now buttressed by compulsory attendance laws, and the state's university system included the dynamic University of Illinois and the Southern Normal School. Other Normals at Charleston, DeKalb, and Macomb were in the planning stages, and private schools like the new University of Chicago were self-consciously jacking up the intellectual level of the state.

Chicago was a world of its own. With a population of 1,698,575, the lake city counted 35 percent of the state's population. A disastrous fire had been turned into a bonanza of new building. City agencies had been enlarged and reorganized, a new sanitary canal was under construction, and a city-owned power plant lit the streets. Sin still ruled the levee, however, and corruption of city officials had become an art form. Unequaled in industrial wealth or power, Chicago towered over the state like Gulliver in Lilliput, while the Lilliputians of downstate spent much time shooting darts at the giant and attempting to tie it down.

Abraham Lincoln continued to be a controversial figure. Lincoln the martyr was an unassailable hero. Draping themselves in his blood-stained mantle, Illinois Republicans guarded elective offices as their sacred preserves and successfully fought off attempted raids by Democrats, socialists, free-silverites, greenbackers, and prohibitionists. Their new Lincoln in 1900 was Governor John Tanner, who kept his bread carefully buttered on both sides and studiously preserved the status quo. Illinois Republicans had lost some influence in Washington by the turn of the century; the heydays of the Grant administration were now merely fond memories, but they were still dominant in the state. Memories of past glory were dutifully and joyfully rekindled each February as the Grand Old Party celebrated Lincoln's birthday and invoked Honest Abe's blessings on their latest pro-business policy or imperialistic venture.

During the thirty-five years after his death, the ghost of Lincoln cast a long shadow over his home state. Biographers squabbled over his past, probed his marriage, his parentage. As life in the state grew increasingly remote from the New Salem cabin and self-education by candlelight, the Lincoln image became a talisman to ward off the fears that accompanied such a drastic change. Friendship with Lincoln, even if cursory, was a guarantee of a share of the reverence, and "he knew Lincoln" became the definitive phrase and highest accolade accorded any man in the public eye.

Memories of the Civil War joined Lincoln in haunting those years. Service in the Union Army was a necessary qualification for elective office—often the only qualification. The war's simplistic and dramatic answer to the complex question of slavery led to the search for an equally simple answer to the more tangled questions facing the new industrial, urban age—but the answer was not to be had.

By 1900 Illinois was pre-eminently an industrial state. More than one-third of her population was jammed into one city, and twenty-four other villages had grown to more than 10,000 persons. The Lincoln mystique had no answers to the problems of urban blight and industrial oppression. It was an anachronism in an age of business consolidation and mechanization. But it was what people believed, and belief is a powerful force. The rural, simple, individualistic values were not easily shaken. Problems of urbanization and industrialization remained to be solved by another set of values and a new set of solutions which were just taking shape.

Illinois in 1900 was building for the centuries. It was forging vast combinations and programs necessary for lasting empire. It was a rich and powerful state. Its natural resources were being exploited with great success; its population was busy and productive. But the problems of this new time were not yet acknowledged, and final solutions were a long way from coming. In the meantime, the tourists and politicians continued to make pilgrimages to Springfield to lay wreaths at the tomb of the fallen hero and bask in the dream of Illinois, already unofficially the Land of Lincoln.

Appendix

Counties of the state of Illinois

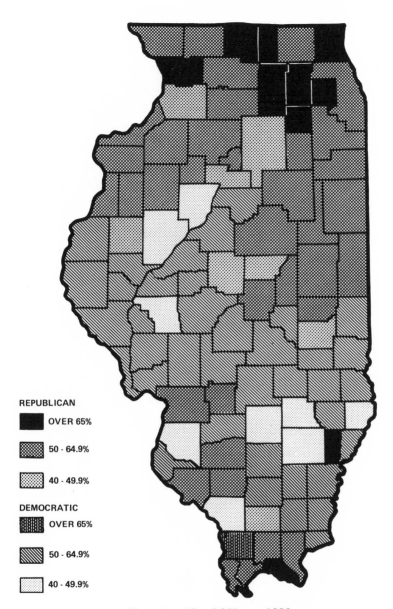

REPUBLICAN

OVER 65%

50 - 64.9%

40 - 49.9%

DEMOCRATIC

OVER 65%

50 - 64.9%

40 - 49.9%

Illinois Presidential Vote—1880
(See opposite page for identification of counties)

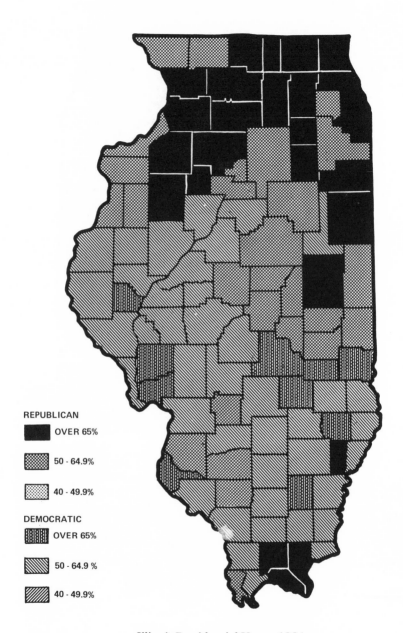

REPUBLICAN

OVER 65%

50 - 64.9%

40 - 49.9%

DEMOCRATIC

OVER 65%

50 - 64.9 %

40 - 49.9%

Illinois Presidential Vote—1864

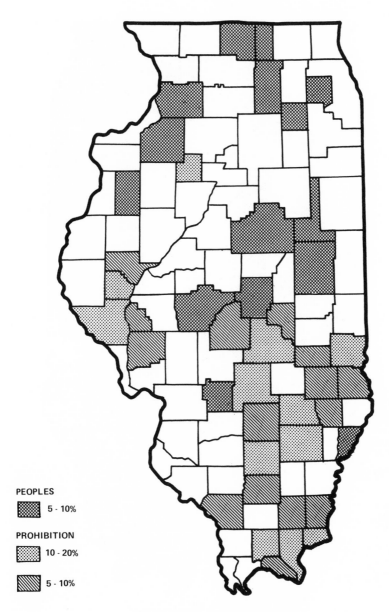

PEOPLES

5 - 10%

PROHIBITION

10 - 20%

5 - 10%

Illinois Presidential Vote—1892

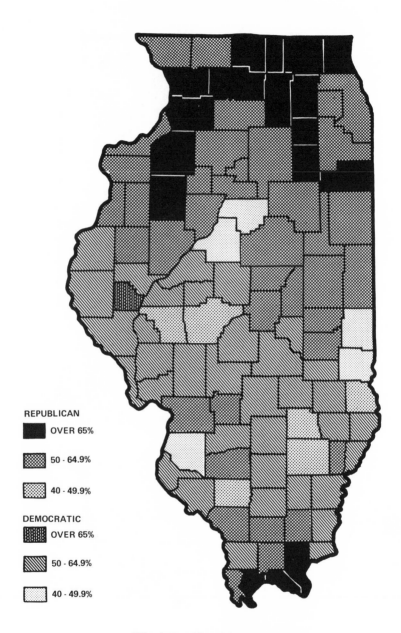

REPUBLICAN

OVER 65%

50 - 64.9%

40 - 49.9%

DEMOCRATIC

OVER 65%

50 - 64.9%

40 - 49.9%

Illinois Presidential Vote—1900

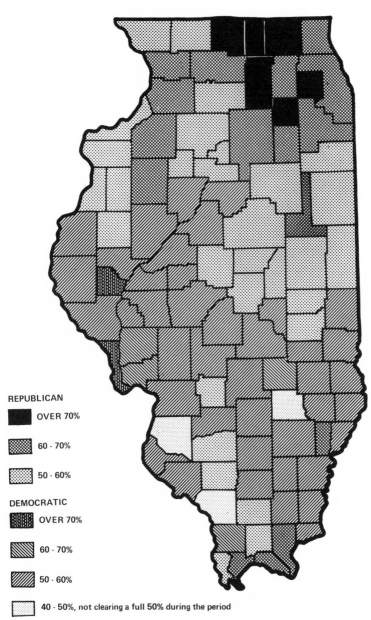

REPUBLICAN
OVER 70%

60 - 70%

50 - 60%

DEMOCRATIC
OVER 70%

60 - 70%

50 - 60%

40 - 50%, not clearing a full 50% during the period

Years When Major Party Did Not Win

Table A. Foreign Born Population of Illinois

BIRTHPLACE	PERCENT OF FOREIGN BORN POPULATION				PERCENT OF TOTAL POPULATION			
	1870	1880	1890	1900	1870	1880	1890	1900
British Isles	37.4535	33.0955	26.9030	20.5739	7.5971	6.2771	5.7383	4.2167
Ireland	23.3234	20.1008	14.7791	11.8458	4.7309	3.8113	3.2532	2.3750
England	10.4564	9.6473	8.3651	6.6579	2.4320	1.8292	1.8414	1.3350
Scotland	3.0545	2.6800	2.4592	2.0702	.6195	.5081	.5347	.4152
Wales	.6106	.6328	.5125	.7512	.1238	.1200	.1081	.0905
Not Specified	.0085	.0346	.0044		.0017	.0066	.0009	
German Empireb	39.5494	40.3901	40.1659	34.3463	8.0223	7.6606	8.8419	6.8891
Prussia	15.9977	14.9355			3.2450	2.8319		
Bavaria	3.4072	2.3384						
Baden	3.0833	2.0446			.6254	.3877		
Mecklenberg	1.3913	1.2207			.2822	.2314		
Hanover	3.9711	3.0765			.8055	.5833		
Saxony	.9293	.1529			.1885	.1427		
Wurttemberg	1.7220	1.3216			.3493	.2506		
Hessen	3.1640	1.4670			.6417	.2781		
Hamburg	.1467	.1369			.0297	.0259		
Nassru	.2349	.1583			.0476	.0300		
Oldenburg	.2624	.2247			.0532	.0426		
Brunswick	.1434	.1142			.0290	.0217		
Neimar	.0491	.0067			.0099	.0013		
Lubeck	.0091	.0043			.0018	.0008		
Not Specified	5.0377	12.5878			1.0218	2.3868		
Austria	.4074	.4467	.9549	1.8831	.0826	.0847	.2113	.3777
Bohemia	1.4266	2.2968	3.1606	3.9881	.2893	.4355	.6958	.7999
France	2.1178	1.4602	1.0131	1.6219	.4295	.2768	.2231	.1615
Italy	.1477	.3022	.9537	2.4323	.0249	.0573	.2099	.4878
India	.0052	.0146	.0144	.0137	.0010	.0028	.0032	.0027
China	.0015	.0512	.0923	.1512	.0003	.0097	.0203	.0303
Japan		.0017	.0028	.0105		.0003	.0006	.0025
Rumania				.0323				.0064
Finland				.0883				.0178
Spain	.0097	.0416	.0180	.0235	.0019	.0079	.0040	.0047
Switzerland	1.7430	1.5213	.9632	.4340	.3535	.2834	.2120	.1873
Holland	.8113	.8585	1.0400	2.2661	.1045	.1628	.2289	.4545
Belgium	.2029	.2508	.3037	.4543	.0421	.0475	.0680	.0911

[a] Based on figures in U.S. Ninth Census, 1870, I, "Population," 336-342;
Tenth Census, 1880, "Population," pp. 492-495; Eleventh Census, 1890,
"Population," pt. 1, 606-609; Twelfth Census, 1900, "Population," pp. 732-735.
[b] Includes states composing German Empire, but not Austria proper.

BIRTHPLACE	PERCENT OF FOREIGN BORN POPULATION				PERCENT OF TOTAL POPULATION			
	1870	1880	1890	1900	1870	1880	1890	1900
Poland	.3292	1.1426	3.4278	7.0254	.0667	.2261	.7546	1.4092
Russia	.0394	.2136	.9479	2.9683	.0120	.0414	.2197	.5953
Turkey	.0025	.0188	.0062	.0296	.0005	.0036	.0013	.0054
Hungary	.0815	.1184	.3710	.6903	.0165	.0224	.0817	.1396
Luxemburg	.1461	.2758	.0331	.0435	.0296	.0523	.0073	.0087
Greece	.0027	.0122	.0301	.1623	.0005	.0023	.0066	.0325
Portugal	.0147	.0726	.0303	.0207	.0029	.0138	.0067	.0041
Malta	.0004	.0027			.0000	.0005		
Gibraltar		.0010				.0002		
Europe- Not Specified	.0070	.0241	.0992	.0163	.0014	.0046	.0218	.0032
Scandinavia	8.8451	11.2055	15.3000	14.9735	1.7941	2.1246	3.3680	3.0033
Norway	2.3058	2.9070	3.6012	3.0998	.4677	.5512	.7927	.6217
Sweden	5.8189	7.2657	10.2672	10.2518	1.1803	1.3776	2.2606	2.0563
Denmark[c]	.7203	1.0328	1.4296	1.6219	.1461	.1958	.3147	.5253
British Amer.	6.3179	5.8316			1.2815	1.1060		
Canada[d]	5.8073	5.5040	4.6916	5.2315	1.1779	1.0436	1.0328	1.0493
New Brunswk.	.1619	.1190			.0328	.0226		
Newfoundland	.0349	.0236			.0070	.0045		
Nova Scotia	.1584	.1405			.0321	.0266		
Pr.Edw.Is.	.0006	.0384			.0001	.0073		
Not Specified	.1549	.0060			.0314	.0011		
West Indies[e]	.0248	.0286	.0330	.0359	.0060	.0074	.0072	.0068
Latin Amer.[f]	.0291	.0388	.0408	.0517	.0059	.0073	.0089	.0103
Australia[g]	.0240	.0356	.0307	.0426	.0048	.0067	.0085	.0085
Africa	.0070	.0098	.0092	.0135	.0014	.0018	.0020	.0027
Asia[h]	.0145	.0060	.0180	.0547	.0029	.0011	.0040	.0119
Miscellaneous[i]	.0046		.0040	.0167	.0009		.0009	.0033

[c] In computing percentages for 1880, foreign born from Greenland are included in total figure for aliens from Denmark.
[d] In U.S. Eleventh Census, 1890, "Population," pt. I, 606, Canada includes Newfoundland. In U.S. Twelfth Census, 1900, "Population," p. 132, Canada includes French and English Canada and Newfoundland.
[e] In U.S. Eleventh Census, 1890, "Population," pt. I, 606, report for West Indies includes Cuba. In U.S. Twelfth Census, 1900, "Population," pp. 733, 735.
[f] In computing percentages for 1870 Latin America included Cuba, Mexico, and South America; for 1880, Central America, Cuba, Mexico, and South America; for 1890, Central America, Mexico, and South America; for 1900, Central America, Mexico, and South America.
[g] Included in report for Australasia in U.S. Ninth Census, 1870, I, "Population," 336.
[h] Includes only persons of Asiatic birth but not China, Japan, and India.
[i] Includes persons whose origin was not stated, or born in the Atlantic Islands, Pacific Islands, Sandwich Islands, or at sea.

Table B. Native Population of Illinois[a]

BIRTHPLACE	PERCENT OF NATIVE POPULATION				PERCENT OF TOTAL POPULATION			
	1870	1880	1890	1900	1870	1880	1890	1900
Old Northwest	72.1845	79.0788	82.8338	84.3678	57.5424	64.0679	64.5911	67.4552
Illinois	58.7495	68.5346	73.5976	75.0666	46.8328	55.5252	57.3890	60.0186
Ohio	8.0512	5.4877	4.2238	3.5579	6.4180	4.4460	3.2936	2.8447
Michigan	.4656	.5206	.7145	1.0164	.3711	.4217	.5571	.8126
Indiana	4.2874	3.6637	3.2286	3.3243	3.4177	2.9683	2.5176	2.6579
Wisconsin	.6308	.8722	1.0693	1.4026	.5028	.7067	.8338	1.1214
Middle Atlantic	12.3637	9.0562	6.7160	5.2593	9.8557	7.3369	5.2368	4.2048
New York	6.5932	4.8188	3.9350	2.8814	5.2558	3.9041	2.8800	2.3037
Pennsylvania	4.8705	3.5867	2.5710	2.0401	3.8826	2.9056	2.0048	1.6311
New Jersey	.8068	.5867	.4036	.3082	.6431	.4754	.3147	.2464
Delaware	.0931	.0640	.0479	.0296	.0742	.0518	.0373	.0236
New England	3.5151	2.4304	1.6982	1.2151	2.8019	1.9692	1.3241	.9712
Connecticut	.5463	.3775	.2565	.1778	.4355	.3059	.2000	.1421
Massachusetts	1.0942	.8211	.6163	.4647	.8723	.6652	.4806	.3715
Vermont	.9144	.5850	.3805	.2587	.7289	.4740	.2967	.2068
Maine	.4336	.2987	.2160	.1593	.3456	.2420	.1684	.1273
New Hampshire	.4056	.2639	.1682	.1066	.3233	.2139	.1311	.0852
Rhode Island	.1208	.0842	.0607	.0480	.0963	.0682	.0473	.0383
South	11.1048	8.3200	6.2481	6.0293	8.8517	6.7409	4.8720	4.8193
Virginia[b]	1.7653	1.1187	.7330	.4985	1.4072	.9066	.5716	.3985
West Virginia		.1089	.1275	.1520		.0883	.0994	.1215
Kentucky	3.3438	2.4823	1.8368	1.6137	2.6655	2.0111	1.4323	1.2902
Missouri	1.5248	1.5833	1.3734	1.7953	1.2155	1.2827	1.0709	1.4354
Maryland	.6217	.4969	.3801	.3110	.4956	.4026	.2964	.2480
Mississippi	.1332	.1229	.0994	.1295	.1061	.0996	.0775	.1035
Louisiana	.1122	.0991	.0943	.1030	.0894	.0803	.0735	.0823
North Carolina	.6504	.3720	.2195	.1526	.5184	.3014	.1711	.1220
Alabama	.1930	.1330	.1009	.1223	.1538	.1078	.0787	.0977
Tennessee	2.3472	1.4997	1.0322	.8423	1.8710	1.2150	.8049	.6734
Georgia	.1132	.0780	.0645	.0896	.0902	.0632	.0503	.0716

[a] Based on figures in U.S. Ninth Census, 1870, I, "Population," pp. 328-335; Tenth Census, 1880, "Population," pp. 480-483; Eleventh Census, 1890, "Population," pt. I, pp. 560-563; Twelfth Census, 1900, "Population," pp. 686-689.
[b] Figures for Virginia and West Virginia are combined in U.S. Ninth Census, 1870, I, "Population," p. 333.

BIRTHPLACE	PERCENT OF NATIVE POPULATION				PERCENT OF TOTAL POPULATION			
	1870	1880	1890	1900	1870	1880	1890	1900
Dist.of Columbia	.0357	.0345	.0439	.0408	.0285	.0279	.0342	.0326
South Carolina	.1482	.0851	.0546	.0419	.1181	.0689	.0426	.0334
Florida	.0052	.0066	.0095	.0185	.0041	.0053	.0074	.0747
Arkansas	.1109	.0990	.0785	.1183	.0883	.0802	.0612	.0945
Trans-Mississippi West	.7931	1.1103	1.5355	2.6798	.6312	.8993	1.1924	2.8507
Iowa	.5622	.6639	.8217	1.2476	.4482	.5317	.6407	.9975
Minnesota	.0582	.0827	.1388	.2451	.0464	.0670	.1082	.1959
California	.0425	.0388	.0518	.0861	.0338	.0315	.0404	.0688
Kansas	.0504	.1744	.2668	.4729	.0401	.1413	.2080	.3780
Texas	.0477	.0522	.0607	.0985	.0379	.0423	.0473	.7873
Oregon	.0094	.0190	.0070	.0132	.0074	.0154	.0055	.0129
Nebraska	.0103	.0402	.0942	.2803	.0081	.0326	.0735	.2244
Nevada	.0021	.0033	.0036	.0046	.0016	.0027	.0028	.0036
Colorado	.0042	.0100	.0249	.0686	.0033	.0081	.0194	.0549
Montana	.0010	.0025	.0070	.0140	.0007	.0020	.0054	.0112
New Mexico	.0010	.0033	.0038	.0067	.0008	.0027	.0030	.0053
Dakota Territory	.0005	.0036			.0004	.0029		
North Dakota			.0180	.0230			.0140	.0183
South Dakota			.0126	.0577			.0098	.0461
Utah	.0015	.0051	.0031	.0096	.0011	.0041	.0029	.0076
Idaho	.0008	.0008	.0011	.0043	.0006	.0006	.0009	.0034
Washington	.0003	.0010	.0052	.0166	.0602	.0008	.0040	.0132
Indian Territory	.0007	.0073	.0045	.0119	.0005	.0059	.0035	.0091
Wyoming	.0002	.0015	.0021	.0069	.0001	.0012	.0017	.0055
Arizona	.0001	.0001	.0010	.0028	.0000	.0005	.0009	.0022
Oklahoma			.0010	.0009			.0005	.0055
Not Stated	.0374	.0004	.8928	.3364	.0298	.0003	.6962	.2689
Miscellaneous[c]	.0004	.0006	.0189	.1057	.0003	.0048	.0148	.0845

[c]Includes figures for persons born in Alaska, at sea under the United States flag, of American parents abroad, and, in 1900, of those born in the Philippine Islands and Puerto Rico.

Table C. Comparative Growth of Manufactures[a]

CATEGORIES	MANUFACTURING AREAS	1870[b]	1880	1890	1900	BY PERCENTAGES			
						1870-1880	1880-1890	1890-1900	1870-1900
Population	Illinois	$ 2,539,891	$ 3,077,871	$ 3,826,351	$ 4,821,550	21	24	26	90
	Chicago	349,966	503,298	1,099,850	1,698,575	44	119	54	385
	Downstate Ill.	2,189,925	2,574,573	2,726,501	3,122,975	18	6	15	43
	Indiana	1,680,637	1,978,301	2,192,404	2,516,462	18	11	15	50
Number of Establishments	Illinois	12,597	14,549	20,482	38,360	15	41	87	205
	Chicago	1,440	3,518	9,977	19,203	144	184	92	1,233
	Downstate Ill.	11,157	11,031	10,505	19,157	-2	-5	82	72
	Indiana	11,847	11,198	12,354	13,015	-6	10	46	52
Average Number of Employees	Illinois	82,979	144,727	280,218	395,110	74	94	41	367
	Chicago	31,105	79,391	190,621	262,621	155	140	38	744
	Downstate Ill.	51,874	65,336	89,597	132,489	26	37	48	155
	Indiana	58,852	69,508	110,590	115,956	18	59	41	166
Total Wages	Illinois	31,100,244	57,429,085	142,873,265	191,510,962	85	149	34	516
	Chicago	13,045,286	34,646,812	104,069,922	131,065,337	166	200	26	905
	Downstate Ill.	15,054,958	22,782,273	38,803,343	60,445,625	26	70	56	235
	Indiana	18,366,780	21,960,888	42,577,258	66,847,317	20	94	57	264
Per Capita Wages of Employed	Illinois	374.79	396.80	509.86	484.70	6	28	5	29
	Chicago	419.39	436.40	545.95	499.06	4	25	-9	19
	Downstate Ill.	348.05	348.69	433.08	456.23	0	24	5	31
	Indiana	312.08	315.94	385.00	428.62	1	22	11	37

Total Capital	Illinois	94,368,057	140,652,066	502,004,512	776,829,598	49	257	55	723
	Chicago	39,372,276	68,831,885	359,739,598	534,000,689	75	423	48	1,256
	Downstate Ill.	54,995,781	71,820,181	142,264,914	242,828,909	31	98	71	342
	Indiana	52,052,425	65,742,962	131,605,366	234,481,528	26	100	78	350
Cost of Materials Used	Illinois	127,600,077	289,843,907	529,019,089	739,754,414	127	83	40	480
	Chicago	60,362,188	179,194,925	409,493,027	538,401,562	197	129	31	792
	Downstate Ill.	67,237,889	110,648,982	119,526,062	201,352,852	65	17	68	199
	Indiana	63,135,492	100,262,917	130,119,106	214,961,610	53	30	65	240
Value of Products	Illinois	05,620,672	414,864,673	908,640,280	1,259,730,168	102	119	39	513
	Chicago	92,518,742	248,995,848	664,567,923	888,945,311	169	167	34	816
	Downstate Ill.	113,101,930	165,868,825	244,072,357	370,784,857	47	47	52	228
	Indiana	108,617,278	148,006,411	226,825,082	378,120,140	36	53	67	248
Value Added By Manufacturing	Illinois	78,020,595	125,020,766	379,621,191	519,975,754	60	196	37	566
	Chicago	32,156,554	69,800,923	255,074,896	350,543,749	117	265	37	990
	Downstate Ill.	45,864,041	55,219,843	124,546,295	169,432,005	20	107	36	269
	Indiana	45,481,786	47,743,484	96,705,976	163,158,530	5	103	69	259
Per Capita Value Added	Illinois	440.24	863.83	1,354.73	1,316.02	-8	53	-3	40
	Chicago	1,033.80	879.20	1,334.12	1,334.78	-15	52	0	29
	Downstate Ill.	884.14	845.16	1,390.07	1,278.83	-4	51	-8	45
	Indiana	772.81	686.87	874.45	1,046.18	-11	27	20	35

a Based on figures in U.S. Twelfth Census, 1900, VIII, "Manufactures," pt. 11, 161, 199, 994-995.

b Figures for 1870 are for Cook County instead of Chicago. U.S. Ninth Census, 1870, III, "The Statistics of Wealth and Industry of the United States," 509.

c "Value Added" is determined by subtracting the "Cost of Materials Used" from the "Value of the Products."

Table D. Comparative Growth of Manufactures—by State[a]

YEARS	NUMBER OF ESTABLISHMENTS	AVERAGE NUMBER OF EMPLOYEES	TOTAL WAGE	CAPITAL	COST MATERIALS USED	VALUE OF PRODUCTS	VALUE ADDED BY MANUFACTURING
1870	Penn. 37,200	New York 351,800	New York 142,466,758	Penn. 406,821,845	New York 452,065,452	New York 785,194,651	New York 333,129,199
	New York 36,206	Penn. 319,847	Penn. 127,976,594	New York 366,994,320	Penn. 421,197,673	Penn. 711,894,344	Penn. 290,696,671
	Ohio 22,773	Mass. 279,380	Mass. 118,051,886	Mass. 231,677,862	Mass. 334,413,983	Mass. 553,912,568	Mass. 219,498,586
	Mass. 13,212	Ohio 137,202	Ohio 49,066,488	Ohio 141,923,964	Ohio 157,131,697	Ohio 269,713,610	Ohio 112,581,913
	Ill. 12,597	Conn. 89,523	Conn. 38,987,187	Conn. 95,281,278	Ill. 127,600,077	Mo. 206,213,427	
1880	New York 42,739	New York 531,533	New York 198,634,029	New York 514,246,575	New York 679,612,545	New York 1,080,696,596	New York 401,084,051
	Penn. 31,232	Penn. 387,072	Penn. 134,055,904	Penn. 474,510,993	Penn. 465,020,563	Penn. 774,818,445	Penn. 279,797,882
	Ohio 20,699	Mass. 352,255	Mass. 138,315,362	Mass. 303,806,185	Mass. 386,972,655	Mass. 631,135,284	Mass. 244,162,629
	Ill. 14,549	Ohio 183,604	Ohio 62,103,800	Ohio 188,939,614	Ill. 289,843,907	Ill. 414,864,673	Ill. 125,020,766
	Mass. 14,352	Ill. 144,727	Ill. 57,429,085	Ill. 140,652,065	Ohio 215,334,258	Ohio 348,298,390	Ohio 132,964,132

1890

Col 1	Col 2	Col 3	Col 4	Col 5	Col 6	Col 7
New York 65,840	New York 752,066	New York 370,380,554	New York 1,130,161,195	New York 871,264,085	New York 1,711,577,671	New York 840,313,586
Penn. 39,339	Penn. 570,393	Penn. 263,375,215	Penn. 991,243,115	Penn. 773,734,637	Penn. 1,331,794,905	Penn. 558,060,264
Ohio 28,673	Mass. 447,270	Mass. 205,844,337	Mass. 630,032,345	Ill. 539,019,089	Ill. 908,640,280	Ill. 369,621,191
Mass. 26,923	Ohio 292,982	Ill. 142,873,265	Ill. 502,044,512	Mass. 473,199,434	Mass. 888,160,403	Mass. 414,960,969
Ill. 20,482	Ill. 280,218	Ohio 128,447,799	Ohio 402,793,019	Ohio 314,016,464	Ohio 641,688,064	Ohio 300,671,600

1900

Col 1	Col 2	Col 3	Col 4	Col 5	Col 6	Col 7
New York 76,658	New York 849,056	New York 408,855,652	New York 1,651,210,220	New York 1,143,791,776	New York 2,175,726,900	New York 1,031,935,124
Penn. 52,135	Penn. 733,834	Penn. 332,072,670	Penn. 1,551,548,712	Penn. 1,042,434,599	Penn. 1,834,790,060	Penn. 792,356,261
Ill. 38,360	Mass. 497,448	Mass. 228,240,442	Mass. 823,264,287	Ill. 739,754,414	Ill. 1,259,730,168	Ill. 519,975,754
Ohio 32,398	Ill. 395,110	Ill. 191,510,962	Ill. 776,829,598	Mass. 552,717,955	Mass. 1,035,198,989	Mass. 482,481,034
Mass. 29,180	Ohio 345,869	Ohio 153,955,330	Ohio 605,792,260	Ohio 447,849,677	Ohio 832,438,113	Ohio 384,588,436

[a]Based on figures in U.S. Twelfth Census, 1900, VIII, "Manufactures," pt. II, 982–989.

Table E. Occupation and Nativity of Employed Persons, 1870, 1880, 1890, 1900—by Percentages[a]

OCCUPATIONS	YEAR	NUMBER TOTAL	% OF TOTAL WORK FORCE	NATIVE BORN			FOREIGN BORN[b]																	
				TOTAL	WHITE	COLORED	TOTAL	GERMANY	GREAT BRITAIN	IRELAND	ENGLAND & WALES	SCOTLAND	BRITISH AMERICA	ENGLISH CANADA	FRENCH CANADA	SCANDI-NAVIA	SWEDEN & NORWAY	NORWAY	DENMARK	ITALY	FRANCE	OTHER NORTH EUROPE	OTHER SOUTH EUROPE	OTHERS
Manufacturing and Mechanical	1870[c]	171,201	23.07	49.54			50.45	20.33	4.52	13.88	4.53	1.28	2.59			4.43	4.95			.05	.76	.31	2.03	.23
	1880	272,562	27.26	11.43 57.52			11.64 42.46	4.69 17.72	1.23 4.15	3.20 8.94	1.04	.29	.60 2.04	1.62 .46	.36 .10	1.02	1.35 15.68		.77 .22	.01	.17	.07	.47	.05 4.28
	1890[d]	385,904	28.51	52.02	50.43	1.59	47.97	17.97		6.62							8.21							1.17 3.50
	1900	580,423	32.17	14.83	14.38	.45	13.68	5.09	1.18	1.89			.55				2.34							8.35 2.38 5.07 .55
Trade	1870	60,732	8.18	65.63			36.33	15.80	4.01	7.43	3.59	.99	1.81			1.41	1.78			.28	.79	.76	1.42	.04
	1880	95,003	9.50	5.37 69.10			2.81 30.84	1.29	.38	.61	.29	.08	.15 2.09	1.88 .46	.20	.11	.17		.52 .05	.02	.06	.06	.11	.00 3.50
	1890	146,892	10.85	6.57 66.58	64.44	2.13	2.93 33.42	1.34	4.09	5.37			.20	.20 .02			3.31							5.07
	1900	252,920	14.02	7.22	6.99	.23	3.62	1.49	.44	4.61 4.50							.36			.02			.11	.55
Domestic and Personal Service	1870	44,403	5.98	57.84			42.15	12.62	2.66	14.29	2.47	.92	1.95	1.05		8.90	7.19		.96	.02	.42	.22	1.37	.10
	1880	56,914	5.69	3.46 69.47			2.52 30.52	.75	.15	.85	.15	.05	.11 1.31	.07	.08 .01	.53	.41 5.66		.06	.00	.02	.01	.08	.01 2.04
	1890	92,268	6.81	3.95 60.03	52.64	7.39	1.74 35.96	8.99	2.92	8.30			2.62				11.33							2.77
	1900	110,279	6.11	4.09	3.59	.50	2.72	.80	.20	.51 9.66 8.97 .49			.11			.11	.77 .29		.06	.00	.02	.01	.08 .19	.14 2.88
Transportation and Communication	1870	29,944	4.03	53.63			46.35	10.91	3.95	23.18	4.53	1.12	2.20	2.15		2.72	4.32		.70	.02	.46	.26	.83	.11
	1880	44,022	4.40	2.16 64.11			1.87 35.86	.44	.09	.93	.18	.04	.09	.11	.08 .01	.11	.19 5.66		.04	.00	.02	.01	.03	.00 1.81
	1890	69,432	5.13	2.82 64.02	12.58	1.44	.45 35.96	9.09	3.46	14.05			2.62	.27			.29							1.48 .08
	1900	101,382	5.62	3.28	3.21	.07	1.84	.58	.18	.62 9.66 .06		.05		.01						.00	.02	.01	.03	2.77 .14
Professional Services	1870	20,875	2.81	86.78			13.20	5.36	2.61	1.78	2.24	.60	1.46	1.48		.52	.65		.12	.02	.36	.15	.56	.13
	1880	34,191	3.42	2.44 86.81	85.70	.86	.37 13.19	.15	.09	.05	.06	.02	.04 1.38	.05	.17	.01	.02		.00	.00	.01	.00	.01	.00 1.49
	1890	46,590	3.44	2.97 86.57			.45 13.41	5.36	2.47	1.70							1.07							1.48 .05
	1900	91,284	5.06	2.98	2.95	.03	.46 1.84	.18 4.83 .16	.08	1.76					.00		.04		.00					
Public Services	1870	4,771	.64	73.25	60.34	.73	26.74	9.45	3.57	9.66	2.70	1.02	1.49	.97		1.28	1.24		.39		.33	.14	.56	.08
	1880	7,256	.72	.47 75.74	.49	.01	.37 24.23	.06 7.20	.02	8.97	.02	.00	.01 1.69	.01	.27	.00	.01		.00		.00	.00	.00	.00 1.56
	1890	10,943	.80	.55 61.07			.17 38.93	7.05	4.37	.06			.01				3.47							.01 2.15
	1900	18,912	1.05	.49			.31	10.03	.03	.13 16.85							.03		.00					.02

This appendix consists of a large rotated statistical table giving census occupational data (1870, 1880, 1890, 1900). The principal figures are transcribed below; the remaining columns consist of percentages (with raised figures indicating the percent of the total in a particular occupation, per footnote e).

Occupation	Year	Number	%
Agriculture	1870	377,084	50.82
	1880	436,810	43.69
	1890	427,953	31.61
	1900	463,954	25.71
Mining	1870	7,760	1.04
	1880	13,098	1.31
	1890	22,195	1.64
	1900	38,184	2.11
Clerical Services	1870	294	.04
	1880	2,211	.22
	1890	61,885	4.57
	1900	102,200	5.66
Itemized Totals	1870	717,564	96.70
	1880	962,067	96.23
	1890	1,264,062	93.39
	1900	1,759,538	97.53
Unclassified and Unknown	1870	24,451	3.29
	1880	37,713	3.77
	1890	89,497	6.61
	1900	44,502	2.46
Grand Total	1870	742,015	66.98
	1880	999,780	70.27
	1890	1,353,559	66.14
	1900	1,804,040	64.39

a Derived from figures in U.S. Ninth Census, 1870, I, "Population," 731; U.S. Tenth Census, 1880, I, "Population," 830; U.S. Eleventh Census, 1890, I, "Population," pt. II, pp. 552-553; U.S. Twelfth Census, 1900, "Occupations," pp. 262-267.
b The percentages for the foreign born represent the percent of the total work force.
c The 1870 and 1880 censuses were not categorized as the 1890 census; hence there are certain classifications for which no figures are available for the earlier years.
d In the 1900 census workers were broken down into those of foreign parentage instead of those of foreign birth as before.
e The percentages in raised figures represent the percent of the total in a particular occupation.

Table F. Occupation and Nativity of Employed Persons, 1870, 1880, 1890—by Numbers

OCCUPATIONS	YEAR	TOTAL	NATIVE BORN			FOREIGN BORN				
			TOTAL	WHITE	COLORED	TOTAL	GERMANY	GREAT BRITAIN	IRELAND	ENGLAND AND WALES
Manufacturing	1870	171,201	84,825	b		86,376	34,811		23,766	
and	1880	272,562	156,774			115,788	48,319	12,333	24,390	
Mechanical	1890	385,404	200,774	194,642	6,132	185,130	68,975	16,008	25,557	7,759
Trade	1870	60,732	39,873			20,859	9,600		4,518	c
	1880	95,003	65,684			29,319	13,385	3,817	5,109	
	1890	146,892	97,793	94,657	3,136	49,099	20,170	6,010	6,775	2,183
Domestic	1870	44,408	25,684			18,719	5,603		6,346	
and	1880	56,914	39,541			17,373	5,121	1,517	4,727	
Pers. Service	1890	92,268	55,377	48,561	6,816	36,891	10,875	2,693	8,278	1,097
Transportation	1870	29,944	16,062			13,882	3,268		6,943	
and	1880	44,022	28,230			15,792	4,006	1,741	6,189	
Communication	1890	69,432	44,460	43,461	999	24,972	7,823	2,407	6,709	1,357
Professional	1870	20,875	18,118			2,757	1,119		372	
Services	1880	34,191	29,679			4,512	1,834	894	582	
	1890	46,590	40,230	39,937	403	6,250	2,252	1,153	823	468
Public	1870	4,771	3,495			1,276	451		461	
Services	1880	7,256	5,497			1,759	523	259	651	
	1890	10,943	6,683	6,603	80	4,260	1,098	478	1,779	129
	1870	377,084	292,720			84,364	37,768		15,625	
Agriculture	1880	436,810	348,143			88,667	42,329	12,321	15,171	
	1890	427,953	339,769	335,945	3,824	88,184	45,846	10,256	11,571	11,254
	1870	7,760	2,018			5,742	820		1,242	
Mining	1880	13,098	5,460			7,638	1,069	4,428	1,202	
	1890	22,195	9,475	8,919	556	12,720	2,777	4,837	1,136	2,566
Clerical	1870	294	218			76	31		11	
Services	1880	2,211	1,880			331	84	95	43	
	1890	61,885	48,863	48,657	206	13,022	3,417	2,923	1,973	19
Itemized	1870	717,564	483,013			234,551	43,471		59,284	
Totals	1880	962,067	680,888			281,179	116,670	37,405	58,064	
	1890	1,264,062	843,534	821,382	22,152	420,528	163,233	46,795	64,601	26,832
Unclassified	1870	24,451	14,030			10,421	4,339		1,963	
and	1880	37,713	21,711			16,002	5,966	2,329	2,837	
Unknown	1890	89,497	51,727	50,169	1,558	37,770	14,350	4,463	4,778	1,416
Grand	1870	742,015	497,043			244,972	97,810		61,247	
Total	1880	999,780	702,599			297,181	122,636	39,734	60,901	
	1890	1,353,559	895,261	871,551	28,710	458,298	177,583	5,258	69,379	28,248

[a] Based on U.S. Ninth Census, 1870, I, "Population," 731; U.S. Tenth Census, 1880, I, "Population," 820; U.S. Eleventh Census, 1890, I, "Population," pt. II, 552-553.
[b] The 1870 and 1880 censuses were not categorized as the 1890 census; hence there are certain classifications for which no figures are available for the earlier years.
[c] The 1870 censuses had the classifications "England and Wales" and "Scotland." In the 1880 and 1890 censuses they appear as "Great Britain."

FOREIGN BORN

SCOTLAND	BRITISH AMERICA	ENGLISH CANADA	FRENCH CANADA	SCANDI-NAVIA	SWEDEN AND NORWAY	DENMARK	ITALY	FRANCE	OTHER NORTH EUROPE	OTHER SOUTH EUROPE	OTHERS[f]
2,197	4,434	d		7,587	e		90	1,311	535	3,480	406
	5,566				13,507						11,673
		6,276	1,409		31,700	2,979					32,226
606	1,102			857			169	479	460	861	24
	1,985				1,697						3,326
		2,763	292		4,872	765					7,452
408	866			3,950			8	188	99	610	44
	747				4,096						1,165
		970	75		10,455	889					2,656
337	659			816			6	138	77	248	33
	1,154				1,902						800
		1,494	191		3,933	491					1,924
126	306			108			7	76	31	117	27
	471				222						509
		691	79		502	58					692
49	71			61			0	16	7	27	4
	123				90						113
		216	30		380	43					236
2,867	4,484			7,386			52	2,483	439	1,869	137
	3,356				8,813						6,677
		1,929	502		10,670	1,488					5,892
719	105			161			8	55	15	43	8
	99				236						604
		78	7		667	33					3,185
4	7			0			0	2	0	0	2
	51				25						33
		1,502	123		1,668	194					1,222
7,313	12,034			20,926			340	4,748	1,663	7,255	685
	13,552				30,588						24,900
		15,919	2,708		64,847	6,940					55,485
378	569			750			54	213	94	487	158
	1,008				1,634						2,228
		1,653	252		5,372	608					6,294
7,691	12,603			21,676			374	4,961	1,757	7,742	843
	14,560				32,222						27,128
		17,572	2,960		70,219	7,548					61,779

[d]The 1870 and 1880 censuses had the classification "British America." In the 1890 census appeared the two headings "English Canada" and "French Canada."
[e]The 1870 census had the category "Scandinavia." In 1880 this is changed to "Sweden and Norway," and in 1890 it appears as "Sweden and Norway" and "Denmark."
[f]Figures for foreign born workers in "all occupations" (they are not broken down as above) for the year 1890 from the countries of England, Wales, Scotland, France, Italy, Russia, Hungary, and Bohemia are in U.S., Eleventh Census, 1890, I, "Population," pt. II, 472-473. The 63,130 unskilled laborers in Illinois in 1870 (the corresponding figures in 1880, 1890, and 1900 are 104,267, 114,051, and 117,550) were listed by the census in the category "Professional and Personal Services." There was no separate classification for "Public Services," "Mining," or "Clerical Services." To make the figures more applicable to twentieth-century understanding, a regrouping of the various classifications used in the census of 1930 has been employed. Accordingly, some 23 percent of the total working in 1870 were in manufacturing and mechanical industries. This number included laborers and those in manufacturing and industries: clerks, miners, fishermen (who in the above classifications appear under "agriculture"), and lumbermen, who in the 1930 census appear in other categories. It should be recognized that the itemized occupations for 1870 add up to a total of only 717,564 in the regrouping, instead of 742,015 as given in the Ninth Census. The latter figure includes 24,451 persons of "unknown and unclassified occupation." This category does not appear in the census. Corresponding figures for Chicago are available in Bessie Pierce, A History of Chicago (New York: Alfred A. Knopf, 1940, 1957), II, 499; III, 517.

Bibliography

PRIMARY SOURCES

COLLECTIONS

John Peter Altgeld papers, Illinois State Historical Library
Sidney Breese papers, Illinois State Historical Library
Broadside Collection, 1865-1900, Illinois State Historical Library
Shelby M. Cullom papers, Illinois State Historical Library
Joseph W. Fifer papers, Illinois State Historical Library
Robert Ingersoll papers, Illinois State Historical Library
Vachel Lindsay papers and paintings, Lindsay home, Springfield, Illinois
Richard Oglesby papers, Illinois State Historical Library
John Palmer papers, Illinois State Historical Library
Lyman Trumbull papers, Illinois State Historical Library
Richard Yates, Jr., papers, Illinois State Historical Library
Richard Yates, Sr., papers, Illinois State Historical Library

GOVERNMENT DOCUMENTS

Federal Writers' Project (Illinois). *Cairo Guide.* American Guide Series. Cairo Public Library, 1938.
————. *Galena Guide.* American Guide Series. City of Galena, 1937.
————. *Hillsboro Guide.* American Guide Series. City of Hillsboro, Ill., 1940.
————. *Princeton Guide.* American Guide Series. Princeton, City of Princeton, Ill. 1939.
————. *Selected Bibliography: Illinois, Chicago and Its Environs.* Chicago: Works Progress Administration, 1937.
Illinois Constitutional Convention. *Debates and Proceedings of the Constitutional Convention of the State of Illinois, Convened at the City of Springfield, Tuesday, Dec. 12, 1869.* Springfield, Ill.: E. L. Merritt and Brothers, 1870.
Illinois Constitutional Convention, 1862. *Journal of the Constitutional Convention of the State of Illinois, Convened at Springfield, January 7, 1862.*
Illinois Bureau of Labor Statistics. *Report,* 1877-1900.
Illinois Department of Mines and Minerals. *Coal Report,* 1883-1919.

Illinois Department of Public Instruction. *Biennial Report*, Vol. 2, 1857-1962.

Illinois General Assembly, 1899. *Official Directory of the Forty-First General Assembly of Illinois, Session of 1899: Including an Appendix Giving a Complete and Accurate Statistical History of Illinois from 1800 to 1899 Inclusive.* John L. Pickering, comp. Springfield: Press of the Illinois State Register, 1899.

———. *Report of the Efficiency and Economy Committee.* Chicago: Windermere Press, 1915.

———. *Report of the Special Committee on Labor.* House of Representatives, 1879.

Illinois Geological Survey. *Economic Geology of Illinois.* A. H. Worthen, Director. 2 vols. Springfield: State Journal Steam Press, 1882.

———. *Geological Survey of Illinois.* A. H. Worthen, Director. 7 vols. Springfield: State Journal Steam Press, 1866-82.

Illinois Historical Records Survey. *Inventory of the Church Archives of Illinois Presbyterian Church.* Chicago, 1942.

Illinois. *Laws*, 1865-1900.

Illinois Legislative Reference Bureau. *Constitutional Conventions in Illinois.* Springfield: Schnepp & Barnes, 1919.

———. *County and Local Government in Illinois.* Springfield: Schnepp & Barnes, 1919.

———. *Farm Tenancy and Rural Credit.* Springfield: Schnepp & Barnes, 1919.

Illinois Military and Naval Department. *Historical Lineage, Illinois National Guard (and) Illinois Naval Militia.* Springfield, 1953.

Illinois Prison Inquiry Commission. *The Prison System of Illinois.* Springfield, 1937.

Illinois School Law, 1889-1901. Springfield, Ill.: Phillips Bros., 1901.

Illinois Secretary of State. *Counties of Illinois: Their Origin and Evolution, with Twenty-three Maps Showing Their Original and Present Boundary Lines of Each County of the State.* Springfield: Illinois State Journal Co., 1912.

———. *History of the Office of Secretary of State.* Springfield, 1961.

Illinois Tax Commission. *The Illinois Revenue System,* 1918-1936. Springfield: State of Illinois, 1936.

Illinois Treasurer's Office. *Biennial Report of the Treasurer,* 1850-1868, 1869-1872. Springfield, 1837-1972.

Millhouse, John G., Director. *A Compilation of the Coal Reports of Illinois, 1882-1930.* Springfield: Department of Mines and Minerals, 1931.

National Convention of Chiefs and Commissioners of State Bureaus of Statistics of Labor. *Proceedings of First Annual Convention.* Columbus, Ohio, 1883.

Powell, Paul, ed. *Handbook of Illinois Government.* Springfield: State of Illinois, 1970.

United States Bureau of Labor. *The Housing of the Working People.* Carroll D. Wright and E. R. L. Gould, eds. Washington, D.C.: Government Printing Office, 1895.

———. *Sixteenth Annual Report, 1901.* Strikes, July 1874-1900.

————. *Tenth Annual Report, 1896. Vol. 1, Strikes, 1887-July, 1894.*

————. Bureau of Labor. *Third Annual Report, 1888, Strikes, 1881-1886.*

————. *Twenty-First Annual Report, 1907.* Strikes, 1900-1905 plus Summary, 1881-1905.

United States Bureau of Labor Statistics. *Employment and Earnings Statistics for the United States, 1909-1960.* Washington, D.C.: Government Printing Office, 1961.

————. *Special Report of the Commissioner of Labor.* Washington, D.C.: Government Printing Office, 1889-1905.

United States Federal Census, 1860, 1870, 1880, 1890, 1900.

Verlie, Emil Joseph, ed. *Illinois Constitutions.* Springfield: The Trustees of the Illinois State Historical Library, 1919.

Works Progress Administration, Federal Writers' Project. *Annals of Labor and Industry.* Chicago Historical Society.

————. *Illinois: A Descriptive and Historical Guide.* Chicago: A. C. McClurg and Co., 1947.

AUTOBIOGRAPHIES AND COLLECTED PAPERS

Addams, Jane. *Twenty Years at Hull House with Autobiographical Notes.* New York: MacMillan Co., 1910.

Altgeld, John Peter. *The Mind and Spirit of John Peter Altgeld.* Henry Christman, ed. Urbana: University of Illinois Press, 1965.

Browning, Orville Hickman. *The Diary of Orville Hickman Browning.* Theodore C. Pease and J. G. Randall, eds. *The Illinois State Historical Library Collections, Lincoln Series, XX and XXII.* Illinois State Historical Library, 1927, 1933.

Cleveland, Grover. "Recollections of Grover Cleveland." *Harper's Weekly,* July 21, 1908.

Cullom, Shelby M. *Fifty Years of Public Service: Personal Recollections of Shelby M. Cullom, Senior Senator from Illinois.* Chicago: Da Capo Press, 1969.

Foner, P. J., ed. *The Autobiographies of the Haymarket Martyrs.* New York: Humanities Press, 1969.

Gage, Lyman. *Memoirs of Lyman J. Gage.* New York: House of Field, Inc., 1937.

Ingersoll, Robert. *The Letters of Robert Ingersoll.* Eva Ingersoll Wakefield, ed. New York: Philosophical Library, 1951.

Koerner, Gustav. *Memoirs of Gustav Koerner, 1809-1896.* T. J. McCormack, ed. 2 vols. Cedar Rapids, Iowa: The Torch Press, 1909.

McDowell, Mary. "A Quarter of a Century in the Stockyards District," *Transactions of the Illinois State Historical Society for 1920.*

Sandburg, Carl. *Always the Young Strangers.* New York: Harcourt, Brace, 1953.

NEWSPAPERS (selected dates, 1860-1900)

Bloomington Pantagraph

Champaign Daily News-Gazette
Chicago Evening Journal
Chicago Evening Post
Chicago Post and Mail
Chicago Republican
Chicago Times
Chicago Tribune
Congressional Globe, 1853-1873
Congressional Record, 1873-1900
Denni Hlasatel
East St. Louis Gazette
Galesburg Republican Register
Galesburg Spectator
Illinois Gazetteer
Illinois Staats-Zeitung
Illinois State Journal
Illinois State Register
The Inter-Ocean
Joliet Daily News
Joliet Daily Signal
Kewanee Independent
Marshall County Republican
Mendota Bulletin
Mound City Emporium
Nation
New York Daily Tribune
Peoria Transcript
Prairie Farmer
Quincy Whig
Rock Island Argus
Workingmen's Advocate
Zgoda

REFERENCE MATERIALS

Angle, Paul McClelland. *A Handbook of Illinois History: A Topical Survey with References for Teachers and Students.* Springfield: Illinois State Historical Society, 1942.

Appleton's Annual Cyclopaedia and Register of Important Events, 1861-1901. New York: D. Appleton & Co., 1865-1901.

Bateman, Newton, ed. *Historical Encyclopedia of Illinois.* Chicago: Munsell Publishing Co., 1905.

Concise Dictionary of American Biography. New York: Charles Scribner's Sons, 1964.

Heitman, Francis B. *Historical Register and Dictionary of the United States Army from Its Organization, September 29, 1789, to March 2, 1903.* 2 vols. Washington, D.C.: Government Printing Office, 1903.

Illinois Historical Records Survey. *Guide to Public Vital Statistics Records in Illinois.* Chicago, 1941.

———. *Inventory of the State Archives of Illinois.* Prepared by Division of Community Service Programs. Chicago: Works Projects Administration, 1942.

Illinois Press Association. *Illinois Newspaper Directory: History of Illinois Press Association.* Springfield: Jartman-Jefferson Printing Co., 1934.

Illinois State Historical Library. *The County Archives of the State of Illinois.* T. C. Pease, comp.

———. *General Index to Collections, Journals, Publications, 1899-1928.* Quincy, Ill.: The Royal Printing Co., 1930.

———. *A List of the Genealogical Works in the Illinois State Historical Library.* Georgia L. Osborne, comp. Springfield: State Journal Co., 1914.

———. *Newspapers and Periodicals of Illinois, 1814-1879.* F. W. Scott, comp.

Illinois State Historical Society. *Papers in Illinois History and Transactions for the Years 1903-1942.* Springfield, 1904-44.

Schlebker, Dr. John T. *Bibliography of Books and Pamphlets on the History of Agriculture in the United States, 1607-1967.* Santa Barbara, Calif.: A.B.C.-Clio Press, 1964.

Warner and Beers. *Atlas of the State of Illinois: General Maps, History, Statistics and Illustrations.* Chicago: Union Atlas Co., 1876.

Weber, Mrs. Jessie Palmer, comp. *An Outline for the Study of Illinois State History: Prepared under the Direction of the Board of Trustees of the Illinois State Historical Library.* Springfield: H. W. Rokker Co., 1905.

SECONDARY SOURCES

PERIODICALS, DISSERTATIONS, SPEECHES, and ARTICLES

Ackerman, William K. "Early Illinois Railroads." *Fergus Historical Series,* No. 23 (Chicago, 1884), 109.

Addams, Jane. "Social Settlements in Illinois." *Transactions of the Illinois State Historical Society* (1906).

Ander, O. Fritiof. "Some Factors in the Americanization of the Swedish Immigrant." *Journal of the Illinois State Historical Society* XXVI (1933).

Andrews, E. "The Sum and Substance of Antiseptic Surgery." *The Chicago Medical Examiner.* N. S. Davis, ed. Chicago, 1869.

Angle, Paul. "Brief History of Chicago." *Illinois Blue Book* (1953-54).

Ayers, Esther Mary. "Art in Southern Illinois, 1865-1914." *Journal of the Illinois State Historical Society* XXXVI (1943).

Babcock, Kendric C. "The Expansion of Higher Education in Illinois." *Transactions of the Illinois State Historical Society* (1925).

Barclay, George A. "The Keeley League." *Journal of the Illinois State Historical Society* LVIII (1964).

Bardolph, Richard. "Illinois Agriculture in Transition, 1820-1870." *Journal of the Illinois State Historical Society* XLI (1948).

Barlow, William. "U.S. Commissioner of Pensions, Green B. Raum of Illinois." *Journal of the Illinois State Historical Society* LX (1967).

Baylan, Josephine. "The Illinois Central Railroad and Its Successors." *Journal of the Illinois State Historical Society* XXX (1937-38).

Belcher, Wyatt Winton. *The Economic Rivalry between St. Louis and Chicago, 1830-1880.* Dissertation Number 529. New York: Columbia University, 1947.

Bigham, T. C. "The Chicago Federation of Labor." Master's thesis, University of Chicago, 1924.

Blair, George S. "The Adoption of Cumulative Voting in Illinois." *Journal of the Illinois State Historical Society* XXXVII (1954).

Bogart, Ernest Ludlow. "The Movement of Population in Illinois, 1870-1910." *Transactions of the Illinois State Historical Society* (1917).

Bogue, Margaret Beattie. "The Swamp Land Act and Wet Land Utilization in Illinois, 1850-1890." *Agricultural History,* XXV (1951).

Bormer, Thomas N. "A Forgotten Figure in Chicago's Medical History." *Journal of the Illinois State Historical Society* XLV (1952).

Bowman, John O. "Trends in Midwestern Farm Land Values." Ph.D. dissertation, Yale University, 1964.

Bronson, Howard G. "Early Illinois Railroads: The Place of the Illinois Central in Illinois History Prior to the Civil War." *Transactions of the Illinois State Historical Society* (1908).

Buck, Solon J. "Agricultural Organization in Illinois, 1870-1880." *Journal of the Illinois State Historical Society* III (1910).

Burjord, Gary Clive. "The Twilight of the Local Passenger Train in Illinois." *Journal of the Illinois State Historical Society* LI (1958).

Bush, Francis X. "The Haymarket Riot and the Trial of the Anarchists." *Journal of the Illinois State Historical Society* XLVIII (1955).

Coleman, Charles H., and Paul H. Spence. "The Normal School Comes to Charleston." *Journal of the Illinois State Historical Society* XLI (1948).

Converse, Henry A. "The Life and Services of Shelby M. Cullom." *Transactions of the Illinois State Historical Society* (1914).

Croll, Rev. Phillip Columbus. *History of the Evangelical Lutheran Church in Illinois and the Middle West.* A paper read at the 50th convention of the Central Illinois Synod at Nokomis, Ill., Oct. 22, 1916.

Culp, Dorothy. "The Radical Labor Movement, 1873-1895." *Transactions of the Illinois State Historical Society* (1937).

Cutshall, Alden D. "A Gazetteer of the Origin of Illinois Nomenclature." A paper for Geography 132 at the University of Illinois.

Dante, Harris L. "The *Chicago Tribune*'s 'Lost Years,' 1865-1874." *Journal of the Illinois State Historical Society* LVIII (1965).

———. "Western Attitudes and Reconstruction Politics in Illinois, 1865-1872." *Journal of the Illinois State Historical Society* XLIX (1956).

Davenport, F. Garvin. "John Henry Rauch and Public Health in Illinois, 1877-1891." *Journal of the Illinois State Historical Society* L (1957).

———. "Natural Scientists and the Farmers of Illinois, 1865-1900." *Journal of the Illinois State Historical Society* LI (1958).

Davis, Allen F. "Jane Addams vs. the Ward Boss." *Journal of the Illinois State Historical Society* LVII (1960).

Debel, N. H. "The Development of the Veto Power of the Governor of Illinois." *Journal of the Illinois State Historical Society* IX (1916).

Derge, David R. "Metropolitan and Outstate Alignments in the Illinois and Missouri Legislative Delegations." *American Political Science Review* LIII (1958).

Dilliard, Irving. "Civil Liberties of Negroes in Illinois since 1865." *Journal of the Illinois State Historical Society* LVI (1963).

Dixon, Harry Mitchell. "The Illinois Coal Mining Industry." Ph.D. dissertation. University of Illinois, 1951.

Dowie, Rev. John Alex. *Doctors, Drugs & Devils . . .or . . . the Foes of Christ the Healer.* Pamphlet. Chicago: Zion Publications, 1894.

Dowling, Rev. Edward J. "Red Stocks in the Sunset." *Journal of the Illinois State Historical Society* XL (1949).

Dukes, E. L. "The Southern Collegiate Institute (1891-1916)." *Journal of the Illinois State Historical Society* XXXVII (1945).

Dunn, F. Roger. "Formative Years of the Chicago Y.M.C.A." *Journal of the Illinois State Historical Society* XXXVII (1945).

East, Ernest E. "The Distiller's and Cattle Feeder's Trust, 1887-1895." *Journal of the Illinois State Historical Society* XLV (1952).

Ellingsworth, Huber W. "John Peter Altgeld as a Public Speaker." *Journal of the Illinois State Historical Society* XLVI (1954).

Ewert, A. F. "Early History of Education in Illinois—The Three Oldest Colleges." *Illinois Blue Book* (1929-30).

Fisher, Miles Mark. "Negro Churches in Illinois, a Fragmentary History with Emphasis on Chicago." *Journal of the Illinois State Historical Society* LVI (1963).

Gates, Paul Wallace. "Cattle Kings in the Prairies." *Mississippi Valley Historical Review* XXXV (1948).

———. "Frontier Landlords and Pioneer Tenants." *Journal of the Illinois State Historical Society* XXXVII (1945).

———. "Large Scale Farming in Illinois, 1830 to 1870." *Agricultural History Journal* VI (1932).

Gertz, Elmer. "Charles A. Dana and the *Chicago Republican.*" *Journal of the Illinois State Historical Society* XLV (1952).

Gordon, Joseph Hinkley. "Illinois Railway Legislation and Commission Control since 1870." *The University Studies* I:6 (March 1904), University of Illinois Press.

"Governor R. J. Oglesby's Pension." *Journal of the Illinois State Historical Society* V (1912).

Griffin, C. E. "Railway History of Illinois." Master's thesis. University of Illinois, 1918.

Griffith, Will. "Egypt, Illinois." *Illinois Blue Book* (1945-46).

Groff, Maurice O. "The Lake Michigan Water Division Controversy: A Summary Statement." *Journal of the Illinois State Historical Society* XXXIV (1941).

Gutman, Herbert G. "The Braidwood Lockout of 1874." *Journal of the Illinois State Historical Society* LIII (1960).

Hall, Andy, M. D. "The Ku Klux Klan in Southern Illinois in 1875." *Journal of the Illinois State Historical Society* XLVI (1953).

Hanley, Sarah Bond. "Political Pioneering in '88." *The Democratic Digest* (1941).

Hardin, Thomas L. "The National Road in Illinois." *Journal of the Illinois State Historical Society* LX (1967).

Hawkins, May Strong. "The Early Political Career of John A. Logan." Master's thesis. University of Chicago, 1934.

Hedges, James B. "The Colonization Work of the Northern Pacific Railroad." *Mississippi Valley Historical Review* XIII (1926).

Heinl, Frank J. "Congregationalism in Jacksonville and Early Illinois." *Journal of the Illinois State Historical Society* XXVII (1934-35).

Hendrickson, Walter B. "Commencement Week in 1876." *Journal of the Illinois State Historical Society* XLII (1950).

———. "Nineteenth-Century Natural History Organizations in Illinois." *Journal of the Illinois State Historical Society* LIV (1961).

Hicken, Victor. "The Virden and Pana Mine Wars of 1898." *Journal of the Illinois State Historical Society* LII (1959).

Hickey, James T. "Oglesby's Fence Rail Dealings and the 1860 Decatur Convention." *Journal of the Illinois State Historical Society* LIV (1961).

———. "Springfield, May, 1865." *Journal of the Illinois State Historical Society* LVIII (1965).

Hildner, Ernest G. "Higher Education in Transition, 1850-1870." *Journal of the Illinois State Historical Society* LVI (1963).

Horney, Helen, and William E. Keller. "The Negro's Two Hundred Forty Years in Illinois—A Chronology." *Journal of the Illinois State Historical Society* LVI (1963).

Huback, Robert R. "Illinois, Host to Well-Known Nineteenth-Century Authors." *Journal of the Illinois State Historical Society* XXXVIII (1945).

Hyneman, Charles Shang. "The Illinois Constitution and Democratic Government." *Law Review of Northwestern University* 46: 4 (1951).

Isaacson, Alfred, and Otto Eisenschiml. "The Virden and Pana Mine Wars of 1898." *Journal of the Illinois State Historical Society* LII (1959).

Johnson, Walter T. "Peter Akers: Methodist Circuit Rider and Educator, 1790-1886." *Journal of the Illinois State Historical Society* XXXII (1939).

Jones, James P. "John A. Logan, Freshman in Congress, 1859-1860." *Journal of the Illinois State Historical Society* LVI (1963).

———. "Trumbull's Private Opinion of the Grant Scandals." *Journal of the Illinois State Historical Society* LIV (1961).

Jones, Stanley L. "Agrarian Radicalism in Illinois' Constitutional Convention of 1862." *Journal of the Illinois State Historical Society* XLVIII (1955).

Keiser, John H. "Black Strikebreakers and Racism in Illinois, 1865-1900." *Journal of the Illinois State Historical Society* LXV (1972).

———. "The Union Miners Cemetery at Mt. Olive, Illinois: A Spirit

Thread of Labor History." *Journal of the Illinois State Historical Society* LXII (1969).

Lambert, Belle Short. "The Woman's Club Movement in Illinois." *Transactions of the Illinois State Historical Society* (1904).

Lochard, Metz T. P. "The Negro Press in Illinois." *Journal of the Illinois State Historical Society* LVI (1963).

Mahon, Ralph. *A Golden Anniversary, 1878-1928: The Story of Fifty Years of the Bell Telephone in Chicago.* Pamphlet. Chicago: Illinois Bell Telephone Co., 1928.

Manfredini, Dalous M. "The Italians Come to Herrin." *Journal of the Illinois State Historical Society* XXXVII (1944).

McClelland, Clarence P. "The Education of Females in Early Illinois." *Journal of the Illinois State Historical Society* XXXVI (1943).

McDowell, Mary E. "A Quarter of a Century in the Stockyards District." *Transactions of the Illinois State Historical Society* (1920).

Merwin, Loring C. "McLean County's Newspapers—Particularly the *Pantagraph.*" *Journal of the Illinois State Historical Society* LI (1958).

Monaghan, Jay. "The Welsh People in Chicago." *Journal of the Illinois State Historical Society* XXXII (1939).

Moore, Margaret King. "The Ladies' Association for Educating Females, 1833-1937." *Journal of the Illinois State Historical Society* XXXI (1938).

"Mrs. Richard J. Oglesby, 1845-1928." *Journal of the Illinois State Historical Society* XXI (1929).

Naeseth, Henriette C. K. "Drama in Swedish in Chicago." *Journal of the Illinois State Historical Society* XLI (1948).

Nevins, Allan. "Not without Thy Wondrous Story, Illinois." *Journal of the Illinois State Historical Society* LXVI (1953).

———. "Sandburg as Historian." *Journal of the Illinois State Historical Society* XXXIV (1945).

Newcombe, Alfred W. "Alson J. Streeter—An Agrarian Liberal." *Journal of the Illinois State Historical Society* XXXIV (1945).

Oglesby, Richard. "Tribute to Corn." *Journal of the Illinois State Historical Society* IV (Oct., 1911).

Panagopoulos, E. P. "Chicago and the War between Greece and Turkey in 1897." *Journal of the Illinois State Historical Society* XLIX (1956).

Pease, Theodore C. "Otto Leopold Schmidt: 1863-1935." *Journal of the Illinois State Historical Society* XXVIII (1935-36).

Pitkin, William A. "Shelby M. Cullom: Presidential Prospect." *Journal of the Illinois State Historical Society* XLIX (1956).

Reid, DeLafayette. "Our State's Public Libraries." *Illinois History* XIX: VIII (May, 1966).

Richardson, Genevieve. "Lorado Taft and Theater." *Journal of the Illinois State Historical Society* XLIX (1956).

Roberts, Sidney I. "The Municipal Voters' League and Chicago's Boodlers." *Journal of the Illinois State Historical Society* LIII (1961).

Schiffler, Harold. "The Chicago Church-Theater Controversy of 1881-1882." *Journal of the Illinois Historical Society* LII (1960).

Schlesinger, Arthur. "Historians Rate U.S. Presidents." *Life* 25:17 (Nov., 1948).

Schwartz, Richard W. "Dr. John Harvey Kellogg as a Social Gospel Practitioner." *Journal of the Illinois State Historical Society* LVII (1964).

Searles, William C. "Governor Cullom and the Pekin Whiskey Ring Scandal." *Journal of the Illinois State Historical Society* LI (1958).

Sigmund, Elwin W. "Railroad Strikers in Court: Unreported Contempt Cases in Illinois in 1877." *Journal of the Illinois State Historical Society* XLIX (1956).

Simonson, Harold P. "Francis Grierson—A Biographical Sketch and Bibliography." *Journal of the Illinois State Historical Society* LIV (1961).

Soderbergh, Peter A. "Charles A. Beard in Chicago, 1896." *Journal of the Illinois State Historical Society* LXIII (1970).

Solberg, Winston N. "The University of Illinois Struggles for Public Recognition, 1867-1894." *Journal of the Illinois State Historical Society* LIX (1966).

Sorenson, Andrew. "Lester Frank Ward: The 'American Aristotle' in Illinois." *Journal of the Illinois State Historical Society* LXIII (1970).

Stallings, Ray. "The Drama in Southern Illinois (1865-1900)." *Journal of the Illinois State Historical Society* XXXIII (1940).

Starke, Aubrey. "The Indigenous Iron Industry of Illinois." *Journal of the Illinois State Historical Society* XXVII (1934-35).

Staudenraus, P. J. "The Empire City of the West—A View of Chicago, 1864." *Journal of the Illinois State Historical Society* LVI (1963).

Tarr, Joel. "The Chicago Anti-Department Store Crusade of 1897." *Journal of the Illinois State Historical Society* LXIV (1971).

Thomas, R. G. "Bank Failures in Chicago before 1925." *Journal of the Illinois State Historical Society* XXVIII (1935-36).

Tompkins, C. David. "John Peter Altgeld as a Candidate for Mayor of Chicago." *Journal of the Illinois State Historical Society* LVI (1963).

Wade, Louise C. "The Heritage from Chicago's Early Settlement Houses." *Journal of the Illinois State Historical Society* LX (1967).

Weber, Jessie Palmer. "The Illinois Centennial Celebration: A Hundred Years of Progress." *Journal of the Illinois State Historical Society* X (1917).

Wilson, Howard A. "William Dean Howells' Unpublished Letters about the Haymarket Affair." *Journal of the Illinois State Historical Society* LVI (1963).

Wish, Harvey. "Altgeld and the Progressive Tradition." *American Historical Review* XLVI (1941).

———. "Governor Altgeld Pardons the Anarchists." *Journal of the Illinois State Historical Society* XXXI (1938-39).

———. "John Peter Altgeld and the Election of 1896." *Journal of the Illinois State Historical Society* XXX (1937-38).

———. "The Pullman Strike: A Study in Industrial Warfare." *Journal of the Illinois State Historical Society* XXXII (1939).

Yates, Richard. "The Jacksonville Centennial." *Journal of the Illinois State Historical Society* XVIII (1925).

———. "Ulysses S. Grant." *Journal of the Illinois State Historical Society* XX (1927).

BOOKS

Adamic, Louis. *Dynamite: The Story of Class Violence in America.* Rev. ed. Gloucester, Mass.: P. Smith, 1963.

Adams, Charles F., Jr. *Railroads: Their Origin and Problems.* New York: G. P. Putnam's Sons, 1878.

Adams, James N. *Illinois Place Names.* Springfield, Ill.: Illinois State Historical Society. Occasional Publications, No. 54, 1968.

Aldrick, Darrogh. *The Story of John Deere.* Minneapolis: Privately printed, 1942.

Allen, John. *Legends and Lore of Southern Illinois.* Carbondale: Southern Illinois University Press, 1963.

Altgeld, John Peter. *The Cost of Something for Nothing.* Chicago: Hammersmark, 1904.

———. *Live Questions.* Chicago: George S. Bowen & Co., 1890.

Andros, S. O. *Coal Mining in Illinois.* Illinois Coal Mining Investigations, Bulletin 13. Urbana: University of Illinois, 1915.

Angle, Paul. *Bloody Williamson: A Chapter in American Lawlessness.* New York: Alfred A. Knopf, 1969.

———, and Mary Lynn McCree. *Prairie State: Impressions of Illinois 1673-1967.* Chicago: University of Chicago Press, 1968.

Anton, Thomas J. *The Politics of State Expenditure in Illinois.* Urbana: University of Illinois Press, 1966.

Atherton, Lewis. *Main Street on the Middle Border.* Chicago: Quadrangle Books, 1966.

Barnard, Harry. *"Eagle Forgotten": The Life of John Peter Altgeld.* Indianapolis, Ind.: Bobbs-Merrill Co., 1938.

Beard, Mary Ritter. *The Making of Charles A. Beard: An Interpretation.* New York: MacMillan, 1955.

Beckner, Earl R. *The History of Illinois Labor Legislation.* Social Science Studies No. 132. Chicago: University of Chicago Press, 1929.

Beinfohr, Oliver Wendell. *The Industrial Potential of Southern Illinois.* Carbondale, Ill.: Southern Illinois University Press, 1954.

Bennet, James O'Donnel. *"Private Joe" Fifer.* Bloomington, Ill.: Pantagraph Printing and Stationery Co., 1936.

Bennett, Clarence Elmore. *History of Employer's Associations in the United States.* New York: Vantage Press, 1957.

Bennett, Francis Cheney. *History of Music and Art in Illinois, Including Portraits and Biographies of the Cultured Men and Women Who Have Been Liberal Patrons of the Arts.* Philadelphia: Privately printed, 1904.

Billington, Ray Allen, with collaboration of James Blaine Hedges. *Westward*

Expansion: A History of the American Frontier. New York: MacMillan Co., 1949.

Biographical Publishing Company. *Biographical Sketches: Illinois 1883; Biographies of the State Officers and the Thirty-Third General Assembly.* Springfield: Biographical Publishing Co., 1883.

Bishop, Glen A., comp. in collaboration with Paul T. Gilbert. *Chicago's Accomplishments and Leaders.* Chicago: Bishop Publishing Co., 1932.

Blaine, James G. *Twenty Years of Congress.* Norwich, Conn.: Henry Bill, 1893.

Blair, George S. *Cumulative Voting: An Effective Electoral Device in Illinois Politics.* Illinois Studies in the Social Sciences, vol. 45. Urbana: University of Illinois Press, 1960.

Bloch, Louis. *Labor Agreements in Coal Mines.* New York: Russell Sage Foundation, 1931.

Bogart, Ernest L., and John M. Matthews. *The Modern Commonwealth, 1893-1918. Centennial History of Illinois,* V. Springfield, Ill.: Centennial Commission, 1920.

Bogart, Ernest L., and Charles M. Thompson. *The Industrial State, 1870-1883. Centennial History of Illinois,* III. Springfield, Ill.: Centennial Commission, 1920.

Bogue, Margaret Beattie. *Patterns from the Sod: Land Use and Tenure in the Grand Prairie, 1850-1900.* Collections of the Illinois State Historical Library, vol. XXXIV, Land Series, vol. 1. Springfield, Ill.: Illinois State Historical Library, 1959.

Bolles, Albert S. *Industrial History of the United States.* Norwich, Conn.: Henry Bill Publishing Company, 1879.

Bonham, Jeriah. *Fifty Years' Recollections with Observations and Reflections of Historical Events, Giving Sketches of Eminent Citizens—Their Lives and Public Services.* Peoria, Ill.: J. W. Franks and Sons, 1883.

Britt, Albert. *An America That Was: What Life Was Like on an Illinois Farm Seventy Years Ago.* Barre, Mass.: Barre Publishers, 1964.

Brooks, John Graham. *The Social Unrest: Studies in Labor and Socialist Movements.* New York: MacMillan Co., 1903.

Brown, Henry J. *The Catholic Church and the Knights of Labor.* Washington, D.C.: Catholic University of America, 1949.

Browne, Waldo R. *Altgeld of Illinois: A Record of His Life and Works.* New York: B. W. Huebsch, Inc., 1924.

Brownell, Baker. *The Other Illinois.* New York: Duell, Sloan and Pearce, 1958.

Brownson, Howard Gray. *History of the Illinois Central Railroad to 1870.* Urbana: University of Illinois, 1915.

Bruce, Robert V. *1877: Year of Violence.* Indianapolis, Ind.: Bobbs-Merrill, 1959.

Buck, Solon J. *The Granger Movement: A Study of Agricultural Organization and Its Political, Economic, and Social Manifestations, 1870-1880.* Lincoln: University of Nebraska Press, Bison Books, 1965.

———. *Illinois in 1818. Centennial History of Illinois,* Introductory vol. Springfield: Centennial Commission, 1917.

Burford, Gary Clive, in collaboration with Guy McIlvaine Smith. *The History and Romance of Danville Junction or When Rails Were the Only Trails.* Danville: Interstate Printers and Publishers, 1942.

Burgess, George H., and Miles E. Kennedy. *Centennial History of the Pennsylvania Railroad Company, 1846-1946.* Philadelphia: Pennsylvania Railroad Company, 1949.

Calkins, Ernest Elmo. *They Broke the Prairie; Being Some Accounts of the Settlement of the Upper Mississippi Valley by Religious and Educational Pioneers, Told in Terms of One City, Galesburg, and of One College, Knox.* New York: C. Scribner's Sons, 1937.

Calmer, Alan. *Labor Agitator: The Story of Albert R. Parsons.* New York: International Publishers, 1937.

Carriel, Mary Turner. *The Life of Jonathan Baldwin Turner.* Urbana: University of Illinois Press, 1961.

Carwardine, Rev. William H. *The Pullman Strike.* Chicago: Charles H. Kerr & Co., 1894.

Casson, Herbert N. *Cyrus Hall McCormick, His Life and Work.* Chicago: A. C. McClurg, 1909.

Catton, Bruce. *U.S. Grant and the American Military Tradition.* New York: Grossett & Dunlap, 1954, by arrangement with Little, Brown.

Chicago Civil Liberties Committee. *Pursuit of Freedom: A History of Civil Liberty in Illinois, 1787-1942.* Chicago Civil Liberties Committee. Illinois Civil Liberties Committee, 1942.

Childs, Mary Louise. *Actual Government in Illinois.* New York: The Century Co., 1917.

Christman, Henry M., ed. *The Mind and Spirit of John Peter Altgeld: Selected Writings and Addresses.* Urbana: University of Illinois Press, 1965.

Church, Charles A. *History of the Republican Party in Illinois 1854-1912, with a Review of the Aggressions of the Slave-Power.* Rockford: Wilson Brothers Co., 1912.

Church, Harry Victor. *Illinois: History, Geography, Government.* Boston, New York, Washington, D.C.: Heath and Co., 1925.

Clark, Neil M. *John Deere: He Gave to the World the Steel Plow.* Moline, Ill.: Privately printed, 1937.

Clayton, John, comp. *The Illinois Fact Book and Historical Almanac, 1673-1968.* Carbondale: Southern Illinois University Press, 1970.

Clemens, Samuel L. *Life on the Mississippi.* New York: Harper and Row, 1917.

Cochran, T. C. *Railroad Leaders, 1845-1890: The Business Mind in Action.* Cambridge: Harvard University Press, 1953.

Colbert, Elias, and Everett Chamberlin. *Chicago and the Great Conflagration: Being a Reproduction of the Original 1871 Edition–The First Hand News and on-the-Spot Views–A Vivid Accounting of the Holocaust and What Directly Followed.* New York: Viking Press, facsimile edition, 1971.

Cole, Arthur C. *The Era of the Civil War, 1848-1870. Centennial History of Illinois*, III. Springfield: Centennial Commission, 1919.

Coleman, McAlister. *Men and Coal.* New York: Farrar & Rinehart, Inc., 1943.

Coletta, Paolo E. *William Jennings Bryan: I, Political Evangelist, 1869-1898.* Lincoln: University of Nebraska Press, 1964.

Commons, John R., *et al.*, eds. *A Documentary History of American Industrial Society.* Cleveland, Ohio: The A. H. Clark Co., 1910-11.

Croll, P. C. *History of the Evangelical Lutheran Church in Illinois and the Middle West.* NI, 1916.

Cullom, Shelby. *Fifty Years of Public Service–Recollections of Shelby M. Cullom.* Chicago: A. C. McClurg and Co., 1914.

Daggett, Stuart. *Railroad Reorganization.* Vol. IV. *Harvard Economics Studies.* New York: Houghton, Mifflin and Co., 1908.

Darrow, Clarence. *The Story of My Life.* New York: Scribner's Sons, 1932.

David, Henry. *The History of the Haymarket Affair: A Study in the American Revolutionary and Labor Movements.* 2nd ed. New York: Russell and Russell, 1958.

Davidson, Alexander, and Bernard Stuve. *A Complete History of Illinois from 1673 to 1884.* Springfield: Illinois Journal Co., 1884.

Davis, N. S., ed. *The Chicago Medical Examiner.* Vol. X. Chicago: Robert Fergus' Sons, 1869.

Debel, Niels Henriksen. *The Veto Power of the Governor of Illinois.* Urbana: University of Illinois, 1917.

Dedmon, Emmett. *Fabulous Chicago.* New York: Random House, 1953.

Destler, Chester M. *American Radicalism, 1865-1901.* New London, Conn.: Quadrangle Books, 1966.

Donald, David. *Lincoln Reconsidered: Essays on the Civil War Era.* 2nd ed. New York: Vintage Books, Random House, 1961.

Doty, Mrs. Duane. *The Town of Pullman . . . Its Growth, with Brief Accounts of Its Industries.* Pullman, Ill.: T. P. Struitsacker, 1893.

Douglas, Paul H. *Real Wages in the United States, 1840-1936.* Publications of the Pollack Foundation for Economic Research No. 9. Boston: Houghton Mifflin, 1930.

Dowie, James Iverne. *Prairie Grass Dividing.* Rock Island, Ill. *Augustana Historical Society Publications,* Vol. XVIII (1959).

Dreiske, John. *Your Government and Mine: Metropolitan Chicago.* New York: Oceana Publications, 1959.

Drury, John. *Old Chicago Houses.* Chicago: University of Chicago Press, 1941.

Dugan, Hugh G., ed. *Village on the County Line: A History of Hinsdale, Illinois.* Chicago: Privately printed, 1949.

DuHamel, Samuel S. *The Illinois School Laws as Found in the Constitution, the Statutory Provisions, the Decisions of the Supreme and the Appellate Courts and the Opinions of the Attorney General.* Tuscola, Ill.: *Tuscola Journal,* 1932.

Dunne, Finley Peter. *The World of Mr. Dooley.* Louis Filler, ed. New York: Collier Books, 1962.

Ebert Roger, ed. *An Illini Century: One Hundred Years of Campus Life.* Urbana: University of Illinois Press, 1967.

El Paso Public Library Board. *El Paso Story.* NI, 1954.

Erickson, Charlotte. *American Industry and the European Immigrant, 1860-1865.* Cambridge: Harvard University Press, 1957.

Evans, Christopher. *History of the United Mine Workers of America.* 2 vols. Indianapolis: The Union, 1918.

Fast, Howard. *The American: A Middle Western Legend.* New York: Duell, Sloan and Pearce, 1946.

Fergus Historical Series, *Chicago and Illinois 3.* Chicago: Fergus Printing Co., 1884.

Fevold, Eugene L., and E. Clifford Nelson. *The Lutheran Church among Norwegian-Americans.* Minneapolis: Augsburg Publishing House, 1960.

Fine, Nathan. *Labor and Farmer Parties in the United States, 1828-1928.* New York: Rand School of Social Science, 1928.

Flinn, John J. *The Standard Guide to Chicago for the Year 1891.* Chicago: Flinn & Sheppard, 1890.

Gage, Lyman J. *Memoirs of Lyman J. Gage.* New York: House of Field, Inc., 1937.

Garraghan, Gilbert. *The Catholic Church in Chicago, 1673-1871.* Chicago: Loyola University Press, 1921.

Garvey, Neil F. *The Government and Administration of Illinois.* New York: Crowell, 1958.

Gates, Paul Wallace. *The Illinois Central Railroad and Its Colonization Work.* Cambridge: Harvard University Press, 1934.

Gephart, William F. *Transportation and Industrial Development in the Middle West.* Studies in History, Economics and Public Law, vol. 34, no. 1. New York: Columbia University Press, 1909.

Gerhard, Frederick. *Illinois as It Is: Its History, Geography, Statistics, Constitution, Laws, Government.* Philadelphia: C. DeSilver, 1857.

Giles, Dorothy. *Singing Valleys, the Story of Corn.* New York: Random House, 1940.

Ginger, Ray. *Altgeld's America: The Lincoln Ideal Versus Changing Realities.* New York: Funk and Wagnalls Co., 1958.

———. *The Bending Cross: A Biography of Eugene Victor Debs.* New Brunswick, N.J.: Rutgers University, 1949.

Gluck, Elsie. *John Mitchell, Miner: Labor's Bargain with the Gilded Age.* New York: Greenwood Press, 1929.

Goodrich, Carter. *Government Promotion of American Canals and Railroads, 1800-1890.* New York: Columbia University Press, 1959.

———. *The Miners' Freedom.* Boston: Marshall Jones Co., 1925.

Goodspeed, Thomas Wakefield. *The Story of the University of Chicago, 1870-1925.* Chicago: University of Chicago Press, 1925.

————. *William Rainey Harper.* Chicago: University of Chicago Press, 1925.

Grant, U. S., III. *Ulysses S. Grant: Warrior and Statesman.* New York: William Morrow and Co., 1964.

Greene, Evarts Boutell. *The Government of Illinois: Its History and Administration.* New York: MacMillan Co., 1904.

————. *Pioneers of Civilization in Illinois: An Address Before the Trustees, Faculty and Students of the Western Illinois State Normal School, Dec. 3, 1907.* Pontiac, Ill.: State Reformatory Printers, n.d.

Greer, Scott A. *Last Man In: Racial Access to Union Power.* Glencoe, Ill.: Free Press, 1959.

Greer, Thomas H. *American Social Reform Movements: Their Pattern since 1865.* New York: Prentice-Hall, 1949.

Grierson, Francis. *The Valley of Shadows.* Boston: Houghton Mifflin, 1948.

Grodinsky, Julius. *The Iowa Pool, a Study in Railroad Competition 1870-84.* Chicago: University of Chicago Press, 1950.

Hadley, Arthur T. *Railroad Transportation: Its History and Its Laws.* New York: G. P. Putnam's Sons, 1886.

Haig, Robert M. *A History of the General Property Tax in Illinois.* Urbana: University of Illinois Press, 1914.

Halsey, John J., ed. *History of Lake County, Illinois.* Philadelphia: R. S. Bates, 1912.

Hamilton, Walton H., and Helen R. Wright. *The Case of Bituminous Coal.* New York: MacMillan Co., 1925.

Handlin, Oscar. *The Uprooted.* 2nd ed. Boston: Little, Brown, 1973.

Haney, L. H. *A Congressional History of Railways in the United States.* Madison: Democrat Printing Company, 1910.

Hansen, Harry. *The Chicago.* New York: Farrar & Rinehart, Inc., 1942.

Harland, Marion (pseud.) (Mrs. Mary Virginia [Hawes] Terhune), ed. *Plain Talks upon Practical Subjects.* New York and Chicago: n.p., 1895.

Harris, Frank. *The Bomb.* New York: Mitchell Kennerley, 1909.

Hayter, Earl W. *The Troubled Farmer, 1850-1890: Rural Adjustment to Industrialism.* DeKalb: Northern Illinois University, 1968.

Higham, John. *Strangers in the Land: Patterns of American Nativism, 1860-1925.* New Brunswick, N.J.: Rutgers University Press, 1955.

Hiller, Ernest Theodore. *Houseboat and River Bottom People: A Study of 683 Households in Sample Localities Adjacent to the Ohio and Mississippi Rivers.* Urbana: University of Illinois Press, 1939.

————. *Rural Community Types.* Urbana: University of Illinois Press, 1930.

Hinchcliffe, John. *Historical Review of Belleville, Illinois, from the Earliest Times to the Present.* Belleville, Ill.: G. A. Harvey, 1870.

Hobart, Chauncey. *Recollections of My Life: Fifty Years of Itinerancy in the Northwest.* Red Wing, Minn.: Red Wing Printing Co., 1889.

Hodges, Carl G., comp. *Illinois Negro Historymakers.* Chicago: Illinois Emancipation Centennial Commission, 1964.

Howard, Robert. *Illinois: A History of the Prairie State.* Grand Rapids, Mich.: W. B. Eerdmans Co., 1972.

Howe, Walter A., comp. *Documentary History of the Illinois and Michigan Canal: Legislation, Litigation and Titles.* Springfield: Illinois Division of Waterways, 1957.

Humphrey, Grace. *Illinois: The Story of the Prairie State.* Indianapolis, Ind.: Bobbs-Merrill Co., 1917.

Husband, Joseph. *The Story of the Pullman Car.* Chicago: A. C. McClurg & Co., 1917.

Hutchinson, William T. *Cyrus Hall McCormick Harvest: 1856-1884.* New York: D. Appleton-Century Co., 1935.

Illinois Centennial Commission. *The Governors of Illinois, 1818-1918.* Springfield: Illinois Journal Co., 1918.

Illinois Central Railroad Company. *Guide to the Illinois Central Archives in the Newberry Library, 1851-1906.* Chicago: Newberry Library, 1951.

Illinois Department of Public Instruction. *Centennial Celebration of the Enactment of the First Free School Law in Illinois, 1825-1925.* Issued by Francis G. Blair. Springfield: Schnepp & Barnes, 1925.

Illinois Gazetteer, 1886. Illinois State Historical Library. Springfield, Ill.: Phillips Bros., 1899.

Illinois Railroad and Warehouse Commission, *Report, 1898.*

Illinois School Laws and Common School Decisions of the State of Illinois. Newton Bateman, ed. Urbana: W. L. Pillsbury, 1880.

Illinois State Normal University. *Semi-Centennial History of the Illinois State Normal University, 1857-1907.* Normal: Prepared under the direction of the faculty, 1907.

Israel, Fred L., ed. *1897 Sears Roebuck Catalogue.* New York: Chelsea House, 1968.

James, F. Cyril. *The Growth of Chicago Banks,* vol. 1, *The Formative Years, 1816-1896.* New York: Harper and Row, 1938.

Johns, Jane Martin. *Personal Recollections of Early Decatur, Abraham Lincoln, Richard J. Oglesby and the Civil War.* Decatur: D.A.R., 1912.

Johnson, Charles B. *Growth of Cook County.* Chicago: Board of Commissioners of Cook County, 1960.

Jordan, Phillip D. *The National Road. American Trails Series.* Indianapolis, Ind.: Bobbs-Merrill Co., 1948.

Josephson, Matthew. *The Robber Barons.* New York: Harcourt Brace, 1962.

Kirkland, Edward C. *Industry Comes of Age: Business, Labor and Public Policy, 1860-1897.* The Economic History of the United States. Vol. vi. New York: Holt, Rinehart & Winston, 1962.

Knox College. *The First Hundred Years of Knox College.* Galesburg, Ill.: Centenary Fund Committee, 1929.

Kobre, Sidney. *Development of American Journalism.* Dubuque, Iowa: Wm. Brown Co., 1969.

Koeper, Frederick, ed. *Illinois Architecture: A Selective Guide from Territorial Times to the Present.* Chicago: University of Chicago Press, 1968.

Kolko, Gabriel. *Railroads and Regulation, 1877-1916.* Princeton, N.J.: Princeton University Press, 1965.

Krug, Mark M. *Lyman Trumbull: Conservative Radical.* New York: A. S. Barnes and Co., 1965.

Lacey, John J. *Farm Bureau in Illinois: History of the Illinois Farm Bureau.* Bloomington, Ill.: Illinois Agricultural Association, 1965.

Landen, John M. *A History of the City of Cairo, Illinois.* Chicago: R. L. Donnelley & Sons Co., 1910.

Lant, Agnes C. *The Romance of the Rails.* New York: R. M. McBride & Co., 1929.

Lee, Alfred E. *The National Road.* Indianapolis, Ind.: Bobbs-Merrill Co., 1948.

Leech, Harper and John Charles Carroll. *Armour and His Times.* New York: D. Appleton-Century Co., Inc., 1938.

Leek, John Halbor. *Government and Labor in the United States.* New York: Rinehart, 1952.

Lentz, E. G. *Seventy-Five Years in Retrospect, from Normal School to Teachers' College to University: Southern Illinois University, 1874-1949.* Carbondale: Southern Illinois University Press, 1955.

Lewis, Lloyd. *John S. Wright, Prophet of the Prairies.* Chicago: The Prairie Publishing Co., 1941.

———, and Henry Justin Smith. *Chicago: The History of Its Reputation.* New York: Blue Ribbon Books, Inc., 1929, for Harcourt, Brace & Co.

Lindsay, N. Vachel. *Collected Poems by Vachel Lindsay.* Rev. ed. with illustrations by the author. New York: MacMillan Co., 1969.

Lindsey, Altmont. *The Pullman Strike.* Chicago: University of Chicago Press, 1967.

Linn, J. W. *Jane Addams.* New York: Appleton-Century, 1935.

Lloyd, Henry D. *A Strike of Millionaires against Miners: Or the Story of Spring Valley.* Chicago: Belford-Clarke, 1890.

Logan, Mrs. John A. *Reminiscences of a Soldier's Wife.* New York: Charles Scribner's Sons, 1912.

London, J. B. *A Tour through Canada and the United States of America.* Coventry: n.p., 1879.

Lusk, D. W. *Eighty Years of Illinois: Politics and Politicians, Anecdotes and Incidents, 1809-1889.* 3rd ed., rev. Springfield: H. W. Rokker, 1889.

Marsh, Charles W. *Recollections, 1837-1910.* Chicago: Farm Implement News Co., 1910.

Masters, Edgar Lee. *Levy Mayer and the New Industrial Era.* New Haven, Conn.: Yale University Press, 1927.

———. *Spoon River Anthology.* New York: Collier Books, 1962.

Mather, Irwin F. *The Making of Illinois: A History of the State from Earliest Records to the Present Time.* Chicago: A. Flanagan Co., 1916.

McBride, John, assisted by T. T. O'Malley. *The Coal Miners in the Labor Movement: The Problem of Today.* George E. McNeill, ed. New York: M. W. Hazen Co., 1888.

McCallum, Henry D. and Frances T. *The Wire that Fenced the West.* Norman: University of Oklahoma Press, 1965.

McClellen, John Little. *Crime Without Punishment.* New York: Duell, Sloan, and Pearce, 1962.

McCulloch, Catharine Waugh. *Chronology of the Women's Rights Movement in Illinois.* Chicago: The Illinois Equal Suffrage Assn., circa 1903.

McDonald, Forrest. *Insull.* Chicago: University of Chicago Press, 1962.

McMurry, Donald L. *Coxey's Army: A Study of the Industrial Army Movement of 1894.* Boston: Little, Brown, 1929.

———. *The Great Burlington Strike of 1888: A Case Study in Labor Relations.* Cambridge: Harvard University Press, 1956.

Millay, Edna St. Vincent. *Collected Poems.* New York: Harper, 1956.

Mills, Harlow Burgess. *Natural History Survey: A Century of Biological Research.* Urbana: University of Illinois Press, 1958.

Mitchell, John. *Organized Labor: Its Problems, Purposes and Ideas and the Present and Future of the American Wage Earners.* Philadelphia: American Book and Bible House, 1903.

Monaghan, James. *This Is Illinois, a Pictorial History.* Chicago: University of Chicago Press, 1949.

Monroe, Harriet. *Poet's Life: Seventy Years in a Changing World.* New York: MacMillan Co., 1938.

Montgomery, Royal E. *Industrial Relations in the Chicago Building Trades.* Chicago: University of Chicago Press, 1927.

Moses, John. *Illinois, Historical and Statistical, Comprising the Essential Facts of Its Planting and Growth as a Province, County, Territory and State: Derived from Original Documents and Papers.* 2 vols. Chicago: Fergus Printing Co., 1889-92.

———. *The White City. The Historical, Biographical and Philanthropical Record of Illinois.* Chicago: Chicago World Book Co., 1893.

Mott, Frank Luther. *American Journalism, a History, 1690-1960.* 3rd ed. New York: MacMillan Co., 1962.

National Farmers' Alliance and Industrial Union. *Minutes of Hart Alliance of Henry County,* May 3, 1890-Aug. 6, 1891.

Neely, Charles. *Tales and Songs of Southern Illinois.* Carbondale: Southern Illinois University Press, 1954.

Neilson, James W. *Shelby M. Cullom: Prairie State Republican.* Illinois Studies in the Social Sciences, vol. 51. Urbana: University of Illinois Press, 1962.

Nevins, Allan. *Illinois.* New York: Oxford University Press, 1917.

Norton, Margaret Cross. *Illinois Census Returns.* Springfield: Trustees of the Illinois State Historical Library, 1935.

Noun, Louise R. *Strong Minded Women: The Emergence of the Woman-Suffrage Movement in Iowa.* Ames: Iowa State University Press, 1969.

Overton, Richard C. *Burlington Route: A History of the Burlington Lines.* New York: Alfred A. Knopf, 1965.

Page, John L. *Climate of Illinois, Summary and Analysis of Long-Time Weather Records.* Urbana: University of Illinois Press, 1941.

Palmer, George T. *A Conscientious Turncoat: The Story of John M. Palmer, 1817-1900.* New Haven, Conn.: Yale University Press, 1941.

Palmer, John M., ed. *The Bench and Bar of Illinois.* Chicago: Lewis Publishing Co., 1899.

Parker, Reginald. *A Guide to Labor Law: Basic Facts, Questions and Answers, Pertinent Statutes.* New York: Praeger, 1961.

Pease, Theodore Calvin. *The County Archives of the State of Illinois.* Springfield: Trustees of the Illinois State Historical Library, 1915.

———. *The Story of Illinois.* Marguerite Jenison Pease, ed. Chicago: University of Chicago Press, 1965.

Pelekoudas, Lois M., ed. *Illinois Political Parties. Final Report and Background Papers, Assembly on Illinois Political Parties.* Urbana: University of Illinois Press, 1960.

Phillips, Isaac N. *Oration of Isaac N. Phillips.* Bloomington, Ill.: Pantagraph, circa 1901.

Pierce, Bessie Louise. *A History of Chicago: The Rise of a Modern City.* 3 vols. New York: Alfred A. Knopf, 1940, 1957.

Plochmann, George Kimball. *The Ordeal of Southern Illinois University.* Carbondale: Southern Illinois University Press, 1959.

Poor, H. V. *Manual of the Railroads of the United States.* New York: H. A. and H. W. Poor, 1868-85.

Putnam, James W. *The Illinois and Michigan Canal. Chicago Historical Society Collections,* X. Chicago: University of Chicago Press, 1918.

Rammelkamp, Charles Henry. *Illinois College: A Centennial History, 1829-1929.* New Haven, Conn.: Yale University Press, 1928.

Rawlings, Isaac Donaldson. *The Rise and Fall of Disease in Illinois.* Springfield: Department of Public Health, 1927.

Riegel, Robert E. *The Story of the Western Railroads.* New York: MacMillan Co., 1926.

Robinson, Luther Emerson. *History of Illinois.* New York: American Book Company, 1909.

Roy, Andrew. *The Coal Mines.* Cleveland: Robinson, Savage and Co., 1876.

———. *A History of Coal Miners of the United States from the Development of the Mines to the Close of the Anthracite Strike of 1902.* 3rd ed. rev. Columbus, Ohio: J. L. Trauger, 1907.

Ruggles, Eleanor. *The West-Going Heart–A Life of Vachel Lindsay.* New York: W. W. Norton and Son, Inc., 1959.

Sandburg, Carl. *Abraham Lincoln: The Prairie Years.* New York: Dell Publishing Co., 1954.

———. *Always the Young Strangers.* New York: Harcourt Brace, 1953.

———. *Harvest Poems, 1910-1960.* New York: Harvest Books, Harcourt, Brace & World, Inc., 1960.

Schaack, Captain Michael J. *Anarchy and Anarchists: A History of the Red Terror and the Social Revolution in America and Europe; Communism, Socialism and Nihilism in Doctrine and Deed; The Chicago Haymarket Conspiracy and the Detection and Trial of the Conspirators.* Chicago: F. J. Schultze & Co., 1889.

Schiabo, Giovanni E. *The Italians in Chicago.* Chicago: Italian American Publishing Co., 1928.

Schlesinger, Arthur M. *The Rise of the City, 1878-1898. A History of American Life*. X. New York: MacMillan Co., 1933.

Schrier, Arnold. *Ireland and the American Emigration, 1850-1900*. Minneapolis: University of Minnesota Press, 1958.

Scott, Roy V. *The Agrarian Movement in Illinois, 1880-1896*. Urbana: University of Illinois Press, 1962.

Seidman, Joel Isaac. *The Needle Trades*. New York: Farrar and Rinehart, Inc., 1942.

Shannon, Fred A. *The Farmer's Last Frontier: Agriculture, 1860-1897. Economic History of the United States*. Vol. 5. New York: Holt, Rinehart and Winston, 1945.

Siegel, Arthur, ed. *Chicago's Famous Buildings: A Photographic Guide to the City's Architectural Landmarks and Other Notable Buildings*. Chicago: University of Chicago Press, 1965.

Simonson, Harold P. *Francis Grierson*. New York: Twayne's United States Authors Series, 1966.

Smith, George W. *A Student's History of Illinois*. Rev. ed. Chicago: Hall and McCreary, 1916.

Spencer, Gladys. *The Chicago Public Library: Origins and Backgrounds*. Chicago: University of Chicago Press, 1943.

Squire, Belle. *The Woman Movement in America*. Chicago: A. C. McClurg & Co., 1911.

Staley, Eugene. *History of the Illinois State Federation of Labor*. Social Science Studies, XV. Chicago: University of Chicago Press, 1930.

Stampp, Kenneth. *The Era of Reconstruction, 1865-1877*. New York: Alfred A. Knopf, 1965.

Stedman, Murry S. *Discontent at the Polls: A Study of Farmer and Labor Parties, 1827-1948*. New York: Columbia University Press, 1950.

Steuernagel, Bella, comp. *The Belleville Public Library: 1836-1936, an Historical Sketch*. Belleville, Ill.: The Library, 1936.

Stevenson, Adlai Ewing. *Something of Men I Have Known: With Some Papers of a General Nature, Political, Historical and Retrospective*. Chicago: A. C. McClurg & Co., 1909.

Stibitz, E. Earle, ed. *Illinois Poets: A Selection*. Carbondale: Southern Illinois University Press, 1968.

Storr, Richard J. *Harper's University, the Beginnings: A History of the University of Chicago*. Chicago: University of Chicago Press, 1966.

Stover, John F. *American Railroads*. Chicago: University of Chicago Press, 1961.

Stroud, Gene S., and Gilbert E. Donahue. *Labor History in the United States, General Bibliography*. Urbana: University of Illinois Press, 1961.

Sullivan, William. *Dunne, Judge, Mayor, Governor*. Chicago: Windermere Press, 1916.

Swados, Harvey. *A Radical's America*. Boston: Little, Brown, 1962.

Swift, Louis, with Arthur Van Vlissingen, Jr. *Yankee of the Yards: A Biography of Gustavus Franklin Swift*. Chicago: A. W. Shaw Co., 1927.

Thornburn, Neil. "John P. Altgeld: Promoter of Higher Education in

Illinois." *Essays in Illinois History: In Honor of Glenn Huron Seymour.* Carbondale: Southern Illinois University Press, 1968.

Townsend, Walter A. *Illinois Democracy: A History of the Party and Its Representative Members–Past and Present.* Springfield: Democratic Historical Association, Inc., 1935.

Trescott, Paul B. *Financing American Enterprise: The Story of Commercial Banking.* New York: Harper & Row, 1963.

Trowbridge, Lydia Jones. *Frances Willard of Evanston.* Chicago: Wellett Clark & Co., 1938.

Upton, George P., ed. *Theodore Thomas: A Musical Autobiography.* 2 vols. Chicago: A. C. McClurg & Co., 1905.

Veach, Rebecca Monroe. *Growing Up with Springfield: A History of the Capital of Illinois.* Springfield: Boardman-Smith, 1974.

Verlie, Emil Joseph, ed. *Illinois Constitutions.* Springfield: Trustees of the Illinois State Historical Library, 1919.

Wade, Louise C. *Graham Taylor: Pioneer for Social Justice, 1851-1938.* Chicago: University of Chicago Press, 1964.

Wakefield, Eva Ingersoll, ed. *The Letters of Robert G. Ingersoll.* New York: Philosophical Library, 1951.

Walton, Clyde, ed. *An Illinois Reader.* DeKalb: Northern Illinois University Press, 1970.

Ward, Estelle Frances. *The Story of Northwestern University.* New York: Dodd, Mead and Co., 1924.

Ware, Norman Joseph. *The Labor Movement in the United States, 1860-1895: A Study in Democracy.* New York: Appleton and Co., 1929.

Warne, Colston Estey. *The Consumers' Co-Operative Movement in Illinois.* Chicago: University of Chicago Press, 1926.

Warne, Frank Julian. *The Union Movement among Coal Mine Workers.* Washington, D.C.: U.S. Labor Statistics Bureau, bull. 51, v. 9.

Webb, Howard, ed. *Illinois Prose Writers: A Selection.* Carbondale: Southern Illinois University Press, 1968.

Weber, Jessie Palmer. *Report of the Centennial Commission.* Springfield: Illinois State Journal Co. Printers, 1920.

Wendt, Lloyd, and Herman Kogan. *Bosses in Lusty Chicago: The Story of Bathhouse John and Hinky Dink.* Bloomington: Indiana University Press, 1967.

Whitman, Walt. *Leaves of Grass.* New York: Aventine Press, 1931.

Wieck, Edward A. *The American Miners' Union.* New York: Russell Sage Foundation, 1940.

Wiebe, Robert. *The Search for Order, 1877-1920. The Making of America.* V. New York: Hill and Wang, 1967.

Wilensky, Harold L. *Intellectuals in Labor Unions: Organizational Pressures on Professional Roles.* Glencoe, Ill.: Free Press, 1956.

Wilkey, Harry L. *The Story of a Little Town: A History of Paloma, Illinois.* NI, 1934.

Wilkie, Frank B. *A Sketch of Richard Oglesby*. Chicago: W. A. Shanholtzer, 1884.

Wilson, H. E. *Mary McDowell*. Chicago: University of Chicago Press, 1928.

Wittke, Carl. *The Irish in America*. Baton Rouge, La.: Louisiana University Press, 1956.

————. *We Who Built America*. New York: Prentice-Hall, 1939.

Well, Matthew. *Labor Industry and Government*. New York: D. Appleton-Century Inc., 1935.

Woodward, W. E. *Meet General Grant*. New York: H. Liveright, 1929.

Workers Education Bureau of America. *Labor and Education: A Brief Outline of Resolutions and Pronouncements of the AFL in Support of the General Principles and Practices of Education from 1881-1938*. Washington, D.C.: AFL, 1939.

Wright, Carrol Davidson. *The Industrial Evolution of the United States*. New York: Flood and Vincent, 1897.

Yearley, Clifton J., Jr. *Britons in American Labor: A History of the Influence of the United Kingdom Immigrants on American Labor*. Baltimore, Md.: Johns Hopkins University Press, 1957.

Yount, Charles A. *William Bross, 1813-1890*. Lake Forest, Ill.: Lake Forest College, 1940.

Index

A. C. McClurg and Company, 191
A. G. Spaulding and Brothers, 191
Abbott, Edith, 282, 284
Abolition: Logan opposed, 95; stops women's rights movement, x, xi, xiii
Adams, Henry, 288
Adams County: gross value statistics, 201
Addams, Jane, 282, 283-284, 287
Adler, Friedrich, 285
Advertising: department stores, 4-5; postwar statistics, 3
Agassiz, Louis, 24
Agitator, The: women's rights weekly, 16
Agriculture: animal products, 138; animal products statistics, 135-136; barbed wire development, 127; boards and institutes control, 133; butter substitutes, 136; colleges affect, 122; corn development, 124; corn statistics, 123; dairy industry statistics, 135-137; decline, 321; dehorning, 129; depression of 1870s, 123; drainage improvement, 129; drainage statistics, 126; economic decline, 186; economics, 139, 140; education, 117, 147; farm animal disease, 131; farmhouse description, 116-117ff.; farm implement development, 125-126; farm implement statistics, 126; farm life, 122, 128, 147-148; farm population statistics, 116-117, 118-119; fish commission statistics, 133; granges, 141-143, 144-145; industry foundation, 6; landholding statistics, 118-119, 120-121; livestock disease, 130-131, 132-133; livestock industry develops, 128, 133; livestock statistics, 128-

130, 131; marketing, 139; oats statistics, 124-125; pasturage, 125; revolutionary atmosphere fails, 146-147; sheep industry, 138; small farm decline, 123; state entomologist, 134; swine production, 137; swine production statistics, 137-138; warehousing, 139; wheat statistics, 124. *See also* Landholding; Railroads; Stockyards; Tenancy
Agriculture, U.S. Department of, 132, 141
Alarm, 237
Albion, 7
Alcoholics Anonymous, 30
Alcoholism: Keeley cure, 29-30
Alexander, John T., 120
Alger, Horatio, 297
Allan, Henry F., 227
Allen Bill, 111, 270
Alliance, 310
Altgeld, John Peter: administers boards, 55; compared to Tanner, 111-112; describes Illinois prosperity, 209; farewell address quoted, 110; Haymarket incident, 108; political career sketched, 101, 103-105, 106-107, 109, 110; success, 73; mentioned, 46, 47, 48, 59, 62, 65, 72, 121, 177, 209, 240, 243-244, 245, 247, 248, 249, 266, 269, 275, 283, 287, 312, 314, 317, 320
Alton: first state prison, 51; glacier soil, 10; mentioned, 60, 202, 204, 305
American Bankers Association, 184
American District Telephone Company, 193
American Federation of Labor (AFL), 236, 238, 241, 250, 322

369